Contested Liberalization

Economic liberalization has been contested and defeated in France to an unparalleled extent in comparison to other leading political economies in Western Europe. Jonah D. Levy offers a historical explanation, centered on the legacies of France's postwar statist or *dirigiste* economic model. Although this model was dismantled decades ago, its policy, party-political, and institutional legacies continue to fuel the contestation of liberalizing reforms today. *Contested Liberalization* offers a comprehensive analysis of French economic and social policy since the 1980s, including the Macron administration. It also traces the implications of the French case for contestation in East Asia and Latin America. Levy concludes by identifying ways that French liberalizers could diminish contestation, notably by adopting a more inclusive process and more equitable allocation of the costs and benefits of liberalizing reform. This book will interest scholars and students of political economy and comparative politics, especially those working on economic liberalization, French politics, and the welfare state.

Jonah D. Levy is a Professor of Political Science at the University of California Berkeley and Director of Berkeley's Center of Excellence in French and Francophone Studies. His research focuses on French politics and political economy. Levy is the author of *Tocqueville's Revenge: State and Society in Contemporary France* (1999) and *The State after Statism: New State Activities in the Age of Liberalization* (2006).

T0384763

Contested Liberalization

Historical Legacies and Contemporary Conflict in France

Jonah D. Levy

University of California, Berkeley

CAMBRIDGE
UNIVERSITY PRESS

Shaftesbury Road, Cambridge CB2 8EA, United Kingdom

One Liberty Plaza, 20th Floor, New York, NY 10006, USA

477 Williamstown Road, Port Melbourne, VIC 3207, Australia

314–321, 3rd Floor, Plot 3, Splendor Forum, Jasola District Centre, New Delhi – 110025, India

103 Penang Road, #05–06/07, Visioncrest Commercial, Singapore 238467

Cambridge University Press is part of Cambridge University Press & Assessment, a department of the University of Cambridge.

We share the University's mission to contribute to society through the pursuit of education, learning and research at the highest international levels of excellence.

www.cambridge.org
Information on this title: www.cambridge.org/9781009283342

DOI: 10.1017/9781009283311

First published 2023

A catalogue record for this publication is available from the British Library.

Library of Congress Cataloging-in-Publication Data
Names: Levy, Jonah D., author.
Title: Contested liberalization : historical legacies and contemporary
conflict in France / Jonah D. Levy, University of California, Berkeley.
Description: First Edition. | New York : Cambridge University Press, 2023. |
Includes bibliographical references and index.
Identifiers: LCCN 2022056274 (print) | LCCN 2022056275 (ebook) |
ISBN 9781009283342 (Hardback) | ISBN 9781009283335 (Paperback) |
ISBN 9781009283311 (eBook)
Subjects: LCSH: Welfare state – France. | Pressure groups – France. |
Proportional representation – France. | Political parties – France. |
Presidents – France. | France – Economic policy – 1945– | France – Economic
conditions – 1945– | France – Politics and government – 1945– |
France – History – 1945–
Classification: LCC JC479 .L49 2023 (print) | LCC JC479 (ebook) |
DDC 361.6/50944–dc23/eng/20230103
LC record available at https://lccn.loc.gov/2022056274
LC ebook record available at https://lccn.loc.gov/2022056275

ISBN 978-1-009-28334-2 Hardback
ISBN 978-1-009-28333-5 Paperback

To Helga, who brings purpose to my life.

Contents

Figures

Tables

Acknowledgments

This book is the culmination of a series of projects, reflections, and research trips to France over the last two decades. Some portions of the book were published previously and are reprinted with permission from the publishers. The account of the shift in France from the *dirigiste* state to the social anesthesia state in Chapter 2 is reproduced with permission from the licensors of "France: Directing Adjustment?" in Fritz Scharpf and Vivienne Schmidt (eds.), *Welfare and Work in the Open Economy: Diverse Responses to Common Challenges* (Oxford: Oxford University Press, 2000): 308–350; "Redeploying the French State: Economic and Social Policy after *Dirigisme*," in Wolfgang Streeck and Kathleen Thelen (eds.), *Beyond Continuity: Institutional Change in Advanced Political Economies* (Oxford: Oxford University Press, 2005): 103–126; "From the *Dirigiste* State to the Social Anesthesia State: French Economic Policy in the *Longue Durée*," *Modern and Contemporary France*, 16(4) (November 2008): 417–435; and "The Transformations of the Statist Model," in Evelyne Huber, Matthew Lange, Stephan Leibfried, Jonah Levy, Frank Nullmeier, and John Stephens (eds.), *The Oxford Handbook of the Transformations of the State* (Oxford: Oxford University Press, 2015): 393–409. The discussion of Nicolas Sarkozy's economic policy in Chapter 3 is reproduced with permission from the licensors of "Directionless: French Economic Policy in the Twenty-First Century," in Dan Breznitz and John Zysman (eds.), *The Third Globalization: Can Wealthy Nations Stay Rich in the Twenty-First Century?* (Oxford: Oxford University Press, 2013): 323–349; and "The Return of the State? France's Response to the 2008 Financial and Economic Crisis," *Comparative European Politics*, 15(4) (June 2017): 604–627.

This book has benefited from many kinds of support. Financially, portions of this research were funded by visiting faculty grants from the Institute of Political Studies of Paris and the University of Paris VIII as well as a University of California Berkeley Faculty Research Grant. Intellectually, I am grateful to a number of scholars who provided helpful comments and criticism on various parts of the project: Ruth Collier,

Richard Deeg, Gregory Jackson, Audrey Mariette, Geoffrey Owen, Martin Schain, Vivien Schmidt, R. Kent Weaver, Douglas Webber, J. Nicholas Ziegler, John Zysman, and two anonymous reviewers for Cambridge University Press.

I want to single out several colleagues and collaborators whose support has been especially valuable. Alice Ciciora provided first-rate research assistance, exceeded only by her care for my canine companions and patient pedagogy about the world of sports. Mark Vail generously read the entire manuscript and helped me reformulate the argument and engage with a broader literature. Chris Howell also read the entire manuscript, pushing me to sharpen the argument, flesh out underdeveloped ideas, and be more intellectually ambitious. Kathleen Thelen helped me improve and reformulate key portions of the book; she also provided much-appreciated guidance and friendship at critical moments.

Several people in France have been especially helpful to my research. Nicolas Véron opened a number of doors to me among French policymakers and elites – not to mention the doors to his Paris apartment, his family, and his keen insights into French politics. Adrien Abecassis also provided entrées to top-level policymakers. Bruno Palier introduced me to the complexities of French social policy, explaining the array of interests and ambitions, putting me in contact with French interlocutors, and challenging some of my most fundamental positions.

Three scholars have played a critical role in shaping my understanding of France's politics and political economy. Peter Hall was my first mentor, who introduced me to the aspirations, achievements, and internal contradictions of France's *dirigiste* state. Suzanne Berger steered me through graduate school and beyond, fashioning my thinking about French politics in general and the travails of French liberalism in particular. In my most immodest moments, I like to think of Chapters 2 and 3 of this book as channeling my inner Peter and Suzanne respectively. Finally, Elie Cohen shared his unmatched expertise on French industrial policy and relations between the state and big business; he also taught me how to tell big stories through targeted case studies and to approach the discourse of French policy elites, however elegantly formulated, with a degree of critical perspective. I hope that Elie will see elements of his own approach in the argument and evidence of this book.

My greatest debt, as always, is to my family. My three children – Julien, Elijah, and Charlotte – are more than any parent could hope for or deserve. As the last of them heads off to college, it will be easier for me to make research trips to Paris, but I would gladly trade the City of Lights for a few more years with my children. My wife, Helga, is also more than I deserve. Helga's irrepressibly cheerful and nurturing personality has filled our home with joy and overcome my most determined efforts at grouchiness and old-world cynicism. Her ability to simultaneously navigate the worlds of corporate America and suburban parenting without missing a beat is nothing short of amazing. It is to Helga, with equal parts love and admiration, that I dedicate this book.

Abbreviations

ANPE	National Employment Agency (Agence Nationale Pour l'Emploi)
APC	Collective Performance Agreements (Accords de Performance Collective)
APLD	Long-Term Partial Employment (Activité Partielle de Longue Durée)
BCG	Boston Consulting Group
BPCE	Banque Populaire Caisses d'Epargne
CAC 40	Benchmark 40 equities listed on the Euronext Paris stock exchange (Cotation Assistée en Continu)
CARE	Contract for Assistance in the Return to Employment (Contrat d'Aide au Retour à l'Emploi)
CCC	Citizens' Climate Convention (Convention Citoyenne pour le Climat)
CCF	Crédit Commercial de France
CDC	Deposits and Consignments Fund (Caisse des Dépôts et Consignations)
CFDT	French Democratic Confederation of Labor (Confédération Française Démocratique du Travail)
CFE-CGC	French Confederation of Management-Confederation of Executives (Confédération Française de l'Encadrement-Confédération Française des Cadres)
CFTC	French Confederation of Christian Workers (Confédération Française des Travailleurs Chrétiens)
CGE	Compagnie Générale d'Electricité
CGT	General Confederation of Labor (Confédération Générale du Travail)
CIASI	Interministerial Committee for the Adaptation of Industrial Structures (Comité Interministériel de l'Aménagement des Structures Industrielles)
CIC	Crédit Industriel et Commercial

CIE	Employment Initiative Contract (Contrat Initiative Emploi)
CIP	Professional Integration Contract (Contrat d'Insertion Professionnelle)
CME	coordinated market economy
CMU	Universal Sickness Coverage (Couverture Maladie Universelle)
CNAM	National Health Insurance Fund (Caisse Nationale d'Assurance Maladie)
CNPF	National Council of French Employers (Conseil National du Patronat Français)
CNRS	National Center for Scientific Research (Centre National de la Recherche Scientifique)
CPE	First Employment Contract (Contrat Première Embauche)
CSE	Social and Economic Committee (Comité Social et Economique)
CSG	General Social Contribution (Contribution Sociale Généralisée)
CSS	Subsidized Supplementary Health Insurance (Complémentaire Santé Solidaire)
CTU	Single Labor Contract (Contrat de Travail Unique)
DATAR	Delegation for the Development of Territory and Regional Action (Délégation à l'Aménagement du Territoire et à l'Action Régionale)
ECB	European Central Bank
EDF	Electricité de France
EDS	Ecology, Democracy, and Solidarity (Ecologie, Démocratie, et Solidarité)
EELV	Europe Ecology – The Greens (Europe Ecologie – Les Verts)
EMS	European Monetary System
EMU	European Monetary Union
ENA	National School of Administration (Ecole Nationale d'Administration)
EPR	European Pressurized Reactor
EU	European Union
FDI	foreign direct investment
FN	National Front (Front National)
FO	Workers' Power (Force Ouvrière)
FSI	Strategic Investment Fund (Fonds Stratégique d'Investissement)

FSV	Solidarity Fund for the Elderly (Fonds de Solidarité Vieillesse)
GATT	General Agreement on Tariffs and Trade
GDF	Gaz de France
GDN	Grand National Debate (Grand Débat National)
GE	General Electric
GPI	Grand Investment Plan (Grand Plan d'Investissement)
HEC	School of Advanced Business Studies (Ecole des Hautes Etudes Commerciales)
ICT	information-communication technologies
IFI	Real Estate Wealth Tax (Impôt sur la Fortune Immobilière)
IFOP	French Institute of Public Opinion (Institut Français d'Opinion Publique)
IGF	Tax on Large Fortunes (Impôt sur les Grandes Fortunes)
ILO	International Labor Organization
IMF	International Monetary Fund
INSEE	National Institute of Statistics and Economic Studies (Institut National de la Statistique et des Etudes Economiques)
INSP	National Institute of Public Service (Institut National du Service Public)
ISF	Solidarity Tax on Wealth (Impôt de Solidarité sur la Fortune)
ISI	import-substitution industrialization
LBD	Flash-Ball riot guns (*lanceur de balles de défense*)
LFI	France Unbowed (La France Insoumise)
LME	liberal market economy
LO	Swedish Trade Union Confederation (Landsorganisationen i Sverige)
LR	The Republicans (Les Républicains)
LREM	The Republic on the Move (La République en Marche)
MEDEF	Movement of French Enterprises (Mouvement des Entreprises de France)
NATO	North Atlantic Treaty Organization
NUPES	New Popular Ecological and Social Union (Nouvelle Union Populaire Ecologique et Sociale)
OECD	Organisation for Economic Co-operation and Development
OPEC	Organization of Petroleum Exporting Countries

PARE	Plan for Assistance in the Return to Employment (Plan d'Aide au Retour à l'Emploi)
PCF	French Communist Party (Parti Communiste Français)
PEJ	Youth Employment Program (Programme Emplois Jeunes)
PERP	Popular Retirement Savings Plan (Plan d'Epargne Retraite Populaire)
PFU	Single Flat-Rate Levy (Prélèvement Forfaitaire Unique)
PIA	Investments in the Future Program (Programme d'Investissements d'Avenir)
PPE	personal protective equipment
PR	proportional representation
PS	Socialist Party (Parti Socialiste)
PSA	Peugeot Group (Peugeot Société Anonyme)
PUMA	Universal Illness Protection (Protection Universelle Maladie)
R&D	research and development
RATP	Autonomous Parisian Transportation Administration (Régie Autonome des Transports Parisiens)
RER	Regional Express Network (Réseau Express Régional)
RIC	Citizens' Initiative Referendum (Référendum d'Initiative Citoyenne)
RIL	locally initiated meeting (*réunion d'initiative locale*)
RMI	Minimum Integration Income (Revenu Minimum d'Insertion)
RN	National Rally (Rassemblement National)
RPR	Rally for the Republic (Rassemblement pour la République)
RSA	Active Solidarity Income (Revenu de Solidarité Active)
SME	small- and medium-sized enterprise
SMIC	minimum wage (Salaire Minimum Interprofessionnel de Croissance)
SMIC-jeunes	lower minimum wage for youths
SNCF	French National Railway Company (Société Nationale des Chemins de Fer Français)
SPD	Social Democratic Party (Germany)
STO	Compulsory Labor Service (Service du Travail Obligatoire)
TEPA	Law for Work, Employment, and Purchasing Power (Loi pour le Travail, l'Emploi, et le Pouvoir d'Achat)
TGV	high-speed train (Train à Grande Vitesse)

TICPE	Domestic Tax on the Consumption of Energy Products (Taxe Intérieure de Consommation sur les Produits Energétiques)
UDF	Union for French Democracy (Union pour la Démocratie Française)
UDR	Union for the Defense of the Republic (Union pour la Défense de la République)
UDR	Union of Democrats for the Republic (Union des Démocrates pour la République)
UD-Ve	Democratic Union for the Fifth Republic (Union des Démocrates pour la Cinquième République)
UIMM	Union of Metallurgical Industries and Professions (Union des Industries et Métiers de la Métallurgie)
UMP	Union for a Popular Movement (Union pour un Mouvement Populaire)
UMP	Union for the Presidential Majority (Union pour la Majorité Présidentielle)
UNEDIC	National Interprofessional Union for Employment in Industry and Trade (Union Nationale Interprofessionnelle pour l'Emploi dans l'Industrie et le Commerce)
UNR	Union for the New Republic (Union pour la Nouvelle République)
VAT	value-added tax
WHO	World Health Organization
WTO	World Trade Organization

1 Three Legacies of *Dirigisme*
The Contested Politics of Economic Liberalization in France

Neoliberalism is the defining economic doctrine of our time. Consigned to the margins of academia and policymaking during the postwar boom period, when Keynesian economics, planning, and the mixed economy held sway (Shonfield 1965), neoliberal ideas were carried into the mainstream by academics like Milton Friedman and economists at the University of Chicago (Burgin 2012; Caldwell 2011; Horn and Mirowski 2009; Overtveldt 2009) as well as by public choice theorists, who recast regulation as capture and public servants as rent seekers (Buchanan et al. 1980; Stigler 1971). In the 1980s, neoliberal ideas entered the policymaking sphere in the UK and the USA under Margaret Thatcher and Ronald Reagan respectively (Campbell and Pedersen 2001; Hall 1992; Hay 2001; King and Wood 1999). These ideas then spread in the wake of the apparent economic success of the Reagan–Thatcher reforms and the difficulties encountered by the various mixed, planned, and coordinated economies of Western Europe and East Asia.

The European Union (EU) provided a further boost to neoliberalism among the advanced European economies. Starting in the 1980s, the European Commission became increasingly aggressive in enforcing antitrust policy, challenging mergers, and clamping down on government aid to businesses, even those owned by the state (Buch-Hansen and Wigger 2010; Jabko 2005). The Commission also spearheaded the expansion of competition in previously sheltered utilities and public services, including railroads, air transportation, gas, electricity, telecommunications, and postal services. Having liberalized public services, the Commission shifted its attention in the 2000s to promoting competition in private services, most notably through the infamous Bolkestein Directive of 2005 that raised the specter of low-wage workers from Eastern Europe displacing the high-wage workers of Western Europe (Crespy 2015; McLauchlin 2005).[1] Other advances in European integration, such as the Single Market Act of 1986, which worked to remove all nontariff barriers to trade by 1992, and the European Monetary Union (EMU), which strives to limit government budget deficits, likewise pushed in a neoliberal direction (De la Porte and Heins 2016; Scharpf 2013; Streeck 1995).

The end of the Cold War bolstered the cause of neoliberalism by discrediting the Communist alternative to neoliberal capitalism and reducing the need to offer protections and benefits to the working class in order to woo it away from communism (Fukuyama 1992; Keating and McCrone 2015). In addition, under the prodding of the USA, international institutions like the International Monetary Fund (IMF), World Bank, and General Agreement on Tariffs and Trade/World Trade Organization (GATT/WTO) increasingly aligned themselves with the neoliberal "Washington consensus" (Stiglitz 2007, 2010; Williamson 1990). Even crises of neoliberal capitalism, most notably the financial meltdown of 2008 and subsequent Great Recession, did little to diminish the influence of neoliberalism (Crouch 2011; Schmidt and Thatcher 2013).

Countries have varied greatly in their enthusiasm for neoliberalism, however. Among the affluent democracies, the USA and the UK were early and far-ranging adopters of neoliberalism. At the other end of the spectrum, France, the subject of this book, stands out for its contestation of economic liberalization.[2] To an extent unparalleled among the leading affluent democracies, economic liberalization is contested in France in a quadruple sense. First, liberalization is contested in the streets, provoking protests, demonstrations, and strikes on a regular basis. To take just one example, French governments have launched seven different pension reforms in the past three decades – in 1993, 1995, 2002, 2007, 2010, 2013, and 2019. Some pension reforms have succeeded, and some have failed, but all have triggered large-scale protests and, in several cases, strikes that shut down the country. The same holds true of just about every significant liberalizing reform in France, whether of social protection, labor markets, or corporate governance and restructuring.

Second, economic liberalization is contested within governing circles. French politicians, including those on the right, display a deep ambivalence toward economic liberalization, concerned that it might erode state power or social order. They also display an enduring attraction to statist and nationalist policies, especially in times of crisis. France stands out, then, for a two-level contestation of economic liberalization – by popular protestors, but also by political leaders from left to right.

Third, economic liberalization is contested in the sense of making relatively limited inroads in France. The French political landscape is littered with liberalizing initiatives, whether to cut public spending or ease labor market regulations, which were defeated by strikes and demonstrations. Such episodes are more than anecdotal. As discussed later in this chapter, France ranks as the least liberal of Europe's advanced political economies along a variety of indicators of fiscal policy, labor market flexibility, and competition in product markets.

Fourth, the contestation of economic liberalization has, on more than a few occasions, spilled over to a contestation of the government itself. French governments have seen their entire agenda or even their capacity to govern derailed by popular opposition to liberalizing initiatives. Alain Juppé's 1995 Social Security reform was the paradigmatic case, triggering the biggest protest and strike movement since May 1968. Not only was Juppé forced to abandon much of his plan, but when he sought to move on to other liberalizing reforms, protestors continued to block his initiatives. Effectively unable to govern, Juppé convinced President Jacques Chirac to call early legislative elections in the hope of winning a mandate for liberalizing reform. French voters had other ideas, however, ousting the right in favor of a Socialist-led coalition.

Much the same story of failed liberalizing initiatives and damaged political prospects could be told of Juppé's conservative predecessor, Edouard Balladur, the prime minister from 1993 to 1995, and Dominique de Villepin, who served from 2005 to 2007. As Chapters 2 and 3 describe, Prime Ministers Balladur and de Villepin both had presidential aspirations, but their political careers were derailed by protests against their liberalizing initiatives. In 1995, after two years of repeated retreats in the face of contestation, Balladur failed to make it beyond the first round of the presidential election. As for de Villepin, he was so politically damaged by an unsuccessful effort in 2006 to loosen job protections for youths that he abandoned the idea of running for president altogether.[3]

The current French president, Emmanuel Macron, has discovered, much to his chagrin, that the contestation of liberalizing reforms, and the governments that propose them, is not just a thing of the past. Early in his first term as president, Macron managed to enact liberalizing reforms in fiscal policy, labor market regulation, and the operation of the public French railroad company. However, in late 2018, Macron's government was rocked by the so-called yellow vest protestors, who sought to reverse many of Macron's liberalizing reforms and compel the president to step down. Although Macron survived the yellow vests' demands for his resignation, he was forced to make a number of expensive concessions. He also emerged politically wounded, with his popularity in the doldrums. Once again, contestation not only defeated specific liberalizing initiatives, but also weakened the leader who proposed them.

Of course, opposition to economic liberalization is not unique to France. Indeed, as the literatures on national models of capitalism and worlds of welfare capitalism demonstrate, some countries have openly rejected the neoliberal model associated with the USA and UK while faring quite well economically. The economies of these countries deviate in important ways from neoliberal principles, in particular through extensive regulation, high wages, and heavy taxes, but these countries possess countervailing strengths that allow them to thrive in international competition. The Germanic Christian Democratic or "coordinated market economy" (CME) competes on the basis of continuous upgrading in manufacturing made possible by highly skilled workers, collaborative industrial relations, and supportive financial and technological institutions (Deeg 1999; Hall and Soskice 2001; Soskice 1999; Streeck 1991; Streeck and Yamamura 2005). The Nordic Social Democratic countries succeed on the basis of public or social investment in childcare, lifelong learning, and technology (Huo and Stephens 2015; Morel et al. 2012; Ornston 2012; Pontusson 2010). Because CME and Social Democratic countries display tremendous economic vitality, political leaders have little reason to discard their economic and social systems in favor of the liberal model.

The same cannot be said for France, however. It has been a very long time since anyone described France as an economic model. As related later in this chapter, the French economy has been mired in slow growth and high unemployment for decades, and its citizens express deep unhappiness with the economy along with pessimism about the future. Thus, France is a case of contested economic liberalization, despite a highly problematic economic and social system. In addition, as discussed later in this chapter, all of the countries held up as alternatives to the neoliberal model have gone through significant episodes of economic liberalization and score higher on most indices of economic liberalism than France. Even compared with the countries held up as alternatives to the neoliberal model, France stands out for its resistance to liberalizing reform.

Admittedly, France is not the only country where liberalizing reforms have been contested. Paul Pierson offers perhaps the most compelling explanation of why liberalizing initiatives may trigger protests that force governments to retreat. Pierson's "new politics of the welfare state" focuses on the obstacles to cutbacks or "retrenchment" of social welfare programs (Pierson 1994, 1996, 2001a). Pierson shows that the existence of massive welfare state policies has changed the political terrain on which reformers operate. In particular, it has created powerful constituencies, whether the recipients of social policies (the elderly, the sick, the unemployed) or the providers of social policies (physicians, nurses, childcare and elderly care workers), who stand ready to mobilize against proposed cuts. In addition, because much welfare reform imposes concentrated, immediate costs in return for diffuse and uncertain benefits, defenders of social programs have stronger incentives to organize and mobilize than advocates of retrenchment. As a result, even in countries where liberal parties are or were strong, like the USA under Reagan and the UK under Thatcher, interest groups and protestors have often been able to block retrenchment efforts.

Pierson's insights contribute centrally to the analysis in this book. That said, French welfare state reform stands out, even by Piersonian standards, for the high level of contestation it provokes and the frequency with which liberalizing initiatives are defeated. In addition, the contestation and resistance to economic liberalization in France extends beyond welfare retrenchment to such areas as industrial relations, economic restructuring, privatization, and corporate control. Finally, at times, French contestation goes beyond specific liberalizing reforms, challenging the legitimacy of the government itself.

This book explains why economic liberalization is so contested in France. While scholars and pundits tend to blame either French leaders or a deep-seated French aversion to the market, this book offers a historical and structural explanation, centering on the legacies of France's postwar economic model. In the postwar period, alone in Europe, France pursued prosperity through a so-called *dirigiste* or statist approach, and the legacies of this statist model – specifically the policy, party-political, and institutional legacies – have fueled the contestation of economic liberalization long after the model itself was dismantled. Although grounded in the unique features of French history, this analysis also points to sources of contestation of economic liberalization that may be present in other countries, suggesting possibilities for extending the argument beyond France.

The rest of this introductory chapter is divided into five sections. Section 1.1 briefly describes the main features of the *dirigiste* model, the achievements and limitations of this model, and France's turn away from the model in the 1980s. Section 1.2 demonstrates that economic liberalization has made less headway in France than in the leading European political economies. Section 1.3 shows that this limited liberalization is not the byproduct of a well-functioning alternative economic model. Section 1.4 presents and critiques three explanations of the French outcome, centered on economic culture, political leadership, and the character of the welfare regime respectively. Finally, Section 1.5 presents the argument and plan of the book.

1.1   The *Dirigiste* Model

Before analyzing the contestation of economic liberalization in France, it is important to understand the postwar *dirigiste* model that has contributed centrally to this contestation. France's postwar economic model concentrated power in the hands of enlightened technocrats, who were charged with steering the direction of economic reconstruction and modernization (Bauchet 1986; Birnbaum 1977, 1978; Bloch-Lainé 1982; Bloch-Lainé and Bouvier 1986; Cohen 1977; Hall 1986; Massé 1965; Rousso 1986; Shonfield 1965; Zysman 1983). The technocrats charted a series of five-year plans prioritizing sectors for development. Later, they launched high-tech industrial projects designed to catapult France to a position of global leadership in cutting-edge industries like aviation, computers, telecommunications, and nuclear energy (Cohen 1992; Cohen and Bauer 1985; Zysman 1977).

French authorities deployed a variety of policy instruments to induce companies to go along with their ambitions, including subsidies, protection from foreign competition, low-interest loans, lucrative government contracts, and free technology developed in public laboratories. They also displayed no hesitation in picking winners, specifically by favoring business over labor, emerging sectors over declining industries, and giant so-called national champions over small- and medium-sized enterprises (SMEs). This *dirigiste* system operated in a top-down, exclusionary manner, sometimes described as a conspiracy between big business and the high-level civil service (Shonfield 1965), which largely ignored the demands and concerns of small business, shopkeepers, and ordinary workers (Levy 1999b).

For three decades after the war, a period that the French refer to as the Trente Glorieuses (Fourastié 1979), or Thirty Glorious Years, France's statist model delivered excellent economic results. There were failures of course, industrial policies that never quite got off the ground, like the Plan Calcul to develop a computer industry, or that yielded technical marvels that were completely unviable from a commercial standpoint, like the Concorde supersonic airplane (Cohen and Bauer 1985; Zysman 1977, 1978). Still, voluntarist initiatives produced many successes as well, from civilian nuclear power to high-speed trains (Trains à Grande Vitesse, TGV), and within a generation, France was transformed from a sleepy, backwards agrarian economy to an advanced industrial society.

Not everyone was satisfied with the *dirigiste* model, however. In May 1968, a series of protests by students and workers, weary of top-down governance and economic exclusion, brought France to the brink of revolution (Berstein 2006; Hoffmann 1978). The specter of revolution, along with the subsequent mobilization of other groups, such as farmers and shopkeepers, placed state authorities on the defensive. In response, *dirigiste* policy shifted from promoting economic modernization to protecting jobs at all costs (Berger 1981; Cohen 1989; Levy 1999b). The statist model grew increasingly dysfunctional, pouring vast amounts of money into uncompetitive companies to prevent them from making layoffs.

In 1983, these growing dysfunctions, along with the pressures of international competition and European integration, led a Socialist government headed by François Mitterrand to make a dramatic U-turn from its voluntarist approach and begin winding down the practices and institutions associated with the *dirigiste* model (Hall 1986, 1990; Levy 1999b; Schmidt 1996). This process would continue under Mitterrand's successors on both the left and the right, and today, little remains of the postwar industrial policy model.

French authorities did not just roll back the *dirigiste* state, however. Fearful of popular protest, Mitterrand and his successors put in place what I have called the "social anesthesia state," that is, a variety of generous social and labor market programs to compensate and demobilize the victims and potential opponents of the break with the *dirigiste* model (Levy 2005a, 2005b, 2008; Levy et al. 2006). In a process that Mark Vail describes as "socialized marketization" (Vail 2010), France would move sharply toward the market, in the sense of putting an end to voluntarist industrial policy, but would simultaneously expand state spending on social protection. Indeed, French social and total government spending as a percentage of GDP rose to the highest level in the Organisation for Economic Co-operation and Development (OECD), surpassing even the Scandinavian countries (OECD 2019c, 2021d).

As Chapter 2 elaborates in greater detail, the reforms of the 1980s and 1990s rolled back the key policies and institutions associated with the *dirigiste* model, from credit rationing, to price controls, to sectoral industrial policy. These liberalizing reforms were arguably as far-reaching as anything seen in Europe at the time. Since then, however, French economic and social reform has slowed or, in some instances, reversed.

1.2   Limited Liberalization

In the early 1990s, as the agenda in France shifted from dismantling *dirigiste* industrial policy to forging new economic strategies and scaling back social spending and labor market regulations (Aghion et al. 2014; Cohen and Buigues 2014), popular resistance stiffened. Reform efforts – from the Juppé Social Security Plan of 1995, to changes in the pension system, to labor market legislation – generated large protests, and governments often responded by abandoning their initiatives. Certainly, governments have introduced important liberalizing reforms, and market forces play a significantly greater role in France's political economy today than four decades ago. Still, France consistently ranks among the least liberal of the advanced European economies along a variety of indicators of fiscal management, labor market flexibility, and competition in product markets.

This section compares France to Europe's leading political economies, in particular Denmark, Germany, the Netherlands, and Sweden. Countries like the UK and Ireland are excluded because they belong to the liberal model of welfare capitalism and would, therefore, be expected to have more liberal economic and social policies than France. The Southern European countries are excluded for the opposite reason: marked by late development, relatively recent transitions to democracy, and corrupt, patronage politics, they would be expected to have less liberal economic and social policies than France (although they, in fact, score roughly the same on indices of economic liberalization).[4] By contrast, Denmark, Germany, the Netherlands, and Sweden have much in common with France. They are advanced economies, with a commitment to quality public services and robust social protection. Moreover, French authorities tend to identify with these countries, especially Germany, seeing them as a yardstick for measuring France's performance. Yet compared with this group, France scores lower across an array of measures of economic liberalization.

Fiscal policy offers perhaps the most striking example of France's distinctive record on economic liberalization. A liberal fiscal stance would entail low levels of public spending, particularly social spending, limited taxation, balanced budgets, and little public debt. Yet looking at the data, even before the COVID-19 crisis, which sent French public spending and government deficits skyrocketing, France stood out for its illiberal fiscal policy.[5] As Figure 1.1 shows, French public spending totaled 55.4 percent of GDP in 2019, the highest figure in the OECD. While spending levels may fluctuate from year to year with shifts in the business cycle, French public spending has been above 50 percent of GDP every year since 1989.

Of course, not all public spending is created equal. Spending that contributes to business productivity, such as infrastructure, education, and research and development (R&D), is less objectionable from a liberal standpoint than spending on the welfare state. Social spending elicits liberal criticism because it not only requires high taxes, but is also claimed to foster idleness and dependency by giving recipients an alternative to

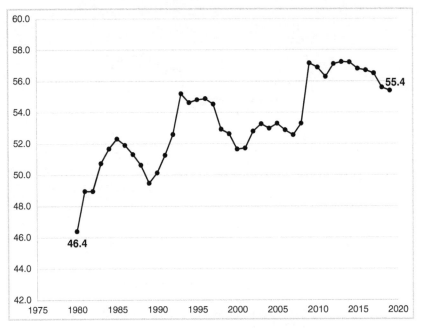

Figure 1.1 French public expenditure as a percentage of GDP, 1980–2019
Source: INSEE (2021c)

paid employment (Fulmer 2010; Murray 1984; Tanner 2008). Although
it is true that historically, France has invested heavily in infrastructure,
education, and R&D, what stands out over the past few decades is the
dramatic progression of social spending.

    In 1981, as Figure 1.2 relates, France was a relatively low social
spender at 15.6 percent of GDP, compared with Denmark (20.1 percent), Germany (22.4 percent), the Netherlands (23.9 percent), and
Sweden (25.6 percent). Even the UK spent more (18.1 percent). In
subsequent years, however, France's welfare state grew rapidly – to
the point that in 1999 France surpassed Sweden as the country with
the most expensive welfare state in the OECD. In 2009, French social
spending topped 30 percent of GDP, where it has remained ever since;
no other OECD country has reached this level in over a quarter-
century (since Sweden in 1996). Between 1981 and 2018, French
social expenditures doubled to 31.2 percent of GDP, making France
the most expensive welfare state in the world by more than 3 percent
of GDP over second-place Denmark (28.0 percent). Germany, which
spent 5.8 percent of GDP more than France on social programs in

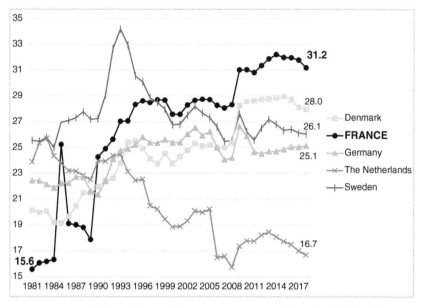

Figure 1.2 Social spending as a percentage of GDP, 1981–2018
Source: OECD (2019c)

1981, spent 7.1 percent of GDP less in 2018, for a massive relative shift of 12.9 percent of GDP.

High levels of government spending, social or otherwise, do not necessarily mean big budget deficits. Historically, the Nordic countries combined large welfare states with high levels of taxation to pay for them (Huber and Stephens 1998, 2001; Steinmo 1993; Stephens 1996; Stephens et al. 1999). They ran budget surpluses, not deficits, and returned to surpluses following a steep recession in the early 1990s. The same cannot be said of France, however. France has high taxes, to be sure. As Figure 1.3 shows, in 2017, France passed Denmark to become the OECD's most heavily taxed country, with public revenues equal to 46.2 percent of GDP.

Yet as Figure 1.4 demonstrates, all this taxation has not produced balanced budgets. Indeed, the last time that France ran a budget surplus was in 1974, that is, before the current president, Emmanuel Macron, was even born! Nor have the strictures of the EMU put an end to French budget deficits. Between 2002 and 2016, France ran a deficit below the EMU-authorized ceiling of 3 percent of GDP just twice, in 2006 and 2007. France has been an "unrepentant sinner," in the choice words of Ben Clift,

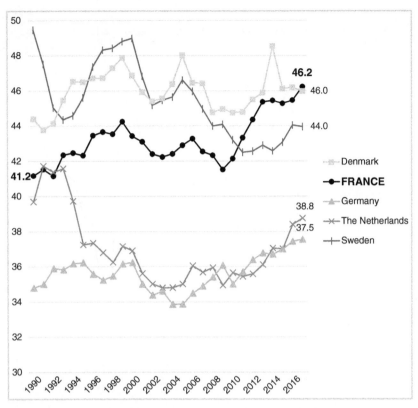

Figure 1.3 Total tax revenues as a percentage of GDP, 1990–2017
Source: OECD (2019d)

consistently flouting EMU budgetary rules (Clift 2006). In 2008, France, like many countries, responded to the financial meltdown with Keynesian demand stimulus, pushing its deficit well above 3 percent of GDP (Levy 2017). Unlike other countries, however, France remained in the European Commission's "excessive deficit procedure" for nine years, from 2009 to 2018 (European Commission 2020). By the time that France exited the excessive deficit procedure, only Spain, still working through the effects of the collapse of its banking system, remained under Commission supervision. What is more, the following year, in 2019 – that is, before the economic and fiscal havoc wreaked by the COVID-19 crisis – the French budget deficit again surpassed the EMU ceiling of 3 percent of GDP.

While France has avoided Commission sanctions for excessive deficits, it has not avoided rising public debt. Even before the COVID-19

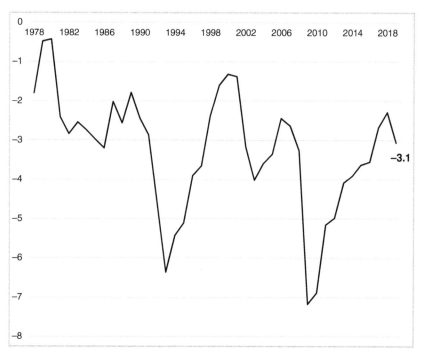

Figure 1.4 French budget deficit as a percentage of GDP, 1978–2019
Source: OECD (2019f)

crisis, French debt was nearing 100 percent of GDP, which Figure 1.5 shows was well above that of the other advanced European economies. Indeed, the only European countries with higher levels of debt are the Southern European countries at the heart of the sovereign debt crisis (Greece, Portugal, Spain, Italy, and Cyprus) along with Belgium, where communal conflict between the Flemish and Walloons has often paralyzed national decision-making.

When it comes to fiscal policy, France could not be further from liberal principles. Compared with the advanced European political economies, it has the highest level of public spending in the OECD, the highest level of social spending, and the highest level of taxation. France has not balanced a budget in nearly fifty years and has spent the last decade fighting with the European Commission over its inability or unwillingness to keep budget deficits below 3 percent of GDP. Thanks to this "unrepentant sinning" (Clift 2006), France's public debt is the largest of any major European country except Italy. France's fiscal policy may be irresponsible and reckless, or it may be justified by the investments

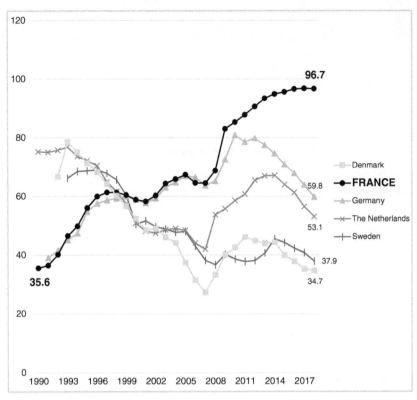

Figure 1.5 Government debt as a percentage of GDP, 1990–2018
Source: IMF (2019)

and services that the state provides. One thing that French fiscal policy is definitely *not*, though, is liberal.

French labor market policy also stands out for its deviation from liberal principles. A liberal labor market policy would let markets set wages, keep unemployment benefits and other forms of income support at low levels so as to preserve work incentives, and give employers the freedom to hire and fire workers and to employ workers on a part-time or fixed-term basis without restriction. Labor market policy is more difficult to measure than fiscal policy because along with quantifiable indicators like average wages or collective bargaining coverage, it involves more subjective judgments about such features as the strictness of employment protection or restrictions on part-time employment. Consequently, any single indicator or set of indicators produced by a single organization should be taken with a grain of salt. Still, a variety of organizations

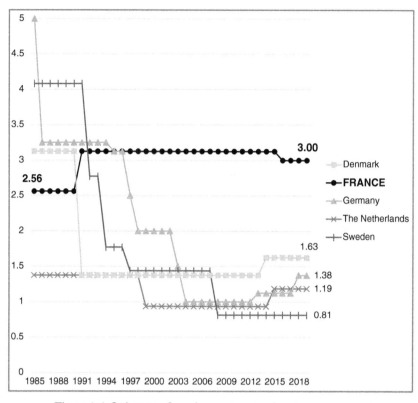

Figure 1.6 Strictness of employment protection, temporary employment, 1985–2019
Source: OECD (2019e)

deploying different metrics all reach the conclusion that French labor market policy is not very liberal.

France scores in the middle of the European pack on most of the OECD's measures of "employment protection," such as the rules governing individual and collective dismissals: 2.56 for France in 2019, compared with an OECD average of 2.06 and 2.60 for Germany (OECD 2019h). However, when it comes to temporary contracts, Figure 1.6 reveals that France is much more restrictive than its peers: 3.00 for France in 2019, versus an OECD average of 1.74 and 1.38 for Germany. In addition, whereas France has become more restrictive since 1985, all of the other countries in the reference group have become less restrictive, often significantly so. Between 1985 and 2019, the strictness of

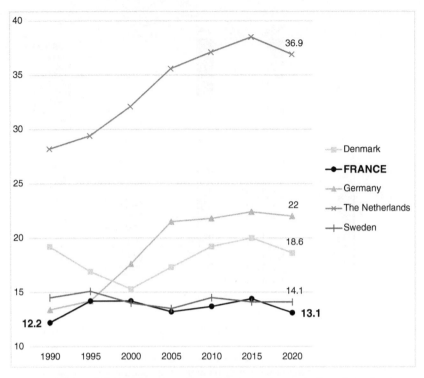

Figure 1.7 Part-time employment as a percentage of total employment, 1990–2020
Note: People in employment (whether employees or self-employed) who work fewer than thirty hours per week in their main job; 2020 figure for Germany is for 2019.
Source: OECD (2019g)

employment protection for temporary workers increased from 2.56 to 3.00 in France, while plummeting from 3.13 to 1.63 in Denmark, 5.00 to 1.38 in Germany, and 4.08 to. 0.81 in Sweden. As a result, France went from having the second most liberal arrangements among the advanced European economies in 1985, behind only the Netherlands, the Mecca of part-time employment, to having the most restrictive regulatory framework by a considerable margin in 2019.

France also restricts part-time employment. Among West European nations, only Greece and Luxembourg have a lower percentage of part-time workers. As Figure 1.7 shows, in 2020, 13.1 percent of French employees worked part-time, compared with 14.1 percent in Sweden, 18.6 percent in Denmark, 22.0 percent in Germany, and 36.9 percent in the Netherlands.

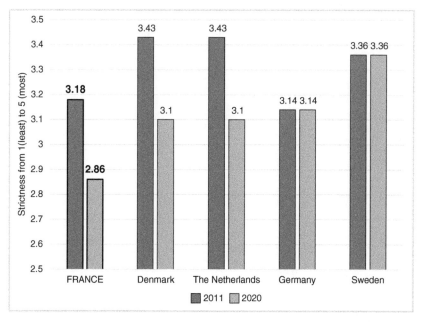

Figure 1.8 Strictness of labor market activation requirements, 2011 and 2020
Note: Strictness of activity-related eligibility criteria for recipients of unemployment and related benefits: the strictness of job search and monitoring procedures, work-availability requirements, and suitable job criteria and sanctions for benefit claimants.
Source: OECD (2021b)

In addition, according to the OECD, France has the least demanding activation requirements for the unemployed, that is, it puts the least pressure on the unemployed to look for work or accept job offers. The OECD index is based on the strictness of job search and monitoring procedures, work availability requirements, and sanctions for benefit claimants. Figure 1.8 shows that in 2020, France had the lowest score for the strictness of activation requirements, 2.86, as against 3.10 for Denmark and the Netherlands, 3.14 for Germany, and 3.36 for Sweden. Moreover, France had eased its demands on the unemployed since 2011, with its strictness score falling from 3.18 to 2.86.

Finally, an "Employment Flexibility Index," based on World Bank data and methods, paints France in an even less liberal light (Lithuanian Free Market Institute 2018). Looking at the rules governing fixed-term contracts, redundancies, and working hours, this index rates France dead last out of forty-one EU and OECD countries, with 38.4 points out of a possible 100, more than 5 points below the next lowest scorer,

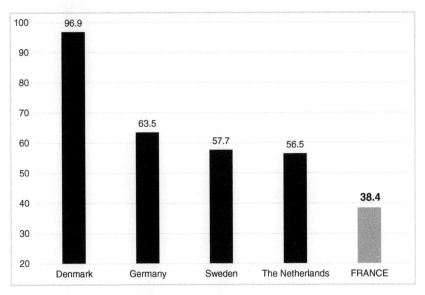

Figure 1.9 Employment Flexibility Index (0–100), 2016
Source: Lithuanian Free Market Institute (2018)

Luxembourg, with 43.6 points. As Figure 1.9 demonstrates, the gap between France and its trading partners is substantial, with the Netherlands tallying 56.5 points, Sweden 57.7, Germany 63.5, and Denmark, the top-ranked country, 96.9. France scores especially low on hiring flexibility (22.3/100) because it prohibits fixed-term contracts for permanent tasks and caps the maximum length of fixed-term contracts at eighteen months. France also scores low on work-time flexibility (25.0/100) because it mandates 30.3 paid workdays per year and requires the payment of premiums for work on a weekly rest day (20 percent), overtime hours (25 percent premium), and night work (8 percent).

Indices of labor market flexibility are obviously more subjective and contentious than the kinds of quantitative measures used to gauge fiscal policy. Indeed, the World Bank stopped ranking countries due to criticism that the metrics reflected a neoliberal bias and neglected the benefits that labor regulation might provide (Aleksynska and Cazes 2014). Although the Lithuanian Free Market Institute claims to still be using the World Bank data, the organization is less well known than the World Bank and less subject to scrutiny. Moreover, its very name raises red flags about potential biases. Still, not all indices of labor market regulation are subjective. A number of objective indicators likewise suggest that the French labor market is the least liberal of the advanced European economies.

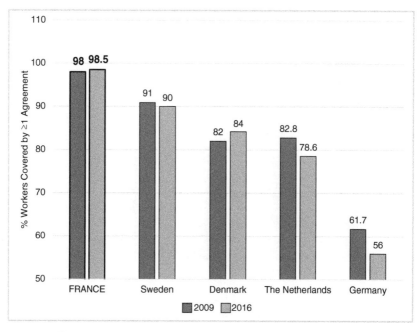

Figure 1.10 Collective bargaining coverage rate, 2009 and 2016
Note: Percentage of workers covered by one or more collective agreements; 2009 figure for Sweden is from 2007 and 2016 figure is from 2015; 2016 figure for France is from 2014; 2016 figure for Denmark is from 2015.
Source: ILO (2016)

The International Labor Organization (ILO) reports that France has the highest percentage of workers covered by one or more collective bargaining agreements of any of the eighty-five countries in its sample. Figure 1.10 shows that in France in 2016, 98.5 percent of workers were covered by at least one collective agreement, as compared with 90.0 percent in Sweden, 84.0 percent in Denmark, 78.6 percent in the Netherlands, and 56.0 percent in Germany. The high rate of French coverage is all the more remarkable given that France has the lowest rate of unionization in Western Europe, at just 7.9 percent of the labor force (ILO 2017). Clearly, French unions are not the driving force behind the high rate of coverage. As Chris Howell has shown, the French state has long substituted for the social partners, notably by extending agreements reached in one sector or even one company to an entire sector or the economy as a whole (Howell 1992a).

The French state has also intervened aggressively to limit low pay. The French minimum wage stands at 62 percent of the median wage, versus

Table 1.1 *Labor income distribution, 2017*

Country	D10/D1 ratio	D5/D1 ratio
FRANCE	10.6	3.2
Sweden	10.3	3.5
Denmark	12.8	4.5
The Netherlands	13.4	3.6
Germany	30.9	8.9

Note: D10/D1 ratio = labor income of highest 10 percent of earners (decile) divided by labor income of lowest 10 percent of earners. D5/D1 ratio = labor income of 5th decile of earners divided by labor income of lowest 10 percent of earners. *Source:* ILO (2021)

47 percent in the Netherlands and 46 percent in Germany (OECD 2021f). The Nordic countries do not have a legal minimum wage, but high levels of collective bargaining coverage and the extension of collective agreements mean that almost every sector has a minimum wage. The collectively bargained minimum wage generally falls between 50 and 60 percent of the median wage, which is still below the French figure.

The combination of a high minimum wage and the use of the extension procedure has led to significant wage compression in France. According to ILO data on labor income in 2017, France has the second-lowest ratio between the income of the top 10 percent of wage earners (D10) and the bottom 10 percent (D1) among the advanced European economies. As Table 1.1 relates, France's D10/D1 ratio is 10.6, compared with 12.8 in Denmark, 13.4 in the Netherlands, and 30.9 in Germany. Only Sweden, with a D10/D1 ratio of 10.3, has a slightly more equal income distribution. Table 1.1 shows that France's D5/D1 ratio, at 3.2, is the lowest among all of these countries, including Sweden.

France's labor market policy, like its fiscal policy, is at odds with liberal principles. The government restricts the hiring of fixed-term and part-time workers, imposes few obligations on the unemployed to look for work, and uses a combination of a high minimum wage and the extension procedure to compress wages and push up the earnings of low-paid workers. As Howell describes, some liberalizing changes have been introduced in France through the substitution of (often one-sided) collective agreements for state rules (Howell 1992a, 1992b, 1996, 2006, 2008, 2009, 2018). Yet, the French state continues to regulate the labor market in critical ways.

France's approach to competition in industry and services is also at odds with liberal orthodoxy. A liberal approach would allow companies to succeed or fail based on their performance in the marketplace, as opposed to their size or political connections. It would also limit anti-competitive regulations that restrict entry into businesses or professions. Finally, it would avoid regulations that hamper business flexibility, innovation, and profitability. Here, again, adherence to liberal principles can be hard to quantify. Still, there is considerable evidence of French resistance to procompetitive reform (Cohen and Buigues 2014).

France has consistently opposed EU Commission efforts to expand competition, whether in industry and finance, public services, or private services. France has run afoul of the Commission repeatedly for bailing out ailing national champions, from the PSA and Renault car companies in the 1980s, to Air France and the Crédit Lyonnais bank in the 1990s, to the Alstom manufacturer of nuclear turbines and high-speed trains in the 2000s, to Renault and PSA (again) along with several banks during the 2008 financial crisis.[6] In addition, starting with a conservative government in 2005, France has reserved the right to block foreign takeovers of French companies in sectors that the government deems strategic (Clift 2009a).

France has also been the most tenacious opponent of EU Commission efforts to expand competition in public services, such as telecommunications, transportation, and electricity (Cole and Drake 2000). In each instance, French authorities have counterposed a French model of "public service" revolving around high-quality services provided by domestic monopolists, often owned by the state (Cole 1999). French governments have not only opposed EU directives to expand competition, but also dragged their feet in complying when such directives were adopted. Not surprisingly, the OECD's 2017 index of "Regulation in Network Sectors," encompassing the energy, transportation, and communications sectors, ranks France as the most heavily regulated of its peer countries. France's score of 1.85 is far higher than that of Sweden (1.35), Germany (1.06), Denmark (1.01), and the Netherlands (0.98) (OECD 2017c).

France has spearheaded opposition to the liberalization of private services as well. The Commission's Bolkestein Directive, expanding competition and the country-of-origin principle in private services, became a political football in France in the run-up to the 2005 referendum on a proposed EU constitution (Marthaler 2005). Critics charged that the Bolkestein Directive would allow detached laborers from Eastern Europe working at cut-rate wages to take jobs away from the French. The apocryphal "Polish plumber" became a staple of no-vote rallies and helped fuel the defeat of the referendum.

Indices of business regulation and competition are generally based on a combination of quantitative and qualitative factors, making them more subjective than measurements of government spending or D10/D1 income ratios. Still, the indices of various organizations all conclude that France regulates business and limits competition more than its peer countries. In the 2019 World Bank rankings for "the ease of doing business" (World Bank 2019a), which focuses on the challenges of starting and expanding a business, France occupied the 32nd position, besting the Netherlands (34th), but trailing Germany (24th), Sweden (12th), and Denmark (3rd).

The World Economic Forum reaches a similar conclusion. In its 2018 "global competitiveness index" (World Economic Forum 2018), France ranked a respectable 17th overall, but was still behind Germany (3rd), the Netherlands (6th), Sweden (9th), and Denmark (10th). What is more, France's performance was very uneven. The country fared well on a number of metrics that are correlated with high levels of public spending, including research institutions (3rd), quality of research publications (5th), public health (7th), infrastructure (8th), and patent applications (12th). By contrast, France ranked much lower on measures of competition and regulation, such as "service trade restrictiveness" (55th) and the "burden of government regulation" (107th). France also scored very low on indices of labor market flexibility, most notably hiring and firing practices (130th) and the labor tax rate (140th).

OECD indices point in the same direction. The OECD's "indicator of product market regulation" is compiled on the basis of six dimensions of government intervention and regulation: public ownership, involvement in business operations, simplification and evaluation of regulations, administrative burdens on start-ups, barriers in service and network sectors, and barriers to trade and investment. The average OECD score is 1.38, with the five most competition-friendly countries averaging 1.00 and the five least competition-friendly countries 1.82. As Figure 1.11 relates, France scores 1.57, meaning that product markets are significantly more regulated in France than among its peer competitors, who are all bunched together between 1.02 (Denmark) and 1.11 (Sweden). Indeed, the French score is much closer to the average of the five countries with the least competition (a difference of 0.25) than to the nearest advanced economy, Sweden (a difference of 0.46).

Although it is possible to quibble with individual metrics and the organizations doing the evaluating, all of these metrics indicate that French policy with respect to business competition and regulation is not very liberal. The same is true of French fiscal and labor market policies. In short, France is a clear outlier when it comes to economic liberalization. France deviates from the prevailing practices of not just liberal exemplars like the USA and UK, but also Continental European countries like Germany, Holland, Sweden, and Denmark that share France's commitment to a mixed economy and robust social protection.[7]

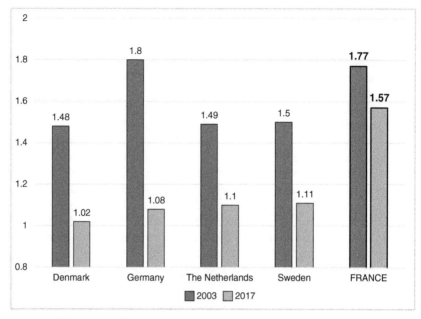

Figure 1.11 Economy-wide product market regulation, 2003 and 2017
Note: Index compiled by the OECD on the basis of six dimensions of government intervention and regulation: public ownership, involvement in business operations, simplification and
evaluation of regulations, administrative burdens on start-ups, barriers
in service and network sectors, and barriers to trade and investment.
Source: OECD (2018a)

France has not always occupied this outlier position. Much of diver-
gence between France and the advanced European political economies
has arisen in the three decades, since the early 1990s. Figures 1.2, 1.3,
and 1.5 show that France's fiscal policy was generally in the middle of
the pack around 1990. Thirty years later, however, France had the highest levels public spending, social spending (Figure 1.2), tax revenues
(Figure 1.3), and general government debt (Figure 1.5).

The figures relating to labor market reform likewise show France
becoming less liberal over time compared with Denmark, Germany, the
Netherlands, and Sweden. The evolution of the strictness of employment protection for temporary workers (Figure 1.6) parallels that of fiscal policy: France occupied a middle-of-the pack position in 1985 but
became the least liberal because it increased restrictions slightly at a
time when Germany, Holland, Sweden, and Denmark were all reducing
their restrictions drastically. The data for the strictness of labor market

activation requirements only go back to 2011 (Figure 1.8), but over this period, France became less demanding and replaced Germany as the country with the weakest activation requirements. The numbers on part-time employment (Figure 1.7) and collective bargaining coverage (Figure 1.10) in France have remained essentially unchanged, and the same can be said for Sweden and Denmark. However, Germany and the Netherlands have become less restrictive, especially with respect to part-time employment. Between 1990 and 2019, part-time employment increased from 13.4 percent to 22.0 percent of total employment in Germany and from 28.2 percent to 37.0 percent of total employment in the Netherlands. Overall, France's labor market indicators are the least liberal of the five countries, and developments since the early 1990s are the main reason why.

The evolution of business regulations points to a different pathway to France's outlier status. Here, regulations have eased in France, but less than in all of the leading European economies. In light of the global push to remove regulations that limit trade along with EU efforts to expand competition in industry and services, it is no surprise that there has been a common trend toward reduced business regulation across Europe. France has generally been less accommodating of this trend than other leading European countries, however. For example, Figure 1.11 shows that the index of product market regulations for France fell from 1.77 in 2003 to 1.57 in 2017, but this decrease of 0.20 pales in comparison to the decreases in the Netherlands and Sweden (0.39), Denmark (0.46), and especially Germany (0.72). Indeed, whereas the German economy was slightly more regulated than the French in 2003, by 2017 France's index of regulation was nearly 50 percent higher than that of Germany (1.57 vs. 1.08).

France has been the most resistant to economic liberalization of Europe's leading political economies. It scores lower on indices of liberalization in fiscal policy, labor market regulation, and product market regulation. This gap cannot be attributed to a historic French aversion to liberalization. On the contrary, much of it has resulted from developments since the early 1990s. Having established that France is an outlier when it comes to economic liberalization, Section 1.3 engages a popular explanation – that French resistance to economic liberalization stems from the success of an alternative, nonliberal economic model.

1.3   An Alternative Economic Model?

Scholars of comparative political economy have long shown that the liberal Anglo-American model is not the only way to organize a modern, dynamic, prosperous economy (Amsden 1989; Hall 1986; Johnson 1982; Katzenstein 1978; Shonfield 1965; Wade 1990; Zysman 1983). In their typologies, France – along with Japan, then later the East Asian "tigers" – incarnates a statist model, in which state authorities direct the course of economic development. Given that economic liberalization would erode the state's capacity to steer the economy, French authorities could be reasonably expected to resist in order to preserve their national model. What is more, from the comparative capitalism perspective, France is not alone in deviating from the liberal model. Every typology of note includes alternatives to liberal capitalism.

Peter Hall and David Soskice distinguish between two "varieties of capitalism" (Hall and Soskice 2001): a British-style liberal market economy (LME) and a Germanic coordinated market economy (CME). Building on earlier depictions of the German model (Gerschenkron 1962; Katzenstein 1989; Shonfield 1965; Streeck 1987, 1991), Hall and Soskice describe the various mechanisms of support among employers, employees, research institutions, and finance that enable CMEs to offset higher labor and welfare costs by moving into high-end, high-profit manufacturing niches. In a similar vein, Gøsta Esping-Andersen's "three worlds of welfare capitalism" includes a liberal model inspired by the USA and UK, but also a Christian Democratic model associated with Germany and a Social Democratic model embodied by the Nordic countries (Esping-Andersen 1990). The Social Democratic model generates egalitarian incomes, backed by a generous welfare state, thanks to high levels of labor force participation, especially among women, and a productive, cooperative workforce.

New ideal types continue to emerge. In recent years, EU reformers have advocated a shift toward a "social investment state" as a way of promoting success in "information-communication technologies" (ICT) and the "knowledge economy" (European Commission 2010; Garritzmann et al. 2022; Hemerijck 2017; Lisbon European Council 2000; Morel et al. 2012). This social investment model bears more than a passing resemblance to the Social Democratic model. The theme again is that high wages and social spending are possible as long as much of that spending goes to various forms of social investment that improve employee skills and capacity to participate in the digital economy. Key social investments, many of which were pioneered and are most developed among the Social Democratic countries, include early childhood education, lifelong learning, active labor market policies, publicly supported R&D, computer literacy, and universal internet access.

If there are multiple alternatives to liberal capitalism and France is one of them, then French resistance to liberalizing reforms would make perfect sense. The French would simply be defending a successful non-liberal model against changes that could potentially undercut the sources of the country's "comparative institutional advantage" (Hall and Soskice 2001). The notion that France is merely defending a well-functioning economic model against ill-advised liberalizing initiatives is problematic on several counts, however. For one thing, France may have incarnated a state-led growth model during the postwar boom period, but as Chapter 2 relates, that model entered into deep crisis in the 1970s and was largely dismantled in the 1980s and early 1990s (Hall 1990; Levy 2008; Schmidt 1996; Vail 2010).

Of course, the French state continues to play a role in the economy. Analyzing the rescue of French banks during the 2008 financial crisis, Nicolas Jabko and Elsa Massoc point to the persistence of elite networks spanning the public and private sectors that allow for give and take between the state and big business (Massoc and Jabko 2012). Ben Clift describes a revival of "economic nationalism" or "economic patriotism" beginning in 2005 and manifested most notably by efforts to protect strategic companies against foreign takeovers (Clift 2009a, 2009b, 2013; Clift and Woll 2012). Vivien Schmidt goes perhaps the furthest in arguing for the continuing economic role of the French state, describing France as a "state-enhanced economy," with the state now supporting business, as opposed to the traditional tack of directing business (Schmidt 2002b, 2003, 2008, 2009, 2012).

Although these works show that the French state still matters, there is less evidence that this intervention adds up to a coherent new or revised economic model. French authorities have dismantled the institutions, policy instruments, and budgets associated with the *dirigiste* model without forging an alternative institutional or cognitive framework. It is also unclear that current state intervention is "enhancing" the economy, especially as social spending has increasingly crowded out public investment in infrastructure and technology. Finally, many of the most significant and costly kinds of state intervention have been defensive in nature, such as one-off (or two-off) bailouts of high-profile companies and the prevention of foreign takeovers. These kinds of ad hoc defensive actions are a far cry from a coherent economic model.

A second limitation to the notion that France represents an alternative to the liberal approach is that by just about any economic measure the French economy has performed poorly for decades. French economic growth has lagged behind that of the advanced economies in Europe. Figure 1.12 shows that from 1990 to 2017, French economic growth averaged 1.57 percent, as compared with 1.65 percent in Denmark,

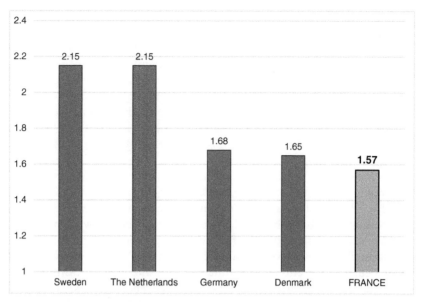

Figure 1.12 Average annual GDP growth, 1990–2017
Source: World Bank (2019b)

1.68 percent in Germany (laboring under the burden of reunification), and 2.15 percent in the Netherlands and Sweden.

Related to slow growth, France has experienced a hollowing out of manufacturing. As Figure 1.13 relates, value added in French manufacturing dropped from 16.3 percent of GDP in 1990 to just 10.1 percent of GDP in 2017. In the latter year, the corresponding numbers were 10.8 percent for the Netherlands (which has historically been a trading and banking economy more than a manufacturing economy), 12.8 percent for Denmark, 13.6 percent for Sweden, and 20.7 percent for Germany, more than double the French figure. Even Italy fared better than France, at 14.7 percent. In fact, the only major country with a lower score was the UK, at 9.2 percent, but the UK is known for having experienced massive deindustrialization since the 1970s. What is more, the UK is home to the City of London, which has generated a large number of high-wage jobs in finance and services (until Brexit at least) and for which there is no equivalent in France.

Slow growth and deindustrialization have fueled persistent high rates of unemployment. As Figure 1.14 relates, French unemployment has exceeded that of other advanced economies of Europe for decades. In 2017, unemployment in France, at 9.1 percent, was significantly

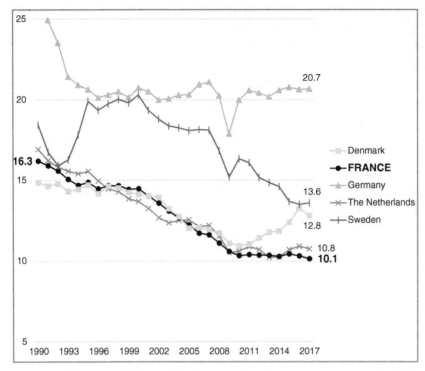

Figure 1.13 Value added in manufacturing as a percentage of GDP, 1990–2017
Source: World Bank (2018)

higher than in Sweden (6.8 percent), Denmark (5.9 percent), Holland (4.9 percent), and Germany (3.8 percent), although the French figure has improved more recently.

In addition, the French employment performance is significantly worse than it appears because France has considerable disguised unemployment. A variety of practices, such as early retirement programs, a guaranteed minimum income, and support for stay-at-home parents, help keep people out of the workforce. Looking at labor force participation rates, as opposed to unemployment rates, the gap between France and the advanced European economies becomes much more pronounced. Figure 1.15 shows that in 2017, the employment rate in France for working-age adults between the ages of 15 and 64 was a mere 64.8 percent, some 10 percentage points lower than in Denmark (74.2 percent), Germany (75.3 percent), the Netherlands (75.9 percent), and Sweden (76.9 percent).

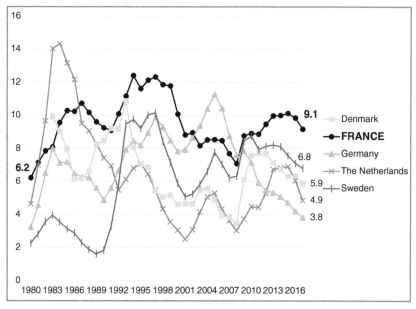

Figure 1.14 Unemployment rate, 1980–2017
Source: OECD (2018b)

The French system has its virtues, of course. State spending and regulation limit poverty and income inequality. Figure 1.16 presents Gini ratios, which measure the extent to which the distribution of income deviates from perfect equality. The combination of a generous minimum wage and high level of collective bargaining coverage has kept French income inequality relatively low. France's Gini ratio (0.292) falls between those of Germany (0.289) and the Netherlands (0.296) and is slightly above the Gini ratios of Denmark (2.63) and Sweden (2.80).

France also fares well on indicators of poverty, defined as income less than one-half the median. As Figure 1.17 reveals, thanks to a high minimum income, wage compression, and an extensive welfare state, France has a poverty rate of just 8.1 percent. Among the reference group of advanced European political economies, Denmark (6.1 percent) and the Netherlands (7.9 percent) boast a lower poverty rate, while Sweden (9.3 percent) and Germany (10.4 percent) have higher rates than France.

France's generous pension system has yielded an especially low poverty rate among senior citizens. Figure 1.18 shows that the poverty rate in France for those above the age of 65 is a mere 4.4 percent. Only

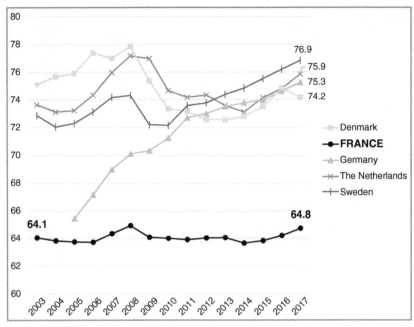

Figure 1.15 Percentage of the population aged 15 to 64 that is employed, 2003–2017
Source: OECD (2018c)

Denmark, at 3.6 percent, outperforms France among the comparison group of advanced European political economies. The Netherlands has a slightly greater rate of senior poverty than France (5.2 percent), while the rate is significantly higher in Germany (9.1 percent) and Sweden (11.4 percent).

The French welfare state does not just help those at risk of poverty. It provides an array of benefits, including lengthy paid parental leave after the birth or adoption of a child, generous family allowances and public childcare, extensive paid holidays, a quality health-care system, high rates of income replacement in the event of job loss, and, as noted, a pension system that keeps almost all senior citizens out of poverty. In addition, the French state has long invested in advanced infrastructure and public services (high-speed trains, civilian nuclear power, advanced telecommunications) that enhance the quality of life along with the business environment.

It also bears mentioning that, as discussed in Chapter 7, having a state that possesses the capacity to take decisive action can prove advantageous

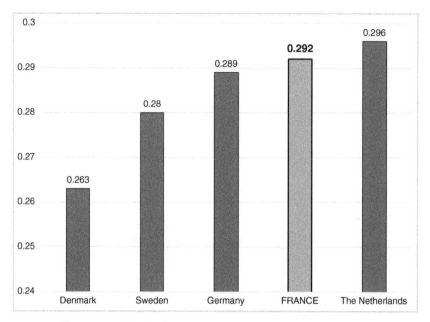

Figure 1.16 Gini ratio
Note: The Gini coefficient is based on the comparison of cumulative proportions of the population against cumulative proportions of income they receive (after taxes and cash transfers), and it ranges between 0 in the case of perfect equality and 1 in the case of perfect inequality. Data are most recent available: 2018 for Denmark and Germany, 2019 for France, the Netherlands, and Sweden.
Source: OECD (2022)

in an emergency like the COVID-19 crisis. In this instance, President Macron deployed a variety of coercive measures that effectively banned the unvaccinated from major aspects of public life. These policies were very controversial and would have been unfeasible in many countries where the executive lacks such discretionary power, but Macron was able to impose them, and in response, France moved from having one of the lowest vaccination rates in Europe to having one of the highest rates. Thus, some of the resistance to liberalizing reforms in France may come from a fear of losing the things that the French system does well, such as limiting inequality and poverty, providing generous benefits and public services, and wielding discretionary authority to combat public-health or other emergencies.

That said, there are limits to France's successes. The generous French welfare state does not cover all citizens equally. A large group of labor market outsiders, who are unable to secure stable, long-term

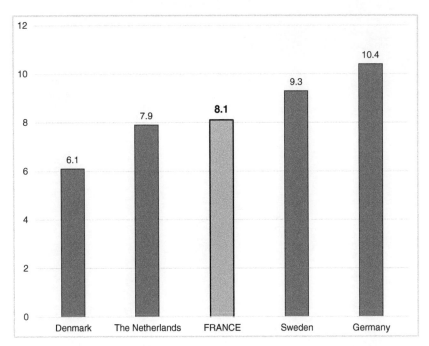

Figure 1.17 Percentage of population below the poverty line, 2019
Note: Percentage of people whose income falls below the poverty line,
taken as half the median household income of the total population.
Data for Denmark and Germany are from 2018 and for France, the
Netherlands, and Sweden are from 2019.
Source: OECD (2021a)

employment, not only earn less than the insiders, but are also ineligible for many of the welfare benefits enjoyed by the stably employed
(Smith 2004). In addition, the vaunted French infrastructure is showing signs of neglect, as the ambitious industrial policies that built this
infrastructure have fallen out of favor and social spending has crowded
out public investment. Finally, as noted, French economic performance has been poor and unemployment painfully high for decades.

Of course, all systems have their strengths and weaknesses, and if the
French were happy with their system, then it might be depicted as a
model of sorts. The French are decidedly unhappy, however. This dissatisfaction is the third reason for questioning the notion of France as
an alternative to the liberal model. French public opinion has clearly
soured on the country's economic system. In comparative opinion polls,
the French consistently rank at the bottom of European countries in

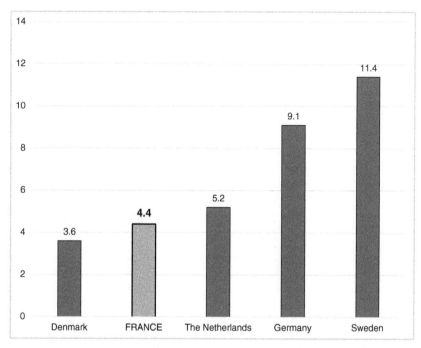

Figure 1.18 Percentage of senior citizens below the poverty line, 2019
Note: Percentage of people above the age of 65 whose income falls
below the poverty line, taken as half the median household income of
the total population.
Source: OECD (2020b)

satisfaction with the economy. Table 1.2 presents Pew Research Center survey results about the state of the economy in different European countries at five-year intervals (2007, 2012, and 2017). In 2007, on the eve of the financial crisis, 70 percent of French respondents felt that the country's economic situation was "bad," compared with 36 percent in Germany, 28 percent in the UK, and 13 percent in Sweden.

With the onset of the financial crisis, the percentages rose everywhere, but in 2017, as Europe's economies began showing signs of recovery, 78 percent of French respondents still described the situation as bad, the second highest figure next to Italy and an order of magnitude above Sweden (15 percent), Germany (13 percent), and the Netherlands (12 percent). Even in Spain, a country wracked by the collapse of its banking system, more than 20 percent unemployment, and a sovereign debt crisis, respondents were slightly less negative (71 percent) than the French.

Table 1.3 shows that the French are, if anything, even more pessimistic about the future. In 2013, a whopping 90 percent of French

Table 1.2 *Percent responding that the economic situation is bad*

	2007	2012	2017
Italy	70	93	83
FRANCE	70	81	78
Germany	36	27	13
Spain	34	94	71
UK	28	84	45
Sweden	13	–	15
The Netherlands	–	–	12

Source: Pew Research Center (2019a)

Table 1.3 *Percent responding that their children's future will be worse than their own*

	2013	2017
FRANCE	90	71
UK	74	68
Italy	73	65
Spain	65	69
Germany	64	52
The Netherlands	–	54
Sweden	–	46

Source: Pew Research Center (2018)

respondents anticipated that their children's situation would be worse than their own. Although 2013 was one of the bleakest years of the Great Recession, the French were the most negative by far. Even respondents in Italy (73 percent) and Spain (65 percent), two Southern European countries ravaged by the sovereign debt crisis, were less pessimistic. In addition, the French remained the most pessimistic about the future in the more recent 2017 survey.

Election results provide another indicator of French dissatisfaction. From the founding of the Fifth Republic in 1958 to 1981, the French right won every national election. From 1981 to 2012, by contrast, the left and the right alternated in power repeatedly, as disgruntled French voters punished the incumbents.

In the two most recent elections, in 2017 and 2022, French voters went a step further, rejecting both governing parties, the mainstream Socialists on the left and Republicans on the right. Neither party managed to place a candidate in the presidential runoff between the two top vote-getters on the first round of balloting.[8] Indeed, in 2022, the candidate of the Republicans received a mere 4.8 percent of the vote and the

Socialist candidate an even worse 1.8 percent (French Ministry of the Interior 2022b). The second round of both the 2017 and 2022 presidential elections featured a contest between Marine Le Pen, the leader of the far-right, xenophobic National Rally (Rassemblement National, RN), which was known as the National Front (Front National, FN) until 2018, and Emmanuel Macron, who had never held elective office before becoming president in 2017 and had formed his party – then known as On the Move (En Marche) or The Republic on the Move (La République en Marche, LREM)[9] – barely a year before the election.

Although Macron was elected president and reelected in 2022, voter disenchantment has by no means abated. In the presidential runoff, Marine Le Pen received a score of 33.9 percent in 2017, nearly double the party's previous all-time high, then increased her score again five years later, to 41.5 percent in 2022 (French Ministry of the Interior 2017b, 2022b). In the ensuing 2022 legislative elections, the two biggest opposition parties were Le Pen's far-right RN and Jean-Luc Mélenchon's far-left France Unbowed (La France Insoumise, LFI), with the mainstream Republicans and Socialists running far behind (French Ministry of the Interior 2022a). In perhaps the most shocking development, Macron became the first newly elected president since presidential and legislative terms were aligned in 2000 to fail to secure an absolute majority in the ensuing legislative elections, leaving it unclear how or even if he will be able to govern.

Thus, French voters have gone to great lengths to voice their dissatisfaction with the leaders and parties that govern them. They first shifted repeatedly from the left to the right and the right to the left. At the same time, they provided increasing support to extremist movements of the left and especially the right. In 2017, they went a step further by electing a president who was not a member of either of the mainstream governing parties. Finally, in 2022, they denied a newly reelected president a majority in the National Assembly.

France is clearly not an economic model. Its economic performance has been poor across a range of indicators, and its population is deeply dissatisfied. Even if France were a model, however, the notion that the alternatives to the liberal model – whether CME, Social Democratic, or social investment – have no place for economic liberalization mischaracterizes the role that economic liberalism plays in these alternative models. As Figures 1.1–1.11 have shown, all of the exemplars of alternatives to neoliberalism score higher on indices of liberalization than France, often substantially higher. Moreover, in response to economic difficulties, all of these countries have enacted significant liberalizing reforms at one time or another.

In the 1970s and 1980s, the Netherlands was the inspiration for the so-called Dutch disease, denoting a country with substantial energy exports, in this case natural gas, which foster an overvalued exchange rate that makes manufacturing uncompetitive and hollows out the industrial base. Over the ensuing fifteen years, Holland was transformed into the "Dutch model" or "Dutch miracle" (OECD 1998; Visser and Hemerijck 1997). The hyperbolic language stemmed from the fact that Holland was able to turn around its economy without massively increasing inequality and poverty, as in the USA and UK. The process of reform, sometimes described as "managed liberalization" (Van der Veen and Trommel 1999), operated through carefully negotiated wage restraint, tax reform, and labor flexibility designed to increase employer profits and investment, while safeguarding employee living standards.

Sweden and other Nordic countries suffered a massive economic crash in the early 1990s, with many pundits proclaiming the death of the Swedish or Social Democratic model (Lindbeck et al. 1994; Lundberg 1986). However, a mixture of liberalization (austerity measures, expanded competition in sheltered sectors, and reduced labor market protections) and public investment (increased spending on education and technology) helped the Nordic countries become "once again a model," in the words of Jonas Pontusson. By the late 1990s, these countries boasted budget surpluses and a wave of high-wage job creation in business services and information industries (Huo and Stephens 2015; Ornston 2012; Pontusson 2010; Steinmo 2003).

Most recently, German Chancellor Gerhard Schröder introduced far-reaching liberalizing reforms into Germany's political economy in the early twenty-first century, unwinding the interlocking directorates of big business and large investment banks, cutting social spending and taxes, dramatically expanding part-time and low-wage employment, and (through the so-called Hartz IV reforms) greatly intensifying the pressure on the unemployed to take jobs (Reisenbichler and Morgan 2012; Thelen 2014). The reforms were very unpopular, and Schröder's Social Democratic Party (SPD) suffered a series of electoral defeats beginning in 2005, from which it has never fully recovered. Even when the SPD finally captured the chancellorship in 2021, its support remained well below historic, pre-Schröder levels. That said, Germany returned to its economic powerhouse status, with strong growth, sound public finances, full employment, and record trade surpluses. Macron has made no secret of his admiration of the German model and its revitalization under Schröder as well as his hopes to do the same for France (*Journal du Dimanche*, September 17, 2017).

The economic turnarounds of the Netherlands, the Nordic countries, and Germany stemmed from many circumstances, including undervalued currencies (the Nordics and Germany) and an inflow of flexible female labor into the workforce (the Netherlands and Germany). It is beyond the scope of this book to determine the extent to which liberalization contributed to these economic recoveries, if it did at all. Parsing the effects of liberalization, favorable circumstances, and other factors is a task better left to the economists. *The French case presents a genuine puzzle for political scientists, though: why have liberalizing reforms that have been widely implemented by France's peer countries – including countries that share France's commitment to social cohesion and robust welfare states and that are touted as exemplars of alternatives to Anglo-American, neoliberal capitalism – provoked so much contestation and incurred so many setbacks in France?*

The suggestion that France has steered clear of economic liberalization because it incarnates an alternative model of capitalism is problematic on multiple fronts. For one thing, France can no longer be characterized as having a coherent economic model. It is neither *dirigiste* fish nor liberal fowl. In addition, whatever the French system may be, it displays none of the hallmarks of a successful economic model: the French economy has performed poorly, and the French public is highly dissatisfied. Finally, having an economic model that is distinct from the liberal model is not the same thing as having no place for economic liberalization at all. The most successful European models all rank higher on indices of economic liberalization than France and, for better or for worse, have all undertaken significant liberalizing reforms. These countries are and have always been *mixed* economies, blending liberal, social, and directive or coordinating elements. There is a real puzzle, then, as to why such mixing has provoked so much contestation in France.

1.4   Existing Explanations

This section presents and evaluates three potential explanations as to why economic liberalization is so contested in France. The first emphasizes a distinctive French outlook and collective psyche when it comes to capitalism and markets. The second points to the defects and miscalculations of France's leaders. The third portrays France's version of welfare capitalism as particularly inertial and difficult to change. Each explanation casts light on features of French society, the economy, and politics that contribute to the contestation of economic liberalization, yet in the end, none can fully account for the dynamics of economic liberalization in France.

1.4.1   Economic Culture

France has long been a favorite of scholars emphasizing political culture. Looking at European economic policy in the 1960s, Andrew Shonfield described a French "étatist tradition," dating back to Colbert,[10] that underpinned the postwar *dirigiste* approach: "The essential French view ... is that the effective conduct of a nation's economic life must depend on the concentration of power in the hands of a small number of exceptionally able people, exercising foresight and judgement of a kind not typically possessed by the average successful man of business" (Shonfield 1965: 71–72). Other scholars rooted state intervention in problematic aspects of French society. Michel Crozier contended that a French aversion to "face-to-face" relations and inability to resolve conflicts through negotiation and dialogue led actors to turn to higher authorities and ultimately the state for resolution (Crozier 1964, 1970). David Landes emphasized the limitations of French business, in particular an unwillingness to take risks, such as borrowing from banks in order to improve equipment or expand market share (Landes 1951, 1957).

In the current era, cultural explanations of France's aversion to economic liberalism come mostly from frustrated liberals struggling to understand why the country will not take their advice. A veritable cottage industry has arisen of books that paint a worrisome picture of France's economic situation, lay out possible solutions, then wonder if and when the French will read the writing on the wall and make the necessary changes (Daniel 2015; Istria 2010; Romanet 2012; Verdier-Molinié 2015). This group is often labeled "declinists" because its members present an alarming array of indicators of French economic decline. Yet the label is somewhat unfair, given that the so-called declinists are not fatalistic, but rather offer an agenda of reform and renewal centered on economic liberalization. In seeking to explain how France has gotten into such dire straits, the declinists tend to emphasize defects and pathologies of French culture or the French psyche.

A recurring theme of this literature is that the French are engaged in denial. Part of the reason why the declinists tend to start their books with a barrage of negative economic statistics is that they feel the need to roust the French from their torpor and get them to take the country's economic problems seriously. One of the recent books by Nicolas Baverez, a proliberalization pundit, who is often described as the leader of the declinist camp, is entitled *Chronicles of French Denial*, and the titles of the first three chapters sound the alarm: "The Specter of the 1930s," "Presidents Come and Go, the Crisis Remains," and "A Catastrophic Balance Sheet" (Baverez 2017).[11] Another of Baverez's books is called, quite simply, *Wake Up!* (Baverez 2012). In it, Baverez argues that the French have spent the last three decades in denial about the country's economic difficulties and need for reform: "They have concluded a tacit accord to not only avoid attacking their problems, but also to not even acknowledge their [problems'] existence or debate them" (Baverez 2012: 11). The only way to reverse France's ominous economic decline is to "wake up," "break with the culture of denial," and introduce a series of liberal economic reforms (Baverez 2012: 190).

The French also suffer from an unhealthy attachment to the state. Jean Peyrelevade traces French resistance to liberalization to cultural traditions forged during the French Revolution: a distrust of independent powers, a refusal to recognize the autonomy and contributions of entrepreneurs, and a belief that the state is the key to wealth creation (Peyrelevade 2014). Peyrelevade sees these cultural traditions as impeding successful economic adjustment. Indeed, he goes a step further, titling his book *History of a Neurosis* and warning that the national neurosis presents a formidable obstacle to the liberalizing reforms that France needs: "The sickness, the neurosis that prevents us from understanding and liberating the economy, is ... profound. We are an old absolutist nation ... that never recognized the autonomy or usefulness of entrepreneurs" (Peyrelevade 2014: 205).

Immaturity is another alleged French defect. Sophie Pedder, the Paris Bureau Chief for the *Economist* magazine, describes the French as "the last spoiled children in Europe" (Pedder 2012). France has been living beyond its means for decades, and during this time, all the other major countries in Europe have introduced significant liberalizing reforms. Pedder calls on politicians to stop "infantilizing the French" (Pedder 2012: 177) and face up to the need for the kinds of liberalizing reforms introduced long ago in countries like Sweden, the Netherlands, and Germany.

A striking number of works in the frustrated liberal camp depict French society in pathological terms. In Peyrelevade's opinion, as described, the French suffer from a "neurosis" that prevents them from understanding basic economic principles. Not to be outdone, Agnès Verdier-Molinié portrays the French attachment to the nation's system of social protection as a case of "Stockholm syndrome":

We are the victims of acute Stockholm syndrome. The more France sinks, the more we struggle to shore up this social model, which has taken us hostage. Because we are petrified at the idea of reforming, we pretend that this model suits us. (Verdier-Molinié 2013: 9)

Critics of France's economic culture are certainly onto something. French culture is distinctive and, more to the point, the French hold distinctively negative views of capitalism and the market. A 2011 poll asked French respondents whether a series of words "evokes in you something very positive, rather positive, rather negative, or very negative" (IFOP 2011). The two options that received the fewest "very

Table 1.4 *Views on the functioning of the market economy and capitalism*

	Are functioning relatively well and should be retained	Are functioning poorly and must be abandoned
FRANCE	15	33
Italy	26	22
The Netherlands	42	20
UK	45	10
Germany	46	12

Source: IFOP (2010)

positive" or "rather positive" responses, at 38 percent, were "capitalism" and "globalization." Even "socialism" fared better with 56 percent, and "the State" scored 64 percent.

When people in different countries are asked questions about the market and capitalism, the French are almost always the most negative, as Tables 1.2 and 1.3 indicate. A December 2010 poll compared economic attitudes in ten countries, including five from Western Europe: France, Germany, the UK, Italy, and the Netherlands (IFOP 2010). Respondents were asked their opinion of how well the "market economy and capitalism" are functioning. As Table 1.4 relates, France had the lowest score by far, a mere 15 percent, for the response that capitalism "functions relatively well and should be retained." Italy was next lowest, at 26 percent, while in the other West European countries, roughly three times as many respondents gave a positive answer as in France (46 percent for Germany, 45 percent for the UK, and 42 percent for the Netherlands). Conversely, France had far and away the highest percentage of respondents (33 percent) choosing the most negative option that capitalism "functions poorly and must be abandoned." Second-place Italy trailed France by 11 points, while only one-third as many respondents in Germany (12 percent) and the UK (10 percent) thought that capitalism should be abandoned.

Clearly, the French hold distinctly negative views of capitalism and market forces, as compared with citizens in other countries. Still, blaming recalcitrant French culture for the contestation and defeat of liberal reforms is a bridge too far. One problem with this explanation is that it offers no understanding of the reasons for French resistance to markets and hankering for state protection, for why the French feel this way more than people in other countries. The French have just always hated the market – or, at least, since Colbert or the French Revolution. This understanding leaves important questions unanswered: why are the French so averse to the market, and why is their economic thinking so infantile or diseased? As noted, part of the reason is that the French have a lot to lose from liberalization. However problematic French state policies may be, these policies provide support and protection to millions of citizens, who are understandably afraid to lose them.

A lack of empathy for French citizens who are wary of economic liberalization can also have problematic policy consequences. Instead of trying to understand the reason for popular unease and seek ways to address it, the dismissive approach encourages leaders to impose reforms from above, secure in the knowledge that the French, like spoiled children, do not know what is good for them and that negotiations are, therefore, a waste of time. As discussed in Chapters 4 and 5, this kind of disdain for the masses has often led French reformers into dangerous political waters. Many of the biggest protests against liberalizing reforms, such as the movement against the 1995 Juppé Plan and the yellow vest protests, occurred in response to a combination of technocratic arrogance, disparaging comments about opponents of liberalization, and a refusal to negotiate when challenged.

Another problem with national cultural explanations is that national cultures are not monolithic. French culture is a complex constellation of values and ideas, in which different and even contradictory strands of economic thought can and do coexist. Of course, one strand, such as statism, may be more prominent than another, such as liberalism, but liberalism has always had a place in France (Vail 2018). Indeed, Richard Kuisel demonstrates that the liberal idea of a limited state prevailed under the Third Republic and that it was not until the Vichy regime and the postwar period that France embarked on a statist economic course (Kuisel 1981). If multiple strands of economic political culture coexist, as presumably statism and liberalism do in France today, then the level of explanation must be pushed back. Instead of saying that the French are averse to liberalism, an explanation is needed as to why a statist or republican economic culture has generally marginalized a liberal culture.

A final related problem of the cultural explanation is that it fails to capture the diversity of French experience with market reform. The cultural interpretation cannot account for moments in French history – the initial postwar decades, the entry into the Common Market in 1958, and the break with the statist model in 1983 – when French authorities introduced dramatic economic change, much of it liberal in nature, without triggering paralyzing contestation. An understanding is needed for why liberal reforms have made headway on some occasions but not others.

1.4.2   Political Leadership

Another popular explanation for the contestation of economic liberalization centers on the defects of French political leaders. The current president, Emmanuel Macron, has certainly provided ammunition for this argument. As described in Chapter 5 of this book, Macron's first eighteen months in office, culminating in the yellow vest protests, were marked by unpopular tactics on behalf of an unpopular agenda.

The unpopular tactics were a top-down reformist strategy tinged with arrogance. Macron quickly earned the nickname "Jupiter" – denoting the supreme Roman god, who rules from the heavens – for his distant and aloof demeanor. Macron felt that since he had won the 2017 presidential and legislative elections, he had a democratic mandate for his entire economic agenda. This reading conveniently overlooked the fact that Macron received less than 25 percent of the vote on the first ballot of the presidential election and that much of his support stemmed from strategic calculations, most of all the desire to prevent the election of the far-right populist, Marine Le Pen, as opposed to an endorsement of Macron's economic policies. The corollary of Macron's supposed democratic mandate was a belief that negotiations with the social partners or other stakeholders were largely unnecessary and would only slow things down. Even when the government held talks, the meetings were often little more than listening exercises, with government representatives refusing to negotiate the actual terms of the reforms.

Aggravating matters, Macron wielded this top-down, Jupiterian mode of governance on behalf of an agenda that struck many in France as unfair. Eager to promote French business and the attractiveness of France as a site for international investors, as a "start-up nation" in one of his favorite phrases, Macron cut taxes on businesses and the affluent. At the same time, in the name of reducing France's budget deficit, he called for sacrifices from the rest of the French. A big increase in the gasoline tax proved to be the straw that broke the camel's back, triggering the yellow vest protests, but these protests came against a backdrop of sizable tax cuts for business and the well-heeled coupled with tax increases and reduced public services for the ordinary population.

It is easy to see how the defects of Macron's leadership were responsible for his difficulties. As Chapter 6 of this book relates, Macron admitted (reluctantly) to having failed to listen and, in January 2019, launched a so-called Grand National Debate (Grand Débat National, GDN) to give citizens a chance to voice their grievances, which he promised to address. Moreover, Macron's predecessors have not exactly excelled as reformers. Indeed, they have all been widely portrayed as failed leaders. President Jacques Chirac (1995–2007) cared about social stability over all else and lacked a vision or national ambition; President Nicolas Sarkozy (2007–2012) had a short attention span and failed to sustain any coherent agenda; President François Hollande (2012–2017) was a party hack, who knew nothing about economics and was in over his head. Books on recent French presidents carry such unflattering titles as *The Fiasco* and *The Curse* on Chirac (Jarreau 1997; Ottenheimer 1996); *The Impetuous One* and *The Zorro Complex* on Sarkozy (Allègre and Montalvon 2012; Nay 2012); *It All Started So Well* and *What Have They Done with Our Hopes?* on Hollande (Germain 2015; Plenel and Dufau 2015); and, for good measure, *Two Presidencies for Nothing* on Sarkozy and Hollande (Barbier 2017). The common thread of these accounts is that French presidents have been incompetent and ineffective.

French presidents have certainly made their share of mistakes. This book presents many of these mistakes and suggests ways that liberal reformers might be more effective. That said, a personalistic account is difficult to square with the tremendous variety of political profiles and leadership styles of France's last few presidents. Indeed, in some ways each president has reacted against the perceived failings of his predecessor. Chirac was cautious and backed down in the face of protests, so Sarkozy would be an activist president, who would seek out confrontation, rather than avoiding it. Sarkozy was impetuous and offended French sensitivities with his vulgar, "bling bling" style, so Hollande would govern cautiously and behave as an everyman "normal president." Hollande was too ordinary, lacking in stature and preferring empty syntheses to bold moves, so Macron would provide decisive leadership in pursuit of his agenda and project a loftier, "Jupiterian" style that the French have traditionally associated with their presidents. For all these efforts to learn from the mistakes of their predecessors, no French president seems to have found the formula for introducing liberalizing reforms without provoking mass contestation or being required to backtrack.

French presidents have differed in other important respects as well. They have spanned the political spectrum, from the Socialist left (Hollande), to some kind of liberal center-right (Macron), to a cautious conservatism (Chirac), to a more confrontational, populist right (Sarkozy). Some have been career politicians (Chirac, Sarkozy), while others had never held national elective office before being elected president (Hollande, Macron). Chirac, Hollande, and Macron graduated from the ultra-prestigious training ground of French elites, the National School of Administration (Ecole Nationale d'Administration, ENA), but Sarkozy worked his way up as a lawyer. If all it took to reform France were the right leader, then somewhere along the line, over the past thirty years, one of these figures should have presumably fit the bill. What is more, all of France's recent presidents were depicted as supremely talented and skillful at the time that they were elected, yet somehow became completely incompetent once they started governing.

France has elected some very impressive individuals as president. These leaders have made their share of mistakes, but it is not as if the leaders of countries now held up as successful reformers never made mistakes. For example, Gerhard Schröder initially expanded social benefits at a time that Germany could not afford them, only to subsequently reverse course (Hinrichs 2010). This fumbling and uncertain trajectory looks a lot like what French presidents have been criticized for doing.

To understand the contestation of economic liberalization in France, it is not enough to blame poor leadership. In comparing French leaders to European leaders who have navigated the politics of liberalization successfully, what is striking is not how much more talented the European leaders are than the French, but rather *how much less room for error France's leaders seem to have than leaders in other countries*. France is a country where one ill-fated initiative, like the Juppé Plan of 1995, can destroy an entire presidency. France is a country where the same top-down approach that initially earned Macron plaudits as an effective reformer can transform him, in the blink of an eye, into an arrogant, out-of-touch, Parisian technocrat. In short, France is a country where economic liberalization is politically fraught, whatever the skills and sensibilities of its president.

1.4.3   A Bismarckian Welfare State

A third explanation of the contestation of economic liberalization in France focuses on the country's labor markets and model of welfare capitalism. France has a classic "insider–outsider" or "dualized" system, in which labor market insiders enjoy secure jobs, high salaries, and excellent social benefits, while labor market outsiders struggle to find stable employment and rely on a less generous tier of welfare programs (Rueda 2007; Smith 2004). The expensive wages and social benefits of insiders dampen job creation as do labor market protections, which make employers wary of hiring workers who may not be easy to dismiss should the need arise. The victims of this system are the outsider groups, that is, the last hired and first fired: young people in search of their first job, the unskilled, women who took time out of the labor force to raise children, and ethnic minorities. These groups all suffer from very high rates of unemployment.

France's system of social protection – variously labeled as "Bismarckian," "Christian Democratic," and "Conservative-Continental" – also presents problems to labor market outsiders (Palier 2010b; Palier and Thelen 2010). In order to qualify for generous "social insurance" benefits, employees must pay into the Social Security system for many years. Those with irregular work histories, typically labor market outsiders, are ineligible for social insurance benefits. They are forced to rely instead on less generous, means-tested "social assistance" programs. Thus, labor market outsiders in France are victims twice over: first, of labor markets that fail to generate enough jobs and, second, of a welfare system that treats them as charity cases, rather than as citizens with rights.

Scholars of insider–outsider labor markets and Bismarckian welfare states portray these systems as extremely difficult to reform because well-connected insiders cling to their privileges, while outsiders lack the political clout to drive the liberalizing changes needed to enhance their employment opportunities (Smith 2004). Economists Assar Lindbeck and Dennis Snower compare labor market insiders to "muggers," who use legislation and force to deprive outsiders of the chance to secure jobs by accepting lower wages and weaker job protections (Lindbeck and Snower 1988). The Social Democratic scholar Gøsta Esping-Andersen steers clear of such inflammatory language, but arrives at much the same conclusion: the Bismarckian model generates "welfare states without work," with too few employees supporting too many welfare claimants; what is more, the system is "frozen" or unable to reform itself (Esping-Andersen 1996a, 1996b).

The literature on insider–outsider labor markets and the Bismarckian welfare state points to important policy challenges in France. The French labor market displays all the hallmarks of dualism described in the insider–outsider literature. Employment rates of young people, the unskilled, and ethnic minorities lag far behind other groups. Many young people, for example, cycle for years through a series of part-time or fixed-term contracts, government internships, and subsidized jobs at low pay and with no job security before finally landing a stable job in their late twenties (Chauvel 2006, 2010, 2013). France also displays all the hallmarks of "welfare states without work." On the welfare side, as related in Figure 1.2, France has the most expensive welfare state in the world. On the work side, French unemployment has generally ranged from 7 to 12 percent, and the numbers are actually worse than they appear because various practices, like early retirement programs, supports for stay-at-home parents, and a guaranteed minimum income, hide the true number of people who cannot find jobs.

If the insider–outsider or Bismarckian welfare state literature identifies important economic problems and policy challenges, it is less effective at elucidating the dynamics of French politics. For starters, recent scholarship suggests that Bismarckian welfare regimes are more reformable than they appear (Levy 1999a; Palier 2000, 2010a; Vail 2010, 2018). Reform has tended to come late to these countries, and the changes that occur are generally piecemeal and incremental. In addition, reform has often been crafted to protect the interests of insiders, concentrating labor market liberalization on outsiders, most notably by expanding part-time employment (Reisenbichler and Morgan 2012; Thelen 2014). Nonetheless, these reforms have cumulated to fundamental change in a number of Bismarckian countries, most notably Holland and Germany. Once paragons of welfare without work, these countries now boast employment levels rivaling those of the Scandinavian countries.

A second problem of the insider–outsider or Bismarckian welfare state literature is that it tends to portray powerful labor market insiders and the unions that represent them as the primary obstacles to reform. France has the lowest rate of unionization in the OECD, however, and unions are almost entirely absent from the private sector. If union power were the main obstacle to liberalization, then France would be at the forefront of liberalizing reform among Bismarckian countries. Yet by just about any measure of economic liberalization, including labor market reform, France has liberalized less than countries like Germany and Holland, where unions are more powerful.

A third issue with the insider–outsider or Bismarckian welfare state literature is that it rests on a questionable attribution of preferences, at least in the French case. The presumption is that labor market outsiders favor economic liberalization because, by reducing rigidities in the labor market, such reform will create more employment. When French governments have acted on this assumption, however, the outsiders have not responded in the predicted manner. As Chapter 2 relates, conservative governments tried to expand job opportunities for young people by introducing a lower minimum wage for youth hires in 1994 and a two-year probationary period during which youths could be fired without justification or compensation in 2006. In both instances, rather than welcoming the changes, young people in France launched protests that eventually forced the government to abandon its reform. French youths did not identify as *current labor market outsiders*, but rather as *future labor market insiders*, rejecting substandard terms of employment that they believed would deepen and perpetuate their second-class status.[12]

French public policy also raises questions about the insider–outsider literature. Many of the most expensive social policy initiatives over the past thirty-five years have aimed to help outsiders. In 1988, a unanimous vote in parliament established a minimum income guarantee, now known as the Active Solidarity Income (Revenu de Solidarité Active, RSA), which provides some 2 million households with an income ranging from €565 per month for a single individual to €1,187 for a couple with two children (plus €226 for each additional child) along with health insurance (DREES 2021). The RSA acts as a kind of backstop for people, mostly labor market outsiders, who have either exhausted or never qualified for unemployment benefits. In addition, even before the COVID-19 crisis,

French authorities were spending over €10 billion annually on subsidies and tax exemptions for employers hiring low-wage, hard-to-place workers, that is, labor market outsiders (INSEE 2018). Finally, France has greatly expanded health benefits for outsiders. In 1999, the government created a Universal Sickness Coverage (Couverture Maladie Universelle, CMU), which was later replaced by two programs, the Universal Illness Protection (Protection Universelle Maladie, PUMA) and the Social Solidarity Supplement (Complémentaire Santé Solidaire, CSS). PUMA provides free basic health insurance to over 2 million French residents, while the CSS offers a supplementary insurance that eliminates co-payments for some 7.5 million people (Complémentaire Santé Solidaire 2021; *Les Echos*, July 29 and October 15, 2019). These kinds of expensive new programs are difficult to square with a claim that labor market insiders are unwilling to do anything for labor market outsiders.

The insider–outsider Bismarckian literature identifies important policy challenges in France, but is less convincing as an explanation of France's response to those challenges. French outsiders have fiercely resisted reforms that would supposedly benefit them, while insiders have reached deep into their pockets to ease the plight of outsiders. Perhaps relatedly, France has resisted liberalizing reform more than other leading Bismarckian countries, even though the supposedly most salient adversaries of liberalization, trade unions, are notably weak in cross-national perspective. Bismarckian welfare regimes are difficult to reform, but an explanation is still needed as to why liberal reform is so much more treacherous and combustible in France than in other Bismarckian countries like Holland and Germany.

1.5   Argument and Plan of the Book

The theories in Section 1.4 offer important insights into why economic liberalization is so contested in France. The French public is distrustful of market capitalism and competition, French leaders have made catastrophic blunders, and France's labor markets and Bismarckian welfare state create a class of insiders with powerful incentives to preserve the status quo. Yet no explanation is provided as to the origin of these features of French politics. Why is the French public so distrustful of liberalization? Why are French leaders so disaster prone? And why have other Bismarckian countries like Germany and Holland managed to overhaul their labor markets and welfare regime, while France has not?

The explanations examined also provide little place for political processes, for the role of political institutions, interest groups, and parties in shaping France's approach to economic liberalization. For the cultural camp, the limits of liberalization in France are simply the byproduct of deeply held values since time immemorial. For those emphasizing leadership, policy is simply a function of the talent (or lack thereof) of France's presidents. And for scholars of the Bismarckian welfare state and insider–outsider cleavages, France's social policy framework produces a characteristic reform dynamic that is essentially the same as that of other Bismarckian systems in Europe (Palier 2010a).[13]

1.5.1   The Argument: Three Legacies of Dirigisme

This book builds on an important premise of the literatures on welfare state retrenchment and the reform of Bismarckian welfare states. Both of these literatures emphasize how policy shapes politics (Campbell 2012; Palier 2010a; Pierson 1993). For Pierson, the postwar welfare states have transformed the political landscape by creating a mass support base for the welfare state composed of the beneficiaries and providers of social programs. For the Bismarckian welfare state literature, the unique features of this kind of welfare regime impel a characteristic agenda and trajectory of reform. In both of these literatures, the existence of mature welfare states strongly shapes the politics of contemporary reform.

This book also emphasizes the salience of policy legacies. However, the postwar welfare state is not the only source of legacies shaping contemporary social and economic reform. The legacies of national models of capitalism also structure the political terrain, even in the case of France, where the national model was more or less dismantled several decades ago. *Indeed, the central claim of this book is that the legacies of France's postwar statist or dirigiste model are the key to understanding the contestation of economic liberalization today. Both the operation of the dirigiste model and the strategies that governments put in place in the 1980s to move away from that model have created powerful obstacles to contemporary liberalization and fueled popular contestation.*

A first source of contestation stems from the policy legacies of the *dirigiste* state. The principal problem confronting reformers, as the Bismarckian welfare literature relates, is that France has a mammoth welfare state supported by powerful insider groups. Yet France did not always have a large welfare state. For most of the postwar period, France was regarded as a "welfare laggard." What changed in the 1980s is that as state authorities broke with the *dirigiste* model, they deployed a variety of social and labor market policies to compensate and demobilize the victims and potential opponents of reform. This "socialized marketization" (Vail 2010) or movement from the *dirigiste* state to the social anesthesia state (Levy 2005a, 2005b, 2008; Levy et al. 2006) enabled governments to unwind the dysfunctional *dirigiste* model, but also created a mammoth, passively oriented welfare state with problems of its own.

Critics rightly point out that other European countries have been able to reform their welfare states and labor markets without compromising their social values (Pedder 2012; Smith 2004). In France, however, the task has been made more difficult by the distinctive reform trajectory stemming from the process of *dirigiste* rollback. Unlike in other European countries, liberalization in France has been a *two-stage* process of reform: a first stage to move away from the *dirigiste* model and a second stage to remedy the dysfunctions of the social anesthesia state that accompanied the first stage. Aggravating matters, the fiscal burden and rigidities of the social anesthesia state offset some of the economic gains from the break with the *dirigiste* model, leaving many in France disappointed with economic liberalization and skeptical of the idea that what was needed was yet another turn of the liberalizing screw. In this context, French reformers have found themselves caught between economic pressures to curb public spending and expand labor market flexibility, on the one hand, and political pushback from a populace that feels that it already engaged in liberalization in the 1980s with little to show for it, on the other hand. In addition, the fiscal burden of the social anesthesia state has left policymakers with few resources to offer compensation or side-payments as a way of mitigating opposition.

The second source of contestation of economic liberalization stems from party-political legacies. Crudely put, France offers a case of liberalization without liberals, in that there is no powerful political voice advocating consistently for liberal economic reform.[14] It is not just the French left that is ambivalent toward economic liberalization, but also the French right. Once again, the legacies of the postwar *dirigiste* experience figure prominently. Whereas in most Western European countries, the governing party of the right supports a market economy and trade liberalization, even if tempered by attachment to a generous welfare state to preserve social cohesion, in France, the governing right has long been economically interventionist and nationalist. Indeed, for much of the postwar period, governments of the right administered the *dirigiste* model and the accompanying top-down mode of governance. The dominant party of the right, the Gaullist movement, was especially tied to voluntarist industrial policy and state activism more generally. The Gaullist movement was also nationalist, and this nationalism has led governments of the right to intervene in markets to protect the nation's leading multinationals from foreign takeovers. Thus, the supposed natural party of market reform in France has as much statism and nationalism in its DNA as liberalism.

Concerns about social order have bolstered the French right's ambivalence toward economic liberalization. In a country with a revolutionary tradition dating back to 1789, governing elites have always feared social upheaval, but the events of May 1968, which were in many ways a revolt against the *dirigiste* model, reactivated these concerns. Jacques Chirac, arguably the most influential Gaullist since de Gaulle, who served as prime minister from 1974 to 1976 and from 1986 to 1988, then as president from 1995 to 2007, cut his teeth politically as state secretary for employment during the May 1968 crisis. So, too, did another Gaullist leader, Edouard Balladur, who held the position of technical advisor for social affairs to the prime minister. Both Chirac and Balladur were marked, indeed traumatized, by the experience of May 1968. Consequently, for Chirac, Balladur, and other French politicians of the right, particularly those who had experienced May 1968, the concern for social order has often trumped the commitment to liberalizing reform. Fearful that protests may snowball into another May 1968, these leaders have repeatedly backtracked when confronted with strikes and demonstrations. Obviously, the French right has changed over the years, but even in the current period French conservatives are much more reticent about economic liberalization and less willing to stare down popular opposition to such reforms than their counterparts in other Western European countries. This thin commitment to liberalism is especially visible in times of economic crisis, when ostensibly promarket leaders have often proven to be what might be called "fair-weather liberals," jettisoning liberal economic principles and launching new interventionist industrial and social policies.

The lack of a strong political voice for economic liberalism stems not only from the postwar practice of *dirigisme*, but also from France's exit from *dirigisme* in the 1980s. French parties of both the left and the right were reluctant to assume responsibility for the break with *dirigisme*. The left presided over the initial shift, but refused to acknowledge the change, speaking of a "pause" in reform as opposed to a U-turn, of budgetary "rigor" rather than austerity, and of "ventilating the public sector" instead of privatization. In addition to linguistic obfuscation and liberalization "by stealth" (Gordon and Meunier 2001), governments of the left and right alike have tended to blame the EU for unpopular economic decisions. Instead of defending liberalizing reforms – like cutting off support to failing national champions or reducing budget deficits – on their own terms, as good for the French economy, politicians have usually claimed that their hand is being forced by the European Commission. In the words of a leading scholar of France's political economy, "French elites thought that they could reform France by invoking European constraints that they themselves had invented" (Interview by author with Elie Cohen, Research Director, National Center for Scientific Research (CNRS) at the Institute of Political Studies of Paris and member of the Prime Minister's Council of Economic Analysis, Paris, March 19, 2019). The predictable result of this approach is that the French have never become fully reconciled to the market and they are increasingly hostile to European integration as well. Vivien Schmidt observes that France has not developed a "communicative discourse" to legitimate liberal economic reform (Schmidt 2002a, 2002b), yet in some ways, Schmidt's claim is an understatement. France has actually developed a *delegitimating discourse* for liberal reform, casting it as an undesirable foreign imposition.

The third legacy fueling the contestation of economic liberalization in France is institutional. Paul Pierson has demonstrated that welfare reform is generally an exercise in "blame avoidance" for unpopular program cuts, as opposed to "credit claiming" for new spending measures (Pierson 1994, 1996, 2001a). This distinction has important implications for the politics of liberalization. Whereas in the era of heroic welfare state construction, concentrated political power and few "veto points" conferred an undeniable advantage on governments seeking to launch ambitious new social programs (Immergut 1992a, 1992b), the logic is somewhat reversed in the era of welfare retrenchment. With concentrated power comes concentrated accountability, making it difficult for French governments to avoid blame for unpopular liberalizing reforms.

Research on welfare reform indicates that many of the most ambitious structural and retrenchment initiatives have been made on the basis of negotiations between the government and other actors to share the blame and defuse potential contestation in the streets (Hinrichs 2000, 2010; Palier 2003b; Schludi 2003, 2005). Sometimes, the government reaches out to its political adversaries: the US Social Security reform in 1983 and the overhaul of the Swedish pension reform in 1998 were both enacted by a joint vote of all the main political parties. Sometimes, the government reaches out to the social partners: the negotiations that produced the 1998 pension reform in Sweden involved the trade unions along with the political parties (Anderson 2001; Anderson and Immergut 2006; Anderson and Meyer 2003). Generalizing from such cases, Martin Rhodes describes a process of "competitive corporatism," under which government, employers, and unions work together to tackle contentious welfare and labor market reforms (Rhodes 1997, 2001).

What is striking about the French experience is that governments have almost never conducted economic liberalization in this inclusive, concertational manner. They have instead hewed to what might be termed a "skinny-politics" approach to reform that admits as few actors as possible. Again, the explanation goes back to the *dirigiste* model. France's postwar *dirigiste* model operated in a top-down, exclusionary measure, channeling resources to the national champions, while largely neglecting other groups, most notably small business, labor, and local officials, who were viewed as the defenders of parochial, backwards-looking interests (Levy

1999b). As a result, in the contemporary period French leaders lack powerful associational partners with whom to negotiate and legitimate controversial reforms; they are also disinclined to turn to existing organizations out of concern that the negotiations will slow down or dilute reforms.

The institutions of the Fifth Republic have bolstered the preference for skinny politics by encouraging a "bipolarization," or sharp divide between rival camps of left and right as well as between the government and the opposition. Indeed, no major liberalization measure has been enacted by a cross-party alliance in the manner of the USA in 1983 or Sweden in 1998. On the contrary, as described in Chapter 4, most French initiatives have been legislated through constitutional strong-arm procedures that are designed to restrict debate, enact change quickly, and minimize the role of the opposition.

Although skinny politics might seem like the shortest distance between two liberalizing points, avoiding the need for lengthy negotiations and compromise, it is a highly combustible approach. Groups that are shut out of the policymaking process have every incentive to take to the streets. Indeed, strikes and demonstrations are often the only way to make the government respond to their concerns and demands. Moreover, contestation in the streets can easily spiral into contestation of the government itself.

In summary, the operation and exit from *dirigisme* have bequeathed three sets of obstacles and sources of contestation of economic liberalization. From a *policy* standpoint, France has a giant welfare state in need of reform, a public that is highly skeptical that liberalizing reform will work, and a cash-strapped government that has little capacity to finance side-payments and compensation. From a *party-political* standpoint, France has generally had no conservative party with a clear promarket outlook or a legitimating discourse to validate liberalization. Finally, from an *institutional* standpoint, French reformers, operating on the basis of skinny politics, lack partners to help demobilize opponents and share the blame for unpopular changes. Taken together, these policy, party-political, and institutional legacies of the postwar *dirigiste* model explain the pervasive contestation of economic liberalization in contemporary France. Again, the claim here is not that liberalization is impossible or that France never changes. Rather, it is that the legacies of France's *dirigiste* model have made economic liberalization an uncertain and politically parlous undertaking, subject to recurring contestation and more than occasional setbacks.

The three legacies of *dirigisme* have also shaped the *substance* of economic liberalization in ways that contribute to contestation. Several lines of analysis in the fields of comparative political economy and welfare state reform suggest that liberalization can take multiple forms. A first varieties-of-liberalization literature consists of comparisons of economic liberalization in different countries. Examples include the rolling back of industrial policy (Vogel 1996), the dismantling of import-substitution industrialization (ISI) (Etchemendy 2011), the privatization and regulation of utilities (Murillo 2009), the liberalization of traditionally illiberal political economies (Vail 2018), and the expansion of labor market flexibility (Thelen 2014). These comparisons are all rooted in the historical-institutionalist, national-models-of-capitalism perspective, which emphasizes the ways that distinctive domestic political and institutional arrangements generate different national responses to common impetuses or shocks. In the case of liberalization, the claim is that different politico-institutional contexts affect not just whether liberalization occurs and at what speed, but also the character of the liberalizing reforms themselves. For example, Kathleen Thelen identifies three kinds of liberal labor market trajectories: deregulation in the USA (a decline in both coordination and solidarity); dualization in Germany (a decline in solidarity, but not coordination); and embedded flexibilization in Denmark (a decline in coordination, but not solidarity). Another implication of this analysis is that economic liberalization need not be synonymous with increased inequality and poverty and that some forms of liberalization (embedded flexibility) are more inclusive and favorable to social justice than others (deregulation and dualization).

A second literature suggesting that liberalization can take multiple forms centers on welfare state "recalibration" (Armingeon and Bonoli 2006; Esping-Andersen 2002; Ferrera and Rhodes 2000; Ferrera et al. 2000; Hemerijck 2013; Pierson 2001b). The starting point is the understanding that welfare reform involves not just reductions in social spending ("retrenchment"), but also changes in the purposes and distribution of spending ("recalibration"). Recalibration addresses problematic aspects of the welfare state, such as the unequal treatment of different social groups or policies that discourage employment. Typically, such reform is enacted through negotiations with the social partners and/or agreements between the government and opposition. Because multiple voices are heard, the resulting recalibrating reforms tend to involve elaborate trade-offs and careful attention to distributional consequences. For example, the Danish version of "flexicurity" eliminated most restrictions on layoffs in return for generous unemployment benefits and retraining opportunities, while the Dutch version of "flexicurity" eased restrictions on part-time and fixed-term employment in return for the equalization of the pro rata wages and benefits of part-time and fixed-term employees with those of full-time workers (Schulze-Cleven 2014; Visser 2002; Visser and Hemerijck 1997). Other deals along these lines reduced the gap between labor market insiders and outsiders by easing the job protections of labor

market insiders in return for improved wages, benefits, and job protections for labor market outsiders. Such deals also characterize many pension reforms that have reduced the subsidies to the pensions of insiders,
while upgrading the pensions of low-income retirees.

A third literature pointing to multiple possibilities for liberalizing
reform is the social or public investment model promoted by a number of scholars (Garritzmann et al. 2022; Hemerijck 2017; Morel et al.
2012) as well as the EU (European Commission 2010; Lisbon European Council 2000). Proponents of this model support forms of social
spending that enhance human capital, productivity, and labor force participation. Key policies include early childhood education, which both
facilitates parents' participation in the labor market and contributes to
higher educational performance of children later in life; increased spending on education and training; opportunities for lifelong learning to
improve social mobility and make workers more employable should their
jobs disappear; and active labor market policies to help displaced workers train for, locate, and move into new jobs. In a similar vein, public
investment in technology – R&D, higher education, computer literacy,
and universal, high-speed internet access – may not yield immediate,
measurable benefits, but it helps countries migrate toward the information economy and develop high-end business services that can support
generous wages and welfare benefits.

In many instances, the arguments of proponents of social investment
bleed into welfare state recalibration. Instead of calling for a massive
increase in spending on human development or technology, proponents
of the social investment model mostly call for a redirection of existing
social spending toward new ends. The recalibration agenda is captured
by calls for shifting from cure to prevention, from old social risks to new
social risks, from retirees to children, from passive to active labor market expenditures, and from redistribution to "predistribution" (Hacker
2011). Nor are these empty slogans. In the 1990s, amidst a deep economic crisis, the Nordic countries made significant cuts in social spending, notably transfer payments, while pouring some of the savings into
increased spending on R&D, higher education, computer literacy, and
internet access (Huo and Stephens 2015; Ornston 2012; Pontusson
2010). Thanks in no small part to this recalibration of public spending,
the Scandinavian countries have enjoyed great success in ICT, creating
a large number of high-paying jobs.

The literatures on varieties of liberalization, welfare state recalibration, and social investment or public investment suggest a richer understanding of the concept of "liberalization" and the options potentially
available to France than a simple dichotomy between no reform and

neoliberal reform. A conventional neoliberal rollback of social spending, taxes, and labor market protections is certainly one possibility (for example, in Thelen's characterization of the US case of labor market reform as "deregulation"). However, there are other possibilities. One, exemplified by the Dutch case, is a renegotiation of social protection and labor market regulation, marked by give and take, that improves efficiency, while addressing inequities and compensating the most vulnerable. Another possibility is a Nordic-style recalibration of the welfare state to permit investments in human capital formation, lifelong learning, and advanced technologies without sending taxes soaring. Both approaches entail a degree of liberalization in the form of lower taxes and social spending, rollbacks of certain benefits like early retirement enjoyed by privileged groups, and a move to more employment-friendly fiscal and labor market arrangements. Compared with the neoliberal approach, however, these alternatives are more attentive to the needs of low-income and vulnerable groups, in some cases increasing their benefits and protections as part of a negotiated reform package. The social investment or public investment approach also directs some of the savings from retrenchment into investments in the future, whether technology or human capital.

Dirigiste legacies in France have worked against such alternatives to conventional neoliberalism, however. Dutch-style concertational give and take goes against the insular, top-down approach characteristic of French politics. Give and take is also difficult in a context in which the fiscal weight of the social anesthesia state limits government resources for side-payments and compensation. *Dirigiste* legacies have likewise worked against the Nordic social or public investment model. Despite the French tradition of sizable public investment, the social anesthesia state has crowded out public investment, and reformers have generally focused on reducing the size of the state, as opposed to recalibrating or redeploying it. The liberalizing measures put forward by French authorities have mainly consisted of painful and one-sided liberal reforms: substantial benefit cuts without compensation, the erosion of labor market protections for insiders and outsiders alike, and tax cuts that are tilted overwhelmingly toward the well-to-do. Such an unappealing agenda is almost an invitation to protest, especially when imposed from above without any kind of negotiation. *Thus, contestation in France stems not just from the way in which reformers have pursued economic liberalization, but also from the substance of that liberalization.*

Of course, French economic liberalization has encompassed dozens of major initiatives and some, particularly those negotiated with the social partners, have been more attentive to distributional concerns. Other reforms have incorporated elements of social or public investment, a priority for current president Macron. That said, French leaders, including Macron, have found it difficult to find resources to fund such initiatives, given the fiscal demands of the social anesthesia state. As a result, French reforms have often hewed to a conventional neoliberal agenda that is long on pain and uncertain on gain. To the extent that reforms have deviated from this agenda, it has been primarily in response to protests and strikes that have forced governments to renegotiate their original proposals.

The claim here is not that French reformers are neoliberal zealots, who never consider any alternatives, but rather that the legacies of the *dirigiste* model have tended to incline French authorities toward conventional neoliberal measures and away from more inclusive, equitable package deals or recalibration in favor of public investment. The literatures on varieties of liberalization, welfare state recalibration, and social or public investment reveal that there are liberalizing trajectories that might serve French interests well and resonate with French traditions and values. The legacies of the *dirigiste* model have pushed against such reforms, however, and toward more conventional, painful, and contested forms of liberalization.

1.5.2   Plan of the Book

This book is organized into eight chapters including the introduction. Chapters 2 to 4 each focus on one *dirigiste* legacy that has fueled the contestation of economic liberalization. Chapter 2 analyzes the *policy* legacy, the social anesthesia state, which accompanied the break with the *dirigiste* model. While an understandable strategy for protecting the vulnerable and demobilizing potential opponents of de-*dirigization*, the social anesthesia state has contributed to the contestation of subsequent liberalizing reforms in three ways. First, it transformed France's liberalizing trajectory into a two-stage process – a shift from the *dirigiste* state to the social anesthesia state, then an overhaul of the social anesthesia state – fueling liberalization fatigue among the French population. Second, the high costs and passive labor market orientation of the social anesthesia state reduced the economic benefits of the break with the dysfunctional *dirigiste* model in the 1980s, fostering the sentiment that economic liberalization does not work. Third, the high cost of the social anesthesia state has limited the fiscal capacity of governments to offer side-payments and compensation in exchange for acceptance of liberalizing reform. Chapter 2 shows how these factors have fostered contestation through two cases of failed labor market liberalization targeted at unemployed youths: the effort to create a lower minimum wage for young people by Prime Minister Edouard Balladur in 1994 and the attempt to reduce layoff protections for youths by Prime Minister Dominique de Villepin in 2006.

Chapter 3 examines the party-political legacy of the *dirigiste* model, in particular the impact on parties of the right. It draws on the experiences of French governments of the right, suggesting that France is, in many ways, a case of liberalization without liberals. The French right ran the *dirigiste* system for much of the postwar period, and the statist and nationalist principles associated with *dirigisme* remain salient today. In addition, many leaders of the right were in power during the upheaval of May 1968 upheaval, which was itself a backlash against top-down governance and *dirigiste* policymaking. Scarred by the upheaval, they emerged with a deep fear of strikes and protests, often leading them to sacrifice reforms in the face of contestation in order to preserve social order. Chapter 3 presents four different dimensions of the French right's ambivalence toward economic liberalization: (1) a nationalist approach to France's economy that prompts conservatives to rig markets for corporate control so as to prevent foreign takeovers; (2) a fear of social upheaval that leads governments to retreat from liberalizing reforms in the face of popular protests; (3) an unwillingness to defend economic liberalization on its own terms, instead delegitimating liberalization by blaming it on outside forces like globalization and European integration; (4) a fair-weather liberalism that gives way to statist revival in times of economic crisis.

Chapter 4 probes the institutional legacy of the *dirigiste* model, the reliance on top-down, insular, skinny politics. Scholars have shown that because liberalizing reforms are often controversial and unpopular, the most effective strategy tends to be for the government to share or avoid blame by inviting parties of the opposition and/or the social partners into the reform process. Enlarging the circle of reformers adds legitimacy to the resulting policies and slims the ranks of opponents and protestors. By contrast, the French skinny approach, a product of both *dirigiste* legacies and the institutions of the Fifth Republic, is marked by top-down imposition, which concentrates blame and fuels the contestation of the government.

Chapter 4 describes how governments of both the left and the right missed an opportunity to reduce this concentration of blame and contestation via the so-called Social Refoundation. Launched by the employer association and reformist unions in 1998, the Social Refoundation sought to move welfare and labor market reform out of the contested political arena and into the corporatist arena of negotiations between employers and unions. Although the right, in particular, shared many of the objectives of the Social Refoundation, neither the right nor the left was willing to cede control over key reforms to the social partners, and the Social Refoundation withered on the vine. Chapter 4 also uses the case of pension reform and other liberalizing initiatives following Chirac's decision to forego the Social Refoundation in 2002 to show how the French skinny-politics approach tends to yield less reform and more contestation than a broader, concertational approach. *Taken together, Chapters 2 through 4 point to three legacies of the* dirigiste *model and its dismantling that make liberalization so contested in France: reform without results or resources (Chapter 2), liberalization without liberals (Chapter 3), and politics without partners (Chapter 4).*

Chapters 5 through 7 apply the argument developed in Chapters 2 through 4 to the current president, Emmanuel Macron. These chapters demonstrate that the three legacies of *dirigisme* continue to fuel the contestation of economic liberalization today. Chapter 5 covers the first eighteen months of the Macron presidency, culminating in the yellow vest protests. It shows that in a context of scarce fiscal resources due to the social anesthesia state, Macron's desire to bolster French business and French attractiveness to international investors through tax cuts while reducing France's budget deficit necessarily entailed tax increases and cutbacks in public and social services for the general population. Further fueling contestation, Macron adopted an extreme form of skinny politics, disdaining negotiations with political elites and the social partners, and imposing reforms from above. The combination of unpopular reform, much of it liberal in nature, and skinny politics sparked the yellow vest protests in fall 2018. The yellow vest movement ultimately forced Macron to backtrack from his agenda, sent his approval ratings plummeting, and weakened his capacity to govern.

Chapter 6 covers Macron's attempt to rebound from the yellow vest protests. On the one hand, signaling a shift in governance, Macron launched two initiatives, the Grand National Debate and the Citizens' Climate Convention (Convention Citoyenne pour le Climat, CCC), which offered an opportunity for ordinary citizens to voice their concerns and preferences. In the case of the CCC, 150 citizens were given the chance to craft legislative and regulatory reforms that Macron pledged to implement. On the other hand, outside the GDN and CCC, Macron continued as before, pursuing an unpopular liberal economic agenda implemented via top-down, skinny methods. Chapter 6 uses Macron's two most important initiatives during this period, a tightening of unemployment benefits and eligibility rules and an overhaul of the pension system, to demonstrate the continuity of his agenda and approach to governing. Both reforms triggered significant contestation, especially the pension overhaul, which Macron eventually abandoned.

Chapter 7 describes Macron's economic response to the COVID-19 crisis since March 2020, which has been strikingly similar to Nicolas

Sarkozy's response to the 2008 financial crisis. Like Sarkozy, Macron retreated from liberal principles and launched new statist initiatives in a crisis. Macron's shift to a statist-protective stance was symbolized by his pledge to spend "whatever it costs" to protect French businesses and workers from the effects of the crisis. Chapter 7 illustrates Macron's shift through four sets of actions: (1) the projection of state power and spending in the area of public health; (2) the creation of expensive new programs to keep French businesses afloat during the crisis along with sectoral policies to protect and direct strategic industries over the long term; (3) a recommitment to social anesthesia policies, including programs that Macron had earlier sought to phase out; (4) a dramatic increase in public spending and borrowing. Chapter 7 also describes Macron's illiberal response to a more recent crisis, the surge in inflation and energy costs beginning in fall 2021, which prompted him to freeze natural gas and electricity rates, subsidize gasoline purchases, launch a €50 billion plan to build a new generation of nuclear reactors, and move to renationalize the country's main electricity provider. Finally, it discusses the ways in which the contestation of liberalization shaped the 2022 presidential and legislative elections. Taken together, Chapters 5 through 7 demonstrate that the three legacies of *dirigisme* – policy, party-political, and institutional – continue to fuel the contestation of economic liberalization in the contemporary period.

Chapter 8 summarizes the evidence in this book, then discusses the implications of the French experience for liberalizing reformers in other countries as well as France. It starts by translating the argument about *dirigiste* legacies into a more general set of hypotheses and showing how these hypotheses may cast light on the contestation of liberalizing reforms in East Asia and Latin America. Next, it identifies changes in the process and substance of liberalization that might reduce contestation. Finally, Chapter 8 discusses the links between France's contested liberalization and the rise of illiberal populist parties. It concludes by suggesting that a more inclusive and equitable form liberalization might help limit the appeal of populist movements.

2   From the *Dirigiste* State to the Social Anesthesia State

This chapter analyzes France's break with the *dirigiste* model in the 1980s and the resulting policy legacies that have contributed to the contestation of economic liberalization in subsequent years. In analyzing these policy legacies, the chapter also addresses a paradox in the debate about French economic and social policy. On the one hand, as related in Chapter 1, France scores relatively low on comparative indices of economic liberalization, and there is a voluminous literature decrying the government's inability or unwillingness to enact liberalizing reform. On the other hand, there is an equally voluminous literature, much of it leftist in orientation, contending that France has succumbed to the neoliberal model. Perhaps the most well-known work in this vein is Viviane Forrester's bestseller, *The Economic Horror*, which argues that a system of "financial totalitarianism" is destroying jobs in France, while spreading poverty and misery in its wake (Forrester 1996). Bruno Amable and Stefano Palombarini offer a more sophisticated argument emphasizing the movement toward neoliberalism of successive French governments, despite the difficulties of enlisting electoral support for such an agenda (Amable and Palombarini 2021).

There are several lines of explanation as to why France has embraced or succumbed to neoliberalism. One emphasizes international and European constraints that supposedly leave little room for the kinds of market-directing or market-resisting policies traditionally favored by French policymakers. European Union (EU) antitrust policy limits government aid to companies, even those that are publicly owned, and often challenges the creation of French-style "national champions" through mergers that reduce competition. Market forces are said to push in the same direction. Globalization, in the form of intensified competition and capital mobility, compels countries to pursue orthodox economic policies, on pain of being sanctioned by internationally mobile investors (Cable 1995; Friedman 1999; Strange 2000). Indeed, the experience of France in the early 1980s, when the leftist government of François Mitterrand rushed headlong into an ultra-voluntarist strategy only to reverse course and initiate market reforms two years later, is often portrayed as the clearest illustration of the loss of economic sovereignty in the face of globalization:

The global economy relentlessly passes judgment on governments and societies.... Consider the lessons learned by a representative middle-ranking nation such as France. Following attempts to reflate in the early 1980s, despite worldwide recession, the Socialist government in France accepted it could no longer go it alone. It subsequently embraced a form of economic liberalism as assiduously as did the rightist opposition. (Horsman and Marshall 1994: xii)

Another line of explanation points to the cramped, insular thinking of French elites. This argument is often put forward by French academics and politicians, especially those of a leftist or voluntarist bent, who criticize elites for having succumbed to *la pensée unique*, loosely translated as economic orthodoxy or the Washington consensus (Chevènement 2011; Montbrial 2000). These critics believe that there are still opportunities for voluntarist policies, but that French leaders, an unusually cohesive cadre trained at the same elite academies and operating in the same closed policy circles, are incapable of thinking outside the box. To an extent unparalleled in other European countries, French elites are chosen, trained, and placed in positions of authority by so-called *grandes écoles*, small ultra-selective public institutions, most notably the Ecole Polytechnique engineering school and especially the Ecole Nationale d'Administation (ENA) or National School of Administration (Birnbaum 1977, 1978; Suleiman 1974, 1978). ENA accepts barely 100 students per year, yet four of the last six French presidents have been ENA graduates: Valéry Giscard d'Estaing (1974–1981), Jacques Chirac (1995–2007), François Hollande (2012–2017), and Emmanuel Macron (2017–present). Indeed, France is only half-jokingly described as an *énarchie*, a fusion of ENA and monarchy, meaning government by graduates of ENA, who wield vast powers like those of French monarchs of long ago.[1] Moreover, alumni from ENA and Polytechnique dominate the top positions in industry and finance along with government and the upper civil service. Leftist critics of the French system argue that Polytechnique and ENA students receive the same orthodox economic instruction, and because alumni of these *grandes écoles* are so influential there is little room for outside voices to challenge the hegemony of *la pensée unique*.

A final explanation zeroes in on the French left, especially the Socialist Party (Parti Socialiste, PS). This literature criticizes Socialist leaders for having abandoned the working class and disadvantaged (Amable and Palombarini 2017, 2021; Germain 2015; Julliard and Michéa

2014; Plenel and Dufau 2015; Rey 2004; Rothé 2013). International economic constraints and the hold of *la pensée unique* are part of the reason, but electoral calculations also enter into play. Socialist leaders have sought to expand their electorate among middle-class and educated voters, while still holding onto a shrinking working class and placating far-left coalition partners. As a result, they tend to combine ambitious, leftist promises on the campaign trail with orthodox economic governance once in office. Lionel Jospin, the Socialist prime minister from 1997 to 2002, campaigned against the terms of the Maastricht Treaty, then implemented an austerity program so that France would qualify for the European Monetary Union (EMU). Jospin also privatized more companies than any French leader before or since (*Le Monde*, November 16, 2009). François Hollande, the president from 2012 to 2017, railed against finance and big business, only to tender sizable tax cuts to business and high-income groups financed by tax increases on ordinary French citizens. To leftist critics, the PS is socialist in name only, acting to accommodate, rather than resist, neoliberalism.

These various explanations of French government actions emphasize different causes, but all agree on the effect: French economic and social policy has moved in a sharply neoliberal direction. The question then becomes how to reconcile this depiction with the evidence in Chapter 1 that fiscal, labor market, and competition policies are less liberal in France than in other leading European countries. The answer, which is also critical for understanding the contestation of economic liberalization today, is that France may have undertaken considerable liberalization, but it has confronted a longer road to travel than other European countries.

Since the 1970s, all of Europe's leading political economies have experienced deep economic problems at one time or another. Typically, reformers have responded by seeking to make labor markets more flexible and improve the returns from employment relative to social benefits. They have also moved to pare the welfare state, so as to get spending and taxation down to more manageable levels. The French agenda diverges from this pattern of reform and is more challenging because before attempting to overhaul labor markets and the welfare state, French leaders engaged in another kind of liberalizing reform: they dismantled the nation's dysfunctional *dirigiste* industrial policy system. As described later in this chapter, the way that successive governments achieved this objective was by deploying a "social anesthesia" strategy, expanding social and labor market policies to cushion the blow and undercut resistance from the potential victims of market-led adjustment, especially those whose jobs were threatened (Levy 2005a, 2005b, 2008; Levy et al. 2006). While understandable, this social anesthesia strategy stretched out the process of economic liberalization. Alone in Europe, the French trajectory of liberalization has entailed two sets of reforms: a first set of reforms to roll back a dysfunctional *dirigiste* model and a second set of reforms to address some of the problems caused by the vehicle used to usher in the first set of reforms, the social anesthesia state.

The contrasting depictions of French economic and social policy stem in part from this two-stage trajectory of reform. To those focusing on the first stage – the break with the *dirigiste* industrial policy model – France has moved in a sharply neoliberal direction, privatizing companies, paring industrial policy budgets, winding down the *grands projets*, lifting price and capital controls, freeing credit channels, and dismantling the key institutions of voluntarist policymaking. By contrast, to those focusing on the second stage – the overhaul of the welfare state and labor markets – France appears more hesitant and blocked, struggling to consolidate public finances, make labor markets more flexible, and expand competition.

France's two-stage trajectory has done more than muddy the debate about how much the country has changed. It has also made contemporary reform distinctly more challenging than in other European countries. For starters, it has required French authorities to initiate controversial liberalizing reforms twice, rather than once. In addition, whereas many European countries experienced significant economic gains from reform, the first stage of reform in France – the rollback of the *dirigiste* industrial policy model – yielded limited benefits, in part because of the costs and rigidities associated with the social anesthesia state that accompanied de-*dirigization*. France never enjoyed a period of rapid economic growth following the liberalizing reforms of the 1980s, nor has France ever risen to the status of an economic model in the manner of Holland, Sweden, Denmark, Germany, and the UK. Because of the country's disappointing economic performance and persistent mass unemployment, much of the French public has grown skeptical of liberalizing reform, feeling that it has been tried and failed. This reform skepticism or reform fatigue has made it politically difficult to introduce further liberalizing measures.

The two-phase trajectory of reform has fostered the contestation of economic liberalization in another way. Because of the high cost of the social anesthesia state, French authorities have generally lacked the fiscal resources to offer side-payments or compensation in exchange for acceptance of new liberalizing reforms. Whereas state authorities deployed social anesthesia spending to smooth the path of de-*dirigization* following the 1983 U-turn, they possess much less fiscal ammunition for accompanying the reform of the social anesthesia state. In the absence of compensation, though, liberalizing initiatives are almost always contested in the streets and, on a number of occasions, persistent strikes and protests have forced the government to back down.

This chapter analyzes France's movement from the *dirigiste* state to the social anesthesia state and the resulting challenges to economic liberalization. Section 2.1 presents the main features of the *dirigiste* model and the reasons for its decline. Section 2.2 describes the movement from the *dirigiste* state to the social anesthesia state. Section 2.3 summarizes the strengths and weaknesses of the social anesthesia state. Section 2.4 illustrates the ways in which the movement from the *dirigiste* state to the social anesthesia state fuels contestation and impedes liberalizing reform, taking as an example the efforts of two French governments to liberalize labor markets for young people.

2.1   The Rise and Fall of the *Dirigiste* Model

In the postwar period, France adopted a *dirigiste* or state-led model of economic reconstruction and development (Bauchet 1986; Cohen 1977; Hall 1986; Massé 1965; Rousso 1986; Shonfield 1965; Zysman 1978, 1983). This *dirigiste* model revolved around two sets of strategies – a strategy toward business and a strategy toward labor. As the verb *diriger* suggests, state authorities sought to direct the strategies of business, to accelerate investment and industrial modernization. At the same time, and less publicized, they sought to squeeze labor, to shift resources from wages and consumption to investment.

France's *dirigiste* model was conceived as a way of creating a modern capitalist economy in the absence of a modern capitalist class (Bloch-Lainé and Bouvier 1986; Hoffmann 1963; Kuisel 1981; Zysman 1983). French employers had been sullied by their wartime collaboration with the Nazi occupiers, but also by their prewar actions. The "Malthusianism" of French employers, denoting a preference for stability over growth and an aversion to risk-taking (Landes 1951, 1957), was widely blamed for having slowed industrialization and left France ill-equipped to face the Nazi war machine. In the postwar period, therefore, a directive, interventionist state would take the economy where Malthusian employers feared to tread.

State efforts to steer the strategies of business were backed by an arsenal of resources, starting with personnel. Following selection through rigorous, meritocratic exams, France's best and brightest students were trained in the *grandes écoles* (notably Polytechnique and ENA), then "parachuted" into key positions within the French state (Birnbaum 1977, 1978; Suleiman 1974, 1978). During the initial postwar period, state technocrats intervened primarily through the multiyear planning process, which channeled resources and guidance to priority heavy industrial sectors, like coal, steel, and electricity (Bauchet 1986; Cohen 1977; Hall 1986; Massé 1965; Rousso 1986; Shonfield 1965). In the 1960s and 1970s, planning was relayed by the so-called *grands projets*, a combination of subsidies, captive markets, and the transfer of technologies developed in public research labs, which catapulted French industry to positions of global leadership in such sectors as nuclear power, high-speed trains (Trains à Grande Vitesse, TGV), and digital telephone switches (Cohen 1992; Cohen and Bauer 1985). Both the planning process and the *grands projets* were facilitated by the existence of a large public sector, a legacy of Liberation-era nationalizations, which the left then expanded in 1982.

The reach of French technocrats extended well beyond the public sector, though. Authorities mobilized a panoply of selective incentives to shape the behavior of private actors, notably protection from foreign competition, exemption from price controls, and subsidized credit. State officials not only "chose winners" in the private sector, but often created these so-called national champions in the first place through state-sponsored mergers and takeovers.

Alongside the various mechanisms for steering business decisions, *dirigiste* policymaking arbitrated between capital and labor. From the perspective of the planners, wages and welfare spending were to be contained, lest they drain resources from industrial investment. Social spending was held in check for many years, increasing by only 2 percent of GDP between 1950 and 1960 (Cameron 1991).

Industrial relations policy also operated in favor of business. Government authorities deployed a variety of techniques to hold down wages, such as turning a blind eye to systematic employer violations of the right to unionize and bringing in immigrant workers from former French colonies to preserve slack in the labor market. They also neutralized wage increases by accommodating rapid inflation and undertaking periodic "aggressive" devaluations of the French franc that were designed to not only restore competitiveness in international markets, but also confer a temporary price advantage on French producers (Hall 1986).

French public finances were likewise organized in a regressive manner, with most revenues generated by sales taxes and payroll taxes (or Social Security charges in the European parlance) that were paid disproportionately by employees.[2] At the same time, more progressive income, inheritance, and corporate taxes were set at low levels and collected unevenly. The combination of a limited welfare state, underdeveloped collective bargaining, and a regressive system of taxation gave France one of the most unequal distributions of wealth of any Organisation for Economic Co-operation and Development (OECD) country. Indeed, by some accounts, inequality in France even exceeded that of the USA (Sawyer 1976).

Beginning in the late 1960s, France's *dirigiste* model confronted a less hospitable political and social environment. Two developments, in particular, undermined *dirigiste* policy: the near-revolution of May 1968 and the emergence in the 1970s of a powerful Socialist–Communist alliance, the "Union of the Left." Although France's break with *dirigisme* was ultimately precipitated by international pressures, the stage for the 1983 U-turn was set by the growing domestically driven dysfunctions of the 1970s and early 1980s.

The events of May 1968 sent a shock wave throughout the French political establishment. Charles de Gaulle, who had dominated French politics for a decade, was no longer the unquestioned leader. Indeed, one year later, de Gaulle resigned from office when a referendum designed to relegitimate his rule failed to secure a majority. May 1968 not only broke de Gaulle's hegemony; it also broke the labor-exclusionary premise of the *dirigiste* model. On the heels of 1968, the marginalization of the French working class would give way to attempts at incorporation. Furthermore, in a country with a relatively new and contested constitution and a long tradition of revolutionary politics, the unrest of 1968 left deep psychological scars. Henceforth, French leaders would become extraordinarily conflict-averse, often backing down at the first sign of street resistance – whether from shopkeepers, farmers, or workers (Berger 1981; Cohen 1989).

The emergence of the "Union of the Left" in the 1970s posed a further challenge to *dirigiste* policymaking. With the left no longer divided, governments of the right found themselves under constant electoral threat. In 1974, the center-right candidate for president, Valéry Giscard d'Estaing, outpolled his Socialist rival, François Mitterrand, by a mere 50.8 percent to 49.2 percent. Giscard's hold on power remained shaky during his entire seven-year term, and he would be ousted by Mitterrand in the 1981 presidential election.

The period from 1968 to 1983 brought an attenuation or even reversal of the traditional probusiness orientation of French policy (Adam et al. 1972; Howell 1992a; Lipietz 1984). Workers benefited from rapid increases in the minimum wage and the use of the so-called extension procedure to make settlements reached in labor strongholds legally binding throughout the economy. Labor registered additional gains through national agreements (*conventions*) that were formally negotiated by the social partners, but in fact largely drafted and imposed by the government. Two such *conventions* were especially significant. One provided unemployment benefits equal to 90 percent of previous wages for up to one year, while the other, the administrative authorization for layoffs, required the approval of an inspector from the ministry of labor for dismissals of ten or more employees for economic reasons. The 1970s were also a time of vigorous growth in social spending, particularly under the Giscard presidency when social transfers increased by over 5 percent of GDP (Palier 2002). Thanks to these and other changes, labor's share of value added expanded from 61 percent in 1967 to 69 percent in 1981 (INSEE 1998: 65).

The contested political environment of the 1970s affected not only social policy, but also the operation of *dirigiste* economic policy. More accurately, political pressures *diverted dirigisme* from its postwar modernizing mission (Berger 1981; Cohen 1989; Levy 1999b). Anxious conservative leaders had no stomach for painful, if much-needed, rationalization of declining or uncompetitive enterprises. Indeed, their initiatives often ran in the opposite direction. While embracing a rhetoric of liberalization and market-driven adjustment, the Giscard administration nationalized the bankrupt French steel industry and created a special agency, the Interministerial Committee for the Adaptation of Industrial Structures (Comité Interministériel de l'Aménagement des Structures Industrielles, CIASI), to bail out companies in difficulty. In 1978, a government-commissioned report revealed that fewer than one-dozen firms, most of them uncompetitive and many in declining sectors, were receiving more than 75 percent of all public aid to industry (*Cahiers Français* 1983: 16). Worse still, these resources tended to be used, not to undertake much-needed restructuring and positioning in viable market niches, but rather to delay layoffs and adjustment.

The diversion of *dirigisme* only intensified when François Mitterrand ousted Giscard as president in 1981. Mitterrand campaigned on a pledge to take *dirigisme* to new heights, to restore growth and employment by running a "real industrial policy." Once in office, the government of the left enacted a sweeping program of nationalizations, covering twelve leading industrial conglomerates and thirty-eight banks (Boublil 1977, 1990; Hall 1986; Stoffaës 1985). Declaring that, "there are no condemned sectors; there are only excessively old factories and equipment" (cited in *Cahiers Français* 1983: 28), Mitterrand launched a series of voluntarist industrial policies designed to "reconquer domestic markets" in all manner of troubled French industries, including electronics, coal, steel, chemicals, textiles, machine tools, furniture, leather goods, and even toys.

Very quickly, however, it became clear that Socialist *dirigisme* was not producing the desired results. Like Giscard, the left found it difficult to shift resources from traditional to emerging sectors. Given its claim that there were no declining sectors, only outmoded technologies, the government was obliged to attempt to turn around lame ducks. Supporting industries like shipbuilding and coal deprived the authorities of resources needed for more promising sectors, however.

Aggravating matters, Mitterrand – like Giscard before him – proved unable to resist pressures to protect jobs at all costs. Indeed, having pledged that *dirigiste* policies would create jobs, rather than eliminate them, Mitterrand was trapped by his own campaign rhetoric. Electoral calculations also entered into play. Job cuts would strike at the core of the left's support base – unskilled and semiskilled blue-collar workers in heavy industry. The government, therefore, opted to buy social peace. This strategy yielded increasingly untenable economic outcomes, however. By 1983, a number of firms were so heavily subsidized that it would have been far cheaper for the government to pay workers *not to produce*. In shipbuilding, for example, it was estimated that each job paying €15,300 in annual wages cost the government between €22,900 and €68,700 in subsidies (Cohen 1989: 230–231).[3] Taken together, these many dysfunctions raised the question of whether *dirigisme* was worth defending.

The crisis of the *dirigiste* model came to a head in 1983, when a weakening French franc threatened to fall below the minimum exchange rate allowed by the European Monetary System (EMS), the precursor to today's EMU (Hall 1990). Under pressure from international financial markets and with growing skepticism about the effectiveness of *dirigiste* industrial policy, President Mitterrand reversed course, abandoning the government's voluntarist industrial policy, loosening state controls over the economy, and introducing austerity measures to defend the franc. A leftist administration that had been elected just two years earlier on a campaign to intensify *dirigisme* began instead to dismantle *dirigisme*.

2.2   From the *Dirigiste* State to the Social Anesthesia State

The 1983 U-turn touched off a range of reforms that struck at the core of the *dirigiste* model (Cohen 1989; Hall 1990; Levy 1999b, 2000; Schmidt 1996). These changes, inaugurated cautiously by the Socialists from 1983 to 1986, were amplified when the right returned to power under a neoliberal banner from 1986 to 1988, then confirmed and completed by subsequent governments on both sides of the political spectrum.

Four sets of changes figured most prominently. In macroeconomic policy, French authorities broke with the traditional "inflationary growth" strategy, marked by deficit spending, lax monetary policy, and periodic "aggressive devaluations" (Hall 1986). The new strategy of "competitive disinflation" prioritized keeping France's inflation rate below that of its trading partners through a combination of fiscal restraint, de-indexation of wages, and tight monetary policy. Although French authorities managed to curb inflation, they did so primarily on the basis of monetary policy rather than fiscal policy, as budgetary restraint remained elusive.

A second important change concerned France's public enterprises. Many of the banks and firms that had been nationalized in the immediate aftermath of World War II and during the Socialists' first years in office were released from their planning targets, instructed to focus instead on profitability, and, in some cases, partially opened to private investors. This movement from state direction to market direction accelerated during a wave of privatizations launched by the right upon its return to power in 1986 and continued by governments of the left and right alike. In the process, the once-vast holdings of the French state were reduced to little more than energy production, public transportation, and some weapons manufacturers.

The third major policy shift after 1983 was a retreat from traditional state efforts to steer private industry. The guiding spirit of this change was that firms would receive less government assistance, but would be subjected to fewer restrictions, so that they could raise the necessary resources by their own means (Hall 1990). The hefty budgets for bailouts of loss-making companies, sectoral industrial policy programs, high-tech *grands projets*, and subsidized loans largely dried up, triggering a wave of bankruptcies. As a counterpoint for the winding down of state support, though, French business gained a number of new freedoms. The deregulation of financial markets, initiated in 1985, enabled firms to raise funds by issuing equity, reducing their dependence on state-allocated credit. The removal of price controls in 1986 allowed companies to reap the full benefits of successful competitive strategies. The elimination of capital controls in the late 1980s facilitated the expansion of production abroad and gave managers an "exit" option if domestic conditions were not to their liking. Taken together, these and other reforms helped boost corporate profitability from 9.8 percent of value added in 1982 to 17.3 percent in 1989 (Faugère and Voisin 1994: 32).

The revival of corporate profits was also fueled by a fourth set of developments, the reform of France's system of industrial relations (Groux and Mouriaux 1990; Howell 1992a, 1992b; Labbé and Croisat 1992). State authorities de-indexed wages and lifted a number of restrictions limiting managerial prerogatives, most significantly the administrative authorization for layoffs. They also expanded the scope of workplace bargaining, which enabled employers to introduce significant labor market flexibility, often in a one-sided manner. Not surprisingly, much of capital's gain in the post-1983 period came at labor's expense. From

1982 to 1989, the share of value added received by capital increased from 24.0 percent to 31.7 percent, surpassing the levels of the early 1970s (Faugère and Voisin 1994: 28–29).

The reforms after 1983 left no *dirigiste* stone unturned. Looking across the wealthy democracies, it would be difficult to find any country that shifted so far away from its postwar economic strategy in the 1980s and early 1990s. Certainly, compared with other statist political economies, such as Japan and Korea, France moved earlier and more aggressively against its postwar statist model (Levy 2015; Levy et al. 2006).

The far-reaching break with the postwar *dirigiste* industrial policy model was not accompanied by a comparable shift in political discourse, however. On the contrary, the Mitterrand government sought to downplay the changes that it was introducing. Officials spoke of a "pause" in reform, rather than a reversal of course, and they used the phrase "rigor," as opposed to austerity. Instead of making the economic and social case for breaking with the *dirigiste* model, the left engaged in what Philip Gordon and Sophie Meunier describe as a kind of adaptation "by stealth" (Gordon and Meunier 2001), maintaining a voluntarist discourse, while conducting liberalizing reforms quietly, under the radar. Moreover, to the extent that the government admitted that it was engaging in economic liberalization, the left presented these reforms as the result of European pressures, rather than domestic choices. In point of fact, the reforms in France after 1983 went well beyond anything necessary for remaining in the EMS, but it was more politically expedient to say that Europe was forcing France to reform than to take responsibility and argue that the reforms were necessary and good for the French economy. This combination of denial and blaming of Brussels may have originated with the left, but it would become a bipartisan strategy, as conservative governments likewise sought to avoid blame for unpopular liberalizing reforms.

The rollback of the *dirigiste* model was not the only shift in French policy touched off by the 1983 U-turn. A second shift, more social in orientation, accompanied and enabled the first shift. State authorities expanded social and labor market programs dramatically, so as to cushion the blow to industrial workers and other groups made vulnerable by the movement away from the *dirigiste* model. These initiatives were motivated by more than social concerns. State authorities feared riots and protests that could block reforms or, worse still, spiral into far-reaching unrest along the lines of May 1968, threatening the regime itself.

The expansion of social and labor market programs was designed to forestall such unrest. It reflected a social anesthesia logic, that is, it sought to permit French firms to reorganize on a more market-rational basis by pacifying and demobilizing the potential victims and opponents of economic liberalization (Levy 2005a, 2005b, 2008, 2013; Levy et al. 2006). In a logic famously articulated by Karl Polanyi, the extension of market forces was softened and made politically acceptable by a simultaneous expansion of social protections for those most affected by liberalization (Polanyi 1944). On the one hand, beginning in 1983, state authorities made a market, imposing liberalization from above. Privatization, deregulation, the phasing out of subsidies to loss-making companies, and the weakening of job protections all heightened the vulnerability of French workers. On the other hand, successive governments, especially those of the left, expanded social and labor market provisions, so as to cushion the blow to the working class and, equally important, undercut the possibilities for union mobilization (Daley 1996; Levy 1999b).

France's social anesthesia strategy centered initially on two sets of policies. The first was the creation of some fifteen "conversion poles" in geographic areas that were especially hard-hit by the industrial restructuring launched in 1984. The government made no effort to hide the link between industrial restructuring and strategies of territorial and worker compensation: the creation of the conversion poles was announced the same day as retrenchment plans in the coal, steel, and shipbuilding sectors. The conversion poles received sizable subsidies to help clean up unsightly abandoned factories, retrain workers, modernize infrastructure, and support new technologies and emerging high-tech startups. From the perspective of displaced workers, the biggest advantage of the conversion pole program was the possibility of retiring on a full pension as early as age 50.

The second, related dimension of the state's social anesthesia strategy was a huge expansion of the possibilities for early retirement, not just in the conversion poles, but in every troubled industrial agglomeration. The expansion of early retirement to accommodate and humanize restructuring began under the Giscard presidency. Between 1974 and 1980, the number of early retirees more than tripled from 59,000 to 190,400 (DARES 1996: 100). The left more than tripled the figure again to over 700,000 workers in 1984. Beyond salving the left's guilty conscience, the widespread recourse to early retirement served the strategic purpose of demobilizing France's working class and undercutting trade union capacity to mount resistance against industrial restructuring. The vast majority of French workers were more than willing to quit smelly, physically taxing, alienating jobs and receive 80 to 90 percent of their previous wages without having to report to work. In such a context, France's already anemic trade unions proved incapable of mobilizing their members against industrial restructuring. The leader of the Communist General Confederation of Labor (Confédération Générale du Travail, CGT) in the Loire Department, a center of coal, steel, and metalworking industries, described his frustration over the demobilizing effects of early retirement programs:

The CGT opposed early retirement programs. We wanted the money to be invested in French industry to maintain and create new jobs. The problem is that the workers loved early retirement: they got paid almost as much as when they were employed, they didn't have to go to work, and they had no risk of being laid off. I would give speeches in the factories, declaring that the CGT demanded more state investment to save the flowers of French industry and create jobs. The guys ate it up; they would stand up and cheer! The problem, though, is that after the speech, a bunch of them would come to me, hanging their heads, and ask if there was some way that I could get them on the list for the next round of early retirements. (Interview by the author with Pierre Gallon, Director of the Industrial and Economic Sector, Loire Department, CGT, October 16, 1992)

The effects of early retirement on the French labor market cannot be overstated. By 1990, fewer than one worker in three was still employed at age 60. What is more, France's labor force participation rate for men aged 55 to 64 fell below 40 percent, one of the lowest rates in Western Europe (Scharpf and Schmidt 2000: 350). In recent years, there have been some initiatives to curtail early retirement, but they have had a limited impact. As Figure 2.1 reveals, whereas in the early 1970s, French men spent roughly the same number of years in retirement as men in other leading OECD countries, the French average began to climb steadily under the effects of early retirement programs, and since 2000, French men have had the longest period of retirement in the OECD. (So, too have French women.)

Social anesthesia policies were deployed not only to facilitate the movement away from *dirigisme*, but also to palliate the perceived limits or failings of economic liberalization, in particular, the persistence of mass unemployment. In 1988, the Socialist government of Michel Rocard established a national guaranteed income, the Minimum Integration Income (Revenu Minimum d'Insertion, RMI). The RMI was transformed into the Active Solidarity Income (Revenu de Solidarité Active, RSA) in 2009, reflecting the aspiration to move claimants into the workforce. As of 2020, the RSA provided a monthly allowance, ranging from €565 for a single individual to €1,187 for a family of four (plus €226 for each additional child), on a means-tested basis to citizens and long-term residents over the age of 25 (DREES 2021).[4] The RMI/RSA replaced a patchwork of local and targeted social assistance programs that had left large segments of the population uncovered, notably the long-term unemployed and persons suffering from psychological problems, alcoholism, and/or chemical dependency. Of particular importance, the RSA often functions as a basic income support for adults who have exhausted or failed to qualify for unemployment insurance.

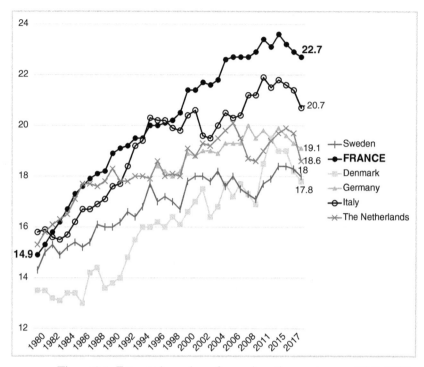

Figure 2.1 Expected number of years in retirement, men, 1980–2018
Source: (OECD 2017a)

The creation of the Universal Health Coverage (Couverture Maladie Universelle, CMU) in 2000 by another Socialist government, that of Lionel Jospin, likewise helped alleviate the effects of mass unemployment. The CMU extended basic insurance to some 1.2 million French citizens who lacked such coverage (almost 2 percent of the population). In addition, it offered supplementary health insurance to 5.3 million people, or 8.8 percent of the population, who did not receive such insurance from their employers and faced sizable co-payments for medical procedures (Boisguérin 2001).

Governments of the left and right alike also multiplied labor market policies to limit the suffering of those who are unable to secure stable employment. The right has tended to focus on subsidies and tax breaks for private employers who agree to hire hard-to-place employees at the bottom of the wage spectrum (youths, the unskilled, older workers). Such programs cost over €10 billion per year (INSEE 2018).

The left has favored training programs as well as public internships. The Jospin government's Youth Employment Program (Programme

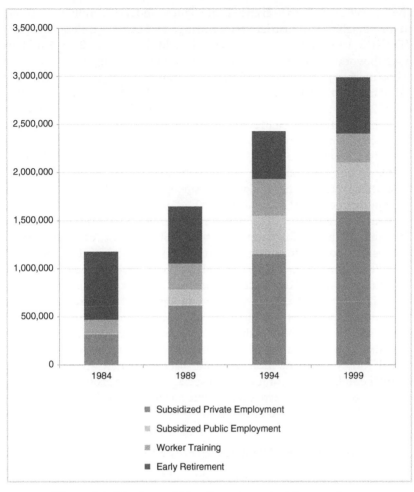

Figure 2.2 Number of French workers in labor market programs, 1984–1999
Source: (DARES 1996, 2000)

Emplois Jeunes, PEJ), for example, provided five-year positions in the public sector to some 350,000 young people at a cost of €5.3 billion, while training and apprenticeship spending totaled €5–6 billion per year. The left also presented its thirty-five-hour workweek reform as a way of creating (or sharing) jobs, although this analysis was hotly contested by many economists along with employers and the parties of the right.

Looking at labor market policy globally, Figure 2.2 reveals that the number of French workers enrolled in some kind of public labor market program expanded two-and-a-half-fold during the fifteen years following the Socialists' U-turn – rising from slightly under 1.2 million in 1984, at the height of industrial restructuring, to nearly 3 million in 1999 (DARES 1996, 2000). This total is in addition to the 2 to 3 million French workers who were formally unemployed. Aggregate spending on labor market policy likewise increased, from slightly over 2 percent of GDP in the mid-1980s to 3.15 percent of GDP in 2003 (OECD 2019b). As of 2022, France spends nearly as much as on labor market programs as Denmark, the Mecca of active labor market policy. The growth of the welfare state has been equally dramatic. Social spending in France rose steadily following the left's U-turn, reaching 28.7 percent of GDP in 2003, which gave France the most expensive welfare state in the OECD. France has retained that ranking ever since, with social spending totaling 31.2 percent of GDP in 2018 (OECD 2019c).

France's break with the *dirigiste* model in the 1980s provided a dual impetus to the social anesthesia state. The *promise* of liberalization induced authorities to commit vast resources to the transition process, to the alleviation of social pain and political resistance, in the expectation that the rollback of dysfunctional *dirigiste* policies and a more flexible labor market would quickly generate enough jobs to make such costly transitional measures unnecessary (or, at least, much less necessary). The *disappointments* of liberalization, the continuing high level of unemployment, not only made it difficult to wind down supposedly transitional early retirement measures, but also drove new spending in the form of employment promotion and social assistance programs. In short, de-*dirigization* and the expansion of the social anesthesia state were two sides of the same very expensive coin.

2.3   Strengths and Weaknesses of the Social Anesthesia State

The social anesthesia strategy brought real benefits to the French economy. Whereas the *dirigiste* state sought to steer the market, the social anesthesia state supported market-led, privately determined adjustment strategies. By protecting French workers from the worst effects of job loss, the state allowed employers to reorganize their companies, closing unprofitable factories and downsizing plants as necessary. In the 1980s, French industry rationalized, returned to profitability, and began to draw down its heavy debt. France's balance of trade shifted into surplus, as French firms met European and global competition with great success. Meanwhile, French productivity surged, ranking among the highest in the world. Indeed, measured as output per hour worked, French productivity exceeded that of the USA during the late 1980s (OECD 2021g).

Another benefit of the social anesthesia strategy is that it enabled French authorities to disengage from dysfunctional *dirigiste* industrial policies. Here, a comparative perspective is revealing. In Japan in the 1990s, despite over a decade of economic stagnation and the discrediting of state guidance in the eyes of the population, government authorities struggled to reform an industrial policy system that, like the French system in the 1970s and early 1980s, had shifted from investing in the industries of the future to mostly supporting uncompetitive industries of the past (Pempel 2010; Tilton 1996; Vogel 2006, 2013). Part of the reason was a reluctance of state authorities to cede traditional powers. In addition, Japanese leaders, perched atop fragile and short-lived governing coalitions, found it difficult to launch controversial reforms. Perhaps the greatest obstacle to reform was the absence in Japan of a French-style social safety net (Gao 2001; Levy et al. 2006; Miura 2002, 2012). Japanese governments instead spent vast amounts to prop up debt-laden banks that were propping up debt-laden companies in turn because, were those banks and their corporate customers to shut down, millions of Japanese workers would lose their jobs, and Japan had no social safety net to take care of them. In the 1990s, Japanese state spending and indebtedness increased even more than French spending and indebtedness – Japanese debt surpassed 200 percent of GDP in 2008, more than twice the French figure (OECD 2017b) – and without the corresponding release from expensive and dysfunctional industrial policies.[5]

The social anesthesia strategy, as the label suggests, offered social as well as economic benefits. French companies were able to reorganize, much like their American or British counterparts, but worker living standards were protected. In other words, the costs of industrial adjustment were socialized to the collectivity, rather than concentrated on those who lost their jobs. French authorities were also attentive to new social needs, establishing programs like the RMI/RSA and CMU to address emerging gaps in the social insurance system. In short, the social anesthesia state moved France toward the market, while offering relatively humane treatment to the victims of industrial restructuring and economic liberalization.

If the social anesthesia strategy facilitated de-*dirigization* and industrial restructuring, it also generated problems of its own. For starters, the social anesthesia state is very expensive. From a fiscal standpoint, the multiplication of social anesthesia measures more than offset the savings from de-*dirigization*. Despite the winding down of expensive industrial policy measures, state spending has increased since the early 1980s, exceeding 55 percent of GDP. Although the effort to protect the poor and vulnerable is certainly laudable, the cost of these programs has pushed the French state to the limits of its fiscal capacity.

The high cost of the social anesthesia state has also compromised public investment, a historic strength of the *dirigiste* model. In the past, French authorities invested heavily in infrastructure and supported industrial development through lucrative government contracts. The result was an impressive array of programs and facilities – highways, high-speed trains, nuclear energy, urban transportation, advanced telecommunications, cutting-edge research and development (R&D) – that enhanced the business climate. More recently, this public investment vocation has been crowded out by social anesthesia spending, as the case of R&D reveals. French public spending on R&D declined from 1.26 percent of GDP in 1992 to 1.03 percent in 2002. This decline occurred at a time when the USA, Scandinavia, Germany, Japan, China, and India were intensifying their investments in the knowledge economy (French Ministry of Industry 2004; French Senate 2006).

Figure 2.3 presents annual R&D spending, including private spending, in a number of leading economies from 1990 to 2019. France was the only country in this group to experience a decline in R&D spending, albeit a small one, from 2.27 percent to 2.20 percent of GDP. During this period, French R&D spending went from above the OECD average of 2.02 percent of GDP in 1991 to below the OECD average of 2.48 percent of GDP in 2019. Among the advanced economies in Figure 2.3, France slipped from the middle of the pack to a near tie with the Netherlands for the lowest level R&D spending, and Dutch outlays grew significantly during the decade prior to 2019. Sweden, Germany, Japan, the USA, and (sometimes) Denmark all pushed their R&D spending above 3 percent of GDP, and the increase was especially dramatic among the Nordic countries.

A second problem of the social anesthesia state concerns the labor market. The social anesthesia state is largely passive; it pays people not to work. If this approach represents an improvement over bailing out uncompetitive companies in order to prevent layoffs, there are better uses for the money. Once again, a comparative perspective is revealing. Social Democratic regimes like that of Sweden have historically spent as much or even more than France on social programs, but the Social Democratic approach is centered around the so-called work line, the notion that every adult should be employed (Esping-Andersen 1990; Huber and Stephens 2001; Huo et al. 2008; Titmuss 1987). As a result, passive measures like early retirement tend to be limited, with much of the spending concentrated on "activating" policies that facilitate employment, such as education and training, relocation assistance, and

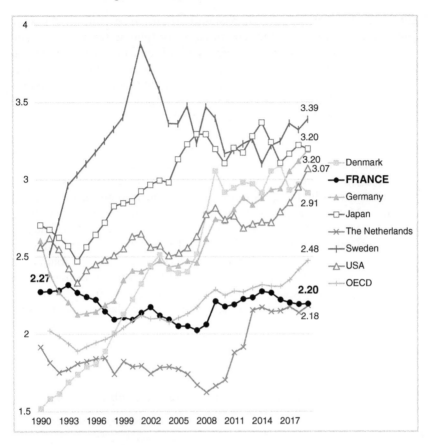

Figure 2.3 R&D spending as a percentage of GDP, 1990–2019
Source: (OECD 2020a)

low-cost public childcare. Under the "active" or "social investment" model, there is an economic payoff beyond simply keeping displaced workers from protesting and blocking layoffs. France's social anesthesia strategy, by contrast, offers relatively few such gains in human capital and employment.

Related to its passive orientation and high cost, the social anesthesia state is widely blamed for pushing up unemployment. Despite the proliferation of early-retirement and make-work programs, the official unemployment rate has remained in the range of 7 to 12 percent for decades. France's minimum wage is quite high (€1,521 per month before taxes in

2019), and Social Security charges add around 40 percent to the wage bill. Critics charge that this combination of high statutory wages and payroll taxes is pricing French workers out of the labor market. One reason why French productivity is high is that the country has not been able to generate many low-wage, low-productivity jobs. Moreover, generous benefits can discourage job search by offering a reasonably attractive alternative to paid employment, particularly to part-time jobs.

The third problem of the social anesthesia strategy is that the anesthetic appears to be wearing off. Social anesthesia is a far cry from social integration. A minimum income of €565 per month may be acceptable as a stopgap but not as a way of life. In the long run, the RSA is no substitute for social integration through a steady job and upward social mobility. Many of the supposed beneficiaries of social anesthesia policies harbor great bitterness toward a government that offers them meager allowances and a succession of dead-end internships and substandard part-time or temporary jobs. This dissatisfaction has fueled all manner of political pathologies, from the November 2005 upheaval in the French suburbs, which was spearheaded by marginalized, unemployed minority youths, to the rise of the far-right, xenophobic National Rally (Rassemblement National, RN, formerly known as the National Front [Front National, FN]), which has become the number one party among both blue-collar workers and the unemployed.

2.4   The Social Anesthesia State and the Problem of Reform

The social anesthesia strategy may have facilitated the movement away from the *dirigiste* model in the 1980s, but the legacies of that strategy pose a significant challenge to liberalizing reformers today. For one thing, the social anesthesia strategy has mostly exhausted the fiscal resources of the French state. In the 1980s, the social anesthesia state offered extensive compensation in return for economic reform: specifically, the state would no longer sustain employment artificially through bailouts to uncompetitive enterprises and restrictions on layoffs, but it would offer generous social protection to those whose jobs were eliminated. With public expenditures now exceeding 55 percent of GDP, however, cash-strapped reformers lack the fiscal means to offer much compensation. Consequently, liberalizing reforms must generally be sold purely on their own terms, with little possibility for side-payments to buy off opposition. Yet such uncompensated initiatives are much more likely to trigger public opposition and protest.

The social anesthesia strategy has also exhausted the patience of the French public. The reforms of the 1980s were supposed to be a one-shot deal to set the French economy right. Of course, there would be some pain in the short term, but once France made the transition from a *dirigiste* political economy to a market-centered political economy, growth and job creation would resume anew. The French economy never really recovered, however, in part because the social anesthesia state itself imposed a significant drag on economic growth and job creation.

The need to reform the social anesthesia state has placed supporters of economic liberalization in a difficult position. France, alone in Europe, has confronted the challenge of two rounds of liberalizing reform: a first round to roll back the *dirigiste* state and a second round to overhaul the social anesthesia state. Given the limited results of the first round of reform in the 1980s, much of the French public has grown skeptical of liberalization and is resistant to the idea that what is needed is more market reform (as Table 1.4 in Chapter 1 demonstrated).

The combination of a skeptical public and limited fiscal resources has made economic liberalization exceptionally challenging. The claim here is not that reform never happens in France, but rather that reform is politically contentious and can be derailed by even small mistakes. Two attempts to deploy liberalizing measures to increase youth employment illustrate these dangers. The first was the 1994 Professional Integration Contract (Contrat d'Insertion Professionnelle, CIP) and the second the 2006 First Employment Contract (Contrat Première Embauche, CPE).

The CIP proposed to allow companies to pay young people under the age of 26 with up to two years of post-secondary education ("Bac+2") 20 percent less than the statutory minimum wage (Balladur 1995; Brigouleix 1995; Paradis and Salmon 1994; Tompson 2010). CIP contracts would run from six to twelve months and be renewable once for a total maximum of two years. Employers had no obligations under the CIP; they did not have to commit to hiring or training young workers. Indeed, if employers offered training, they could pay young employees even less: 30 percent of the minimum wage for 16–17-year-olds, 50 percent for 18–20-year-olds, and 65 percent for 21–25-year-olds.

The CPE likewise targeted unemployed youths (Chiroux 2006; Friedberg 2006; Geay 2009; Michon 2008; Ross 2006). The premise behind the CPE was that restrictions on layoffs discourage employers from hiring less skilled and inexperienced workers, for fear of being unable to shed these workers should they fail to pan out. The CPE proposed to introduce a two-year probationary period for workers under the age of 26. During this probationary period, employers would be free to dismiss young employees without providing any justification or compensation. The government reasoned that by making it easier to fire young people, the CPE would also make it more attractive to hire young people.

Both the CIP of 1994 and the CPE of 2006 were motivated by concerns about high unemployment, especially youth unemployment. At the end of 1993, French unemployment exceeded 12 percent. What is more, the number of households claiming RMI had increased by 18.1 percent in 1993 and was approaching the politically sensitive figure of 1 million (Mathieu 1994). The CPE emerged out of similar concerns. In 2006, youth unemployment exceeded 20 percent, and in the blighted suburban projects the rate was nearly double (Statista 2022). The dangers of this situation had been brought home in November 2005, when weeks of riots by marginalized and excluded young people, many of them ethnic minorities, rocked the suburban projects and prompted President Chirac to declare France's first state of emergency since the Algerian War more than forty years earlier.

Political ambitions also drove the CIP and CPE reforms. Both sitting prime ministers at the time, Edouard Balladur in 1994 and Dominique de Villepin in 2006, had presidential aspirations. Balladur, a Gaullist, had been expected to serve as a caretaker prime minister during the two-year run-up to the 1995 presidential election and help his long-time mentor and ally, Jacques Chirac, become the next president. Once in office, however, as described in Chapter 3, Balladur was able to get several reforms enacted, notably of the pension system. He gained popularity as a cautious reformer, who understood that in a country traumatized by wrenching economic change and mass unemployment, it was important to move gradually and consensually. His approach was even described as "the Balladur method" and contrasted with Chirac's confrontational tack when the latter had served as prime minister from 1986 to 1988. Buoyed by his initial popularity, Balladur double-crossed Chirac, announcing his intention to run for president. The CIP would be another illustration of the Balladur method. It was not an ideologically driven, across-the-board reduction in the minimum wage, but rather a narrowly targeted, pragmatic measure aimed at helping a disadvantaged population – unskilled youths – who found it especially difficult to secure jobs.

Like Balladur, Dominique de Villepin was eyeing the Elysée Palace when he launched the CPE in 2006. The outgoing president, Jacques Chirac, did not plan to run again in 2007. The frontrunner, Nicolas Sarkozy, although hailing from Chirac's Gaullist Party, had been at odds with Chirac for over a decade. Sarkozy had supported Balladur in the 1995 presidential election; he had captured the Gaullist Party against the wishes of Chirac in 2004; and he was openly critical of Chirac, portraying him as a failure and calling for a "rupture" with Chirac's policies and governing style. Chirac was, therefore, looking for someone who could derail Sarkozy's presidential candidacy, and de Villepin, a

Chirac loyalist, seemed to fit the bill. De Villepin had made a name for himself as minister of foreign affairs, spearheading the opposition to a UN authorization for the US invasion of Iraq and openly criticizing the George W. Bush administration, a position that played very well with the French public. The CPE was intended to add a domestic achievement to de Villepin's foreign policy credentials.

It is worth noting that the CIP and the CPE were not the work of neo-liberal ideologues. Balladur was a cautious, pragmatic reformer, while de Villepin was associated with the socially oriented wing of the Gaullist movement. More important, both the CIP and CPE were carefully targeted, limited liberalization measures. Balladur and de Villepin were not looking to deregulate French labor markets across the board, but rather to carve out an exception, whether in the form of lower wages or weakened job protections, for young people struggling to secure employment.

Despite these relatively modest aspirations, both the CIP and CPE triggered a wave of protests centered on the very people whom they were supposedly helping – French youths. Critics decried the CIP as a SMIC-jeunes (a lower minimum wage for youths), and hundreds of thousands of demonstrators, mostly young people, took to the streets in a succession of protests during March 1994. Toward the end of the month, French unions joined the protests. What is more, public opinion ran strongly against the government, with 55 percent of respondents opposing the CIP and just 36 percent favoring it (IFOP 2014).

The combination of rising contestation and unpopularity finally induced Balladur to back down. On March 30, 1994, he withdrew the CIP. What is more, he replaced it with a program that would pay employers €153 per month for nine months if they hired a young person who had never held a job and €305 per month if they made the hire before October 10, 1994. Instead of the liberal approach of pushing youth wages down, Balladur retreated to the traditional French tack of having the state pay employers to hire hard-to-place young people.

De Villepin's CPE fared no better with French youths. Once again, opponents organized quickly. The initial demonstration on February 7 numbered some 400,000 protestors, which was more than the largest demonstration against the CIP. From there, the protests continued to grow, reaching 3 million demonstrators on March 28 according to the organizers, 1 million according to the ministry of the interior (*Les Echos*, January 11, 2013). In addition, two-thirds of French universities went on strike, as did many high schools, while public-sector unions disrupted transportation and postal services.

The anti-CPE movement was the biggest French protest in a decade, and in an ominous sign, the Sorbonne University was occupied by students (briefly) for the first time since May 1968. As the conflict dragged on, public opinion turned increasingly against the government. Whereas in January 2006, 54 percent of respondents believed that the CPE would increase worker vulnerability and casual employment (*précarité*), in March, the figure rose to 62 percent, while only 35 percent believed that the CPE would increase youth employment (IFOP 2014). With the government losing in both the streets and the opinion polls, President Chirac forced de Villepin to withdraw the CPE.

The CIP and CPE dealt a serious blow to the presidential aspirations of Balladur and de Villepin respectively. Balladur's popularity had been declining, as his policies had been contested and defeated by other protesters (including Air France workers, supporters of public schools, and fishermen), but the CIP sent his approval rating into negative territory for the first time. Whereas in December 1993, Balladur had a 58 percent approval rating, versus 32 percent disapproval, by April 1994, his approval rate had fallen to 43 percent, while his disapproval had surged to 49 percent. One year later, Balladur would be outpolled by Jacques Chirac in the first round of the presidential election, failing to qualify for the runoff. Chirac's comeback was widely attributed to his denunciation of Balladur as a servant of *la pensée unique* and hard-hearted neoliberalism.

Dominique de Villepin did not even make it to the presidential election. The CPE completely destroyed his popularity. De Villepin's approval rating plummeted from 52 percent in January 2006 to 24 percent in April 2006, while his disapproval numbers jumped from 45 percent to 74 percent (IFOP 2014). Facing certain defeat against Sarkozy, de Villepin opted not to run for president.

Balladur and de Villepin certainly made their share of mistakes. Their reforms were poorly prepared politically: rather than negotiating with the unions and political opposition to build support, they announced their reforms with no prior consultation. Consequently, the left and the unions were free to denounce and mobilize against proposals that they had played no part in formulating. Balladur and de Villepin were also slow to take the protest movements seriously, instead trying to wait them out. As Chapter 4 relates, the propensity of French politicians to impose controversial liberalizing reforms from above in a heavy-handed, skinny-politics manner has often fueled protests and strikes against such initiatives.

De Villepin's behavior represented an extreme form of this kind of top-down imposition. The prime minister announced the CPE reform during school holidays in the hope of making it difficult to mobilize student opposition. De Villepin also deployed a constitutional device, the

Article 49.3 confidence procedure, which allowed him to limit debate and enact the reform without a vote in the National Assembly. Finally, the same self-confident and defiant tone that the French so enjoyed when it was deployed against the Bush administration went over less well when directed at youthful protestors. As late as March 21, after protests exceeding 1 million demonstrators, de Villepin declared that he would accept neither the "retraction," "suspension," nor "denaturing" of his law.

Still, even a more flexible and responsive approach than that of de Villepin offered no guarantee of success. Balladur made a series of concessions to the demonstrators. On March 3, 1994, he announced that young skilled workers (holders of a Bac+2 BTS degree, Professional Bac, or Technical Bac) would receive 80 percent of the (usually higher) collectively bargained wage, rather than 80 percent of the minimum wage (*Libération*, March 11, 1994). Two weeks later, Balladur promised that the CIP would apply only if training were provided to the youth hires (*Le Monde*, March 16, 1994). He added that young workers who received 80 percent of the minimum wage would only work 80 percent of the statutory workweek and would receive training during the remaining 20 percent (*Libération*, March 19–20, 1994). Finally, Balladur promised to establish a committee to evaluate the CIP at the end of the year and to include young people among the committee members. None of these concessions slowed the protestors, who did not trust Balladur (or an eventual successor) to keep his promises and felt that they had the prime minister on the ropes. Thus, it is by no means certain that a less arrogant and impositional de Villepin would have been any more successful with the CPE than Balladur had been with the CIP, although de Villepin's approval rating might not have fallen as precipitously.

A key problem for both the CIP and CPE was a disconnect between government reformers and the youths whom the government was purporting to help. Whereas French authorities saw the CIP and CPE as allowing young people to get a foot in the door, French youths regarded the reforms as consigning them to the margins of the labor market. A clearly frustrated Balladur later wrote that French youths had been manipulated and were ignorant of their own interests: "Why the CIP? To combat youth employment. Why its failure? Because established interests opposed it and youths, influenced [by them], did not understand their true interest" (Balladur 1995: 165).

Yet young people had good reason to oppose Balladur's reform. The CIP would have required them to work for substandard wages, and employers would have been free to lay them off as soon as the special provisions expired, then hire new youth employees at substandard wages in their place. Similarly, de Villepin's CPE would have forced young people to toil for two years, with absolutely no rights and in constant fear of dismissal, making them vulnerable to all kinds of abuses, from unpaid overtime to sexual harassment. As with the CIP, employers would have been able to dismiss CPE hires just before the two-year probationary period ended, then take on new probationary employees in their place. In the eyes of youthful protestors, the CIP and CPE did not give them a foot in the door, but rather replaced stable, secure jobs with revolving-door, substandard jobs.

Dissatisfaction was particularly pronounced among students in Bac+2 technical programs, who formed the core of the protestors (*Le Monde*, March 21, 1994; *Libération*, May 3, 1994). Bac+2 programs were designed to give technically oriented youths access to practical training that would lead to good jobs after just two years. These programs had a strong placement record and were expanding rapidly. Yet by lumping Bac+2 students with high-school dropouts, the Balladur and de Villepin governments were essentially telling Bac+2 students that their training was worthless. This message was completely at odds with the cherished notion of the "Republic of merit" and upward social mobility through education.

The failure of the CIP and CPE was due to more than the miscalculations of Prime Ministers Balladur and de Villepin, however. Both initiatives ran up against the legacies of the movement from the *dirigiste* state to the social anesthesia state. One such legacy was financial. The expansion of the social anesthesia state increasingly deprived French authorities of the fiscal resources for negotiating deals. Whereas in the 1980s, governments were often trading one benefit for another – plant closings in return for early retirement, fewer industrial policy subsidies in return for greater managerial autonomy – by the mid-1990s, cash-strapped governments had little to offer in the way of side-payments. Yet zero-sum reforms, requiring claimants to give up benefits, with only the vague promise of a healthier economy or public finances in return, are among the most politically difficult to sell. In the case of the CIP and CPE, French youths were offered nothing more than the hope that reducing their wages or job security would lead to increased hiring. There was no compensation, such as guaranteed training, income supports, or access to unemployment benefits when the jobs came to an end, since any of these measures would have cost money that the government felt it could not afford. Instead, French youths were asked to take a neoliberal leap of faith, which they were understandably reluctant to do.

This reticence was bolstered by a second legacy of France's break with the *dirigiste* model: "reform fatigue" or "liberalization fatigue" stemming from France's two-phase trajectory of reform. The experience of de-*dirigization* had led many in France to feel that they had *already* been subjected to liberal economic reform – and had little to show for it, particularly in the labor market. Since 1983, French citizens had reluctantly accepted a series of painful liberalizing measures. Each time, they were told by government authorities or employers that the reforms in question would relaunch growth and bring down unemployment: if French inflation were held below that of Germany or Italy, then French workers would get the jobs that were going to German and Italian workers; if the state spent less on uncompetitive firms, then fast-growing startups would arise in their place; if wages gave way to profits, then investment and jobs would follow; if French employers gained the freedom to fire, then they would be more inclined to hire (Berger 1985). The reforms were implemented one after the other, yet economic growth remained anemic and high unemployment persisted. Given these disappointments, the idea embodied by the CIP and CPE that what was needed was another turn of the liberal screw, labor market rollback on top of *dirigiste* rollback, did not elicit great popular enthusiasm. In a sense, rather than spilling over sequentially from economic policy to social policy, the bitter experience of de-*dirigization* stiffened resistance to further liberalizing measures.

The point of these examples is not to suggest that economic liberalization is impossible in France. Balladur and, to a lesser extent, de Villepin enacted some important reforms. As noted, the CIP and CPE might have fared better if Balladur and de Villepin had consulted more and dictated less. That said, they had little room for error. Although de Villepin might not have been the right person for the job, Balladur had a reputation for pragmatism and sought to recalibrate his reforms in response to protests. Yet Balladur would not be afforded a chance to modify the CIP, and the reform would ultimately be dropped.

2.5   Conclusion

In the 1980s, French authorities determined that the postwar *dirigiste* industrial policy model, whatever its previous achievements, had become counterproductive and needed to be dismantled. Whether out of social solidarity or fear of protest or even revolution, the authorities also determined that this turn to the market needed to be accompanied socially. *Pace* Polanyi, market forces and social protection would be expanded in tandem. The expectation was that social measures would be of short duration. Once France had reorganized on a market-rational basis, the country would return to full employment, and social measures could be rolled back.

The Polanyi strategy was entirely understandable, and it did indeed allow France to break with its *dirigiste* industrial policy model. As mass unemployment persisted, however, French authorities felt compelled to expand, rather than roll back, social protection and labor market measures. What was supposed to be a temporary accompaniment to *dirigiste* retrenchment morphed into the social anesthesia state, and France found itself with the most expensive and one of the most passively oriented welfare states in the OECD.

The movement from the *dirigiste* state to the social anesthesia state has cast a heavy shadow over contemporary reform. On the one hand, high levels of public spending and labor market regulations have fueled calls to curtail social spending and expand labor market flexibility. On the other hand, the apparent failure of market reform to deliver growth and employment has stiffened popular resistance. In addition, in contrast to the 1980s, the high cost of the social anesthesia state means that would-be reformers generally lack the fiscal resources to offer significant side-payments and compensation. Instead, they have been forced to try to sell liberalizing reform on its own terms, which is a very risky undertaking, as the CIP and CPE episodes demonstrated. Thus, contemporary French reformers are not operating with a clean slate: rather, their initiatives have often triggered contestation due to the policy legacies of decisions made in the 1980s.

Policy legacies are not the only challenges confronted by contemporary liberalizers. The *dirigiste* model and the manner in which France moved away from it in the 1980s have also shaped the economic outlook and discourse of France's governing political parties. The next chapter shows how these party-political legacies, like the policy legacies of the *dirigiste* model, have fueled the contestation of economic liberalization.

3   Liberalization without Liberals
The French Right's Ambivalence
toward Economic Liberalization

Chapter 2 described how the policy legacies of France's postwar *dirigiste* model have fueled the contestation of economic liberalization. This chapter turns to the party-political legacies. It is well known that economic liberalization has historically commanded more political support among the exemplars of neoliberalism, the USA and UK, where powerful neoliberal parties like the Republican Party and the British Conservatives govern on a regular basis, than in Continental Europe, where free-market, neoliberal parties are generally small, junior coalition partners (Vail 2018: 264).[1] Yet even by the standards of Continental Europe, French parties of the right have long stood out for their ambivalence toward economic liberalization. Put crudely, France offers a case of liberalization without liberals, meaning that the parties and governments responsible for social and economic reform have been ambivalent at best and, in many instances, hostile to an agenda of economic liberalization.

Looking at the left of the political spectrum, most European leftist parties either began the postwar period as Social Democratic (among the Nordic countries) or evolved in that direction fairly soon thereafter (the German Social Democratic Party's (SPD's) conversion at Bad Godesberg in 1959). The French left, by contrast, was long dominated by a Stalinist Communist Party (Parti Communiste Français, PCF). What is more, the Socialist Party (Parti Socialiste, PS) was only able to supplant the Communists in the 1970s by embracing the Communists' Marxist economic agenda via the joint PCF–PS "Common Program of the Left." At the time, the PS routinely dismissed Scandinavian Social Democrats for pursuing a welfare state instead of structural change through the socialization of the means of production. As Mitterrand wrote in 1978, "Sweden is not Socialist enough, in spite of a redistribution of income without parallel among social groups and individuals, because it has not struck capitalism in the heart of its power, the private ownership of the most important means of production" (cited in Palme 2014: 90).

Even when the French Socialists oversaw the beginnings of the move to the market in 1983, they did so grudgingly, downplaying and hiding the extent of their shift. The PS never underwent a Bad Godesberg. What is more, as the Socialists moved away from the statist model and the Communist Party entered into decline, new self-styled "anti-capitalist," "anti-globalization," and "anti-liberal" political movements emerged to fill the void. Consequently, for the left to win national elections, the PS continued to need the support of far-left parties.

Whether by ideological choice or coalitional necessity, the PS has tended to voice strong hostility to competition and market reform, as compared with the governing left in other European countries (Spector 2017). The Socialists' governing record has been more accepting of liberalization than its discourse, a point of criticism for many on the left (Amable and Palombarini 2017, 2021; Germain 2015; Julliard and Michéa 2014; Plenel and Dufau 2015; Rey 2004; Rothé 2013). Still, Socialist-led governments have generally undertaken economic liberalization with great reluctance, while seeking to mask or downplay their actions.

Of course, in most countries, it is the right, not the left, which is the primary voice and vehicle for economic liberalization, so the antipathy of the French left would not necessarily constitute an insurmountable obstacle were the French right strongly committed to economic liberalization. The commitments of the French right have run in a very different direction, however. Certainly, Continental center-right governing parties, such as the Christian Democrats, have been more tempered in their enthusiasm for the market than Anglo-American conservatives, in particular by insisting on robust welfare states to protect the vulnerable. However, the Gaullist movement, the main political force of the French right under the Fifth Republic, has been more than ambivalent. As the party that long administered the *dirigiste* model, it wholly identified with state direction of the economy, making it an unlikely agent of economic liberalization. Thus, the contestation of economic liberalization in France can be found, not just among leftist parties and demonstrators in the streets, but also within conservative governing circles.

This chapter analyzes the party-political forces behind the contestation of economic liberalization in France. It focuses on governments of the right, rather than the left since the left is not expected to support liberalization in the same way as the right. In other words, governments of the right present a critical or hard case for the claim that French political parties harbor deep misgivings about economic liberalization.

The analysis of the ambivalent French right begins with Section 3.1, which discusses the ways in which France's *dirigiste* model and the break with that model in the 1980s shaped the ideology and strategy of the right. The rest of the chapter, drawing on the governing experiences of conservative leaders, most notably Jacques Chirac, Edouard Balladur, and Nicolas Sarkozy, shows how four resulting political legacies have undercut economic liberalization and fueled contestation under governments of the right. Section 3.2, which analyzes French privatizations and the doctrine of "economic patriotism," highlights the right's nationalist approach to corporate ownership and its willingness to manipulate markets for corporate governance in order to prevent French companies from coming under foreign control. Section 3.3, focusing on the initiatives of the Balladur government in the 1990s, demonstrates how concerns about social order have led governments of the right to retreat from liberalizing reforms in the face of protests and strikes. Section 3.4 describes the initial period of the first Chirac presidency, punctuated by the failed Juppé Social Security reform, which illustrates the right's difficulty formulating an effective legitimating discourse for economic liberalization. Section 3.5 then examines the evolution of economic policy under Nicolas Sarkozy, highlighting the French right's fair-weather liberalism, that is, its willingness to cast aside liberal principles and launch neo-*dirigiste* initiatives in times of economic crisis. Although governments of the right have certainly undertaken important measures of economic liberalization, many of their most high-profile liberalizing initiatives have spawned popular contestation and/or been checked by the right's own ambivalence stemming from the ideological and political legacies of the *dirigiste* model.

3.1   *Dirigiste* Legacies and the French Right

The Gaullist movement has been the dominant force of the French right under the Fifth Republic. The movement, which has gone by a number of different names,[2] has almost always been the largest force of the right. Its hegemony was challenged when Valéry Giscard d'Estaing, who hailed from the centrist, liberal wing of the right, outpolled the Gaullist candidate in the first round of the 1974 presidential election. Giscard won the presidential runoff against the Socialist candidate François Mitterrand, then served as president from 1974 to 1981. During that time, he federated several small center and center-right parties into the Union of French Democracy (Union pour la Démocratie Française, UDF), which briefly ran ahead of the Gaullist Rally for the Republic (Rassemblement pour la République, RPR). Following Giscard's defeat in the 1981 presidential election, however, the Gaullists once again became the biggest party of the right, and the UDF entered into decline. In 2002, the *coup de grace* was administered when most of the UDF joined forces with the Gaullists behind Jacques Chirac in a Gaullist-dominated Union for a Popular Movement (Union pour un Mouvement Populaire, UMP). Nicolas Sarkozy, the president from 2007 to 2012, also hailed from the UMP, which changed its name in 2015 to The Republicans (Les Républicains, LR).

The Gaullist movement forged by Charles de Gaulle in the 1950 and 1960s was different from other European center-right parties of the time (De Gaulle 2007; Fenby 2010; Hoffmann 1963, 1978). It was not confessional like the Christian Democrats, nor cautiously promarket like other European conservatives. Rather, it was nationalist and statist. De Gaulle sought to concentrate power in the executive, so that he could enact the far-ranging and controversial reforms he believed were needed to modernize the economy and restore France's international rank. His ultimate objective was to project French influence and grandeur throughout the world, balancing between the superpowers and offering a civilizational alternative to the USA. Economic modernization spearheaded by an activist state was the means to this nationalist end; it would give France the economic and industrial might to make its voice heard in international affairs.

Obviously, the Gaullist movement has experienced significant changes over the years, and not just in its name (Berstein 2002; Knapp 1994). Following de Gaulle's departure from the political scene in 1969, the movement became more internationalist, supporting European integration and eventually rejoining the North Atlantic Treaty Organization (NATO) integrated command. The nationalism of the movement also evolved: it became less self-confident and inclusive and more defensive and exclusionary, especially toward immigrants. Finally, on the economic front, the Gaullists have become more supportive of economic liberalization. For all the changes, though, the Gaullist commitment to economic liberalization – and, by extension, that of the governing right – has been qualified in important ways. Four party-political legacies of the postwar *dirigiste* model have limited the French right's support for economic liberalization.

First, the French right ran the *dirigiste* model for decades. The right and left shared power under the Fourth Republic from 1946 to 1958, but the right governed alone for roughly the first quarter-century of the Fifth Republic. During this time, the French right did not operate a free-market economy, nor a social market or ordoliberal economy combining a liberal market order with a generous welfare state like German Christian Democrats, but rather a *dirigiste* economy. The prevailing economic view of the French right was that the state, through extensive direction and manipulation of all manner of policy instruments, could improve upon the performance of the market (Shonfield 1965). The limited state of the Third Republic had led to economic decline and military defeat, while the *dirigiste* state of the postwar period was transforming France into one of the most technologically advanced and affluent countries in the world, thereby seemingly proving the superiority of French statism. It is scarcely a stretch to say that short of embracing socialism, the post-war French right could not have positioned itself further from the ideals of economic liberalism.

The *dirigiste* model was nationalist as well as statist. For de Gaulle, *dirigiste* economic policy was the means to reconstitute French national power and grandeur. The *dirigiste* model was also nationalist in the sense of believing that companies have strong national identities and favor the interests of their home country over those of other countries. Tellingly, French authorities refer to the country's giant companies not as multi-nationals or conglomerates, but rather as "national champions." The language suggests that these firms do more than pursue profits; they also champion the interests of the nation. Given this sentiment, French conservatives have gone to great lengths to protect national champions against foreign takeovers by restricting or rigging markets for corporate control.

A second party-political legacy stemmed from a backlash against the top-down governance of the *dirigiste* model and Fifth Republic. In May 1968, French students launched a wave of protests and university occupations against restrictions on free speech and sexual mores as well as alienating, abstract, hierarchical education (Berstein 2006; Hoffmann 1978). While students protested in many countries during the 1960s, the French case was unusual – and more destabilizing – because French workers, angered by decades of labor-exclusionary *dirigiste* policies and authoritarian governance in the workplace, threw in their lot with the students. Workers occupied factories throughout the country, bringing the economy to a standstill and France to the verge of revolution. At one point, President de Gaulle left the country, and many believe that he seriously considered stepping down. Although France ultimately averted revolution, the previously invincible de Gaulle was politically wounded, and he would leave office less than one year later.

The revolt against the top-down governance of the Gaullist political order and *dirigiste* economic model traumatized a generation of French leaders on the right. Both Jacques Chirac and Edouard Balladur began their political careers as disciples of Gaullist prime minister and later president, Georges Pompidou, and held positions in social affairs at the time of the May 1968 upheaval. Balladur served as technical adviser for social affairs in Pompidou's cabinet and Chirac as state secretary for employment (Nay 1994). Both were heavily involved in negotiations with the unions to try to end the crisis. Balladur even authored a book about May 1968 (Balladur 1979). Although France has a long revolutionary tradition, for Chirac and Balladur the fear of revolution was not some hazy historical memory, but rather the product of a lived experience at the formative moment of their political careers. Scarred by this experience, Chirac and Balladur were reluctant to push reforms too forcefully, often backing down in the face of protests. From their perspective, sacrificing the potential benefits of economic liberalization was a small price to pay for preventing another May 1968. The problem is that this understandable reluctance to forge ahead in the face of popular contestation had the perverse effect of encouraging further contestation, as opponents of reform learned that they could make the government reverse course if they mobilized enough strikers and demonstrators to threaten social order.

A third party-political legacy that has fueled the contestation of economic liberalization stems from the manner in which French governments presented the break with the *dirigiste* model following the 1983 U-turn. The left was understandably uncomfortable acknowledging its shift in policy, minimizing the extent of change and suggesting that the shift was merely temporary. Those reforms that the left could not hide it blamed on European integration, as opposed to defending them on their own terms as good for the French economy.

After a brief flirtation with neoliberalism in the mid-1980s, the French right adopted a similar discourse to the left, engaging in a combination of denial and blaming of Brussels for unpopular decisions (Clift 2006; Schmidt 2002b, 2007). When governments declined to throw money away on a firm that was heading for bankruptcy, the reason given was not that such spending would be foolish. Instead, it was that the EU Commission, blinded by its neoliberal ideology, would not let the French government do what was good for French industry. When governments sought to reduce France's budget deficit, they again blamed the Commission – in this case, for embracing an arbitrary deficit limit and slavishly following the German obsession with balanced budgets. The effect of such denial and blame shifting was to delegitimate economic liberalization, which was portrayed as a nefarious European Union (EU) imposition, and to delegitimate European integration as well.

The fourth legacy of the postwar *dirigiste* model is a shallow, fair-weather liberalism that tends to dissipate in hard economic times. Conservative governments have varied over the years, with some more committed to liberal economic principles than others. However, even ostensibly promarket governments have shown a remarkable willingness to turn away from liberal principles and return to France's *dirigiste* roots in times of economic crisis. Of course, governments everywhere have felt compelled to respond to deep economic crises like the 2008 financial meltdown in interventionist ways, stimulating demand and bailing out financial institutions and firms deemed "too big to fail." That said, French conservatives have gone a step further, treating economic crises as opportunities to launch new interventionist policies to steer French business.

In sum, the French *dirigiste* model bequeathed four sets of obstacles to Gaullist-led liberalization. First, many on the right had spent their entire careers operating from a statist perspective that disdained free markets, and statist and nationalist reflexes by no means disappeared in 1983. Second, the right and its top leadership were scarred by the upheaval of May 1968 and therefore wary of pressing economic reforms in the face of popular protests that threatened social order. Third, the right (along with the left) failed to develop a legitimating discourse around economic liberalization; indeed, successive French governments delegitimated liberalization by portraying it as an unwelcome foreign imposition. Fourth, leaders of the right have often proven to be fair-weather liberals, casting aside liberal principles and returning to their statist roots in hard economic times. As the following sections demonstrate, these four legacies have fed contestation and undercut economic liberalization in France.

3.2   Fear of Foreigners: From Balladur to Macron

French conservatives have displayed persistent concern about foreign ownership of important French companies. The right's privatization campaign from 1986 to 1988 offers a telling illustration. During these years, France experienced its first "cohabitation," denoting a partisan divide between the president and the National Assembly, as legislative elections produced a conservative majority, while the Socialist François Mitterrand remained president. In practice, cohabitation meant that the leader of the legislative majority, Jacques Chirac, was in charge of domestic affairs, but Mitterrand did his best to limit or discredit Chirac, as the two prepared to face off in the 1988 presidential election.

The period from 1986 to 1988 represented the high-water mark of liberalism in France. From 1983 to 1986, the Mitterrand government had begun cautiously moving France away from the *dirigiste* model. The Chirac government that followed took a much more aggressive and ideological approach (Berger 1986). Having described himself in the 1970s as socially progressive along the lines of the British Labor Party (*travaillisme à la française*), Chirac, who was not exactly known for his ideological constancy, pivoted and became a champion of neoliberalism in the 1980s. In 1984, as the mayor of Paris, he even awarded the gold medal of the city to Friedrich Hayek, arguably the most important champion of free-market capitalism and critic of government intervention in the post-war era. At the ceremony, Chirac declared, "Know, Professor Hayek, that you have served as a guide to the Pilgrims of Freedom that we want to be" (Frazier 1986).

Chirac turned to neoliberalism for a variety of reasons. The experiences of the USA under Ronald Reagan and the UK under Margaret Thatcher appeared to offer real-world validation of neoliberal reform, as the economies of these two countries prospered. Beyond its apparent economic virtues, neoliberalism was attractive to Chirac on political grounds. Reeling from its historic defeat in 1981, when the right lost power for the first time under the Fifth Republic, the conservative camp was searching for a new vision to revive its electoral fortunes. Neoliberalism offered an ideological rallying point, and the electoral success of Reagan and Thatcher did not go unnoticed. Neoliberalism also gave Chirac a club with which to beat the incumbent Socialist administration: the right's embrace of the market stood in sharp contrast to the left's alleged attachment to *dirigisme*, even if the left's stance had evolved considerably since 1981.

The right's economic platform for the 1986 legislative election contained all manner of neoliberal promises (Berger 1986). On the fiscal front, the right pledged to slash taxes and spending, including eliminating the left's wealth tax, the Tax on Large Fortunes (Impôt sur les Grandes Fortunes, IGF). On the financial front, the right promised to abolish capital controls, credit rationing, and price controls. Finally, on the labor market front, the right announced its intention to ease restrictions on temporary work and abolish the administrative authorization for economic layoffs. If ever there was a time when the French right embraced neoliberalism, it was the period from 1986 to 1988.

The centerpiece of the right's agenda was an ambitious campaign of privatizations. The right pledged that during the course of the five-year legislature, it would privatize sixty-six companies, employing a workforce of 900,000 and representing one-quarter of the capitalization of the French stock market (Bauer 1988). The list of companies to be privatized included not only those nationalized by the left in 1982, but also some that had been nationalized by de Gaulle in 1945.

Chirac entrusted the privatization campaign to his loyal ally, Edouard Balladur. Balladur was the only cabinet member who held the rank of minister of state, making him the undisputed second in command. Balladur organized the privatization of nine major industrial and financial groups: Paribas, Crédit Commercial de France (CCF), Compagnie Générale d'Electricité (CGE), Havas, Matra, Suez, Saint Gobain, Société Générale, and the TF1 television network. He also privatized three medium-sized banks. The privatizations netted over €18 billion in revenues or roughly 10 percent of the capitalization of the Paris Bourse.

While impressive in their scale, Chirac and Balladur's privatizations hardly attested to the triumph of free-market principles. Despite their neoliberal rhetoric, Chirac and Balladur had cut their political teeth as protégés of Georges Pompidou, in an age of heroic industrial policy. Although much had changed since their formative years, the two remained wary of ceding control to the market (Bauer 1988; Griotteray 1994; Guyon 1995; Schmidt 1996). In addition, as Gaullists, Chirac and Balladur approached issues of corporate governance from a nationalist perspective. They were determined to keep the crown jewels of the French economy from falling into foreign hands.

Chirac and Balladur protected the privatized companies in two ways. First, foreign investors were barred from acquiring more than a 20 percent stake in the privatized companies. Second, as against a liberal logic of auctioning companies to the highest bidder, the government allocated a controlling stake of 20 to 30 percent of the shares in each company (a so-called *noyau dur* or stable nucleus) to a select group of investors. In a chapter that Balladur later authored on his term as minister of finance, the only justification that he provided for the *noyaux durs* was to protect privatized companies against foreign takeovers: "Since it was decided that we would sell nationalized companies ... there had to be constituted, among the shareholders, groups that were determined to defend them [the companies], so as to avoid having them fall under foreign control" (Balladur 1995: 48).

The members of the *noyaux durs* were barred from selling their shares for two years and could only sell in years three through five with permission from the company's board of directors. In addition, the determination of who received the *noyaux durs* and at what price was the result, not of open competitive bidding, but rather of government fiat. As Michel Bauer relates, such practices could scarcely be described as the substitution of markets for politics:

The Minister [of Finance] intervened not only to define the new rules of the game but also to fix the price, choose the shareholders, and decide on the composition of the board. There never was so powerful a Minister of Finance in France: never did the rue de Rivoli [the Ministry of Finance] matter so much in the business world. The French privatisation programme did not represent any great break with the past. Quite the contrary: it fully illustrated the State's interventionist tradition and even reinforced it. (Bauer 1988: 57)

The privatizations were conducted during the only time under the Fifth Republic when the right openly embraced neoliberal ideals (Berger 1986). As the privatization campaign illustrates, the government did not always live up to those ideals. Nor was it the only instance. In order to preserve social order and social cohesion, Chirac announced that he would not touch the French welfare state, limiting the possibilities for cutting spending and, with it, taxation. Rather than a break with past practice and embrace of neoliberalism, Chirac was basically accelerating the social anesthesia strategy inaugurated by the Socialists, combining de-*dirigization* with expansive social protection. This social anesthesia approach enabled Chirac to roll back key elements of the postwar *dirigiste* model, including price controls, credit rationing, and many restrictions on layoffs and temporary employment. That said, on the issue of corporate control, nationalism and statism clearly trumped liberalism.

The French right's commitment to neoliberalism, even in a limited, socially compensated form, proved to be short-lived. During the cohabitation, President Mitterrand denounced the right for its alleged neoliberal excesses. The abolition of the IGF, while insignificant from a fiscal perspective, was very damaging to Chirac politically. So, too, were sluggish French economic growth and persistent high unemployment, which belied Chirac's promises of a Reagan- or Thatcher-style boom. In 1988, Mitterrand easily defeated Chirac in the presidential election, and the French right's brief infatuation with neoliberalism was over. Since then, scholars have taken to describing the 1986–1988 period as "the liberal moment" (Baudoin 1990) or "the liberal parenthesis" (Perrier 2015), attesting to the brevity of the French right's attachment to neoliberalism.

The RPR–UDF alliance's platform in the 1993 legislative elections contained none of the messianic liberalism of 1986. Instead of sweeping economic reform, the platform offered schemes for tinkering with retirement pensions and the family allowance system. Chirac himself underwent no less striking a conversion. In 1995, his successful campaign for president would center around denunciations of hegemonic neoliberal orthodoxy (*la pensée unique*) and appeals for heightened state intervention to reduce unemployment and heal France's "social fracture."

The nationalism that refashioned the right's ostensibly neoliberal privatizations during the 1986–1988 cohabitation did not disappear, however. Rather, it resurfaced in the waning years of Chirac's political career in the form of restrictions on foreign acquisitions of French companies. In 2005, in response to a rumored effort by the American giant Pepsi to acquire the French food and water company Danone,

Chirac's prime minister, Dominique de Villepin, proclaimed a doctrine of "economic patriotism" (Clift 2009a, 2009b, 2013; Clift and Woll 2012, 2013; Cohen 2007). Although it may have seemed strange for a government to become agitated over a rumored takeover bid of a company best known for its yogurt, Danone held a special place in governing circles as a French multinational that was both highly successful and a model of inclusive social relations (Riboud 1987). In addition, Chirac and de Villepin were not just responding to a specific threat – indeed, Pepsi never actually made a bid for Danone – but also seeking to position de Villepin as an alternative to Chirac's hated rival, Nicolas Sarkozy, in the forthcoming 2007 presidential election. The doctrine of "economic patriotism," echoing Gaullist and nationalist traditions, was designed to woo conservative voters away from Sarkozy, who was regarded as more receptive to liberal economic ideas.

The doctrine of economic patriotism was also a response to the vulnerability of France's erstwhile national champions. While the system of *noyaux durs* and interlocking directorates protected privatized companies against hostile takeovers initially, after a few years these arrangements began to come apart, as French multinationals, seeking to specialize and free up capital for new investments, sold their shares (Levy 1999b; *Le Monde*, October 12, 1995). What is more, most of France's national champions were undercapitalized. During the *dirigiste* era, the main vehicle for external expansion had been state-rationed, low-interest loans, so these companies carried high levels of debt. Adding to their financial woes, with the end of the *dirigiste* model the national champions lost many state supports, including subsidies, free technology from state research labs, captive public procurement markets, and advance payments for government contracts (Cohen 2018).

Responding to the vulnerabilities of the national champions and under the banner of "economic patriotism" (Clift 2009a, 2013; Clift and Woll 2012; Cohen 2007), Prime Minister de Villepin enacted laws to protect strategic French sectors against takeovers by foreign companies. The government drew up a list of strategic sectors subject to special protections. Henceforth, any non-EU company acquiring more than 33 percent of a strategic French firm would have to announce its intentions to the French government and submit a formal request to conduct a takeover. The government was free to deny the request or to require the foreign bidder to make concessions, whether by ceding parts of its business to French firms or committing to preserve research and development (R&D) or employment in France.

De Villepin's "economic patriotism" had a limited impact at the time. His restrictions focused on militarily strategic sectors, such as defense, weapons, national security, and counterterrorism, which have always been treated differently in France and are protected in many countries, including the USA (*Le Monde*, May 16, 2014; *Le Figaro*, July 10, 2018).[3] Nor did de Villepin's embrace of economic patriotism change the French political context. As described in Chapter 2, de Villepin's mishandling of the First Employment Contract (Contrat Première Embauche, CPE) destroyed his political popularity, and he would ultimately choose not to run for president against Sarkozy.

De Villepin's "economic patriotism" did not disappear with the end of his tenure as prime minister, however. In 2014, another high-profile takeover bid for a French national champion prompted new additions to the list of protected sectors, this time by Socialist president François Hollande. The US conglomerate General Electric (GE) made a bid for the energy business of the French national champion Alstom. Alstom had benefited from two of France's most successful *grands projets*, civilian nuclear power and high-speed trains (*Trains à Grande Vitesse*, TGV). The government had also rescued Alstom from bankruptcy in 2004 (Cohen 2004). Given this history of government support, many in Hollande's administration balked at ceding Alstom's valuable technology to a US company.

Arnaud Montebourg, the minister of the economy at the time, favored the German conglomerate Siemens as a partner for Alstom since Siemens was a European firm and was willing to exchange its railroad business for Alstom's energy business. Failing a deal with Siemens, Montebourg wanted to negotiate more favorable terms with GE. In order to boost the French state's leverage with GE as well as with future bidders for strategic French businesses, he convinced Hollande to enact a decree adding five broad infrastructural sectors – energy, water, transportation, telecommunications, and public health – to the list of protected industries:

I was opposed to GE's purchase of Alstom's energy business. I thought that Siemens would be a better partner and that we should create an "Airbus of energy and transportation." Siemens was offering to cede its railroad business to Alstom. The Montebourg decree, which was named after me, was a direct response to GE's initiative. It allows the minister of the economy to block any undesirable foreign takeover in a strategic sector. [President] Hollande had already agreed to the GE takeover before I got involved. Still, I was able to use the Montebourg decree to make GE improve its offer. More important, thanks to the Montebourg decree, France has an instrument for preventing undesirable foreign takeovers in a number of strategic activities. (Interview by author with Arnaud Montebourg, Minister of Productive Renewal, 2012–2014 and Minister of the Economy, Productive Renewal, and Digital Affairs, March–August 2014, May 2, 2017)

Beyond the specific case of Alstom, Montebourg's initiative stemmed from a growing concern that France's national champions were ripe for foreign takeover. More than 40 percent of the shares in the benchmark forty companies of the Paris Bourse were held by foreign investors (Guette-Khiter 2020; *Les Echos*, September 26, 2013). Aggravating matters, France had not created large pension funds, which often act as a stable, long-term source of capital (Saint-Etienne 2014). Lacking the protection of either stable nuclei or long-term investors, several undercapitalized French household names were acquired by foreign firms, in some cases with disastrous consequences. In 2003, the Pechiney aluminum company was bought by a Canadian firm, Alcan, which was acquired, in turn, by the Australo-Brazilian giant Rio Tinto in 2007. In the process, Pechiney was essentially dismantled, and a number of French factories were closed. Much the same happened to the Usinor steel company after it merged with Aceralia of Spain and Arbed of Luxembourg in 2002 to create Arcelor, which was then taken over in 2006 by the Indian enterprise, Mittal Steel Company.

Another big expansion of the government's capacity to regulate foreign takeovers occurred under the ostensibly promarket Emmanuel Macron. Despite the protections of the Montebourg decree, foreign companies continued to acquire French national champions. Macron was especially concerned about what happened after the acquisitions, in particular, the failure of acquiring enterprises to honor their commitments (Cohen 2017). For example, when Nokia took over the French telecom manufacturer, Alcatel, its leadership pledged to retain employment and 5G research in France, but Nokia quickly reneged. Likewise, when a Swiss company, Holcim, entered into what was billed as a "merger between equals" with the Lafarge cement producer, Holcim pledged to preserve French management and capacities. Yet Holcim soon got rid of the French management team and later shut down the Paris office (*Les Echos*, April 7, 2019).

In 2019, Macron expanded the protection of French companies in several ways (Clifford Chance 2020; Jones Day 2020). He added a number of new activities to the list of strategic sectors: the editing, publication, and distribution of political and general information both in print and online; energy storage; biotechnologies; quantum technologies; and the production, transformation, and distribution of agricultural products insofar as they contribute to national food security objectives. In addition, the threshold for triggering a government review was reduced from 33 percent of voting rights to 25 percent; it would be "temporarily" reduced to 10 percent in response to the COVID-19 crisis. What is more, the ministry of the economy gained important powers to punish acquiring companies that fail to obey their promises or French rules. If a foreign acquisition is carried out without prior government authorization, the ministry can issue orders and injunctions, including to revert to the preexisting situation at the foreign investor's expense. If a foreign owner fails to keep the promises made as a condition of government authorization of an acquisition, the ministry can penalize that owner or even unwind the deal altogether at the foreign owner's expense. The ministry can also impose stiff financial penalties, specifically the largest of three options: (1) twice the amount of the defaulting investment; (2) 10 percent of the annual turnover (excluding taxes) of the target company; (3) €1 million for an individual or €5 million for a company.

Macron's law provides new grounds for refusing a foreign investment, notably if the acquiring investor has any kind of relationship or links with foreign governments or foreign public entities. This provision was clearly aimed at Chinese investors. In addition, Macron extended French restrictions to all foreign companies, including EU companies, whereas the law previously applied only to companies outside the EU. Finally, the government expanded the list of protected activities to include space operations and food production along with a third kind of strategic sector – R&D activities relating to cybersecurity, artificial intelligence, robotics, additive manufacturing, semiconductors, energy storage, biotechnology, and dual-use goods. At this point, the list of strategic sectors has become so long and open-ended that almost any acquisition could potentially be challenged by the French government. A brief summary of the list includes media, space, energy, water, transportation, public health, electronic communications, agriculture and food, advanced R&D, defense, dual-use goods and technologies, IT security, data processing, and cryptography.

The growth of France's foreign direct investment (FDI) control regime has been driven by economic concerns about French competitiveness and holes in the industrial fabric. It is a response to the weakness and vulnerabilities of France's national champions following privatization, the dissolution of the *noyaux durs*, and the end of the *grands projets*. It also stems from frustration with what has happened to a number of national champions in the wake of foreign takeovers. That said, the growth of this protectionist regime resurrects the Gaullist, nationalist approach to the economy, with a clear delineation between national champions, who are presumed to be acting in French interests, and foreign predators, who are believed to be concerned only with short-term profits and/or advancing the interests of the countries where they are headquartered. It is also a continuation of the aversion to market forces and fear of foreign takeovers that marked the Chirac–Balladur privatizations of 1986–1988.

Time and again, ostensibly promarket French leaders have chosen domestic protection over the principles of economic liberalism and market regulation, especially when it comes to corporate control. In the view of these leaders, the ownership of large French companies, successful or otherwise, is far too important to be left to the vicissitudes of the market.

3.3   The Sanctity of Social Order: Balladur

The French right's commitment to economic liberalism has been undermined by domestic as well as foreign threats. France has a long history of popular protests and revolutions. Historically, for conservative elites, including liberal luminaries like Alexis de Tocqueville, preserving social and political order against revolutionary upheaval has trumped all other considerations (Tocqueville 1893). This concern for social order is more than a distant historical memory. It was reactivated by the near revolution of May 1968. French conservatives, who thought that de Gaulle's Fifth Republic had finally brought democratic stability to France, were shocked to discover the seething discontent among French students, workers, and other subordinate groups. Conservative leaders who experienced May 1968 firsthand, most notably Valéry Giscard d'Estaing, Jacques Chirac, and Edouard Balladur, were scarred by the experience. Once in power, these leaders would repeatedly respond to protests by sacrificing liberalizing reforms for the sake of social order.

In 1974, Giscard d'Estaing won the presidential election on pledge to create a "society of advanced liberalism," both in social affairs and the economy (Giscard d'Estaing 1976). Giscard enacted a number of important societal reforms, reducing the voting age to 18, scaling back state control of TV broadcasts, introducing no-fault divorce, and legalizing abortion. On the economic front, Giscard also aspired to introduce far-reaching liberalizing change. In the 1960s, he had been an orthodox minister of finance, and from 1976 to 1981 Giscard's prime minister was a professor of economics, Raymond Barre, whom he described as "the best economist in France." The Giscard–Barre tandem advocated a less directive state role in the economy, allowing market forces, as opposed to *dirigiste* fiats, to steer France's economic development.

Yet Giscard and Barre did not scale back state intervention. Rather, in an effort to preserve employment, they shifted from supporting advanced technologies and the industries of the future to bailing out uncompetitive lame ducks in declining sectors like coal and steel (Berger 1981; Cohen 1989). Part of the motivation was electoral: Giscard and Barre faced a formidable challenge from a PS–PCF "Union of the Left." No less important was the fear of another May 1968. This fear was brought home by recurring worker protests whenever troubled national champions sought to close plants or lay off workers. As Elie Cohen puts it, the protests transformed the modernizing, *dirigiste* state into a "stretcher-bearer state" (Cohen 1989) that threw money at lame-duck companies with little prospect of recovery in order to forestall layoffs and preserve social order. In short, the conservative fear of social disorder, of another May 1968, led Giscard and Barre to abandon their agenda of economic liberalization in favor of protecting employment in hopelessly uncompetitive businesses. This shift was one of the central problems that would lead the Socialists to break with the *dirigiste* model in 1983 (Cohen 1989; Levy 1999b).

Fear of another May 1968 continued to shape the actions of French conservative governments after the break with the *dirigiste* model. As noted, the Chirac government, from 1986 to 1988, embraced neoliberal reform across a range of areas but pledged to leave the welfare state intact, so as to preserve social cohesion. Even at the height of its commitment to neoliberalism, the French right would not risk social upheaval for the sake of reduced public spending.

The next conservative government, the Balladur administration from 1993 to 1995, did seek to reform the welfare state. Prime Minister Balladur made some important reforms, most notably of the pension system. Still, Balladur was scarred by May 1968, and he would repeatedly abandon key liberalizing initiatives in the face of contestation in the streets.

Balladur made no secret of the fact that he had been traumatized by May 1968: "I lived through the ordeal of May 1968 close to him [Prime Minister Pompidou]. I say ordeal because we saw, at that moment, how state authority rested on so little" (Balladur 1995: 13). Balladur published a book on May 1968, a peculiar mixture of his own experiences and accounts by wholly fictitious characters (Balladur 1979). He also drew a direct link between May 1968 and his approach to governing: "I was profoundly influenced by what I lived, the irrational and the violent behaviors. My method of governing is the fruit of my reflections about then" (Balladur 1995: 20).

Balladur drew several important lessons from May 1968 (Nay 1994). First, the French political system is more vulnerable than it appears. A seemingly strong state, like the Gaullist regime of the 1960s, can turn out to be a colossus with feet of clay. Second, France is susceptible to violence. It is very easy for the masses to get angry and for the situation to spin out of control, so governments must proceed with caution. Third, the courageous position in a crisis is not necessarily to stick to one's guns when challenged, but rather to make concessions or even back down entirely for the sake of social order. Although Chirac did not theorize the lessons of May 1968 in the manner of Balladur, he shared many of the same instincts, in particular the need to proceed with caution and even reverse course in the face of protests.

Balladur's propensity for caution was reinforced by his reading of French social conditions in the 1990s. In Balladur's view, French society was traumatized by persistent high unemployment. As if to confirm his view, the very day that his government was named, official unemployment in France hit 3 million for the first time (*Le Monde*, April 1, 1993). Balladur contended that governing an anxious France required taking a gradual, cautious approach, seeking to explain and win people over, rather than ramming unpopular reforms down their throats: "We are in a society in which many sensibilities are upset and worries awakened. We are dealing with men, not machines. We must convince. We must make time" (cited in Chiroux 1994: 104).

Balladur got the chance to put his approach into action in 1993. Following the right's landslide victory in the 1993 legislative elections, Chirac seemed the logical choice to serve as prime minister, since he was still the leader of the right, but he had no stomach for a second cohabitation with Mitterrand. Not wishing to see his popularity eroded by the daily grind of governing, Chirac endorsed his longtime ally, Balladur, for the position of prime minister.

During his first six months as prime minister, Balladur implemented several important reforms. Confronting a budget deficit of some 6 percent of GDP, Balladur raised taxes by over €10 billion and cut spending, in part by freezing social benefits and the pay of civil servants. Balladur also introduced limited austerity measures into the health-care system, reducing patient reimbursement rates along with the budget for public hospitals (Hassenteufel 1997).

In August 1993, Balladur enacted his most significant reform, a retrenchment of the French pension system for private-sector employees (Bonoli 1997; Palier 2000, 2002, 2003a). The changes made by Balladur diminished the generosity of pensions in three ways: shifting the calculation of the reference wage for pensions from the average of the best 10 years to the average of the best 25 years of earnings; indexing pensions to prices instead of wages; and requiring employees to work for a minimum of 40 years to receive a full pension, as opposed to 37.5 years previously. To limit opposition to his reform, Balladur applied the changes in pension rules only to workers in the private sector, avoiding the potentially explosive challenge of reforming civil-service pensions and so-called special regimes, notably in public transportation and energy, that allow employees to retire in their mid- to late fifties. In addition, Balladur made an important, if somewhat complex, tax concession to the unions.

France's unions had long complained about the practice of making "Bismarck pay for Beveridge" (Bonoli 1997; Palier 2000, 2002, 2003a). Bismarckian programs, evoking the early German social insurance programs established by Otto von Bismarck in the 1880s, cover wage earners and are funded by the Social Security charges paid by employers and employees. Beveridgean programs, referencing William Beveridge, the architect of the postwar British welfare state, are available to all citizens and financed by general taxation. The union complaint was that the government was using payroll taxes on wage earners (Bismarck) to pay for social assistance or national solidarity benefits that permitted all citizens to receive a decent pension (Beveridge), even those with a limited record of payments into the system.

Balladur's reform addressed the union complaint by creating a Solidarity Fund for the Elderly (Fonds de Solidarité Vieillesse, FSV) to cover noncontributory benefits. Funding for these benefits would come, not from payroll taxes, but instead from a recently established General Social Contribution (Contribution Sociale Généralisée, CSG) levied on all sources of income, including from capital and property. Henceforth, taxes on wage earners (Bismarck) would serve to finance only the pensions of wage earners (Bismarck), while the CSG, a universal tax (Beveridge), would pay for solidarity benefits (Beveridge). This shift lowered the tax burden on wage earners, who were no longer required to cover the costs of noncontributory benefits. Even though Balladur's pension reform was an undeniable austerity measure – the first French reform ever to cut pension benefits and raise the retirement age – the "separation of Bismarck from Beveridge" and resulting reduction of the tax burden on wage earners softened the blow and gave the unions a face-saving concession.

Balladur was very popular initially. After one month in office, he had a 56 percent approval rating, the highest rating to date of any prime minister under the Fifth Republic and 20 points higher than Chirac at a similar moment in his tenure as prime minister (*Le Monde*, April 20, 1993). In a *Globe-Hebdo* poll conducted August 27–28, 1993, 67 percent of respondents favored Balladur for president, whereas only 20 percent endorsed Chirac (Nay 1994). Balladur's popularity was surprising, given his rather bland and austere image. In contrast to Chirac, who loved to press the flesh and work a crowd, Balladur was a quiet technocrat, who generally preferred to labor outside the public eye. Still, his calm, pragmatic demeanor struck a chord with a population traumatized by mass unemployment and the ideological battles of the 1980s.

For a time, Balladur seemed immune to the laws of political gravity. Despite raising taxes, cutting spending, and presiding over a period of negative economic growth and double-digit unemployment, he remained popular. Even mistakes and setbacks redounded to his advantage. One such instance was the government's mishandling of a crisis at Air France, France's nationalized airline.

Air France had lost over €1.5 billion during the previous five years and would lose another €1.1 billion in 1993. The company also carried a debt of €5.6 billion. To try to turn Air France around, its CEO, Bernard Attali, prepared a "plan to return to equilibrium" that would reduce costs by €625 million, primarily by cutting salaries. Balladur's minister of transportation, Bernard Bosson, felt that the plan was not ambitious enough, though, and demanded an additional €150 million in cuts (*Libération*, October 27, 1993). What is more, fearful of the powerful unions representing pilots and cabin crews, Bosson insisted on largely sparing in-flight workers from austerity, which meant concentrating the losses on the ground personnel, who were already earning much less than the flight crews. Attali's plan was, therefore, not only painful but, in the eyes of the low-paid ground crews, inequitable. In response, the ground crews launched a two-week strike and took the unprecedented step of occupying runways at the Roissy and Orly airports (*Les Echos*, May 4, 2018).

Minister of Transportation Bosson tried to draw a line in the sand, declaring Attali's plan to be "the only means" to save Air France (*L'événement du jeudi*, October 28–November 3, 1993) and "irrevocable" (*Libération*, November 6–7, 1993). Faced with rising protest, however, the government reversed course, dropping both Attali and his plan. Having compelled Attali to present an unfair and unpopular plan, Bosson now dismissed him with the justification that "we cannot save Air France while clashing with its employees" (*New York Times*, October 25, 1993). Bosson also raised the specter of May 1968, asserting that the government was not facing a strike, but rather "a revolt" and adding, "It is a movement the likes of which has never occurred since 1968" (*Le Monde*, October 27, 1993). The hint of a movement that might escalate into broader contestation along the lines of May 1968 was more than enough to convince Balladur to abandon the Air France reform.

Balladur later defended the government's retreat from Attali's plan as necessary to avoid a social crisis (Balladur 1995: 171–172). He was worried about the unrest at Air France, but also the possibility that the unrest could spread to other public enterprises where tensions were running high, notably the French National Railway Company (Société Nationale des Chemins de Fer Français, SNCF) and France Télécom. In addition to saving France from a potential May 1968, Balladur noted that the new CEO whom he had appointed, Christian Blanc, was able to enact a major cost-saving plan and get it ratified by more than 80 percent of Air France personnel in an April 1994 referendum. In other words, discretion was the better part of valor when confronted with a possible rebellion, and the government got its way in the end.

Balladur's characterization is not entirely accurate, however, or at least, it is incomplete. The government committed over €3 billion to rescue Air France – at the time, one of the most expensive bailouts in French history. Moreover, the aid was conditioned on employee ratification of the Blanc Plan, which is the main reason why more than 80 percent of employees voted for it. Far from a retreat followed by successful reform, Balladur's handling of the Air France crisis was a retreat followed by a massive government bailout.

Despite the Air France fiasco, Balladur remained very popular. Indeed, his willingness to retreat in the face of protest was viewed by many as a strength (Marian 1993: 164). It showed that Balladur was willing to listen and admit when he was wrong. Although Balladur believed in liberal economic principles, he would not destabilize French society for the sake of a grand ideological vision. Pundits began describing this pragmatic willingness to listen and back away from controversial reforms as "the Balladur method" and a new way of unblocking France. The problem with the Balladur method, though, was that it sent the message that government reforms could be stopped, provided that opponents put enough demonstrators in the streets and caused enough disruption to threaten social order. It did not take long for opponents of reform to act on this message.

In December 1993, Balladur moved to lift a cap on local government funding for private, mostly Catholic, schools (Chiroux 1994). Balladur tried to calm criticisms of the move by offering an extra €380 million to public schools over a five-year period, but opponents were not placated. On January 16, 1994, some 600,000 demonstrators took to the streets to protest the government's effort to increase public spending on religious schools. In response, Balladur backed down, pulling the plug on the law and opening negotiations with the unions on a multiyear financing plan for French public schools. The failure of the private school reform marked a turning point, with Balladur's approval rating dropping for the first time (*Libération*, April 19, 1994).

One month later, Balladur engaged in another climbdown, this time with Breton fishermen. Angered by low fish prices and cheap imports, protestors rioted in the streets of Rennes, where Balladur had been attending a meeting, burning down the regional parliament, a masterpiece of seventeenth-century architecture. A number of treasured tapestries and paintings were also destroyed. Balladur's response to this act of vandalism was not to stand his ground and denounce lawlessness, but rather to loosen the government's purse strings, boosting aid to the fishermen (*L'Express*, February 10, 1994). Key concessions included a minimum income for workers in the fishing industry (whose income at the time depended on the value of the catch), price supports for seven critical varieties of fish, and financial assistance to help fishermen modernize their boats and equipment (*Les Echos*, February 7, 1994).

As described in Chapter 2 of this book, Balladur backed down yet again one month later, in this case, from the proposed lower minimum wage for youths, the Professional Insertion Contract (Contrat d'Insertion Professionnnelle, CIP). Once more, protests derailed a liberalizing initiative. After a promising beginning, the Balladur method was faltering as a strategy for reforming France.

The Balladur method proved no more successful as a political strategy. Balladur had been expected to support Chirac's run for president in 1995 then serve as Chirac's prime minister. Buoyed by impressive public opinion polls, however, Balladur decided to run for president instead, betraying Jacques Chirac. At the time, Chirac appeared to have no chance of catching Balladur. Yet as protestors discovered how to use the Balladur method to their advantage, reforms mostly ground to a halt. What is more, despite a slew of make-work programs and other initiatives to keep down unemployment, France's unemployment rate remained above 12 percent.

Balladur's difficulties provided a political opening for Chirac, who denounced Balladur for his alleged subservience to neoliberal orthodoxy (*la pensée unique*), but also for immobilism, a product of Balladur's disinclination to risk social conflict and protests for the sake of liberal economic reforms (Allaire and Goulliaud 2002; Griotteray 1997). As against Balladurian orthodoxy, whether real or imagined, Chirac promised to ramp up social spending, so as to reduce unemployment, renew the "republican pact," and heal France's "social fracture." These promises proved popular, and by the middle of February 1995, Chirac had pulled ahead of Balladur in the polls (Buffotot and Hanley 1996).

On the first round of balloting of the 1995 presidential election, Lionel Jospin, the Socialist candidate, placed first with 23.3 percent of the vote. Chirac came in second, with 20.8 percent, while Balladur, with just 18.6 percent, was eliminated from the runoff (Maus 1995: 192). The cautious Balladur method had fallen short as political strategy as well as a reform strategy, and Chirac would secure election as president easily in the runoff against Jospin.

Balladur's economic and social policy was fashioned by fears of social disorder as much as any commitment to liberal economic principles.

Balladur abandoned important reforms, like that of Air France and the youth labor market, in the face of protests. He also loosened the purse strings following protests by supporters of secular public education and a riot by Breton fishermen. Time and again, the preservation of social order took precedence over the cause of economic liberalization. While preserving social order, Balladur was unable to prevent contestation. He was also unable to preserve his popularity, as Chirac deployed criticisms of *la pensée unique* and "immobilism" to close the gap then surpass his rival.

3.4   Liberalization without Legitimation: Chirac

Jacqueqs Chirac's election as president and subsequent travails point to another limitation of the French right's commitment to economic liberalization – the absence of a legitimating discourse for such reform. As Vivien Schmidt observes, "Since 1983, with the adoption of a moderate neoliberal political-economic policy programme, French governments have been markedly unsuccessful in constructing a legitimating discourse capable of projecting to the public a convincing vision of how France fits within an integrating Europe and a globalizing world" (Schmidt 2002b: 271). That the French left would experience such difficulty is unsurprising, given the left's historic opposition to free-market capitalism (Spector 2017). Following the 1983 U-turn, the Mitterrand administration offered a combination of denial, rhetorical sleight of hand, and blaming of Brussels.

The left has not been alone in acting this way, however. The French right has likewise proven reluctant to defend economic liberalization, often feigning opposition and blaming liberalizing reforms on forces beyond the government's control, most notably European integration. Indeed, the election of Chirac as president represented the culmination of a decade-long retreat by the French right from liberal economic principles: the brief embrace of (socially compensated) neoliberalism during the 1986–1988 cohabitation gave way to the cautious and oft-revoked reformism of Balladur from 1993 to 1995 and finally to the election of Chirac in 1995 on what was essentially an anti-liberal platform.

During the 1995 election campaign, Chirac presented himself as a radical alternative to Balladur and economic orthodoxy (*la pensée unique*). As against Balladur's cautious approach, Chirac promised to be a bold, activist president: "I am a candidate for the Presidency of the Republic because I have in me the force and will to implement real change. Small steps, half-measures are just a form of immobilism, the worst danger for France" (cited in Maus 1995: 110). Restoring the French economy would require an activist state, not a cautious or minimal state.

Chirac also argued that Balladur had his priorities wrong. Instead of trying to reduce France's budget deficit, the government should prioritize bringing down unemployment to heal the social fracture. In his first public statement upon assuming the presidency, Chirac declared: "Above all, I will engage all my forces to restore France's cohesion and renew the republican pact among the French. Employment will be my preoccupation at all times" (*Le Monde*, May 18, 1995). Fighting unemployment was not only more important than reducing the budget deficit, according to Chirac, but also *the most effective way* to reduce the deficit, since unemployment drives up social spending, while reducing tax revenues. Chirac went so far as to claim that, "With a 3 percent lower unemployment rate, there would be no deficit" (cited in Ottenheimer 1996: 269). Chirac also argued that raising taxes to reduce deficits was counterproductive. One of his favorite lines on the campaign trail was "too much taxation kills taxation," that is, higher taxes reduce economic growth and, with it, tax revenues.

Finally, Chirac took issue with Balladur and *la pensée unique* over the appropriate remedy for mass unemployment. Whereas Balladur had sought to reduce the minimum wage for young people to stimulate hiring, Chirac regularly declared when campaigning that "the paycheck is not the enemy of employment" (cited in Allaire and Goulliaud 2002: 114). In other words, wages need not be reduced in order to create jobs. Rather, the state would expand employment by stimulating demand, increasing its own hiring, and giving employers generous incentives to take on additional workers.

Chirac's successful election campaign amounted to an across-the-board assault on economic liberalism: the government is the solution to the problem, not the source of the problem; France needs more public spending, not less; cutting wages to create jobs is cruel and unnecessary; and the road to fiscal recovery is to multiply subsidized jobs at a time when the state was already subsidizing one job in ten. Whether Chirac actually believed his own rhetoric is impossible to tell; he was nothing if not ideologically flexible. What is knowable, though, is that *many French voters* believed Chirac's rhetoric, and they were not about to let him blithely dismiss it once he became president.

As president, Chirac did honor one major campaign promise. One month into his term in office, his government announced an "emergency plan for employment" (*plan d'urgence pour l'emploi*) costing an estimated €7 billion per year. The centerpiece was an Employment Initiative Contract (Contrat Initiative Emploi, CIE) for companies hiring workers who had been unemployed for at least one year (*Le Monde*, June 23 and 24, 1995; *Libération*, June 23, 1995). Under the CIE, the government paid roughly 40 percent of the wages and payroll taxes of each hire for up to two years. Employers were required to commit to the jobs for at least one year, but there were no other obligations. The government rolled out similar, if less generous, programs for companies hiring young people in search of their first job or low-wage employees earning less than 120 percent of the minimum wage. Chirac was thus true to his word in increasing state spending to try to expand employment.

While honoring a key campaign pledge on the spending side, Chirac violated his promise on the revenue side. Concerned about France's budget deficit, he raised a number of visible, painful taxes. The government increased the corporate tax from 33.3 percent to 37.0 percent, the wealth tax by 10 percent, gasoline taxes by 2.7 percent, tobacco taxes by 3.0 percent, and most controversially, the sales tax or value-added tax (VAT) from 18.6 percent to 20.6 percent (Allaire and Goulliaud 2002: 110–111; Ottenheimer 1996: 132). These tax hikes contradicted Chirac's campaign slogan that "too much taxation kills taxation."

The government's tax increases were very unpopular, especially the VAT hike. They also dampened consumption, slowing French economic growth. So, too, did another retreat from Chirac's campaign rhetoric, in this case regarding wages. In September 1995, the government announced a wage freeze for civil servants in 1996, which it would later extend to 1997. The wage freeze was difficult to reconcile with Chirac's claim that "the paycheck is not the enemy of employment," although Chirac attempted to justify his position by noting that the paycheck of civil servants "is the tax bill of the French" (*Le Monde*, September 22, 1995).

The biggest renunciation by Chirac would come one month later. In a television interview on October 26, Chirac stunned the French public by announcing that his top priority was to reduce France's budget deficit (*Le Monde*, October 27, 1995). Chirac's main justification for this U-turn, the most significant since that of the Socialists in 1983, was that France's public finances were in worse shape than he had realized (Allaire and Goulliaud 2002: 110; Domenach and Szafran 1997: 302–303). Given that Chirac's prime minister, Alain Juppé, was a former budget minister and that the right had been in power since 1993, the claim that the new administration had no idea of the extent of the deficit was not very convincing.

Another justification offered by Chirac was that the newly independent Bank of France, headed by the future president of the European Central Bank (ECB), Jean-Claude Trichet, was keeping interest rates high out of concern that budget deficits would trigger inflation or an attack on the French franc (Domenach and Szafran 1997: 304–305). Trichet had indicated to Chirac that he would lower interest rates only in conjunction with reductions in the budget deficit. Chirac argued, therefore, that the way to stimulate the economy was not to run a big budget deficit in a Keynesian manner, since Trichet would respond by raising interest rates, but rather to reduce the budget deficit, so that Trichet would reduce interest rates, thereby providing support to investors and borrowers. Of course, Trichet's orientation was also nothing new to Chirac.

Although Chirac emphasized economic considerations, it was no secret that he was motivated first and foremost by European considerations (Domenach and Szafran 1997; Jarreau 1997). Chirac was determined to place France among the first group of countries to qualify for the European Monetary Union (EMU). Under the terms of the Maastricht Treaty, France needed to reduce its budget deficit below 3 percent of GDP by the end of 1997, whereas the deficit at the time was running above 5 percent of GDP, meaning that Chirac would have to implement an austerity plan. Austerity flowed from Maastricht more than from any reading of the French economy. Indeed, as Chirac had pointed out during the 1995 campaign, the combination of low inflation and high unemployment suggested that the French economy needed demand stimulus, not belt tightening.

Chirac was determined to have France qualify for the EMU out of European solidarity, but also because the EMU was central to the Franco-German relationship (Domenach and Szafran 1997; Jarreau 1997). Chirac felt that the relationship could thrive only if it were roughly balanced, which would not be the case if Germany qualified for the EMU while France did not. What is more, Chirac had given repeated assurances to German Chancellor Helmut Kohl that he would do whatever it took for France to meet the Maastricht criteria. Chirac himself later acknowledged that the primary reason for the U-turn was to qualify for the EMU, although he also argued that Maastricht played a useful role in pressuring France to get its fiscal house in order:

The main thing ... was to get through the next stage in the construction of Europe in keeping with the conditions established by Maastricht. We have developed bad habits since the beginning of the 1980s: we spend more than we produce. The euro will impose sound management practices on us and force us to finally manage our affairs seriously. It is, therefore, in our national interest. (Cited in Giesbert 2014: 653)

One month after Chirac's U-turn, Prime Minister Juppé presented a highly ambitious "Social Security Plan" to parliament that spanned pensions, health care, and taxation (Allaire and Goulliaud 2002: 137–140; Laot 1997). The Juppé Plan aimed to reduce France's budget deficit to 4.5 percent of GDP in 1996 and 3.0 percent in 1997. It included a number of tax hikes, which brought the total tax increase under Chirac to €18.3 billion in a full year (Jarreau 1997: 171–172). On the spending side, the Juppé Plan froze family allowances in 1996 and subjected the benefits of high earners to taxation beginning in 1997. It also saved €3 billion by postponing the launching of a program to help the dependent elderly for one year.

The Juppé Plan proposed a major overhaul of the French health-care system. France's nineteen different health regimes were to be merged into a single, universal system. To rationalize and contain costs, Juppé sought to clamp down on spending by tightening controls on physicians, patients, and hospitals. Of particular note, he proposed to reward or punish physicians by adjusting fees annually, from one region to the next, according to each region's success in meeting government spending targets. In addition, the reform would require patients to get a referral from a general practitioner before seeing a specialist and expand the use of generic drugs. At an aggregate level, Juppé proposed a constitutional amendment subjecting the Social Security budget to a parliamentary vote. Juppé's hope was that by imposing an annual budget from above, rather than accommodating a series of autonomous spending decisions below, the government would be better able to limit health-care spending. At the subnational level, state "regional hospitalization agencies" would be established to give the state the ability to control the flow of money to both public and private hospitals.

The Juppé Plan aimed to curtail spending on pensions as well as health care. Whereas the Balladur pension reform had targeted private-sector workers, Juppé focused on employees in the public sector. Civil servants would be required to work 40 years instead of 37.5 years in order to qualify for a full pension, the same requirement as in the private sector. In addition, Juppé proposed to eliminate the various *régimes spéciaux* that allowed employees of some public enterprises, notably in transportation and energy, to retire as early as age 50. Henceforth, no public employee would be allowed retire before age 60.

The initial response to the Juppé Plan was very positive (Jarreau 1997: 132–134; Laot 1997). Juppé's presentation of his plan to the National Assembly was interrupted repeatedly by applause. To ensure that he had the support of the legislature, Juppé posed the confidence question, which was approved overwhelmingly by 436 to 87, with 10 abstentions (Allaire and Goulliaud 2002: 140). Pundits praised Juppé for having taken an ambitious approach to overhauling France's social programs and putting public finances on a stable footing. They also praised his commitment to "equality of sacrifice." Taxpayers, doctors, civil servants, pharmaceutical companies – everyone would be made to contribute their fair share.

Despite the initial positive reception, the Juppé Plan would ultimately provoke the biggest protest movement since May 1968. Part of the problem was that Juppé made little effort to get buy-in from key stakeholders. Indeed, his approach was almost a caricature of the insular, technocratic Gaullist methods of the 1960s. The government's role was to modernize the country, to pursue the general will, not to cater to the particularistic concerns of self-serving interest groups. The Juppé Plan was conceived in this spirit – prepared in complete secrecy, lest it be contaminated by special pleading. The prime minister openly bragged that not ten people had seen his plan prior to its presentation to parliament. As Chapter 4 of this book relates, this kind of top-down, skinny policymaking often provokes strikes and protests by groups that have been excluded from the reform process and feel that the only way to influence policy is to take to the streets.

The Juppé Plan was also too ambitious. Juppé boasted that, "Nobody has ever dared to do this kind of reform since 1945" (cited in Allaire and Goulliaud 2002: 138), but perhaps Juppé's predecessors had been cautious for good reason. More ambition meant more potential opponents of reform. By pursuing the "equality of sacrifice," Juppé ensured the equality of enmity toward his government and its objectives. His plan gave every group in society a reason to be unhappy. As a result, groups that normally had little in common, such as physicians and transportation workers, found themselves united in their opposition to the Juppé Plan.

One decision that Juppé probably came to regret was a last-minute addition to his plan. Pension reform was not in the plan originally, but Juppé felt that with Balladur having reformed the pensions of workers in the private sector, it was only fair that the pensions of public-sector workers also be reformed. President Chirac warned against the idea, describing it as a "minefield," before adding, "Don't overload the boat. Think about it carefully" (cited in Giesbert 2014: 611) and, "In your place, I would not do everything" (cited in Allaire and Goulliaud 2002: 143). Juppé went ahead with the pension reform anyway.

Juppé's pension reform was a red flag for France's powerful transportation workers, who stood to lose their early retirement pensions. Adding to their anxiety, two days after the announcement of the Juppé Plan, the government opened negotiations with the SNCF over a five-year planning contract (*Libération*, November 20, 1995). In exchange for absorbing the SNCF's debt of €26 billion, the government wanted to decommission some 3,700 miles of unprofitable railroad lines and sharply reduce SNCF employment. SNCF workers, threatened by the planning contract as well as the Juppé Plan, had ample motivation to go on strike. When joined by employees of the Paris agglomeration's subway and suburban train system, the Autonomous Parisian Transportation Administration (Régie Autonome des Transports Parisiens, RATP), SNCF strikers brought French public transportation to a standstill for more than three weeks, paralyzing the country.

Workers in France's private sector, where unions were weak and jobs scarce, were not in a position to go on strike, but the transportation workers had other allies. Public-sector unions in gas, electricity, postal services, and telecommunications walked out to defend their pensions. University students, who often regard antigovernment strikes as a rite of passage, likewise joined the movement. The students were motivated by financial concerns as well as tradition, seeking to reverse university budget cuts that the right had imposed in previous years. Public opinion was also friendly to the strikers, despite the disruptions to people's lives. A December 2 opinion poll commissioned by *Le Parisien* and RTL showed 62 percent approval for the strikers (Ottenheimer 1996: 264). By contrast, another poll on November 21 revealed that negative opinions exceeded positive opinions by 64 to 27 percent for Chirac and 65 to 26 percent for Juppé (*Le Monde*, November 21, 1995).

Alongside the public-sector strikes, opponents of the reform organized a series of ever-larger one-day protests (Allaire and Goulliaud 2002: 127–150). On November 16, 1 million demonstrators took to the streets according to the organizers, 400,000 according to the police. The numbers on December 5 were 800,000 and 500,000 respectively. The biggest protest occurred December 12, with 2 million demonstrators according to the organizers and 1 million according to the police.

At first, Juppé stood his ground. He did not speak publicly about the protest for eleven days and showed little willingness to engage in serious negotiations. In a meeting of the Council of Ministers, he declared, "We have not been elected to organize the decline of France. There is no alternative" (cited in Allaire and Goulliaud 2002: 148). Juppé also deployed Article 49.3 to cut off debate in the National Assembly.

Faced with growing opposition in the streets and the opinion polls, however, the government began to backtrack. On December 10, Chirac announced that SNCF and RATP personnel who worked on the trains (but not office employees) would be exempted from the pension reform. He also postponed the negotiations for a new five-year planning contract with the SNCF. In addition, the government made a U-turn on university funding: instead of cutting the budget, it offered a new "emergency plan" for the universities. Still, opponents of the Juppé Plan were not swayed and on December 12 they organized their largest demonstration yet.

Three days later, at Chirac's insistence, Juppé abandoned his pension reform altogether. Although he maintained a tougher line toward the physicians, ultimately this part of the reform also unraveled. The system of penalties lacked effective enforcement mechanisms, and after a brief pause, medical spending was again increasing at two to three times the level of inflation. In the end, all that was left of the Juppé Plan were a number of unpopular tax increases and the annual parliamentary vote of the Social Security budget, which did little to slow the growth of spending.

Juppé's missteps certainly contributed to the failure of his reform. His plan was too ambitious, especially with the inclusion of the pension reform. Juppé's high-handed and secretive ways deprived him of allies, who felt no responsibility for an unpopular reform that they had played no part in drafting. The biggest problem, though, was that Chirac lacked a mandate for the kinds of reforms that Juppé was proposing. Indeed, Chirac had a kind of *anti-mandate*, given that he had criticized precisely these kinds of liberal policies during his campaign for president.

Chirac's entire election campaign had delegitimated the economic arguments that he was now making. The top priority was supposed to be to heal the social fracture, not to reduce the budget deficit. Deficit reduction was supposed to be the *result* of economic recovery, not the *precondition* for it. State spending, not austerity, was supposed to bring down unemployment. Finally, the paycheck was supposed to be compatible with employment growth, yet the government was freezing wages in the public sector and shrinking purchasing power by raising VAT. In many ways, Chirac's new agenda looked a lot like Balladur's old agenda, that is, the agenda that Chirac had done so much to discredit while running for president.

With the Juppé Plan, Chirac was quickly and, in the eyes of many, cynically betraying the promises that had been central to his election campaign just a few months earlier. Sociologist Emmanuel Todd, who had coined the phrase "social fracture," described Chirac's U-turn as "a rape of Republican legitimacy" (cited in Domenach and Szafran 1997: 309). The prevailing sentiment was that Chirac had said whatever it took to get elected but never intended to honor his campaign promises. The fact that Chirac reversed course so quickly, after just five months, added to suspicion around his intentions. As one critic observed wryly, "The country was invited to release [Chirac] from his promises before he even attempted to honor any of them" (Jarreau 1997: 135). The country refused the invitation, however, and Chirac was forced to abandon the Juppé Plan.

The difficulties of Chirac and Juppé did not end with the abandonment of the Juppé Plan. Weakened by its defeat and lacking any legitimating discourse for its actions, the government was contested at every turn and forced to withdraw other liberalizing proposals. Some of these proposals involved the remnants of the Juppé Plan (Mouriaux 1997: 18). In January 1996, in the face of protests by family associations, the government abandoned its plan to tax the family allowances of high earners; that same month, it withdrew collective penalties on physicians for overspending.

The government also retreated from several planned privatizations (Mouriaux 1997: 77–78). As part of the government's privatization campaign, Juppé sought to sell Crédit Industriel et Commercial (CIC), France's eighth-largest bank, to one of its larger competitors. Juppé wanted to place a political ally with questionable qualifications as CEO of the company. In response, more than one-half of all CIC employees took to the streets, and the government wound up retracting its nominee for the CEO position and postponing the privatization.

Juppé also planned to privatize the electronics conglomerate Thomson by selling its weapons business (Thomson CSF) to a much smaller French company, Matra, and its consumer electronics business (Thomson Multimédia) to a Korean company, Daewoo, for just 1 franc. Juppé justified the giveaway to Daewoo by saying that, "Thomson is not worth anything" (cited in Mouriaux 1997: 78). Thomson employees, outraged by both the transaction and Juppé's depiction of their company as worthless, struck in masse, and the government was forced to cancel the privatization.[4]

Protest was not confined to privatization decisions. In November 1996, truckers unhappy with working conditions and pensions blocked France's highways on two separate occasions. In response, the government agreed to allow truckers to retire at age 55. The government also promised to issue decrees limiting the working hours of truckers (Mouriaux 1997: 13–14).

In April 1997, after eighteen months of protests and blockage, Chirac decided to dissolve the National Assembly and call early elections. The move was somewhat surprising given that the right held 475 out of 577 seats in the National Assembly, the largest majority in over 150 years, and that the outgoing legislature still had another year to run. Chirac later told a biographer that he felt he had no choice but to call early elections because France had become ungovernable and was at risk of a 1968-style social explosion:

[If I had not called early elections] everything would have ended up in the streets. We needed to purge it all. We were no longer able to govern. Everything would have exploded. We were in a system in which the French refused all constraints.... If I had let things continue without dissolving the National Assembly, I cannot even imagine what would have happened. (Cited in Giesbert 2014: 653)

Chirac's hope was that a new election, even if it resulted in a diminished majority, would give him a mandate to pursue the economic reforms necessary to qualify for the EMU (Ross 1997). The right still had to win the legislative elections, but it started off with a big advantage: given the right's historic majority in the outgoing legislature, it could survive significant losses. In March 1997, a secret poll by the ministry of the interior forecast that the right would lose around 100 seats, but even under this scenario, the right would still have more than twice as many seats as the left (*New York Times*, April 21, 1997). In addition, the left's leader, Lionel Jospin, had already lost to Chirac in the 1995 presidential election and lacked Chirac's charisma and zest for campaigning. Finally, the left was caught unawares by Chirac's snap dissolution and had little time to resolve the thorny issues of the campaign platform and the allocation of ministerial positions among the several parties composing its Plural Left (La Gauche Plurielle) alliance.

The right also had problems, though (Northcutt 1998). Many conservative voters did not understand why they were being called to the polls one year early when the right already enjoyed a huge majority. In addition, voters on both sides of the political spectrum were fed up with Prime Minister Juppé, who seemed to combine arrogance with incompetence. The government's discourse on economic reform for the economy's sake had fallen flat, hoisted on the anti-liberal petard of Chirac's own presidential campaign, so the right needed to come up with a new justification. This time, Chirac made explicit what been implicit at the time of his U-turn: his economic and social agenda was being driven by the imperatives of European integration. Regardless of whether liberal reforms helped or hindered the economy, they were necessary if France was to be among the first group of EMU members and maintain its standing in Europe.

Jospin was more ambivalent about the EMU. The Socialist leader supported European integration, but he felt that the Maastricht criteria were too focused on inflation and public spending at the expense of growth and employment. The right seized upon this reticence to depict the left as the enemy of Europe (Hainsworth 1998). While the strategy might have worked in the past, European integration was not as popular as it had once been. Here, too, a legacy of the 1983 U-turn figured prominently. Many French voters were tired of being asked to make sacrifices on behalf of a Europe that seemed to deliver only hardship and frustration in return (Schmidt 2007).

The left had justified the 1983 U-turn primarily on the basis of European solidarity, as opposed to the economic need to break with a *dirigiste* model that was failing. In addition, the left had presented the embrace of Europe as a means to extend EU programs that were popular with the French, most notably support for farmers and successful Euro-industrial policies like civilian aircraft (Airbus) and rocket launchers (Ariane) (Schmidt 2002b, 2007). By the 1990s, however, such initiatives had fallen out of favor with France's European partners, and little had been accomplished. Meanwhile, the biggest advances in European integration had been in the area of economic liberalization: reducing internal European barriers to trade with the Single Market; clamping down on the creation and support of national champions through vigorous enforcement of competition policy; and, with the Maastricht Treaty, pressuring governments to implement austerity in order to qualify for the EMU.

Not surprisingly, the disappointments of an EU associated increasingly with neoliberalism and the repeated evocations of European pressures to justify unpopular policies led many in France to question whether European integration was worth the trouble (Schmidt 2002b, 2007). Already in 1992, the referendum on the Maastricht Treaty had passed by the slimmest of margins, despite support from all the mainstream governing parties. In the 1997 legislative elections, French voters showed that they were unwilling to accept substantial economic sacrifice for the sake of the EMU. Instead of endorsing the right and an expected austerity package, French voters elected a Plural Left coalition headed by Lionel Jospin and encompassing the Socialists, Communists, Greens, and a few smaller movements. A legitimating discourse for liberal reform centered on European integration had become a delegitimating discourse for both liberal reform and European integration.

The unwillingness of French voters to sacrifice for Europe extended beyond 1997. In 2005, the French overwhelmingly rejected a proposed EU constitution in a referendum, by nearly 55 percent to 45 percent (Marthaler 2005). The proposed constitution had been drafted by a committee headed by former French president, Valéry Giscard d'Estaing, and was backed by both the governing UMP and opposition Socialists. Electoral analysis showed that supporters of the referendum voted mainly out of a general commitment to European integration (Amable and Palombarini 2017: 85–86). Opponents, by contrast, focused on economic and social issues, voting against what they saw as a neoliberal Europe that was acting as a Trojan horse for global capitalism. Thus, the repeated use of the European blame game had poisoned the appeal of European integration for many voters, especially those on the left. Bruno Amable and Stefano Palombarini note that in the 2005 referendum, 94 percent of Communists, 61 percent of Socialists, and 61 percent of Greens voted "no," as did 76 percent of blue-collar workers (Amable and Palombarini 2017: 87).

More recently, the Pew Research Center reports that France is among the most pessimistic countries about the economic impact of European integration (Pew Research Center 2019b). In 2015, only 31 percent of French respondents felt that the economic integration of Europe had been good for the country. The figures for Germany and the UK were 59 percent and 49 percent respectively. Shockingly, in a survey taken the very year that UK voters elected to leave the EU, a significantly lower percentage of French citizens (31 percent) than British subjects (49 percent) felt that European integration had benefited their country's economy.

In the postwar period, the French right, especially the Gaullist movement, championed a *dirigiste* model whose underlying principles were directly at odds with those of economic liberalism. Since the break with the *dirigiste* model in 1983, the right has struggled to come up with an alternative more market-centered outlook like that of other European conservative parties (Schmidt 2002b, 2007). In the extreme case, Chirac's 1995 campaign actually sounded an anti-liberal note, denouncing *la pensée unique* and calling for increased state spending to combat unemployment and heal the social fracture. Once in office, Chirac tried to pivot away from his discourse by invoking the imperatives of European integration. The French did not buy Chirac's explanation however, suspecting him of having never intended to honor his campaign promises and balking at further sacrifices on the altar of European integration. Lacking a legitimating discourse, Chirac's government was mostly checked in its liberalizing initiatives – first by strikers and protestors, then by French voters, who refused to sign up for a new round of austerity from a president who had promised to make the fight against unemployment and the social fracture his top priority. The combination of dishonesty and reliance on an increasingly unpopular European scapegoat left Chirac's liberalization without legitimation.

3.5   Fair-Weather Liberalism: Sarkozy

A final limitation of the French right's commitment to liberalism has been a willingness to cast aside liberal principles in times of economic crisis. Promarket conservatives have often turned out to be "fair-weather liberals," jettisoning their thin commitment to liberal principles when economic ill winds blow. Of course, economic crises invariably place pressure on governments to intervene, whether to stabilize aggregate demand, clean up the financial system, or rescue companies deemed too big to fail. The French right has gone a step further, though, responding to crises by launching new voluntarist programs.

The case of Giscard d'Estaing described earlier in this chapter illustrates the tendency of the right to abandon liberal principles in hard economic times. Despite the liberal bona fides of Giscard and his economist prime minister, Raymond Barre, the government responded to the economic disruption of the 1970s by bailing out lame ducks and nationalizing the steel industry. It also created a new, interventionist institution, the Interministerial Committee for the Adaptation of Industrial Structures (Comité Interministériel pour l'Aménagement des Structures Industrielles, CIASI) for the express purpose of rescuing companies on the verge of bankruptcy (Buigues and Cohen 2020; Cohen 1989).

The interventionism of Giscard and Barre took place during the waning days of the *dirigiste* model, and French economic policy has changed dramatically since the 1970s. Still, the experience of France's most recent president of the right, Nicolas Sarkozy, offers another case of fair-weather liberalism. Sarkozy was elected president in 2007 on a probusiness, liberalizing agenda. He did not speak glowingly of economic liberalization in the manner of Chirac in 1986, but his depiction of France's economic and social difficulties echoed liberal critiques. Although the French generally refer fondly to their "social model" or "system of social protection," which they contrast to the heartless, lean-and-mean American model (Smith 2004), Sarkozy countered that a system that generates mass unemployment could in no way be viewed as a "social model." Sarkozy hammered away at the failings of France's system of social protection: "Today, there are three certainties: the [French social] system is not financially sustainable, it discourages employment ... finally, it does not provide equality of opportunity" (*Libération*, September 18, 2007). In Sarkozy's view, the French welfare state produces "more injustice than justice.... We must change it." Sarkozy was especially critical of the thirty-five-hour workweek, blaming it for everything from "killing French industry" (*Libération*, March 4, 2010) to causing mass unemployment:

Why is there so much more unemployment in our country? Because we chose to share jobs rather than pursue growth ... [This] choice of the thirty-five-hour workweek has revealed itself to be a catastrophe. (*Libération*, February 1, 2010)

Sarkozy did not just denounce the failings of France's social system; he also ran for president on a pledge to overhaul it. Already in 2004, while serving as minister of the economy, Sarkozy had tasked Michel

Camdessus, a former head of the International Monetary Fund (IMF) known for his neoliberal orientation, to head a commission to identify solutions for renewing French economic growth. The Camdessus Report proposed to "jumpstart" the French economy through a series of mostly neoliberal reforms: cutting public spending by 1 percent of GDP every year; bringing tax rates down to the level of France's European competitors; eliminating the distinction between highly protected permanent workers and unprotected temporary workers; reducing the costs and uncertainties encountered by firms making layoffs; limiting increases in the minimum wage; introducing flexibility into the thirty-five-hour workweek; and allowing employees to "work more to earn more" through generous tax treatment of overtime hours (Camdessus 2004). Sarkozy referred to the Camdessus Report as his "bedside reading" or "bible," and most of its proposals made it into his fifteen-point presidential program (Sarkozy 2007). In addition, the phrase "work more to earn more" became a staple of Sarkozy's campaign speeches.

Upon assuming the presidency, Sarkozy launched several liberal economic initiatives. In the summer of 2007, his government enacted the Law for Work, Employment, and Purchasing Power (Loi pour le Travail, l'Emploi, et le Pouvoir d'Achat, TEPA), a package of tax cuts totaling roughly €15 billion per year (Greciano 2008; Monnier 2009). Honoring Sarkozy's promise to "be the president of purchasing power" and to enable employees to "work more to earn more," the TEPA Law exempted overtime hours from income and payroll taxes, at a cost of approximately €6 billion per year. The other important provision in the TEPA Law concerned the so-called fiscal shield, a cap on total direct tax liability. The Chirac government had established the fiscal shield in 2006, setting the ceiling at 60 percent of earnings. Arguing that, "one should not take from someone more than half of what he earns," Sarkozy reduced the ceiling to 50 percent (*Libération*, March 31, 2010). He also incorporated various Social Security taxes into the fiscal shield along with the income tax.

To finance the TEPA tax cuts, Sarkozy pledged to reduce public spending by 1 percent of GDP every year. As a symbol of his commitment to shrinking the state, Sarkozy instituted a policy of not replacing one retiring civil servant out of two. This attrition policy eliminated nearly 100,000 positions in the civil service from 2007 to 2009, with about 40,000 job reductions in the national education system. The ministry of the interior (police) and ministry of defense were also hard hit, and in 2009, employment in public hospitals shrank for the first time ever (*Libération*, January 21, 2010). Sarkozy extracted further savings through a modest reform of the France's "special pension regimes" (*régimes spéciaux*), requiring beneficiaries to work longer to receive a full pension and shifting the indexation of public pensions from wages to prices (Cahuc and Zylberberg 2009; French Senate Commission on Social Regimes and Retirement 2010; Howell 2008).

Along with a liberal fiscal policy of tax and spending cuts, Sarkozy sought to make French labor markets more employment-friendly. The government reduced opportunities for early exit from the labor market through the reform of the *régimes spéciaux* and the phasing out of several early retirement programs. The administration also made it easier for employers to make layoffs, arguing that this facility would encourage greater hiring in the first place. In addition, the government moved to slow the growth in France's minimum wage (Salaire Minimum Interprofessionnel de Croissance, SMIC), which it blamed for pricing young, unskilled, and minority workers out of jobs. Starting in 2008, Sarkozy halted the tradition of providing a "nudge" (*coup de pouce*) to the SMIC beyond the legally mandated adjustment for inflation, which meant that the minimum wage grew only about one-half as fast as average wages (OECD 2009).

In another move to increase employment, the government ratcheted up the pressure on the unemployed to take jobs. The August 2008 Law on the Rights and Duties of Job Seekers established the requirement that all recipients of unemployment benefits devise individualized "employment plans" in cooperation with their case workers. The law also provided for the reduction or even elimination of unemployment benefits for claimants who refused more than two "reasonable offers of employment" (OECD 2009: 48–49). The law did contain one advantage for the unemployed – the possibility of becoming eligible for benefits after four months on the job, rather than six months as previously required.

The government deployed other carrots as well. The overhaul of the Minimum Insertion Income (Revenu Minimum d'Insertion, RMI), a means-tested minimum income for residents over the age of 25, sought to boost employment in this way (Greciano 2010). In 2009, the government replaced the RMI with the revealingly named Active Solidarity Income (Revenu de Solidarité Active, RSA). Aside from more assistance with job search, the main change introduced under the RSA was to allow recipients to combine government benefits with earnings from employment, with the goal of ensuring that there would always be a significant financial gain from working, even in a part-time, minimum-wage position. The RSA also made subsidies available to offset the costs associated with working, such as transportation and childcare.

Barely one year into his presidency, Sarkozy's commitment to liberal reform was tested by the 2008 financial crisis. To be fair, the crisis challenged liberal economic beliefs and policies everywhere, especially given that the crisis centered, at least initially, on the exemplars of the neo-liberal model, the USA and UK. To address the crisis, governments of all political stripes intervened in a variety of ways, launching stimulus packages, rescuing financial institutions that posed "systemic risk," and bailing out strategic sectors, notably the auto industry. Sarkozy was no exception.

Like the leaders of most other leading countries, Sarkozy engaged in deficit spending. A €26 billion package, announced in December 2008, emphasized investment in public infrastructure and aid to small business (OECD 2009). Sarkozy also primed the pump through tax cuts. He initially announced a one-year holiday for the local business tax (*taxe professionnelle*), then decided to eliminate the tax altogether as of 2010, saving French businesses between €7.8 and €8.2 billion per year (Guené 2012: 17).

Sarkozy likewise hewed to a common pattern by bailing out companies that were too big to fail or posed a systemic risk, notably in the banking sector (Massoc and Jabko 2012; Woll 2014). In October 2008, the French government joined with the Belgian and Luxembourg governments to rescue Dexia, the leading lender to local authorities in France and Belgium, at a cost of €6.8 billion (€3 billion from France). The government also orchestrated a merger and injected €5 billion into two French banks, the Caisse d'Epargne and Banque Populaire, that had been brought to their knees by exposure to the US subprime market and the collapse of Lehman Brothers.

On a grander scale, in October 2008, Sarkozy announced a €360 billion rescue package for the banking industry as a whole (OECD 2009). The package included €40 billion in fresh capital to bolster the solvency of France's leading banks and €320 billion in loan guarantees to improve liquidity and lending. That said, in comparative perspective, this rescue package was not terribly distinctive or large. Germany committed €480 billion and the UK €382 billion to their respective financial institutions (*Libération*, February 9, 2009).

The Sarkozy administration also intervened to help the French auto industry (Clift 2013; Greciano 2010). In early 2009, the government provided €7.8 billion in subsidized loans to the main domestic manufacturers (Renault, Peugeot, Citroën, Renault Trucks) along with their subcontractors. The government extended further support to the industry through a French version of "cash for clunkers" programs seen in the USA and Germany, offering rebates of up to €1,000 for the replacement of cars older than ten years with new, fuel-efficient models. Once again, though, France was not alone in rescuing an auto industry deemed too big to fail. The USA likewise supported domestic auto manufacturers through a combination of capital injections and incentives for new car purchases.

Sarkozy went well beyond measures to stabilize a French economy in crisis, however. What distinguished him from other leaders and made him a fair-weather liberal was that he took the crisis as an opportunity to pivot away from his initial cautious liberalism and embrace state direction of the economy. Sarkozy heaped scorn on the neoliberal model, railing against the *laissez-faire* excesses of the neoliberal age. In his first public speech following the outbreak of the crisis, he pronounced the neoliberal model dead: "*Laissez-faire* is over. The market that is always right is over" (Sarkozy 2008). Sarkozy denounced unchecked speculation by financial institutions, the excessive pay of executive and traders, and the provision of golden parachutes to CEOs who had ruined their companies. Sarkozy sought not only to tame the market, but also to rehabilitate the state, calling for "a new balance between the State and the market" (Sarkozy 2008). Sarkozy demanded no less than a "refounding of capitalism," starting with a global summit "to go back to square one with the global financial and monetary system, just like we did at Bretton Woods after World War II" (Sarkozy 2008).

Sarkozy's embrace of statism was more than verbal. In addition, he undertook a revival of voluntarist industrial policy. Some industrial policy initiatives were attached to the bailouts. The government did not just recapitalize French automakers, for example, but also sought to shape their long-term competitive strategies. The vast majority of the subsidized loans that Sarkozy provided to the automakers (€6.5 billion out of €7.8 billion) were earmarked for the development of clean hybrid and electric vehicles (French Presidency 2009). The government favored clean vehicles for economic as well as environmental reasons, seeing them as a potential growth industry and source of high-tech jobs and exports. In other words, Sarkozy's administration was using its leverage to try to make automakers invest in what it judged to be the automotive markets of the future.

Sarkozy also imposed social quid pro quos on French automakers. In return for the subsidized loans, auto manufacturers were barred from making any layoffs for one year or closing any factories in France for the duration of the loans (*Libération*, February 11, 2009). As Sarkozy put it, "We are going to mobilize a lot of money" to save the French auto industry, "but we will battle to ensure that the [production] sites that represent French identity are preserved" (*Libération*, January 15, 2009).

The government's rescue of the financial sector likewise went beyond the prevention of bankruptcy. Sarkozy took advantage of the crisis to install loyalists at the helm of several of France's leading financial institutions, including Société Générale and the Franco-Belgian Dexia (Clift 2013; Massoc and Jabko 2012). The most egregious case involved Sarkozy's chief economic adviser, François Pérol. Pérol organized the merger between Caisses d'Epargne and Banque Populaire along with the injection of €5 billion in fresh capital by the state. In defiance of deontological standards and French conflict of interest laws, Sarkozy then appointed Pérol as CEO of the new Banque Populaire Caisses d'Epargne (BPCE) (*Libération*, February 24, 2009).

Sarkozy also used the bank recapitalization program for industrial policy purposes, most notably for bolstering the international presence of BNP Paribas. In spring 2009, BNP Paribas CEO, Michel Pébereau, requested that the government speed up delivery of the second tranche of state financial support. Sarkozy, who was close to Pébereau, approved the request. The day after the second tranche arrived, BNP Paribas announced that it was buying the subsidiaries of Fortis bank in Belgium and Luxembourg, making it the largest bank in the eurozone. Thus, French state aid had served not just to save BNP Paribas from bankruptcy, but also to underwrite the bank's aggressive international expansion plan to pick up bargains during the crisis. As a scholar of France's economic patriotism notes, "French state actors were keen not to waste a good crisis and took advantage of the opportunities to advance international champions" (Clift 2013: 114). Interestingly, with Sarkozy's support, BNP Paribas did exactly what French authorities have been so worried that foreign companies might do in France – buy up undervalued national champions on the cheap during an economic crisis.

The most striking evidence of Sarkozy's statist turn was his creation of three new industrial policy programs. In November 2008, Sarkozy announced the establishment of the Strategic Investment Fund (Fonds Stratégique d'Investissement, FSI), modeled on the sovereign wealth funds of several foreign countries (Greciano 2010). The FSI was given €20 billion in capital to invest in companies that are critical to the competitiveness of the French economy based on their potential for growth, technological mastery, savoir-faire, export potential, or brand value. In a neo-mercantilist tilt, Sarkozy also charged the FSI with protecting "companies that may become the prey of [foreign] predators" (*Le Monde*, October 25, 2008).

One year later, the government launched the Grand National Loan (Grand Emprunt National). Sarkozy commissioned a study by two former prime ministers, one on the right (Alain Juppé) and one on the left (Michel Rocard), to identify priority measures for promoting French industry (Greciano 2010). Based on the recommendations of Juppé and Rocard, Sarkozy launched a state loan campaign in November 2009 to raise €35 billion. At that time, the Grand National Loan was renamed Investments in the Future Program (Programme d'Investissements d'Avenir, PIA), emphasizing how the money was spent, as opposed to how it was raised. Of the €35 billion in the PIA, €11 billion went to help five to ten institutions of higher education reach world-class level, €7.9 billion to promote technology transfer from research to industry, €6.5 billion to support industrial small- and medium-sized enterprises (SMEs), €5.1 billion to fund sustainable development initiatives, and €4.5 billion to encourage France's transition to a digital economy (French Ministry of the Economy and Finance 2012).

In November 2009, the government convened a series of meetings, the Estates General of Industry (Etats Généraux de l'Industrie), to analyze the problems of French industry. At the conclusion of the Estates General in March 2010, Sarkozy announced over €1 billion in new aid, declaring "France must keep its factories; France must keep its instruments of production" (*Libération*, March 4, 2010). The government also spelled out a series of specific targets in the purest 1960s industrial policy style. These targets included increasing industrial production by 25 percent in five years, boosting France's share of European industry by 2 percent by 2015, sustaining employment in industry at existing levels, and returning to a trade surplus in manufactured goods (excluding energy) by 2015 (French Presidency 2010).

While all the major Organisation for Economic Co-operation and Development (OECD) countries suffered deep economic trauma in 2008, only Sarkozy took this trauma as an opportunity to rehabilitate the statist model. A fair-weather liberal, Sarkozy shifted on a dime from the cautious liberalism of his first year in office to a full-throated embrace of statism. Sarkozy denounced neoliberal capitalism in hellfire-and-brimstone terms. He called for a new economic order, characterized by a greater role for the state in regulating capitalism. Sarkozy also turned bailouts into an instrument of industrial policy, pushing the auto industry to invest in green technologies and underwriting the international expansion of one of France's largest financial institutions. Most strikingly, Sarkozy launched several industrial policy programs wrapped in the kind of *dirigiste* discourse not heard in decades.

Ironically, some of the same legacies of France's break with the *dirigiste* model that impeded liberal economic reforms also impeded Sarkozy's effort to revive voluntarist industrial policy. The most important such legacy was the expansion of the social anesthesia state, which deprived the government of the fiscal means to finance hefty new programs. As a result, Sarkozy's main industrial policy initiatives were constructed with an eye to limiting the government's financial outlays.

For example, the aid to the auto industry consisted of loans, not grants or subsidies.

Even when Sarkozy provided fresh capital, the money did not necessarily come from the budget. The first €10.5 billion capital infusion for French banks was provided by the state's allied financial institution, the Deposits and Consignments Fund (Caisse des Dépôts et Consignations, CDC). The CDC also paid one-half of the €20 billion cost of the FSI. The CDC receives cheap capital, primarily in the form of tax-exempt funds collected by savings banks and post offices. In return, it performs various public missions, most notably funding the construction of public housing and acting as a long-term investor in many of France's most prominent companies (including about one-half of the CAC 40 [Cotation Assistée en Continu], or the benchmark 40 equities listed on the Paris stock exchange).

The state's fiscal bind likewise shaped the €35 billion PIA. The PIA was launched precisely because government authorities feared that they would be unable to preserve public investment in an economic downturn (interview by author with Emmanuel Moulin, Economic Adviser to the President, April 11, 2011). Sarkozy's special adviser, Henri Guaino, who was widely depicted as the architect of Sarkozy's statist turn, claimed that the PIA was designed to safeguard public investment against the growing demands of the social anesthesia state:

> We needed to de-budgetize investment. Social spending was crowding out investment. If we left investment in the budget, it would become the adjustment variable crowded out by other priorities. (Interview by author with Henri Guaino, Special Adviser to the President, April 13, 2011)

Guaino wanted the PIA to be a €100 billion initiative, but in another sign of the government's limited financial resources, Sarkozy cut the figure by two-thirds to €35 billion (Duval 2009; Poncins 2009). Moreover, the Grand National Loan, as the program was originally called, was financed through long-term borrowing, rather than direct outlays. In addition, the initiative provided for less new spending than the €35 billion price tag indicated. Some €19 billion of the €35 billion was committed to higher education at a time when the government was reducing educational spending and employment from year to year. In practice, according to a parliamentary report, much of the PIA spending simply filled the holes caused by cuts in the government's regular budgets (Claeys et al. 2011). Sarkozy's plan to revive French manufacturing was even more tightfisted. Despite the ambitious objectives (increasing industrial production by 25 percent in five years, returning to a trade surplus in manufacturing, etc.), the administration committed a paltry €1 billion to the undertaking.

The combination of the Great Recession and Sarkozy's spending programs sent French debt and deficits skyward. The deterioration of French public finances raised concerns that government debt was reaching an unsustainable level, while the ongoing Greek sovereign debt crisis offered a searing lesson in the perils of excessive indebtedness. In response, Sarkozy shifted policy once again, making deficit reduction his new top priority. Initially, he proposed to meet fiscal targets solely through spending cuts, while avoiding tax increases. In particular, Sarkozy doggedly defended his fiscal shield, which he viewed as *the* defining reform of his administration and a symbol of his commitment to reining in French taxation. Sarkozy drew a line in the sand, declaring that he would not abandon the fiscal shield under any circumstances.

One year later, however, Sarkozy crossed that line. Unable to reduce France's budget deficit sufficiently by spending cuts alone and facing charges of unfairness, Sarkozy reversed course on tax increases. In short order, virtually all of the TEPA tax cuts, including the fiscal shield, were sacrificed. Other taxes were raised as well. An August 2011 austerity plan was the polar opposite of earlier plans that had focused on spending cuts: of the €12 billion in deficit reduction measures, €11 billion came from tax increases (*Le Monde*, November 7, 2011).

Sarkozy's fiscal record in office was scarcely that of a liberal reformer. On his watch, tax revenues went up not down, increasing from 42.5 percent of GDP in 2007 to 44.4 percent of GDP in 2012 (OECD 2021e). Public spending surged even more, from 52.6 percent of GDP in 2007 to 57.1 percent of GDP in 2012 (OECD 2021e), and Sarkozy left office with a budget deficit of 5 percent of GDP. While the 2008 crisis was partly to blame, so too was Sarkozy's response – a revival of statist industrial policy and an inability or unwillingness to reduce public spending. Other advanced economies were hit hard by the 2008 crisis, yet these countries did not embrace statist industrial policy, and they brought spending and budget deficits under control much more quickly than France. By contrast, the French right's fair-weather liberalism was cast aside in a crisis.

Sarkozy's notoriously mercuric personality was certainly part of the reason for his statist turn. Sarkozy was more of an activist than an ideologue (Allègre and Montalvon 2012; Cohen 2008; Nay 2012). He was often referred to as the "omnipresident" or "hyperpresident" for his perpetual activism and micromanagement (Foucault 2007). What mattered to Sarkozy was making bold decisions, whatever their nature. When the situation seemed to call for liberal economic reform, Sarkozy was a liberal activist, and when it seemed to call for statist reform, he was a statist activist. Activism, not neoliberalism, was Sarkozy's North Star.

That said, Sarkozy is not the only French leader to have jettisoned liberal economic principles in a crisis. As described, Giscard did much the same in the 1970s. Moreover, as Chapter 7 relates, France's current president, Emmanuel Macron, who came to power with a reputation as a liberal reformer, made a similar statist turn in response to the COVID-19 crisis. With three different presidents having responded to economic crises in much the same way, it is clear that fair-weather liberalism stems from more than personal foibles of this or that leader. Rather, it reflects the tenuous commitment of France's ostensibly promarket reformers to liberal economic principles and their penchant for turning to statist remedies in times of crisis.

3.6   Conclusion

Postwar French conservatism was fashioned in the crucible of the *dirigiste* model and Gaullist nationalism. It was also marked by the May 1968 upheaval that nearly toppled the regime. Although the French right has changed over the years, the legacies of the past have continued to weigh on its economic and social policy and to fuel the contestation of economic liberalization. An enduring Gaullist, nationalist approach to the economy has led French conservatives to restrict foreign ownership of cherished national champions, whether via the *noyaux durs* of the Chirac–Balladur privatizations or an increasingly lengthy list of sectors that require foreign bidders to obtain French government approval for any takeover. The shadows of protest against the Gaullist and *dirigiste* regime also remain salient. Fearing another May 1968, cautious liberalizers like Edouard Balladur have backed down in the face of strikes and demonstrators. The problem of this cautious tack is that it has tended to encourage further popular contestation by opponents of the government's agenda, who understand that they can prevail provided that they cause enough disruption.

The French right's discourse on economic reform has likewise contributed to contestation. The right's inability to formulate a legitimating discourse for France's economic liberalization and its blame-shifting to Brussels have delegitimated both liberalization and European integration. In 1995, Chirac profited from the weak legitimacy of economic liberalization by campaigning for president on a statist agenda and denouncing his rival, Balladur, for supposed subservience to *la pensée unique*. However, Chirac was then impaled on his own anti-liberal rhetoric when he attempted to pivot back to an orthodox fiscal policy to enable France to qualify for the EMU. Chirac was also impaled on the blame-shifting rhetoric of French politicians, who persistently blamed

Brussels for unpopular decisions. His evocation of the EMU as justification for austerity measures failed to move French voters, who saw little reason for further sacrifices on behalf of a European project that many French politicians, Chirac among them, had portrayed as a Trojan horse for neoliberalism.

Finally, the French right's shaky, fair-weather liberalism has repeatedly dissipated in hard economic times. The Organization of Petroleum Exporting Countries (OPEC) oil shocks of the 1970s prompted Giscard and Barre to multiply bailouts of uncompetitive enterprises in order to preserve employment. Similarly, the 2008 financial crisis led Sarkozy to abandon his initial liberalization and embrace statist solutions. Sarkozy responded to the crisis by launching an array of statist initiatives: imposing industrial strategies on the automotive industry; placing allies at the helm of major financial institutions; creating a sovereign wealth fund to invest in French companies; establishing a program to invest in innovative industries and universities; and setting targets for industrial production, employment, and market share in the purest 1960s style. As Chapter 7 relates, Macron has likewise responded in a statist and voluntarist fashion to the COVID-19 crisis, illustrating the persistence of fair-weather liberalism among France's ostensibly promarket reformers.

4   Skinny Politics
Reforming Alone

Chapters 2 and 3 analyzed the policy and party-political reasons why economic liberalization is so contested in France. This chapter turns to the institutional reasons. The striking feature of French economic reform is that governments almost always act alone. French reform is invariably conducted on the basis of what might be called "skinny politics." Whereas many governments tackling sensitive and contentious reform have sought allies, whether the political opposition or the trade unions, in order to build a broad basis of support and defuse opposition, French governments have pursued reform on the basis of the narrowest or skinniest majority possible. No major initiative to reduce social spending or make labor markets more flexible has been enacted on the basis of an all-party agreement. On the contrary, governments of the left and right alike have relied heavily on strong-arm provisions that allow for the enactment of legislation with little or no input from parliament. They have shown the same disdain for the social partners, pursuing reforms via top-down imposition, as opposed to negotiations.

This chapter demonstrates how skinny politics has fueled contestation and impeded the pursuit of liberalizing reform. Section 4.1 discusses the literature on the conditions that permit controversial reform, particularly welfare reform. This literature emphasizes the need for reformers to avoid or share blame by reaching out to the political opposition and/or social partners. Section 4.2 relates that France's postwar *dirigiste* policymaking system was organized on the exact opposite set of principles, emphasizing the concentration of power in the state and the marginalization of societal actors. The establishment of the Fifth Republic in 1958 accentuated this exclusionary orientation by creating a powerful president, backed by an arsenal of weapons to control the legislature, who has little need to work with the political opposition. Section 4.3 focuses on a missed opportunity to bring the social partners into the heart of the reform process through the so-called Social Refoundation. The Social Refoundation aimed to overhaul French labor markets and the welfare state on the basis of bilateral negotiations between employers and reformist unions, but was undermined by governments of both the left and the right. Finally, Section 4.4 shows that the reliance on skinny politics by the right following the demise of the Social Refoundation produced inadequate half-measures that failed to resolve the problems that had motivated reform in the first place. A comparison of pension reform in France and Sweden further illustrates the limitations of the skinny French approach as a strategy of economic liberalization.

4.1   The Politics of Blame Avoidance

Liberalizing reforms that reduce welfare benefits and labor market protections are invariably contentious. In a pathbreaking analysis of welfare retrenchment in the USA and UK under Ronald Reagan and Margaret Thatcher respectively, Paul Pierson describes powerful obstacles to such initiatives (Pierson 1994). Pierson identifies two main reasons why it is so difficult to cut social spending, even for leaders like Reagan and Thatcher who were elected on pledges to do just that.

The first reason is that retrenchment generally imposes immediate, direct costs on specific groups in return for diffuse, long-term, and uncertain benefits for the population as a whole. Consequently, opponents of program cuts have much stronger incentives to mobilize than supporters. They stand to suffer significant losses: their pensions will shrink; their guarantee of affordable health care may be taken away. These are important issues. People will take to the streets to prevent such losses. Many of the biggest demonstrations in Western Europe have occurred in response to proposed welfare state cuts, such as the Berlusconi pension reforms in Italy in 1994 and the Juppé Social Security Plan in France in 1995 (Baccaro and Locke 1996; Bonoli 1997). In both of these instances, the government was forced to withdraw its proposed reforms. Even in the USA, the public pension system, Social Security, is commonly referred to as the "third rail" of American politics – touch it, and you die.

In contrast to targets of cutbacks, the average taxpayer has little to gain from social program cuts. While the costs of retrenchment are concentrated on certain groups, the benefits are diffused throughout society. For the average citizen, welfare cuts may diminish taxes and Social Security charges a little bit, but not significantly. These kinds of small savings do not provide much incentive for mobilizing. Not many people are going to take to the streets to cut their tax bills by a few euro per month.

The second reason why welfare retrenchment is so difficult, according to Pierson, is that reformers confront powerful legacies from the past. Postwar welfare programs have reshaped the terrain on which contemporary reformers operate. In particular, they have created powerful "policy-takers," that is, interest groups created by the existence of a policy, who have a shared interest in the preservation and expansion of this policy (Kocka 1981; Offe 1981, 1985; Skocpol 1992).

Two sets of policy-takers bolster the welfare state against would-be budget-cutters. The first consists of the recipients of government services and transfer payments, such as pensioners, patients, the disabled, and the unemployed. These groups may tap additional support from family members, whose burden is lessened by social programs, or from citizens who know that they too are likely to benefit some day from these programs. For example, just about everyone expects to eventually retire and receive a pension. The second set of policy-takers consists of the providers of social services, such as physicians, nurses, childcare and elderly care workers, and assistants to the disabled. These service providers can be expected to resist retrenchment out of a combination of belief in their missions and defense of their budgets and incomes. Since many providers are highly skilled professionals, who are seen as committed to the public good, their views are often more credible with the public than those of the budget-cutters.

Taking a step back, Pierson contends that the contemporary period is marked by a "new politics of the welfare state" that impedes efforts at retrenchment (Pierson 1996, 2001a). Whereas the expansion of the welfare state during the postwar boom may have driven primarily by the strength of parties of the left and trade unions, proponents of retrenchment today confront a much more complex political environment. Their decisions are constrained by the need to honor the pledges of previous governments (for example, that health care will be provided to all citizens at little or no cost or that public pensions will be available when workers retire) and by the new interest groups that have arisen around existing social programs (policy-takers). Thus, when it comes to the defense of the welfare state, pensioners, patients, doctors, nurses, and social workers may be just as important as left parties and trade unions.

Pierson's logic can also be extended to labor market reform. Changes to introduce more "flexibility" into the labor market typically impose concentrated cuts on employees, such as weaker job protections or lower wages, in the hope that such cuts will lead to the creation of more jobs. Reforms along these lines have rarely gained the support of job holders or those aspiring to hold jobs, at least in France. As related in Chapter 2, initiatives to create a lower minimum wage for youths (SMIC-jeunes) in 1994 and a less protective First Employment Contract (Contrat Première Embauche, CPE) in 2006 were conceived of as ways to promote youth employment. If employers could pay lower wages to young workers or lay them off more easily should the arrangement not pan out, they would be more willing to give youths a chance. Yet young people, the purported beneficiaries of these initiatives, were the ones who spearheaded the French protests. Rightly or wrongly, they identified not as currently unemployed workers desperate for any kind of job, but rather as future employed workers, who feared being relegated to a new underclass. In response to youth-led protests, governments in both instances eventually withdrew their proposals.

Given the depth of opposition to welfare and labor market retrenchment, Pierson notes that navigating such reform is generally an exercise in blame avoidance or blame-sharing, as opposed to credit-claiming. Governments are no longer extending popular new benefits, as during the postwar "golden age" of rapid economic growth and welfare state expansion. Instead, they are engaging in unpopular and contested efforts to curtail those benefits. They, therefore, try to either hide what they are doing from the public eye or share the blame with other actors.

Pierson describes several techniques of obfuscation designed to mask the government's responsibility for program cuts. The most important such technique, which Pierson refers to as "decrementalism," is to shift to a less generous indexation formula, such as indexing pensions to inflation instead of wages. Because pensions are growing at the rate of inflation, governments can argue that they are still increasing pensions, even if pensions are increasing less rapidly than if they had remained indexed to wages. Moreover, in any given year, the difference between the two indexation formulae is relatively small, of the order of 1 or 2 percent. Over time, however, the cuts compound and become quite significant. Using such techniques, pension promises in European Union (EU) countries were reduced by about one-quarter during a two-decade period from the mid-1980s to the mid-2000s (Glennerster 2010). The first important pension reform in France, Prime Minister Balladur's 1993 initiative described in Chapter 3, included a shift in pension indexation from wages to prices.

Another way to hide the government's responsibility is to compel other actors to do the cutting. The 1996 welfare reform in the USA is a classic example. Instead of guaranteeing federal funding for all welfare recipients, the government transferred block grants to the fifty states and left it to them to establish funding levels. Given that the block grants were not even indexed to inflation, the amount of federal support eroded in real terms year after year. Yet it was up to the states, rather than the federal government, to make the necessary program cuts to manage with diminishing federal support. The government's hope was that any political heat over welfare program cuts would be directed at state authorities, rather than federal authorities.

A third strategy for dealing with the unpopularity of retrenchment is to divide and conquer by imposing welfare cuts on some groups, while sparing others or even providing them additional benefits. For example, the Thatcher government sold public housing at a steep discount to renters, and this side-payment split the natural constituency for increased spending on housing policy. Those who purchased their homes were unaffected by and, therefore, less likely to resist the cuts in housing allowances or increases in rents that the government imposed on those who remained in public housing.

Another divide-and-conquer technique is the delayed implementation of cuts. So-called grandfather clauses are an especially common technique to defuse popular opposition, especially in the case of pension reform. Typically, existing workers and those approaching retirement are exempted from new, less generous pension rules, which apply only to future hires. Given that negotiations involve present workers, not future workers, exempting the former demobilizes the group that is most likely to protest, while the costs of retrenchment fall on workers not yet hired (or, in some cases, born) who, for obvious reasons, are difficult to mobilize. In France, pension reforms are typically phased in, sparing those already retired or near retirement. Another common grandfathering practice has been to allow existing employees in the civil service or public enterprises to retain their privileged labor status, while new employees are hired under less generous, private-sector rules.

Pierson points to several limits and risks of the obfuscation strategy. Changes in indexing take time to cumulate to significant savings and may be reversed by future governments. The same is true of grandfathering, which only generates savings in the distant future and may be reversed or attenuated in the interim. Dividing the opposition through side-payments tends to be effective, but it is also expensive, with the side-payments offsetting much of the savings. Finally, offloading responsibility for program cuts to other actors, such as the fifty states, devolves control, and local authorities may not agree to do the government's bidding; there is also a risk that voters will see through the ploy and blame the national government, irrespective of who does the actual cutting. Taken together, these limitations suggest that techniques of obfuscation offer a less than perfect solution. Obfuscation runs the risk of being exposed, saddling the government with blame for unpopular reforms, limited financially by the cost of side-payments, and attenuated or reversed by future governments. Obfuscation also violates norms of democratic accountability since the fundamental purpose is to hide the government's responsibility for controversial reforms from public view.

An alternative to this top-down, go-it-alone approach is to open up the reform process by expanding the circle of participants to include the political opposition or social partners. These actors are the most inclined to mobilize against reform, whether out of dislike of benefit cuts or a desire to score political points against the government. For this reason, if the government can involve them in the reform process, it may be able to preempt contestation, ensuring that its reforms are not defeated by strikes or demonstrations.

Of course, there are downsides to this maximum-winning-coalition approach. For one thing, negotiations can take a long time. The Swedish pension reform of 1998, admittedly a major overhaul, was some fifteen years in the making. In addition, governments must tender concessions to the opposition or the social partners in order to gain their support. In the case of pension reform, for example, unions tend to demand that the new rules be grandfathered, that high-income employees pay a greater share of the costs than low-income employees, and that those who started working earliest in life (mostly unskilled, manual laborers, who began their careers during or shortly after high school) be allowed to retire early if they have paid into the system for a requisite number of years.[1] Still, these delays and concessions seem to be the cost of doing retrenchment business. Welfare scholars note that most major pension and health-care reforms have been enacted on the basis of some kind of agreement between the government and the opposition or between the government and the social partners (Hinrichs 2000, 2010; Palier 2003b; Schludi 2003, 2005).

The Swedish pension reform is perhaps the paradigmatic case of the promise of widening the circle of participants (Anderson 2001; Anderson and Meyer 2003; Palme and Wennemo 1998; Scherman 1999; Wadensjö 1999). As noted, the reform took fifteen years to negotiate, but the process yielded an all-party agreement that was also supported by nation's largest trade union, the Swedish Trade Union Confederation (Landsorganisationen i Sverige, LO). More important, it created what many pension scholars and politicians regard as the model pension system (World Bank 1994). The new Swedish pension system is a points-based regime that treats all contributors equally: 1 Swedish krona paid into the system yields the same number of points, regardless of who is contributing.

The Swedish pension regime is more sustainable as well as equitable. The value of points is adjusted automatically, via the "automatic balancing mechanism," also known as the "brake," depending on demography and economic growth rates. As a result, Swedish governments are not required to constantly tinker with the system to keep it in balance (although, in response to severe economic downturns like that of 2008, the government has limited the immediate decline in pensions by spreading the effects of the "brake" over several years).

The Swedish pension system has become the model that many other countries, including France, seek to emulate. Meanwhile, despite seven, mostly top-down, efforts to reform the pension system since 1993, the French system remains highly fragmented, treats some groups far more generously than others, and is operating in the red. Indeed, the goal of the unsuccessful Macron pension reform of 2019, which is discussed in Chapter 6, was to merge France's forty-two different pension systems into a single points-based regime, modeled on that of Sweden.

The Swedish pension reform is an extreme, but not an isolated, example. The Italian pension reform of the 1990s, which also reduced many inequities and laid the foundation for a points-based system, was negotiated between technocratic or left-leaning governments and the trade unions, then ratified by a vote of the union membership (Baccaro and Locke 1996). Even in the USA, the last major Social Security reform in 1983 was drafted by a blue-ribbon panel headed by future Federal Reserve Chair, Alan Greenspan, then enacted via a bipartisan agreement between the Democrats and Republicans.

The concertational approach has also proven its mettle as a means for overhauling labor markets. The transformation of the so-called Dutch disease into the "Dutch miracle" or "Dutch model" (OECD 1998; Visser and Hemerijck 1997) occurred on the basis of a foundational labor market agreement in 1982, the Wassenaar Accord. The agreement committed Dutch unions to accepting the wage restraint necessary to revive corporate profits and investment in return for a slightly shorter workweek and is credited with having launched Holland's economic turnaround. While the initial deal favored business and was signed by the unions only in response to a thinly veiled threat by a right-wing government to pursue a Thatcherite approach to industrial relations if wages were not brought under control, the terms became more balanced as the Dutch economy revived and the governing coalition shifted to the left. During the 1990s, when Holland was governed by a Labor Party-led "purple coalition" (combining the red of Labor with the blue of the Liberal Party), the unions agreed to continue restraining wages, despite tight labor markets, in return for employee payroll and income tax cuts that significantly increased take-home pay. Other agreements facilitated the hiring of fixed-term and temporary employees in return for guaranteeing those employees the same hourly wages and benefits as full-time workers.

The Dutch industrial relations model was not an isolated incident. Martin Rhodes describes an analogous development across much of Southern and peripheral Europe in the 1990s. In a process that he labels "competitive corporatism," governments and the social partners negotiated far-reaching reforms of the welfare state, fiscal policy, and labor market regulations (Rhodes 2001). Echoing the seminal work of Philippe Schmitter and Wolfgang Streeck (Schmitter 1979; Streeck and Schmitter 1985), Rhodes suggests that competitive corporatism offers an alternative form of governance for countries seeking to overhaul dysfunctional labor markets and welfare states, while steering clear of the divisive and polarizing approach associated with Thatcherism.

Paradoxically, then, in a world of blame avoidance, expanding the sphere of participants often produces the most far-reaching reforms. Agreements with the opposition and social partners may involve tortuous negotiations, but they reduce the likelihood of protest, so that the announced reforms can actually be implemented. Concertational processes also spread the blame for unpopular retrenchment measures, providing political cover for reformers pursuing bold changes like the Swedish pension reform or the Dutch Wassenaar Accord. Governments are less likely to be punished at the polls if the opposition is equally complicit in painful changes. Finally, from a democratic perspective, negotiated reforms bring retrenchment into the open, making it less conspiratorial and more transparent and participatory.

The retrenchment literature thus identifies two main pathways of reform (Levy 2010). The first is a top-down, semi-conspiratorial approach that tries to hide what the government is doing through a variety of practices, including technical adjustments that are not easily understood, devolution of responsibility for program cuts to other actors, and grandfathering to impose costs on future groups that are not yet fully formed and, therefore, unable to mobilize. The second pathway is a more inclusive approach that incorporates a range of stakeholders beyond the governing majority. The first approach has tended to generate targeted, limited reforms and is vulnerable to protest by unions and policy-takers who see through the government's obfuscation. The second approach, while slow and cumbersome at times, has been the primary source of far-reaching systemic reforms that produce a major shift in the nature of the welfare state or the labor market. *What is striking about the French case is that when it comes to controversial welfare or labor market reform, governments have relied almost exclusively on the first approach, on skinny politics, while foreswearing concertation with opposition parties or the social partners.* The following section explains why French authorities have gravitated toward the skinny-politics approach.

4.2   Concentrated Power, Concentrated Blame

Arguably, no democracy in the world is less suited to the politics of blame avoidance than France. Instead of sharing power, the French system concentrates power in the executive branch. It places the executive above the legislature, the government above the opposition, and the state above society, thereby dissuading authorities from pursuing reform on the basis of broad political or social coalitions. The tendency of French reformers to go it alone stems from three sources: (1) the republican model; (2) the *dirigiste* economic model; (3) the institutions of the Fifth Republic.

4.2.1 The Republican Model

The "republican model" dates back to the French Revolution of 1789 (Cole et al. 2003). In the republican conception, all citizens are created equal and are members of a national political community. They owe their allegiance to the nation as a whole, rather than to local or religious communities, ethnic groups, or producer and labor associations. Interest groups are regarded as the bearers of particularistic agendas, who have little regard for the common good.

Interest groups also pose a threat to national identity and cohesion. They promote economic, religious, or ethnic identity at the expense of national identity. The principal mass opposition to the Revolution of 1789 came from the Church and practicing Catholics, who took up arms against the secular agenda of the revolutionaries.

From the republican perspective, intermediary associations are not to be trusted. This distrust of interest groups is exemplified by Le Chapelier Laws enacted in 1791, which banned most intermediary associations, such as guilds and trade unions, for nearly a century. Nor is this distrust confined to the distant past. Even today, French law bars the state from collecting ethnic, racial, or religious data on its citizens. Part of the reason is to prevent state authorities from engaging in discrimination, a response to the abuses of the Vichy regime during World War II. That said, the ban is also motivated by the belief that such data are not needed, since the "universal" or "colorblind" republic treats all citizens equally. Indeed, from the republican perspective, collecting and disseminating ethnic, racial, or religious data could even be harmful by encouraging dangerous group identification at the expense of national integration.

French scholars from Alexis de Tocqueville to Michel Crozier have lamented the subordination of societal and local interests to the central state (Crozier 1964, 1970, 1979; Tocqueville 1955, 1969). Interest groups and local authorities have met with broad and sustained suspicion. At best, they have been regarded as "private wills" in a political culture that values the "general will," a common good believed to exist above and beyond the vector sum of the partial interests composing French society. At worst, they have been branded *corporatiste*, a characteristically French conception of the term, denoting parasitic, protected groups, who receive undeserved advantages at the expense of the common good.

4.2.2   *The* Dirigiste *Model*

France's postwar *dirigiste* or state-led economic model took this historic concentration of power in the central state to new heights (Levy 1999b, 2000). The *dirigiste* system – often described as Colbertiste in reference to the mercantilist finance minister of Louis XIV, Jean-Baptiste Colbert – was forged on the presumption that the state represented an oasis of enlightenment and integrity amidst a desert of selfish, narrow-minded societal actors: a "Malthusian" or risk-averse employer class that was more interested in preserving family control than in expanding profits and market share; *corporatiste*, self-serving trade unions and other interest groups; and parochial and change-resistant local authorities. In a fusion of the Rousseauian notion of the "general will" with a Saint-Simonian faith in enlightened technocratic leadership, state officials based their strategy on the premise that rapid economic development could be pursued most effectively without the participation of narrow interest associations that might stand in the way of rationality and modernization. "Private wills" could not be allowed to impede "the general will."

Given France's unpromising societal materials, state technocrats felt justified in their *dirigiste* outlook – in pursuing the "general will" without or even against the bearers of "partial wills." One can, of course, debate the merits of this position. To the charges of Malthusianism and *corporatisme*, critics of state intervention since Tocqueville have responded with indictments of stifling statism. French civil society is weak, they maintain, because state officials will not let it develop, preferring to monopolize power and clamp down on autonomous initiatives. It is Colbert who has created Malthus. If the state were less invasive and more willing to share its authority, groups in French civil society would learn to exercise power responsibly.

Whether it was Malthus who created Colbert or Colbert who created Malthus, the hallmark of the postwar *dirigiste* system came to be a concentration of authority in Parisian ministries, with minimal input from societal and local organizations. The initial Liberation-era hopes for a new, more cooperative system of industrial relations, for example, quickly gave way to a set of policy arrangements in which organized labor was reduced to the role of disgruntled spectator. This shift resulted from a number of factors: the pervasive distrust between French employers and unions; the weakness and divisions among French unions; the radicalization of the largest union, the communist General Labor Confederation

(Confédération Générale du Travail, CGT), with the ramping up of the Cold War; and perhaps most important, a fundamental disagreement over economic and social priorities, with planners and industrialists favoring corporate investment, while union officials sought to alleviate pent-up consumer demand and to repair a damaged and underdeveloped social infrastructure (Kuisel 1981). There was plenty of blame for all parties, from *dirigiste* technocrats, to Malthusian employers, to politicized and *corporatiste* union officials. Whatever the exact balance of causes and responsibilities, within a few years after the Liberation, French unions were essentially absent from the policymaking scene.

The collective organizations of business fared scarcely any better. Many of these associations had originated as recession cartels under the Third Republic, restraining and coordinating production to prop up prices, and remained faithful to their Malthusian founding mission. They represented a segment of French industry, small- and medium-sized enterprises (SMEs), that was widely regarded as hopelessly backwards (Piore and Sabel 1984). What is more, they tended to view the state as the enemy, the source of their problems, with its excessive spending and commitment to market opening (Brizay 1975; Bunel and Saglio 1979; Ehrmann 1957). State officials returned the disdain and focused their attentions on an alternative set of interlocutors. The overriding share of subsidies and cheap credit were channeled to "national champions," a select group of multinationals, constructed through a series of mergers, with whom planners could negotiate directly. Once again, the logic of both Colbert and Malthus pointed in the same direction: an organized interest – in this case, business associations – became marginalized, not only due to its own incapacity and ambivalence toward state modernization projects, but also as a result of technocratic considerations. From a planner's perspective, it was far easier to implement industrial policy measures through direct negotiations with one or two corporate giants than through bargaining with a weak industry association that had different objectives and could not always control its members.

Economic relations between Parisian technocrats and local elected officials unfolded according to a similar dynamic. Provincial elites were concerned primarily with preserving the stability of the community. They tended to perceive state-sponsored economic development as a threat or nuisance, bringing pollution and Communist voters, rather than a desirable good. Such antipathy did not deter Parisian officials, however. Instead, they intervened directly in the provinces, via technocratic agencies such as the Delegation for the Development of Territory and Regional Action (Délégation à l'Aménagement du Territoire et à l'Action Régionale, DATAR), which encouraged and helped finance the transfer of factories from the Paris region to areas targeted for development. The government also created new institutional channels, most notably regional administrations, to help implement state economic policy at the local level.

Although the statist economic model was largely dismantled in the 1980s and early 1990s, the statist spirit has carried over to social and labor market policy (Levy 2000). France has the most expensive welfare state in the world, and as described in Chapter 2, the dramatic expansion of social spending was driven largely by government efforts to manage the winding down of the *dirigiste* economic model. In addition, while the social partners ostensibly play a leading role in the management of social programs, in most cases, it is state authorities who make critical decisions regarding eligibility rules and contribution and benefit levels. Moreover, the trend of late has been for the state to gain greater control over the Social Security system, particularly in health care and, more recently, unemployment insurance (Bonoli and Palier 1997). Relatedly, while French labor market policy has been liberalized to a degree (Howell 2018), the state still has its hand on critical levers (Howell 1992a, 2009). The state sets a high minimum wage that compresses earnings across the economy, uses the "extension" procedure to generalize agreements in lead sectors to workers throughout the economy, and provides an array of costly subsidies to encourage employers to hire low-wage or hard-to-place workers. Consequently, in contemporary social and labor market policy, as in postwar economic policy, an activist central state makes most of the important decisions, often with little or no input from key stakeholders like the social partners.

4.2.3   The Institutions of the Fifth Republic

The institutions of the Fifth Republic have both empowered and isolated executive leadership. Seeking to break with the inertia and weakness of the Fourth Republic, the framers of the Fifth Republic drafted a number of constitutional features to create a strong president. The president possesses significant powers, including the right to appoint the prime minister (Article 8), organize a referendum (Article 11), dissolve the National Assembly and call new legislative elections (Article 12), and declare a state of emergency (Article 16). A referendum in 1962 bolstered the democratic legitimacy of the president by providing for the direct election of the president via universal suffrage.

Alongside these specific powers, the president was strengthened by the shift from proportional representation (PR) under the Fourth Republic to a two-round, winner-take-all electoral law in both legislative and presidential elections under the Fifth Republic. Whereas the Fourth Republic was governed by shifting coalitions of parties around the center, the two-round, winner-take-all electoral law polarized French representatives into two rival camps. In addition, thanks to the majoritarian element, National Assembly elections tend to produce a clear governing majority, obviating the need for the government to work with the opposition.

The ability of the majority to operate on its own is further bolstered by the absence of a powerful second chamber, like the US Senate or German Bundesrat. The French Senate is elected indirectly, so it does not have the same democratic legitimacy as the president and National Assembly. More important, while the Senate can delay legislation, it cannot prevent legislation from being adopted if the National Assembly votes to override it. In practice, the Senate has tended to operate as a source of expertise and criticism to enhance the quality of National Assembly bills, but in the end, its assent is not required.

Finally, the framers of the Fifth Republic, notably Michel Debré, introduced several provisions, referred to as "rationalized parliamentarism," that were designed to allow the executive to govern even in the absence of a solid legislative majority. Three such provisions figure most prominently: the ordinance procedure (Article 38), the package vote (Article 44.3), and the confidence vote (Article 49.3). All three allow the government to enact legislation quickly and with limited debate or parliamentary input.

Under Article 38, the government can ask the National Assembly to vote on a framework law (*loi d'habilitation* or *loi cadre*) granting it permission to issue ordinances or decrees within a domain defined by the bill. Once the framework bill is passed, the government can issue ordinances that have the force of law and take effect as soon as they are published. The only requirement is that the government go back to the legislature within a time period specified in the initial law (usually from three to eighteen months) and present a single bill to ratify all of the ordinances after the fact. If a bill is not presented by the deadline or if the National Assembly rejects the bill, all of the ordinances cease to operate, and the law reverts to the status quo ante. The advantage of the ordinance procedure for the government is that instead of having to hold a vote for each provision of a complex set of reforms, such as the privatization of a number of French companies or the overhaul of a set of labor market regulations, all that is needed is one vote to authorize the issuing of ordinances and a second vote to ratify all of the ordinances at a later date. Obviously, such a process greatly limits the possibilities for input from the opposition or even National Assembly members in the government's own camp.

Article 44.3 enables the government to limit amendments to its bills by the National Assembly or Senate (Huber 1992, 1996). At any point during the parliamentary debate, the government can call for a so-called package vote (*vote bloqué*). Under the terms of the package vote, the legislative assembly considering a bill must decide by a single vote on all or part of the text under discussion, retaining only the amendments proposed or accepted by the government. The government decides whether the legislature votes on the original bill, the bill as amended at the time that the package vote is called, or the bill with only the amendments that the government chooses to include. The legislature must support or reject this bill, but it cannot amend the bill. The package vote does not completely shut down the legislative process: even though the bill cannot be modified, all of the amendments on the agenda when the package vote is called must still be debated.

Article 49.3 offers a third way for the government to enact laws quickly and overcome dissent. Although all parliamentary regimes have some kind of confidence vote procedure, Article 49.3 serves primarily to allow French governments to enact legislation without even holding a vote. When the government engages its responsibility, a vote is held only if one-tenth of the members of the National Assembly sponsor a no confidence motion.[2] Assembly members may sponsor only three such motions per legislative session, so they are reluctant to sign up for motions that have little chance of success. As a result, in many instances, important bills become law without so much as a vote by the legislature.

A reform in 2008 did narrow the opportunities for using Article 49.3. The confidence procedure can be deployed without limit to ratify the annual budget and the Social Security spending bill, but beyond those two areas, it can be used only once per parliamentary session. That said, the French legislature typically holds two sessions per year, so there are still many opportunities for the government to use Article 49.3 to ram through important legislation.

The major vulnerability of the president under the Fifth Republic is the possibility of conflicting presidential and legislative majorities, which the French call "cohabitation." Under the original constitution, the president's term in office lasted seven years, while that of the legislature lasted five years, raising the possibility that elections in different years might yield different majorities. From 1958 to 1986, France's president and prime minister were always from the same political coalition. For all intents and purposes, it was the president who was in charge, naming and dismissing prime ministers at his pleasure.

The situation changed in 1986, however. That year, the right won regularly scheduled parliamentary elections, while Socialist President Mitterrand remained in office, with two years left on his seven-year term. As a result, from 1986 to 1988, a Socialist president and a Gaullist prime minister (Jacques Chirac) were forced into an uneasy cohabitation. The right possessed the bulk of the power, but Mitterrand was able to check the right's reforms occasionally and retained some authority, particularly in foreign policy. Subsequent cohabitations occurred from 1993 to 1995 and 1997 to 2002.

Cohabitations weakened presidential leadership in two ways (Levy 1999b; Levy and Skach 2008). The most obvious was when the opposition won legislative elections and selected a prime minister who became the de facto leader of the country. Even in the absence of such a scenario, however, the mere threat of cohabitation could shorten presidential time horizons. In effect, cohabitation meant that there were two ways that the president could lose power: by losing a presidential election or by losing a legislative election. Since these elections were often held in different years, French presidents essentially confronted twice as many chances to lose power as under a typical European parliamentary regime.

Prime ministers under a cohabitation also had short time horizons, since the president possesses the authority to dissolve the National Assembly and call new legislative elections as often as once per year. For example, although the Chirac–Jospin cohabitation lasted a full five years, from 1997 to 2002, Prime Minister Jospin operated under a perpetual sword of Damocles, never knowing whether or when President Chirac might call early elections. Consequently, Jospin was wary of taking any kind of controversial or unpopular action, for fear that a resulting drop in his popularity could lead Chirac to call early elections that would oust him from office.

In order to minimize the likelihood of cohabitations, the left and the right united to pass a constitutional reform in 2000 that shortened the presidential term in office from seven years to five years. Paradoxically, this reform was designed to bolster, not weaken, the president. By aligning the presidential and legislative mandates, newly elected presidents were almost sure to enjoy a full five years before having to face a national election. What is more, to reduce the possibility of split-ticket voting, the legislative elections are held a month or two after the presidential election in the expectation that the voters will validate the presidential election by electing a sympathetic legislative majority.

The expectation of the reformers was borne out in every election after the constitutional amendment went into effect – until 2022. The right won both the presidential and parliamentary elections in 2002 and 2007 and the left won both in 2012. Even in 2017, when Emmanuel Macron was at the helm of a newly created party, his Republic on the Move (La République en Marche, LREM) received a majority in the legislative elections. In 2022, however, Macron was both better known and less popular than in 2017. As discussed in Chapter 7, even though Macron was reelected president, many voters harbored deep misgivings about his agenda. They also wanted him to govern in a less top-down manner and collaborate with other parties. As a result, in the legislative elections, Macron's three-party coalition emerged as the largest group, but was denied an absolute majority. No other group earned a majority either, so the result was not a cohabitation, but rather a hung parliament.

Only time will tell if Macron can find a way to pursue his agenda and what kinds of concessions he might be compelled to make in order to govern. Still, it is important to keep the 2022 legislative elections in perspective. They were very much the exception, not the rule. In all other cases since the 2000 constitutional reform, the institutional logic of the Fifth Republic combined with the sequencing of presidential and legislative elections has given the newly elected president a parliamentary majority for the duration of his presidential term.

4.2.4   Skinny Reform

The combination of republican and *dirigiste* traditions, on the one hand, and political institutions that concentrate power in the executive, on the other hand, has created a seemingly irresistible temptation for French governments to pursue reform in a skinny, top-down manner. Consultation with the social partners tends to be pro forma at best. In many instances, the government prepares reforms behind closed doors before announcing them to the public. Even when the government solicits input from the social partners, its representatives tend to engage in listening exercises, as opposed to negotiating the actual terms of the reform.

Consultation with the legislature and the opposition parties is also limited. Indeed, many of the most important welfare or labor reform initiatives of the past three decades have been enacted via Article 49.3 (confidence vote), Article 44.3 (package vote), or Article 38 (ordinances). A partial list includes the 1993 Balladur pension reform, the 1994 SMIC-jeunes, the 1995 Juppé Social Security Plan, the 2004 Law on the Energy Sector that transformed Gaz de France (GDF) and Electricité de France (EDF) into private companies and opened the French gas and electricity industries to foreign competition, the 2006 CPE, the 2010 and 2013 pension reforms, the 2016 El Khomri labor market reform, the 2017 Pénicaud labor market reform, the 2018 reform transforming the national train agency (Société Nationale des Chemins de Fer Français, SNCF) into a company and moving all new hires from civil service to private contracts, and the 2020 pension reform. The confidence vote, package vote, and ordinance procedure serve to curtail debate and limit parliamentary involvement in the making of legislation. Article 49.3 is also a vehicle for enacting bills when the government has a slim legislative majority and fears defection by members of its coalition. In other words, rather than reach out to the opposition and build a broader coalition, French governments have opted to use Article 49.3 to ram through controversial bills in the face of resistance from not only the opposition, but also members of the government's own majority.

France's insular, top-down policymaking system was well suited to the postwar boom period, when governments were launching heroic industrial policies and establishing popular new social programs (Immergut 1992a, 1992b). When it comes to reforming welfare states and labor markets, however, this approach is highly problematic. Instead of defusing or sharing blame, the skinny French approach concentrates blame. It is the government and the government alone that is responsible for unpopular program cuts or reductions in labor market protections. The government cannot hide behind or share blame with opposition parties or the social partners because these actors have not been brought into the reform process.

Skinny politics also encourages protest. Opposition partners and unions have no stake in government initiatives that do not include them and that harm their members and supporters. On the contrary, for unions in particular, protesting against the government offers a way to signal to members that they are standing up for their interests.

Another reason why skinny politics prompts protest is that alternative channels of influence that operate in other countries are largely nonexistent under the insular French system. It makes no sense to "write your congressman," in the US manner, in a system in which the National Assembly has no significant autonomy and voting is tightly controlled by the government. Nor can opponents of reform place their faith in German-style collective bargaining in a country where unions have few members and are largely excluded from policymaking. Rather, the most effective way to influence the French government is to put large numbers of protestors in the street and shut down critical public services, most notably public transportation and energy, where unions are strongly represented.

Skinny politics is understandably attractive to French reformers. The shortest distance between two points would seem to be to skip negotiations with prickly political opponents and social partners, instead imposing reforms from above. France's republican and *dirigiste* traditions certainly point in that direction. What is more, the institutions of the Fifth Republic, especially the tools of rationalized parliamentarism (Articles 38, 44.3, and 49.3), make it easy to enact controversial reforms quickly, even when support for the government is wavering. However, in the world of welfare and labor market retrenchment, where governments seek to avoid or share blame for unpopular reforms, skinny politics can be fool's gold. Reform from above triggers protest from below, while reforming alone frees the opposition parties and social partners from any obligation to help the government out of its predicament. On the contrary, the top-down, insular approach gives opposition politicians and union leaders every incentive to add fuel to the fire, pillorying the government's "heartless" reforms and encouraging strikes and demonstrations.

The claim here is not that skinny politics never yields liberalizing reforms. Sometimes, French governments have won their showdowns with the streets. What is more, a timely concession at the right moment may be enough to defuse protests, enabling a contested reform to survive. Still, the skinny approach can be quite risky. It is prone to triggering protests and strikes, which in many cases are fatal to reform and can threaten the government as well.

4.3   The Social Refoundation

For all the limits of skinny politics, the top-down, insular approach has proven remarkably resistant to change. Perhaps the greatest missed opportunity of the past few decades involved the so-called Social Refoundation (Adam 2002; Roger 2001). The Social Refoundation was launched in 1998 by French employers and unions as a vehicle for reforming labor markets and the welfare state independently of – and, at times, against – the government. It offered the opportunity to shift highly sensitive liberalizing reforms from the political arena to the corporatist arena. Yet despite the obvious advantage of leaving often-unpopular reform to others, governments of both the left and the right disdained or even actively undermined the Social Refoundation.

The Social Refoundation sprang from three developments. The first was an emerging alliance between the French employer association, the National Council of French Employers (Conseil National du Patronat Français, CNPF) and the main reformist trade union, the French Democratic Confederation of Labor (Confédération Française Démocratique du Travail, CFDT). Historically, employers worked primarily with Workers' Power (Force Ouvrière, FO), which focused on bread-and-butter benefits for workers and had little interest in politics. By contrast, the other main trade unions, the communist CGT and the CFDT, pursued far-reaching transformation – to communism for the former and to a socialism based on worker self-management (*autogestion*) for the latter. CNPF support allowed FO to occupy the presidency of several welfare state administrations, providing a source of employment for hundreds of the union's militants.

Beginning in the 1970s and accelerating in the 1980s and 1990s, the CFDT moved away from broad, transformative aspirations, "recentering" its efforts on worker empowerment at the company or factory level (Adam 2000; Hamon and Rotman 1982; Palier 2002). In addition, the CFDT showed a willingness to consider the economic constraints under which French companies were operating and to make concessions when the competitive context seemed to call for it. The CFDT was also willing to revisit and reform social and industrial relations institutions that had become problematic. FO, by contrast, continued to doggedly defend employee wages, benefits, and workplace organization, with little regard for corporate profitability, in a manner much like the communist CGT. Highlighting the union divide, CFDT General Secretary Nicole Notat supported the 1995 Juppé Plan, despite the secretive and heavy-handed methods of the government and the pain that the reform threatened to inflict on CFDT members.

The reformist position of the CFDT turned it into the privileged interlocutor of the French employer association. In addition, the CFDT had long been wary of excessive state power and advocated a bottom-up approach to reform, which also dovetailed with the CNPF's concerns about state intervention. Support from the employers allowed the CFDT to capture the presidencies of the unemployment insurance fund, the National Interprofessional Union for Employment in Industry and Commerce (Union Nationale Interprofessionnelle pour l'Emploi dans l'Industrie et le Commerce, UNEDIC) in 1992 and the National Health Insurance Fund (Caisse Nationale d'Assurance Maladie, CNAM) in 1996, both held previously by FO. As the CFDT General Secretary at the time, Nicole Notat, relates, the Social Refoundation grew out of this emerging alliance with the CNPF:

The backdrop to the Social Refoundation was a shuffling of the cards in favor of the CFDT. Historically, FO was the privileged partner of employers in organizations run by the social partners. In 1992, the CFDT replaced FO at the helm of UNEDIC. In 1995, health insurance was being run by an FO representative who opposed the Juppé Plan. We did not oppose it, so employers gave us the health insurance presidency as well. The correlation of forces among the unions had shifted. The employers supported the CFDT. (Interview by author with Nicole Notat, General Secretary of the CFDT, 1992–2002 and President of UNEDIC, 1992–1998, April 21, 2012)

The second development that fueled the Social Refoundation was a battle between the CNPF and the Jospin government over the left's signature reform, the thirty-five-hour workweek (Seillière 2005). French employers were unhappy about the reform, but to mute their opposition, the government provided a combination of subsidies on the order of €10 billion annually and flexibility in reorganizing work time within the thirty-five-hour rule (INSEE 2018). For example, many enterprises were able to annualize working hours, so that the average was thirty-five hours per week over the course of the year, but with peaks of up to forty-eight hours per week depending on company needs. A number of businesses, especially the larger ones, made out quite well in these negotiations and were willing to go along with the thirty-five-hour reform.

Despite such win-win arrangements, the thirty-five-hour reform touched off a major conflict between the government and the CNPF. The flash-point occurred in October 1997, when the government and the social part-ners met to discuss the way forward. At the meeting, Prime Minister Jospin announced that the government intended to impose the thirty-five-hour workweek via legislation, rather than wait for the results of collective bar-gaining. Jospin felt the need to move quickly because, operating under a cohabitation, he feared that President Chirac might call early legislative elections before he had a chance to enact the reform. Still, the head of the CNPF, Jean Gandois, was aghast. Declaring that he had been "duped," Gandois resigned in protest, adding that the employer association needed a "killer," rather than a negotiator (*Le Monde*, October 15, 1997). The CFDT was also displeased by Jospin's action.

The social partners were further antagonized when the government attempted to redirect funds from the UNEDIC unemployment insur-ance program that Notat was presiding to help finance the thirty-five-hour workweek. The government argued that the creation of jobs resulting from a shorter workweek would reduce unemployment insur-ance payouts, but employers saw the thirty-five-hour workweek as a job killer, not a job creator. Moreover, UNEDIC is technically administered by employers and unions alone, so the government had no legal basis for taking the money. Thus, the Social Refoundation was created in a climate of anger and resistance to several heavy-handed actions by the Jospin government. Denis Kessler, who spearheaded the Social Refoun-dation on behalf of the employers, contends that the thirty-five-hour workweek brought the employers and the CFDT together:

The thirty-five-hour workweek drove the employer association and CFDT into an alliance against the government. Following the thirty-five-hour workweek, the raid on Social Security funds, I told Notat, "We can't get anything done with the government. Let's work with each other." The thirty-five-hour workweek drove the CFDT into an alliance with us. The thirty-five-hour workweek was the cause of the Social Refoundation. (Interview by author with Denis Kessler, Vice-President of the French Employer Association from 1998 to 2002, June 19, 2002)

The third development that contributed to the Social Refoundation was the transformation of the French employer association follow-ing Gandois' resignation. The employer association changed its name from the CNPF to the Movement of French Enterprises (Mouvement des Entreprises de France, MEDEF). Beyond eliminating the archaic term of *patronat*, which conjured images of cigar-smoking "bosses," this name change sought to convey that the employer association was more than an interest group, defending the narrow interests of French employers. Rather, it was a social movement, a source of ideas, seeking to frame public debate and advance new reforms (Woll 2006). In a scarcely veiled dig at France's political parties, Jacques Creyssel, the general director of MEDEF, asserted that MEDEF was, in fact, the *only* source of new ideas:

We are the only source of fresh ideas, the only one making new proposals on a range of subjects. There is a force of the majority, a force of the opposition, and we are the force of new proposals. We are the only source of new ideas. It shouldn't be this way, but nature abhors a vacuum. We are the only remaining revolutionary movement in France. (Interview by author with Jacques Creyssel, General Director, MEDEF, June 14, 2000)

MEDEF made major changes to its leadership as well as its name. Ernest-Antoine Seillière became the new president. Seillière defended the movement's right to criticize the government and speak out on matters of interest to business. In practice, Seillière's proclamations tended to have a political edge, contesting the left-leaning Jospin government and working in favor of leaders of the right, whom Seillière clearly hoped to see return to power (Lagneau-Ymonet 2002).

Seillière's vice-president, Denis Kessler, was the driving force behind the Social Refoundation. An intellectual and former university professor, Kessler established a "Summer University" for employers in 1999, featuring a range of speakers on important issues (Quénel 2016). Although Kessler had held many positions, most recently as the head of the French Insurance Association, he had a consistent record of engagement with societal organizations going all the way back to his student days at the elite School of Advanced Business Studies (Ecole des Hautes Etudes Commerciales, HEC), where he was a left-leaning student leader. An admirer of Tocqueville, Kessler crafted the Social Refoundation as a way to expand the role of civil society and clip the wings of an overbearing state. Kessler also had close ties to CFDT leader Notat. Indeed, Notat would later succeed him as the president of Le Siècle, a prestigious association bringing together leaders from the worlds of politics, the state, business, society, and the media to share and discuss their ideas.

The Social Refoundation sought to overhaul the French system of social protection and industrial relations on the basis of bilateral agreements between the employers and trade unions. The initial agenda encompassed nine areas of reform, including unemployment, health care, pensions, collective bargaining, workplace health and safety, and employee training. MEDEF portrayed the Social Refoundation as a means to narrow the scope of the state, denouncing the alleged interventionist excesses of the Jospin government in the harshest terms. MEDEF also negotiated very aggressively, challenging central components of France's system of social protection and threatening to withdraw from the Social Security system and renounce collective bargaining agreements if the unions did not agree to its proposals.

All of the major French trade unions participated in the Social Refoundation, including the CGT and FO. The unions were motivated partly by fear. If MEDEF withdrew from organizations that were nominally independent of the state, like UNEDIC, the unions would lose resources – both subsidies and employment positions – for their militants. In addition, if MEDEF renounced collective agreements, workers would lose the benefits and protections provided by these agreements, which typically went well beyond the statutory requirements of the labor code. Union leaders were well aware that one of Kessler's first actions in his position as head of the French insurance industry had been to renounce all of the collective agreements in the industry and renegotiate a less protective set of arrangements with employees.

The unions were motivated by more than fear, though. They also saw an opportunity in the Social Refoundation. There were problems to be solved: the French pension system was underfunded and inequitable; the health-care system was expensive and increasingly offloading costs on patients; and the unemployment insurance system covered barely one-half the workforce. In addition, the largest unions, the CGT and CFDT, wanted to roll back what they saw as a major problem in collective bargaining: the possibility for minority unions to ratify collective agreements, as a CGT negotiator in the Social Refoundation related:

> The issue of representativeness is very important to both the CFDT and CGT. Recently, the UIMM [Union of Metallurgical Industries and Professions/ Union des Industries et Métiers de la Métallurgie] signed a deal on the thirty-five-hour workweek with FO and the CFTC [French Confederation of Christian Workers/Confédération Française des Travailleurs Chrétiens], who together represent less than 20 percent of the workforce. The CFDT and CGT believe that if collective bargaining is to take root, the signatories must be truly representative. They must represent more than 50 percent of employees. (Interview by author with Jean-Christophe Le Duigou, Member of the Executive Committee and Confederal Bureau in Charge of Economic Questions and Pensions, CGT, June 12, 2000)

The Social Refoundation reached some important agreements based on give and take between MEDEF and the unions. A "common declaration on the channels and means of collective bargaining" established the principle that collective agreements, to be valid, must be signed (or not opposed) by unions representing a majority of workers. The benefit to employers was the opportunity to bargain on a greater range of issues at the workplace level. Although this "common declaration" did not resolve the thorny legal issue of union representativeness, it pointed toward an eventual solution.

Another significant agreement increased payroll taxes to fund supplementary pensions, which are layered on top of the basic public pension. In return, the unions pledged to support a reform of the entire pension system (basic and supplementary alike) without any new increases in employer contributions. Finally, a deal on worker training mandated increased employer spending on training and created a right for workers to receive at least twenty hours per year of training along with the right to initiate the training. As a counterpart, employers would be allowed to require that some of the training take place outside working hours.

The most important agreement to come out of the Social Refoundation concerned the unemployment system. MEDEF sought to "activate" the unemployment system by establishing a Contract for Assistance in the Return to Employment (Contrat d'Aide au Retour à l'Emploi, CARE). Under the CARE, those on unemployment insurance would be required to sign a contract committing to specific job search and training activities as a condition for receiving unemployment benefits. In addition, they could lose their benefits if they refused to accept multiple job offers. The CARE was MEDEF's top priority. Indeed, at one point, MEDEF halted all the other negotiations (on pensions, representativeness, etc.) until an agreement on the CARE was reached.

The CFDT pushed back against the language of "contract," so the CARE became a "plan" instead, the Plan for Assistance in the Return to Employment (Plan d'Aide au Retour à l'Emploi, PARE). The unions extracted more than symbolic concessions. Job search requirements were softened, and workers gained several important benefits. For starters, they could qualify more quickly for unemployment benefits. In addition, these benefits were improved. A reform in 1992 had made unemployment benefits "degressive," that is, they declined in stages the longer a recipient remained unemployed. Under the PARE, degressivity was eliminated, the logic being that if the PARE was making sure that the unemployed were genuinely looking for jobs, then those who were unable to find a job through no fault of their own should not see their benefits diminished.

MEDEF was jubilant over the PARE agreement. The statement by General Director Creyssel that MEDEF was "the only source of fresh ideas ... the only remaining revolutionary movement in France" was made the morning after the PARE was signed. A MEDEF publication likewise depicts the PARE as a revolutionary development:

The PARE is a veritable revolution in the conception of the treatment of unemployment. A collective mechanism dedicated essentially to anonymous payment is giving way to individualized attention based on help returning to employment. As against insurance payments that underwrite waiting, the PARE emphasizes the activity of searching for a job. It puts employment at the heart of the unemployment insurance system. It marks a rupture with the lack of respect for work exemplified by the thirty-five-hour workweek and passive assistance to the unemployed. [It is also] a stinging rebuttal of those who condemned the unions and the very idea of joint management of programs by the social partners as obsolete. (Seillière 2005: 75)

Jean-François Trogrlic, a member of the Executive Commission of the CFDT, credits the PARE with shifting the center of gravity of the French unemployment system toward job placement: "The PARE established that UNEDIC is not just for writing checks. It also has a role to play in helping the unemployed find jobs" (interview by author with Jean-François Trogrlic, Member of the Executive Commission of the CFDT, Responsible for External Relations and Societal Questions, June 21, 2002). Others were less enthusiastic. Marc Blondel, the leader of FO, which did not sign the PARE agreement, compared it to the Vichy Regime's Compulsory Labor Service (Service du Travail Obligatoire, STO), which conscripted young French men for work in German factories during World War II (*Les Echos*, May 17, 2000). The CGT also declined to sign the PARE. Le Duigou, the CGT negotiator, chose a historical reference from a more distant time:

UNEDIC negotiations are not just about unemployment. MEDEF's real agenda is to change the functioning of the labor market. They want workers to be forced to accept low-paid jobs on pain of losing their benefits. They want to make the jobless into a reserve army of the unemployed. They are trying to go back to the world of Marx, to the nineteenth century. (Interview by author with Jean-Christophe Le Duigou, Member of the Executive Committee and Confederal Bureau in charge of Economic Questions and Pensions, CGT, June 12, 2000)

The signing of the PARE was not the end of the story, however. The PARE was not self-implementing. It needed the government's formal approval (*agrément*) in order to enter into effect. In addition, a number of laws concerning contribution rates, unemployment benefits, and job search requirements had to be changed.

The government's approval would be long in coming (Adam 2002). Genuine concerns about the PARE were part of the reason. The PARE was a minority agreement, signed by two of the main unions (CFDT and CFTC), but opposed by three others (CGT, FO, and the French Confederation of Management-General Confederation of Executives [Confédération Française de l'Encadrement-Confédération Générale des Cadres, CFE-CGC]). The PARE also challenged the historic division of labor between UNEDIC, which pays benefits, and the National Employment Agency (Agence Nationale pour l'Emploi, ANPE), which helps the unemployed find jobs. Of particular concern, UNEDIC is technically a private organization which, under the PARE, would be given the authority to impose punishments on the unemployed, a power that is reserved for public agencies like ANPE. Finally, the PARE threatened to create a two-tier system: those unemployed with a long contribution record, who qualified for unemployment insurance, would be accompanied in the search for employment by UNEDIC, while those with a shorter contribution record would receive less generous social assistance benefits and be accompanied in the search for employment by ANPE. In effect, the PARE was cherry-picking the easiest cases for UNEDIC, which MEDEF General Director Creyssel openly acknowledged:

There are three categories of unemployed. The first are people with little work experience who do not qualify for unemployment insurance. They're not our problem. We are in a contribution-based system. You don't have rights if you haven't contributed financially. This group is the state's problem. The second category is the short-term unemployed with long contribution records. These are the ones we care about. The third category is the unemployed who have exhausted their benefits. They belong to the solidarity regime. They aren't our problem either. (Interview by author with Jacques Creyssel, General Director, MEDEF, June 14, 2000)

The government, therefore, had plenty of legitimate reasons for rejecting the PARE as constructed. That said, the fine points of the PARE were a secondary consideration. The government had more fundamental objections. The Social Refoundation had been constructed as an alternative to the government; it was designed to evict an overbearing state from the management of social protection and industrial relations. In many ways, it was the exact opposite of the most extreme conception of the republican or *dirigiste* model: instead of the state being everything and ignoring the social partners, under the Social Refoundation the social partners would be everything and ignore the state. In this spirit, the government was deliberately excluded from the entire process, including the negotiations that produced the PARE. Consequently, there was little incentive for the government to approve the PARE. Indeed, according to CFDT General Secretary Notat, the government used the approval process for the PARE as a way of sabotaging the Social Refoundation and punishing the unions:

The government was not trying to accompany the efforts of the social partners. On the contrary, the government engaged in guerilla warfare against the agreements of the social partners. The refusal to ratify the PARE was the means for the government to wage guerilla warfare against the unions. Relations with the government were strained, strained, strained. (Interview by author with Nicole Notat, General Secretary of the CFDT, 1992–2002 and President of UNEDIC, 1992–1998, April 21, 2012)

Opposing the Social Refoundation also made good electoral sense. Prime Minister Jospin, who was preparing to run for president in 2002, was a centrist figure seen by many on the left as insufficiently Socialist. From this perspective, standing up to the employers, and getting into a fight with MEDEF offered a way to burnish his leftist credentials, all the more so given that the majority of French unions, including FO and the CGT, opposed the PARE as well. Thus, the longer the battle over the PARE dragged on and the nastier it became, the more it would boost Jospin's claim to represent the working class against the employers. A social affairs adviser to Jospin, interviewed the day that the PARE was signed, made it clear that the government was more than willing to do battle with MEDEF:

Nothing can happen without our agreement, and we will approve the accord only if it is signed by unions that represent a large majority of workers. We won't submit to blackmail. If they are looking for a fight, they will get one. (Interview by author with Jacques Rigaudiat, Social Adviser to Prime Minister Jospin, June 14, 2000)

Nor did the government harbor warm feelings toward the unions, especially the CFDT. According to Notat, the government and the CFDT were more or less at war: "We [the CFDT] were regarded as having taken part in a war against the government. No actor within the Social Refoundation could find favor in its eyes. Relations were very tense." (Interview by author with Nicole Notat, General Secretary of the CFDT, 1992–2002 and President of UNEDIC, 1992–1998, April 21, 2012).

In response to government criticisms, the social partners modified the PARE, shifting responsibility for job search and penalties from UNEDIC to ANPE, but this change was not enough to secure government approval (Adam 2002). The government rejected the PARE barely one month after it had been signed, sending a five-page letter replete with criticisms. A slightly modified version was presented to the government in September and rejected again October 1. This "ping pong match between the government and the social partners," as Notat described it, finally came to an end when Jospin and MEDEF President Seillière worked out an agreement over the phone on the night of October 15–16. Employers were allowed to retain some of the payroll tax reductions in the PARE, but not all, and UNEDIC would have to write a €3 billion check to the government as "part of the clarification of complex financial relations between the State and the unemployment insurance system" (Adam 2002: 59). In the end, a process that was supposed to evict the state from social and industrial relations reform could be completed only through direct negotiations with the prime minister and a sizable payment to the government.

To add insult to injury, when the Jospin government finally enacted the legislation to "implement" the PARE in June 2001, it removed the principal punishments relating to job search requirements, such as the reduction or loss of benefits for unemployed workers who refuse to sign a personalized plan to return to employment or who decline a job beneath their qualifications (Adam 2002). The government also mandated that all unemployed workers, whether receiving unemployment benefits or not, receive the same support for finding a job and receive it only from the public ANPE. In addition, the legislation removed a provision designed to encourage the unions to sign that had stipulated that only signatories to the PARE could be represented on the boards that manage UNEDIC. In the end, all that remained of the PARE were a shorter contribution period for workers to become eligible for unemployment benefits, the elimination of benefit degressivity, slightly reduced payroll taxes for employers and employees, and the €3 billion check from UNEDIC to the state. For all intents and purposes, the "activation" strategy designed to move the unemployed into jobs had disappeared.

The Social Refoundation never had much of a chance under the Jospin government. The proponents, particularly on the employer side, made no secret of their hostility to the government, which returned the favor by blocking then eviscerating the PARE. In addition, MEDEF's hardball tactics – the constant threats to withdraw from welfare state institutions or renounce collective bargaining agreements as well as the refusal to share control over the agenda, insisting that the only issues up for discussion were those prioritized by MEDEF – irritated and alienated the union representatives, who came to unite on many issues against the employers. Finally, most of the topics under negotiation involved liberalizing measures that reduced social and labor market protections (Lallement and Méraux 2003; Renard and Cleyre 2001). These reforms had a zero-sum character, with the gains of employers from the losses of employees, and therefore held little appeal to the unions, even the reformist CFDT (Jacot 2001/2). Although the Social Refoundation yielded some joint declarations and statements of intent, substantive agreements were harder to come by.

The PARE was, in a sense, the exception that proved the rule. At the time of the Social Refoundation negotiations, the unemployment insurance fund enjoyed a substantial surplus, thanks to relatively strong economic growth and falling unemployment. This surplus created the opportunity for a win-win game, making it possible for the PARE to both increase unemployment benefits for workers and reduce payroll taxes for employers. Even with this advantage, the PARE barely survived the guerilla war waged by the Jospin government, and its activation measures largely fell by the wayside. Still, the going was even tougher for other items on the Social Refoundation's agenda. The unions balked at one-sided cutbacks, such as reductions in pensions, and negotiations bogged down. In fall 2001, MEDEF announced that it was pausing the Social Refoundation until after the 2002 presidential and legislative elections. Although MEDEF did not officially endorse a candidate, it was clearly pinning its hopes on a victory of the right that could produce a government more supportive of the employers' agenda.

4.4   Business as Usual: The Second Chirac Presidency (2002–2007)

The 2002 elections delivered a victory to the French right, but in a way that few, if any, had expected. Prior to the election, it had been almost a foregone conclusion that incumbent President Chirac and incumbent Prime Minister Jospin would face off on the second ballot, with Jospin a slight favorite. To the surprise of all, however, on the first round of voting, Jospin was edged out for second place by Jean-Marie Le Pen, the founder and leader of the far-right, xenophobic National Front (Front National, FN). Many voters on the left, confident that Jospin would make the runoff, had either not bothered to vote or cast their ballots for far-left candidates with no chance of winning. No doubt, had they been aware of Jospin's vulnerability, they would have behaved more strategically, but nothing could be done once Jospin polled third, as under the rules of the Fifth Republic only the top two candidates qualify for the presidential runoff.

Jospin's debacle meant that despite receiving less than 20 percent of the vote on the first round, the worst showing of any incumbent president in the history of the Fifth Republic, Chirac was assured of a landslide reelection as president. All of the other candidates and leaders of the major political parties quickly came together in a "Republican Front" to support Chirac, warts and all, against Le Pen, who was seen as a threat to decency and democracy. On the second ballot, Chirac received 82 percent of the votes, the highest total by far in the history of the Fifth Republic. French voters then followed through on the presidential election by giving Chirac's party an absolute majority in the National Assembly.

Despite Chirac's massive victory, the 2002 elections were a warning to France's governing parties that they could not continue as before. At the same time, the highly unusual circumstances surrounding the 2002 elections opened the door to new governing approaches. Indeed, two possible blame-sharing reform strategies became available to Chirac.

The first was to extend the Republican Front into a governing strategy, a kind of *union sacrée* or grand coalition with the Socialist Party (Parti Socialiste, PS). Chirac's reelection as president had been something of a fluke – he may well have been the second-most popular candidate behind Jospin – and owed much to support from leftist voters. Given Chirac's weak mandate and reliance on leftist voters, the way to reform France, some believed, was to reach out to the left and offer to work together (Giroux 2013). Such a strategy was all the more plausible in light of the PS's movement away from statism and socialism since the 1983 U-turn. Indeed, Jospin had publicly declared that his 2002 campaign platform was not Socialist. In addition, Jospin had commissioned far-reaching reform proposals for health care (the Johanet Plan) and pensions (the Charpin Report) that had support among conservatives and employers (Charpin 1999; Johanet 1999). Jospin ultimately decided not to implement these reforms, at least not until after the 2002 elections, for fear of alienating leftist voters. Following the elections, though, Chirac had a chance to possibly construct a Republican Front government, integrating moderate center-left politicians, behind an agenda of reform along the lines suggested by Johanet and Charpin. Under the bipolar logic of the Fifth Republic and on the heels of a humiliating five-year cohabitation, however, Chirac had no desire to share power with the left, opting to govern alone instead.

The second possible blame-sharing strategy operated through the corporatist channel rather than the political channel, entrusting controversial reforms to the Social Refoundation. Chirac had embraced the ideals of the Social Refoundation in his election campaign. In July 2000, he had called for a French social democracy "that does not leave it to the government or the central State to direct everything, but rather gives social actors, unions, professions, associations, the possibility, within a framework guaranteed by the State, to move things along" (cited in Adam 2002: 97). In fall 2001, four Chirac allies, including future Prime Minister Jean-Pierre Raffarin, published a book setting out Chirac's "contract" for his second term (Barnier et al. 2001). Each of the four authors wrote one section of the book. The section penned by Jacques Barrot, a former minister of labor and social affairs, was entitled, "To Open Chances for an Authentic Economic and Social Democracy," and its first sentence declared, "The establishment of new social relations must not be done via laws and regulations, but must be conceived, as often as possible, by social and economic actors themselves, through negotiations, and implemented via contracts" (Barnier et al. 2001: 101). It is hard to imagine a clearer endorsement of the Social Refoundation.

Beyond campaign promises, the Social Refoundation seemed attractive as a vehicle for economic liberalization under a government of the right. Chirac had tried top-down imposition with the Juppé Plan, and that approach had blown up in his face. Whatever the government of the day, welfare and labor market reform proposals seemed to be political dynamite, triggering mass protests that forced governments to make costly concessions or back down altogether. Consequently, there was good reason to move the reform process out of the political arena. The Social Refoundation was all the more tempting given that MEDEF was pushing an ambitious, probusiness agenda that appealed to many conservative politicians and voters (Jacot 2001/2; Lallement and Méraux 2003). In the name of "social democracy," the government could simply step aside and let MEDEF do its dirty work – or, more accurately, its politically contentious work.

Although the Social Refoundation had made relatively little headway under Jospin, a government of the right offered more promising conditions. The Jospin government had opposed and even sabotaged the Social Refoundation, but with the right in power, bargaining between MEDEF and the unions could have taken place under the shadow of a very different hierarchy. Instead of sabotaging MEDEF's initiatives, the government could have lent its support. Facing a MEDEF backed by a government of the right, France's unions might well have experienced their Wassenaar moment. Like their Dutch counterparts in 1982, they would have confronted the choice between negotiating reforms with the employers, thereby bolstering corporatist institutions and perhaps extracting some concessions along the way, or refusing to negotiate and risking the collapse of the corporatist channel and the takeover of the reform process by a hostile conservative government (Hemerijck and Vail 2006; Visser and Hemerijck 1997). Like the Wassenaar Accord, the Social Refoundation might have provided the vehicle for renewing collective bargaining and launching a process of carefully managed and negotiated liberalization.

Denis Kessler certainly thought that the moment had finally come for the Social Refoundation. Kessler anticipated that Chirac would strike quickly, enacting a framework law to give the social partners the authority to overhaul French industrial relations and social protection: "We expected Chirac to enact a framework law, pass a number of ordinances, then the social partners would rebuild the system: the thirty-five-hour workweek, pensions, union representativeness, the civil servant statute, collective bargaining" (interview by author with Denis Kessler, Vice-President, MEDEF, April 12, 2011). Kessler even told his wife not to plan a summer vacation because he "would be busy establishing the new system."

In hindsight, Kessler would have been better off taking that vacation. Despite the discourse of social democracy that filled his campaign, President Chirac was no more interested than Jospin in sharing power with the social partners. Chirac also had a different understanding from Kessler of France's needs. For Kessler, an ailing French economy needed bold, radical reform. For Chirac, by contrast, a traumatized French society, wracked by decades of mass unemployment and displaying an alarming willingness to vote for the FN, needed reassurance and cautious governance. Once again, the concern of French conservatives for social order was a higher priority than economic liberalization.

Chirac's choice of prime minister revealed his clear preference for not rocking the boat: Jean-Pierre Raffarin was a centrist politician with a reputation for consulting widely, advancing incrementally, and seeking consensus wherever possible. With Raffarin, Chirac would never have to worry about a Juppé-style social explosion. Chirac wanted to avoid such a disaster at all costs, and from his perspective, Denis Kessler, with his strong ideological positions and aggressive negotiating style, was a social explosion waiting to happen.

When MEDEF officials met with Raffarin in June, Kessler urged the prime minister to act quickly and decisively in the manner of de Gaulle in 1958. Raffarin temporized instead, asking for time to reflect. Three months later, MEDEF officials met again with Raffarin, and that is when Kessler saw the writing on the wall:

In September, Raffarin convened us. Nothing had been done all summer. Raffarin told us, "I need one year. During that year, I will consult widely and conduct studies." I was crushed. I told Seillière, "It's f--ked. I don't believe in it anymore." The conditions were in place – political, social, and economic. Yet the government fell back into narrow ambitions and petty politics. (Interview with Denis Kessler, Vice-President, MEDEF, April 12, 2011)

To be fair to the government, Kessler also received less than full support from MEDEF. Seillière had always been more of a political creature than Kessler, supporting the Social Refoundation primarily as a club to wield against Jospin's government of the left. When the right returned to power, Seillière saw less need for the political club, even as Kessler aspired to kick the Social Refoundation into high gear to overhaul social protection and rebuild the French economy. Seillière also shared the government's wariness of Kessler's brusque, confrontational negotiating style (Giroux 2013), a concern that was echoed by many leaders or "barons" within MEDEF, most notably, Kessler's principal rival, Denis Gautier-Sauvagnac.

Gautier-Sauvagnac and the barons had never thought much of the Social Refoundation, preferring traditional bread-and-butter negotiations with the unions over wages and working conditions. They were also less interested in evicting the government from social and economic reforms than in getting a now ideologically aligned government to enact the reforms that they favored. In fall 2002, Seillière seemed to side with the barons when he took away some of Kessler's negotiating responsibilities and distributed them among Kessler's rivals. Whether because of internal MEDEF machinations or the government's unwillingness to support the Social Refoundation, Kessler left MEDEF in November 2002 to become the CEO of a French reinsurance company. The Social Refoundation was effectively over.

With Seillière's rediscovery of the virtues of legislation, as opposed to negotiation, MEDEF returned to its traditional role as a lobbyist for narrow employer interests. Seillière issued a series of demands to the government – to weaken the thirty-five-hour workweek, reduce employer Social Security charges and corporate tax rates, and reform the pension system. Seillière constantly urged the government to take action and move faster "on behalf of the urgent reform that needs to happen" (Seillière 2005: 79). At the same time, he refused to take any responsibility for helping advance such reform. When the government invited MEDEF to negotiate with the unions on the modernization and pruning of the country's 2,579-page labor code, Seillière declined, calling on the government to "take up its responsibility" and "propose, via a law, the modification of the legislation" (*La Tribune*, July 7, 2004; *Le Monde*, July 8, 2004). Finally, Seillière complained continuously about the government's failure to deliver enough favors to employers. Despite a law making it easier and cheaper to extend the workweek beyond thirty-five hours, he stated that "People have talked a lot [about the thirty-five-hour workweek], but nothing has been done" (*Les Echos*, October 7, 2004). On another occasion, Seillière declared, at a time when Raffarin had been prime minister for more than two years, that "since Mr. Raffarin has been in power, companies have gained nothing" (*Libération*, August 31, 2004).

Having rejected both the political and corporatist modes of blame-sharing, the Chirac administration took up a kind of cautious liberalism calibrated according to the level of street protests that was reminiscent of the "Balladur method." The reform of the French public pension system in 2003 under Minister of Social Affairs, Solidarity, and Labor François Fillon illustrated the modalities and limits of this approach (Palier 2003b; Palier and Bonoli 2007; Tompson 2010). Facing a growing deficit in the pension system, the government sought to cut spending primarily by bringing the pensions of civil servants more into line with those of employees in the private sector.

The government presented the main lines of its reform in February 2003. The reform focused on the pensions of civil servants, while excluding the "special pension regimes" for certain professions, like public transportation and energy workers (employed by the Autonomous Parisian Transportation Administration [Régie Autonome des Transports Parisiens, RATP], SNCF, EDF and GDF). Although the special pensions were even more generous than the public pensions, permitting retirement as early as age 50, the government wanted to avoid uniting civil servants and employees in the transportation and energy sectors against the reform, as Juppé had done in 1995 (Tompson 2010: 98). Consequently, Fillon focused on the civil servants, leaving the reform of the special pensions to a future government. His reform proposed to index the pensions of civil servants to prices instead of wages. In addition, the required number of years of contributions for civil servants to receive a full pension would be aligned with that of employees in the private sector, increasing from 37.5 years in 2003 to 40 years in 2008.

Private-sector workers were not entirely spared by the reform. Once the contribution period between the public and private sectors was aligned, the required years of contributions for both civil servants and private-sector workers would increase to forty-one years in 2012 and forty-two years in 2020. In addition, a bonus/malus system would be introduced to encourage workers to defer retirement – boosting pensions by an extra 3 percent per year for those working beyond age 60, while reducing pensions by 5 percent per year for those retiring before age 60. A further innovation was the creation of a system of voluntary private pension funds, the Popular Retirement Savings Plan (Plan d'Epargne Retraite Populaire, PERP), supported by tax breaks. The private pension funds were supposed to offset some of the losses that employees experienced in their public pensions – at least those employees with sufficient earnings to be able to put money into private pensions – as well as deepen French capital markets.

While preparing the Fillon Plan, government officials met with the unions, but engaged in little more than a listening exercise, refusing to negotiate the actual terms of the pension reform. In a presentation of his reform to a national television audience April 24, Fillon then sought to foreclose any negotiations by declaring that his bill was "the only possible reform." The unions, feeling otherwise, responded by launching a series of protests and strikes. The movement culminated May 13, when 2 million protestors took to the streets according to the unions, 1.1 million according to the police, and public transportation was paralyzed (*Les Echos*, January 11, 2013). At this point, a government fearful of the growing disorder finally agreed to negotiate with the unions.

The government's goal was to split the opposition by winning over the main reformist unions, the CFE-CGC, the CFTC, and especially the CFDT. The price of the CFDT's support would be nineteen modifications to the original plan. Most were relatively minor, but one proved quite significant: workers who had begun their careers at a very young age (14–16 years) would be allowed to retire before age 60 if they had made the requisite number of years of contributions. These concessions induced the CFDT to switch its position and endorse the Fillon reform, and the demonstrations petered out.

Although the government was able to implement its pension reform, it was a very limited victory. The government had considered a bold reform to move the French pension system toward the Swedish or Italian points-based model but decided against it because it was considered too contentious. For the same reason, the government did not touch the special pension regimes. Since the private sector had already been reformed by Balladur in 1993, there were not many places to extract savings. According to official estimates, in 2020, the Fillon reform would cover only €5 billion of the expected €15 billion financial shortfall for private-sector pensions and €13 billion out of the expected €28 billion shortfall for public-sector pensions (Tompson 2010: 98). Moreover, these estimates were predicated on economic growth and unemployment numbers that were widely viewed and would prove to be unrealistic. In addition, the government underestimated the number of workers who would be eligible to retire before age 60, raising the cost of this concession to the CFDT. In the end, the strategy of privileging skinny politics over political or corporatist concertation did yield a reform, but one that was both contested – indeed, that encouraged those seeking a different reform to mobilize in the streets – and far from sufficient to meet the financial challenge at hand.

This pattern of limited, contested, inadequate reforms has been repeated again and again in the case of French pensions. Pension reforms have been launched seven times in the past three decades: in 1993, 1995, 2002, 2007, 2010, 2013, and 2019. All of the reforms have been conducted on the basis of skinny politics, excluding the opposition parties and engaging in no more than "consultation without negotiation" with the unions, at least in the initial crafting of the reforms. Relatedly, all of the reforms have prompted major protests and, in several cases, paralyzing strikes.

The most ambitious reforms, the 1995 Juppé Plan, which would have extended the Balladur reform of private-sector pensions to both public-sector pensions and the special regimes, and the 2019 Macron reform, which proposed to merge France's forty-two different pension system into a single Swedish-style points system, were both abandoned. Other less ambitious pension reforms have been more successful. In some instances, notably under the Sarkozy presidency in 2010, governments stared down the protestors and implemented their reforms with few or no concessions. In others, like the Balladur reform of 1993, the Fillon reform of 2003, and Sarkozy's 2007 pension reform, the government made enough concessions to split the unions and see their initiatives through. Altogether, skinny politics has enabled French leaders to successfully complete five different pension reforms.

Taking a step back, though, the record of skinny politics is less impressive. Although French reformers racked up some wins, these victories have fallen well short of resolving France's pension problems. In the extreme case, the 2007 reform of the "special regimes" was accompanied by so many concessions that it had virtually no impact on overall spending (Cahuc and Zylberberg 2009; *La Tribune*, October 18, 2010). After more than one-quarter century and five successful pension reforms, France still spends more on public pensions, 13.6 percent of GDP in 2018, than Germany, Denmark, Sweden, or Holland (OECD 2019a). Only the notoriously patronage-ridden systems of Italy and Greece exceed French public pension spending. Nor is high cost the only problem. The French pension system remains in deficit, is fragmented into forty-two different regimes, and continues to treat different groups differently in ways that are difficult to justify.

The Swedish concertational approach may have involved tortuous negotiations and compromises. It may have taken fifteen years to negotiate. Yet the Swedish reform was completed more than a quarter-century ago, in 1998. It delivered more change than the seven skinny-political reform initiatives over three decades in France combined – and with nothing like the French level of contestation.

The strategy of privileging skinny politics over political or corporatist concertation imparted a similar pattern to other reforms of the second Chirac presidency from 2002 to 2007. Reforms were implemented, but they were inadequate to the task at hand. Prime Minister Raffarin's government was able to enact legislative changes in a number of areas. A

health-care law increased patient contributions, encouraged the substitution of generic drugs for brand name drugs, and began to set up a gate-
keeper system that would require patients to see their primary caregiver
and receive a referral before being authorized to see a (more expensive)
specialist. Raffarin also took much of the bite out of the thirty-five-hour
workweek, reducing the wage premium for the 36th through 39th hours
from 50 percent to 25 percent and increasing the number of overtime
hours allowed annually from 130 to 180. Finally, the government cut
income taxes three times by a total of 10 percent, expanded tax breaks
and write-offs for the hiring of low-wage and household employees, and
phased out the wage component of the local corporate income tax (*taxe
professionnelle*).

For all the Raffarin government's activity, its skinny-politics approach
yielded only limited reform. Lacking partners with whom to share the
blame for painful or unpopular reforms, the government was wary
of going too far and triggering mass protests. As a result, its reforms
tended to fall well short of what was needed; they were inadequate, stopgap, even symbolic, as opposed to comprehensive. The Fillon pension
reform covered barely 40 percent of the projected shortfall in the system
(Tompson 2010). Similarly, the health-care reforms saved only €5 billion, at a time when the annual deficit in the health insurance program
was €12.9 billion, and French health-care costs were rising much faster
than inflation. The government reformed the thirty-five-hour workweek
but did not repeal it, for fear of protests. Because the law was still in
place, the government had to continue paying over €10 billion annually
in compensatory subsidies to employers (INSEE 2018). Gaëtan Gorce,
a Socialist deputy (the title of members of the National Assembly),
criticized the government's pursuit of minor reforms that failed to solve
France's problems:

> The government is constantly enacting reforms, but they are half-measures that
> don't fix problems like our budget deficits and public debt. It's dangerous to tell
> people that reforms are significant when they are not. It feeds a sense of injustice
> and ineffectiveness, and people become cynical about politics. What we need
> instead is for the government to work with the opposition to enact reforms that
> actually solve problems. (Interview by author of Gaëtan Gorce, Socialist Deputy
> in the National Assembly, April 6, 2011)

The limited liberalization produced by skinny politics failed to turn
around the French economy. Economic growth lagged behind that
of France's trading partners, while unemployment remained higher.
France's public finances also deteriorated. In 2003, for the first time
since the creation of the eurozone, France breached the Maastricht
budget deficit ceiling of 3 percent of GDP. France also breached the

Maastricht debt ceiling of 60 percent of GDP. These developments occurred at a time when most other eurozone countries were reducing their budget deficits and public debt.

While skinny politics may have seemed the expedient strategy in 2002, it put French reform on what might be called a "perverse Goldilocks" trajectory of limited liberalization. On the one hand, the government introduced enough change – and did so in a sufficiently high-handed and regressive manner – to alienate large swathes of the French population. On the other hand, the government did not introduce enough change to resolve the fiscal and economic problems that had motivated reform in the first place. In short, limited liberalization imposed social and political pain for scant economic gain, alienating voters while failing to resolve France's deep-seated problems.

4.5   Conclusion

The politics of welfare and labor market retrenchment is fundamentally different from the politics of establishing new forms of social protection and labor market regulation. The agenda involves taking away popular benefits from groups who have strong incentives to mobilize against such losses. Contemporary welfare and labor market reform is, therefore, mostly an exercise in blame avoidance or blame-sharing, rather than credit-claiming.

France's policy regime, fashioned by the republican model, the postwar *dirigiste* model, and the institutions of the Fifth Republic, is geared toward the "old politics of the welfare state," not the "new politics of the welfare state." It concentrates blame, rather than avoiding or sharing it. As a result, French authorities have found it difficult to navigate the politics of social and labor market reform. The strategies that they have deployed, the various forms of "skinny politics," from the Balladur method, to consulting the social partners without actually negotiating, to calibrating reforms to the level of street protests, have yielded limited and contested change. The factors described in Chapters 2 and 3 – the frustration of French citizens with earlier rounds of reform that produced disappointing results, the paucity of resources for crafting win-win games due to the fiscal burden of the social anesthesia state, and the tepid commitment of conservative politicians to economic liberalization – have only added to the dangers and difficulties of skinny-politics reform.

Still, the 2002 elections were a potential critical juncture, offering France an opportunity to shift onto a different reform path, whether based on political concertation or corporatist concertation. Where those paths led is, of course, unknowable. Maybe Socialist or Green leaders would have rebuffed offers from Chirac to cooperate and govern together. Maybe MEDEF's Seillière had no intention of using the Social Refoundation for anything more than a political weapon against the left. What *is* knowable is that the path chosen by President Chirac, the path of least resistance and skinny politics, led to the perverse Goldilocks world of reforms that antagonized voters without providing effective solutions to France's fiscal and economic problems.

Nowhere is this perverse Goldilocks pattern more evident than in pension policy: five supposedly major pension reforms in the last three decades, each triggering protests and strikes, have failed to resolve the problems of the French pension system. French pension spending remains the highest in Europe outside the notoriously corrupt cases of Greece and Italy; French citizens spend more years in retirement than citizens in any other European country; the French pension system continues to run a deficit; and France's forty-two different pension regimes still produce all manner of inequities. Sweden may have needed fifteen years of hard bargaining to overhaul its system, but that process established a financially sustainable, points-based system in 1998. More than a quarter-century later, as Chapter 6 relates, French reformers are still chasing the Swedish pension model.

Chapters 5, 6, and 7 focus on another potential critical juncture, the election of Emmanuel Macron as president in 2017. Macron upended the French political system, displacing the governing parties of the left and the right that had alternated in office for the entire history of the Fifth Republic. He also embraced a language of "revolution," pledging to overhaul France's ailing economy and restore the country to international prominence. Most important for the purpose of this book, Macron made no secret of his belief that France needed liberalizing economic reforms. That said, the next three chapters show that the policy, party-political, and institutional legacies of the *dirigiste* model that fueled the contestation of economic liberalization in the past continue to weigh on Macron's efforts in the contemporary period.

5   Jupiter's Limits
From Initial Achievements to the Yellow Vest Crisis

Economic liberalization has been a parlous political exercise in France. More than in any other affluent democracy, it seems that liberalization in France is politically contested and, in many cases, defeated by protests and strike movements. The previous chapters have offered three main reasons why economic liberalization is so contested in France, all traceable to legacies of the country's postwar *dirigiste* economic model.

When Emmanuel Macron was elected president in 2017, it looked like he might be able to break with the French pattern of contested liberalization. A former minister of finance, who had shepherded a law expanding competition in business services that bears his name, Macron had an undeniable proliberal identity. He also claimed a democratic mandate for policies of economic liberalization. Indeed, almost all of the major reforms that he has launched figured prominently in his 2017 presidential platform. Yet Macron has been arguably more contested than any other president in recent French history, confronting multiple mass protests that disrupted or even shut down France for lengthy periods. In some cases, these protests have forced Macron to make concessions or withdraw his proposals altogether, and the so-called yellow vest protests of 2018 fundamentally challenged both his agenda and capacity to govern. As Chapter 7 relates, Macron has also been contested in the ballot box, failing to secure a legislative majority in the 2022 elections.

This chapter analyzes Macron's economic and social policy agenda and his efforts to implement that agenda during the first eighteen months of his presidency. It also analyzes the yellow vest protests that rocked France in the winter of 2018. Finally, it shows that Macron's liberalizing efforts have provoked large-scale protests and, in some cases, defeat for the reasons emphasized in this book, notably the French trajectory of reform via the social anesthesia state and Macron's skinny-politics approach to governing.

The contention here is not that Macron has failed to carry out any measures of economic liberalization. His government has introduced significant reforms. In addition, after securing reelection as president in

2022, Macron has five more years to implement his agenda, albeit without a legislative majority (as of this writing). That said, it is clear that the three legacies of *dirigisme* described in this book have weighed heavily on Macron's liberalizing initiatives, contributing to a high level of contestation and several significant setbacks.

The rest of this chapter explores Macron's election, early actions, and contestation by the yellow vests. Section 5.1 describes Macron's profile and economic agenda as president. Section 5.2 covers the reforms enacted during the first eighteen months of Macron's presidency. Section 5.3 reviews the yellow vest protests of winter 2018–2019. Sections 5.4 and 5.5 shows how the social anesthesia state and skinny politics respectively contributed to the yellow vest movement. Finally, Section 5.6 examines the government concessions that brought the yellow vest crisis to an end.

5.1   Macron's Agenda

Emmanuel Macron came to power with a firm belief that the French economy was lagging behind its European peers economically. In the words of a top economic adviser, "The general idea was that France had not managed to make the major transformations that other leading European countries had undertaken" (interview by author with a high-level Macron economic adviser, March 2019). France's failure to reform was not just an economic problem, but also a geopolitical problem. French influence had waned vis-à-vis Germany, as the German economy raced ahead of the French. In his 2016 book *Révolution*, which launched his campaign and laid out his intentions if elected president, Macron contended that France had lost credibility with Germany because successive governments had failed to honor promises to reduce public spending and budget deficits (Macron 2016: 237). The only way for France to wield influence at the European Union (EU) level was to get its fiscal and economic house in order:

France has an immense responsibility. If we want to convince our German partners to go forward, we absolutely must reform ourselves. Germany today is hesitant, blocking a number of European projects out of distrust toward us. (Macron 2016: 236–237)

Macron's hope was that if France reformed and turned around its economy, he could then get Germany to go along with some of his ambitious ideas for Europe, such as the establishment of an EU minister of finance and the launching of a program of public investment for the eurozone. Macron's support for liberal economic reforms was motivated by more than a need to win over Germany, though; he also believed that these changes would be good for France. Indeed, Macron broke with the

French miserabilist discourse that blamed the EU for foisting neoliberal reforms on France. Instead, he offered a more optimistic vision that such reforms would be good for France, restoring the country's economic health. In the words of a top economic adviser:

The discourse in the past was that we are doing a reform either because we didn't have money or because of external constraints. Macron, by contrast, incarnates an optimistic vision. We are doing reforms because it will take us to a better place. (Interview by author with high-level Macron economic adviser, March 2019)

Macron saw the root problem of France's economic difficulties as what this book calls the "social anesthesia state." Arguing that, "real prosperity can only be created by producing first and redistributing afterward," Macron blasted past French governments for privileging social spending over measures to promote economic growth:

For 30 years ... we have chosen to substitute public spending for economic growth. We have been very generous with social support, but we have never attacked the roots of mass unemployment.... We have constructed a model of palliative social spending, rather than productive spending. (Macron 2016: 76)

Macron pledged to reduce public spending by €60 billion and all but eliminate France's structural budget deficit by the end of his five-year term in office (Macron 2017). Reforming the social anesthesia state would involve more than cutting spending, however. Macron believed that the social anesthesia state had crowded out both public and private investment. To revive private investment and risk-taking, he promised a variety of tax cuts for business and wealthy individuals. Macron also committed to over €50 billion of public investment in worker training, apprenticeships, environmental transformation, and new technologies (Macron 2017).

It is easy to see why many regard Macron as a conventional neoliberal (Amable and Palombarini 2021). He served as an investment banker for the Rothschild Bank from 2008 to 2012. During that time, Macron was also a rapporteur for the Attali Commission, which offered a number of recommendations, many neoliberal in orientation, for "liberating French growth" (Attali 2008). As deputy secretary general of the Elysée, Macron proposed temporarily raising the workweek from thirty-five to thirty-seven hours and famously quipped that President Hollande's 75 percent income tax bracket would turn France into "Cuba without the sun" (*Le Figaro*, August 26, 2014). As minister of the economy and finance from 2014 to 2016, Macron championed a law, enacted via Article 49.3, that expanded Sunday work and competition in regulated professions and transportation (*Le Monde*, August 6, 2015). He also stated repeatedly that he was not a Socialist and founded his own political party to run for president, rather than seeking the Socialist Party (Parti Socialist, PS) nomination.

Macron's cabinet appointments likewise conveyed a neoliberal image. As part of an effort to woo conservative voters, Macron gave some of the most important ministries to members of the conservative party, The Republicans (Les Républicains, LR). Edouard Philippe, the prime minister, Bruno Le Maire, the minister of the economy and finance, and Gérald Darmanin, the minister of the budget, all hailed from LR.[1] Philippe, Le Maire, and Darmanin received cabinet positions that were not only important, but also central to economic and social policy. Macron's selection of the three men, therefore, seemed to indicate his intention to pursue a conservative, neoliberal agenda.

Yet to call Macron a neoliberal would be simplistic and inaccurate. Jean Pisani-Ferry, an economist who played a leading role in putting together Macron's economic platform in 2017, believes that the president is cut from the same ideological cloth as the former Socialist minister of finance and head of the International Monetary Fund (IMF), Dominique Strauss-Kahn (interview by author with Jean Pisani-Ferry, March 14, 2019). Before becoming the head of the IMF, Strauss-Kahn had been a very successful minister of finance in the Jospin government and was widely expected to run for president on a centrist, social-liberal platform in 2007. However, Strauss-Kahn's career was derailed by allegations that he raped a chambermaid in a New York hotel and that he participated in sex parties with prostitutes. Ten years later, Macron moved into the social-liberal space that Strauss-Kahn had occupied. Pisani-Ferry notes that Macron shares Strauss-Kahn's "desire to push the left to break with its ideological taboos and be more reformist." In addition, rather than aligning with either the left or the right, "Macron prefers to pick and choose what works from both sides" (interview by author with Jean Pisani-Ferry, March 14, 2019).

Many have noted the parallels between Macron's 2017 campaign themes and the Attali Report of 2008, which Macron helped write (*L'Opinion*, January 23, 2018). Here, too, there is more ambiguity than the conventional depiction suggests. Although the Attali Report is often caricatured as a neoliberal wish list, alongside neoliberal recommendations to expand competition and labor market flexibility it contained a number of social and public investment recommendations. Indeed, the first six of the twenty "fundamental decisions" in the Attali Report revolve around increased public spending to promote innovation and productivity (Attali 2008: 14–15):

(1) Enable all students to master reading, writing, arithmetic, computer skills, and the English language by the sixth grade.
(2) Create ten poles of excellence in research and training among institutions of higher learning.

(3) Give France the means to be a leader in the technologies of the future (digital, health, renewable energy, tourism, biotechnology, nanotechnology, and neuroscience).
(4) Establish ten "Ecopolises," small towns or neighborhoods of fewer than 50,000 inhabitants that integrate advanced environmental and communication technologies.
(5) Make high-speed internet available to all individuals, companies, and public administrations.
(6) Install infrastructure (ports, airports, financial centers) to support business and improve the quality of public housing.

Whether out of social-liberal convictions or the need to win over left-leaning voters, Macron offered a number of social promises on the campaign trail. He regularly pledged to "protect" as well as "liberate" (*libérer, protéger*) (French Government 2018) and was known for using phrases that conveyed a balanced agenda like "at the same time" or "on the other hand" (*en même temps*) (Bigorgne et al. 2017). More concretely, Macron's program contained a number of important social investment measures designed to expand opportunities for the disadvantaged. He pledged to cut maximum class sizes in half for first- and second-graders in low-income school districts (Macron 2017). In addition, he promised to establish some 2 million training and apprenticeship positions to help people with poor job prospects, especially those who had left school without a diploma (Macron 2017).

Macron also promised to help those at the bottom more directly. He pledged to increase the minimum pension by 10 percent and to boost the take-home pay of ordinary workers by phasing out the local housing tax for the bottom 80 percent of earners. He also vowed to increase take-home pay by replacing certain payroll taxes, which are levied only on wages, with the General Social Contribution (Contribution Sociale Généralisée, CSG), a tax that is imposed on all sources of earnings, including pensions, investments, annuities, rental income, and capital gains. Finally, Macron depicted his planned pension overhaul as a social justice measure. The reform aimed to merge France's forty-two different pension regimes into a single system, with the same rules for all, thereby putting an end to opaque cross-subsidies that cause low-income, blue-collar workers to subsidize the pensions of more affluent white-collar workers and civil servants (Macron 2016: 147–149; 2017).

Macron's agenda clearly involved more than neoliberalism. There were certainly pledges to cut spending, taxes, labor market regulations, and restrictions on competition. However, inspired by the Attali Report and Pisani-Ferry, Macron also pledged to undertake costly public investments in education and skill formation, research, advanced technologies, and infrastructure. In addition, he promised a number of reforms to improve the living standards of low-income workers and pensioners. Of course, it is one thing to have a campaign platform and another to enact the promised measures once elected. In the case of Macron, the agenda of economic liberalization dominated his early actions, and the limited public investment and social initiatives that he put into place failed to dispel the notion that he was a neoliberal reformer, concerned only about the well-being of corporations and the well-to-do.

5.2   Initial Reforms

Macron wasted no time in converting electoral victory into liberal economic reform. The most dramatic changes were in the area of fiscal policy. Macron's budgets delivered several sizable tax cuts to business and the affluent. The corporate tax rate was placed on a four-year glide path, declining from 33.3 percent to 31 percent in 2019, 28 percent in 2020, 26.5 percent in 2021, and 25 percent in 2022 (French Government 2018). The government also created the Single Flat-Rate Levy (Prélèvement Forfaitaire Unique, PFU) at a low rate of 30 percent for financial income (dividends, interest, capital gains on the sale of shares). Previously, the tax rate could be as high as 46.5 percent on dividends and 64.5 percent on capital gains for movable assets (France 2018).

In a very controversial move, Macron significantly scaled back France's wealth tax, the Solidarity Tax on Wealth (Impôt de Solidarité sur la Fortune, ISF). The ISF was imposed on holdings of over €1.3 million, starting at a rate of 0.5 percent and rising to a maximum of 1.5 percent. Macron had called for a "tax system that rewards risk taking, enrichment through talent, work, and innovation" and singled out the ISF as a tax that penalized "those who succeed during their lives by investing in companies and innovation" (Macron 2016: 87). One of his first acts as president was to replace the ISF with a much narrower tax on real estate wealth only, the Real Estate Wealth Tax (Impôt sur la Fortune Immobilière, IFI). Whereas in 2017, the ISF was paid by 350,000 households and generated €4.2 billion in revenues, in 2018, the IFI was paid by only 120,000 households and raised a mere €1.3 billion in revenues (Vandepitte 2019: 63). Macron defended the overhaul of the ISF on the grounds that the tax penalized those who work hard and take risks, but many of the beneficiaries of his reform came by their wealth through inheritance, as opposed to hard work and risk-taking.

Macron sought to improve the business climate through labor market liberalization as well as tax cuts (*Les Echos*, August 31, 2017; *Capital avec Management*, May 23, 2017). The Pénicaud Law, named after Minister of Labor Muriel Pénicaud, was enacted via ordinances in fall 2017 and offered several advantages to business. Although the law raised the minimum compensation for unfair dismissals, it also established a ceiling and tied the level of compensation to the number of years worked. Employers were more than happy with this trade-off, which limited their financial exposure and put an end to lengthy, uncertain legal conflicts. The Pénicaud Law also extended the primacy of company-level agreements, where French unions are typically weak or absent, over sectoral agreements, where unions have greater leverage. In addition, the law made it easier for companies to lay off workers for economic reasons. Previously, if a company was losing money in France, but making profits globally thanks to strong results in other countries, it could not invoke economic difficulties as a reason for laying off workers. With the Pénicaud Law, poor economic performance in France became sufficient to justify layoffs, even if the company as a whole remained highly profitable.

The Pénicaud Law provided a further benefit to small businesses with fewer than fifty employees, authorizing employers to negotiate directly with employees on working hours, pay, and overtime, whereas previously there had to be a union representative present. The law also reduced costs and red tape in businesses with more than ten employees by merging several in-company worker organizations – personnel delegates, enterprise committees, health and safety committee representatives – into a single organization, the Social and Economic Committee (Comité Social et Economique, CSE). Finally, the Pénicaud Law created the possibility for companies experiencing economic difficulties to negotiate so-called Collective Performance Agreements (Accords de Performance Collective, APC) with employees that reduce pay, increase working hours, and/ or reorganize job duties in return for a promise to preserve employment.

On September 12, 2017, the neo-communist trade union, the General Confederation of Labor (Confédération Générale du Travail, CGT), organized a protest against the Pénicaud Law. Some 223,000 demonstrators took to the streets according to the police, 400,000 according to the CGT (*Le Parisien*, September 12, 2017). There would be no other major protests, however, in part because the CGT was acting alone. The other unions did not join the CGT for a variety of reasons. They liked some provisions of the Pénicaud reform, notably the increase in the minimum compensation for unfair dismissals. The government had also made some small concessions: bargaining over health-care rules was not decentralized beyond the sectoral level, as the government had contemplated, and instead of all employers, only employers in companies with fewer than fifty employees were authorized to negotiate without a union representative. Most important, the largest union, the French Democratic

Confederation of Labor (Confédération Française Démocratique du Travail, CFDT), was not entirely opposed to the reform. The CFDT has long favored a decentralization of bargaining as a way of reducing state control and opening a space for worker participation and flexibility. The CFDT's support was conditioned, though, on the requirement that decentralized agreements be signed by forces representing a majority of employees, rather than by a minority union, as had often been the case in the past. Without the support of the CFDT, the protests did not go far. Still, that did not stop Macron, while visiting Greece, from making the kind of dismissive remark that would later come back to haunt him: "I am of an absolute determination, and I will cede nothing – not to the slackers, not to the cynics, and not to the extremes" (Young 2018).

Macron confronted significantly more union resistance over another liberalizing initiative, the 2018 reform of the French National Railway Company (Société Nationale des Chemins de Fer Français, SNCF) (*Le Monde*, June 5, 2018). The SNCF carried a huge debt (€54.5 billion), had lagged in maintaining and modernizing the railroad network, and had a high-cost structure. With the EU requiring that French railroad lines be fully open to competition by the end of 2019, Macron felt it imperative to overhaul the SNCF. The law adopted June 14, 2018, provided that the government would take over €25 billion in SNCF debt in 2020 and €10 billion in 2022, but subject to two liberalizing measures that raised red flags with the unions. The first put an end to the special "railroad employee status," which provides job security and the right to retire between the ages of 50 and 55, for all new hires. Existing employees would retain their status. The second controversial provision transformed the SNCF into a "company with public capital" (*société anonyme à capitaux publics*). Although the state still held 100 percent of the SNCF's capital, this transformation was widely viewed as a first step toward privatization.

Even before the SNCF reform was enacted, the powerful railroad workers went on strike (*Libération*, April 3, 2019; *Le Figaro*, June 27, 2018). While the CGT is the biggest union among the railroad workers, this time the other unions joined the movement. The first strike was organized April 3, 2017, and to make the movement last longer, strikes were scheduled for just two days per week, so that strikers could continue to collect part of their salaries. The first day, nearly 40 percent of the railroad workers went on strike. More important, the strike rate for conductors was close to double that figure (77 percent). Without conductors, the trains ground to a halt, leaving passengers stranded and generating massive traffic jams, as commuters took to their cars to get to work (*Le Figaro*, May 22, 2018). The conductor strike rate remained above 50 percent for six weeks, and there was a lot of public sympathy for the strikers.

The railroad workers mounted an impressive movement, with thirty-six strike days spread over three months. In terms of strike days per worker, it was the largest movement since the 1995 protests against the Juppé Plan (*Le Monde*, June 28, 2018). The strike inflicted losses of €790 million on the SNCF (*Capital*, July 20, 2018). Still, a determined Macron was able to stare down the strikers, and the reform entered into effect without any modification.

For all the tax cuts, labor market reforms, and confrontations with the unions, Macron's agenda went beyond economic liberalization. True to his campaign platform, shortly after taking office Macron announced a massive public investment program, the €57 billion Grand Investment Plan (Grand Plan d'Investissement, GPI), covering the period 2018–2022 (French Government 2017b; Pisani-Ferry 2017). The plan had been drafted by the economist, Jean-Pisani Ferry, who was also the central figure behind Macron's economic platform. It devoted €15 billion to training, in particular targeting 1 million long-term unemployed and 1 million young school dropouts, with the hope of finding permanent jobs for at least 300,000 of them. The plan also pledged €20 billion for accelerating France's ecological transformation, with much of the money going to subsidies for the renovation of homes to make them more energy-efficient and for the purchase of hybrid and electric automobiles. The GPI pledged a further €13 billion to enhance French competitiveness through innovation, focusing on joint projects between industry and universities, the provision of high-speed internet service throughout France, and subsidies for innovative projects, including in agriculture. Finally, the plan budgeted €9 billion to "build the digital state," with the goal of making all public services available online by 2022 as well as modernizing and digitizing French public hospitals.

Along with public investment, Macron tendered a number of measures to help low-income households. Some of these measures reflected a social investment logic, such as cutting class sizes in half for first- and second-graders in disadvantaged school districts. The reform was in keeping with Macron's belief that "the state should privilege intervention up-front, which is less costly and more effective" (Macron 2016: 139). The presumption in this case was that early intervention to provide additional, individualized attention to students from low-income families would reduce dropout rates in the higher grades, thereby improving the academic and employment prospects of students from disadvantaged backgrounds.

Other reforms entailed direct transfers to average and low-income groups. Macron boosted the minimum pension by 10 percent or roughly €80 per month. His government also began phasing out (over a three-year period from 2018 to 2020) the local housing tax for 80 percent of the population, while excluding the wealthiest 20 percent.[2] In a more complicated move, Macron eliminated remaining payroll taxes for unemployment and health insurance, shifting their funding to the CSG, which is levied on all sources of earnings, not just wages. With other groups sharing the cost of the unemployment and health insurance programs, the burden on wage earners was reduced, resulting in a net increase in take-home pay of 1.45 percent (*Les Echos*, October 1, 2018).

Macron's initial actions, particularly the liberalizing reforms, were well received by business groups and their supporters. No less a proponent of free markets than *The Economist* magazine named France its "country of the year" for 2017, declaring that, "before he [Macron] turned up, France looked unreformable … [but] in 2017, France defied all expectations" (*The Economist*, December 23, 2017–January 5, 2018). Macron also appeared on the cover of the May 31, 2018 edition of *Forbes*, with the headline, "Leader of Free Markets" and a statement by Macron that, "I want this country open to disruption." Macron declared repeatedly that "France is back" and that he was turning the country into a "start-up nation." French political scientist Pascal Perrineau summarizes the prevailing sentiment at the time that Macron had found a long-elusive path of reform in France:

In the space of a few months, the new government in power gave the impression that political representatives had rediscovered their capacity to speak for and change society. The reforms of the SNCF and the labor code which, in other times, would have encountered hostility and blockage by social forces, were voted by national representatives. The new political power appeared, for a time, to be effective. (Perrineau 2019: 57)

International investors also responded to Macron's message. Foreign direct investment (FDI) in France jumped from €22.0 billion in 2017 to €35.4 billion in 2018 (INSEE 2021a). In 2018, France passed Germany to occupy the second position in Europe for the number of FDI projects, and in 2019, France passed a UK hobbled by Brexit to assume the top spot (Business France 2020).

5.3   The Yellow Vest Protests

Macron's top-down, skinny-politics approach may have won the plaudits of the Anglo-American and business press, but just eighteen months into his term, it triggered arguably the most significant protests since May 1968, the so-called yellow vest movement, which shook Macron's government to its foundations. The protests were touched off by anger over a planned increase in diesel gasoline taxes, totaling €0.28 per liter (around $1.40 per gallon), beginning January 1, 2019, which came on the heels of an even bigger increase in 2018 (French Ministry of

Environmental Transition 2020). The tax on diesel was especially exasperating, given that the government had long encouraged French drivers to switch to cars with diesel engines in order to improve gas mileage and reduce fuel consumption. In addition, the tax was occurring at a time of rapidly rising world oil prices, making the extra cost visible and painful. Between October 2017 and October 2018, the price of diesel gasoline increased by 22.6 percent and that of regular unleaded by 14.6 percent (Vandepitte 2019: 56). Beyond the diesel tax hike, the yellow vests were angry about a host of other measures that penalized car owners: more expensive and demanding technical inspections that made it harder to keep older cars on the road, higher tolls, increased parking fees, a lower speed limit on secondary roads, and an explosion in the number of tickets issued automatically via speed detection cameras installed at toll booths (Vandepitte 2019: 58–59).

The label "yellow vest" referred to the yellow safety vests that French drivers are required to keep in their cars in case of breakdown or accident. All of the protestors donned these yellow vests when demonstrating. However, the yellow vest protests went well beyond the costs of car ownership, spiraling into a broader critique of the government's economic agenda and mode of governance.

The movement started in May 2018, when Priscillia Ludosky, a 32-year-old woman, posted a petition on change.org. Ludosky's petition called for "a reduction in the price of gasoline at the pump!" (Vandepitte 2019: 10). It amassed 300,000 signatures by October and 1.2 million by January 2019. The next step occurred in November 2018, when two truck drivers outside Paris launched a Facebook event to "block all roads." The truckers also came up with the idea of wearing yellow vests.

Beginning November 17, the yellow vests held protests every Saturday, organizing demonstrations on the Champs-Elysées and major arteries of provincial cities. The first protest drew nearly 300,000 demonstrators. The yellow vests also blocked highways and many entrances to city centers, becoming a ubiquitous presence at roundabouts on the edge of French cities.

According to the historian Gérard Noiriel, the yellow vests reintroduced the "social question," which Noiriel contends had been ignored in favor of identity politics, into the heart of French political life (Noiriel 2019: 24). The yellow vests were generally people of modest means, employed in low-paid and precarious jobs, and struggling to make ends meet (Depraz 2019). One of their criticisms of the use of gasoline taxes to combat global warming was that "The elites speak of the end of the world, while we worry about [having enough money for] the end of the month" when paychecks are issued in France (*Le Monde*, November 24, 2018). The average income of the protestors was around €1,700 per month (under $25,000 annually), and they resented Macron for his policies, which they believed favored the rich (Farbiaz 2019: 33; Noiriel 2019; Plenel 2019).[3] Along with the gasoline tax, they wanted to roll back the reform of the ISF, which symbolized in their minds Macron's bias toward the wealthy (Plenel 2019: 38–39). Their preferences for redistribution ran in an altogether different direction from Macron's, with 87 percent agreeing with the statement that "in order to establish social justice, we must take from the rich and give to the poor" (Perrineau 2019: 99).

The yellow vest movement had a territorial component as well as a class component. It drew primarily from people living in rural or peri-urban areas (Bruneau et al. 2019; Lussault 2019). One reason was that unlike city dwellers, who benefit from France's excellent public transportation system, rural and peri-urban inhabitants are wholly dependent on their cars to get to work, take their children to school, and do their shopping. Consequently, they were especially sensitive to measures that increased the cost of car ownership: "It's the revolt of the employee who has no choice but to go to drive to work and feels unfairly taxed" (*Le Monde*, November 6, 2018). Another reason was that these territories had experienced a host of cuts to public services – the elimination of unprofitable rural train and bus lines, the consolidation of courthouses in large cities, and the closing of post offices, schools, and public hospitals – that forced inhabitants to drive more (Farbiaz 2019: 23–24). Sociologist Alexis Spire notes that using tax incentives to discourage people from driving is only legitimate to the extent that they have alternatives to getting behind the wheel:

This idea of using green taxation to orient behavior is plausible in urban areas where people can choose between the subway, tram, bus, bicycle, and car, but when the car is the only means of transportation, it does not have the same meaning. And when one adds the vaunting of this green taxation to recent decisions to close train lines and more generally the disinvestment in public transportation, it becomes intolerable for the affected populations. They feel doubly penalized: on the one hand, in terms of access to public transportation; on the other hand, concerning the only remaining means of transportation, the automobile. (Spire 2019: 19–20)

The yellow vests harbored a deep antipathy toward governing elites in general and Emmanuel Macron in particular (Plenel 2019). Attesting to their dissatisfaction with French governance, in the first round of the 2017 presidential election, 42 percent of yellow vests had voted for the far-right candidate, Marine Le Pen, and 20 percent for the far-left candidate, Jean-Luc Mélenchon (Lorriaux 2018). Indeed, one of the recurring demands of the demonstrators was for Macron to resign, often expressed in profane language or with images of a guillotine (Vandepitte 2019: 42–44).

The yellow vests wanted to do more than get rid of Macron. They also sought to forge a different kind of politics in France, a more bottom-up democracy. The yellow vests frequently voiced their disdain for centralized governance by out-of-touch Parisian elites. In order to check Parisian power and give a greater voice to the people, they called for the creation of a Citizens' Initiative Referendum (Référendum d'Initiative Citoyenne, RIC), which would allow referenda to be held on a wide range of issues, including to propose or repeal a law, amend the constitution, or remove an elected official from office (Vandepitte 2019: 70–72).

Any explanation of the yellow vest protests starts with Macron's arrogant and dismissive behavior. When Macron became president, his demeanor changed dramatically. During the campaign, he had projected a fresh, open image. He had been very accessible and eager to debate his ideas with anyone. Once Macron became president, however, he became distant, formal, and aloof – almost a caricature of the imperious Fifth Republic president. Macron also concentrated power in the purest Fifth Republic presidential style, making all decisions, big and small, and imposing a tight discipline on cabinet members and Republic on the Move (La République en Marche, LREM) politicians. The combination of icy formality and far-reaching power earned Macron the nickname "Jupiter," after the all-powerful god of Roman mythology, the god of the sky, thunder, and lightning (*Politico*, June 16, 2017). In his postelection incarnation, Macron often came off as arrogant, dismissive, and indifferent to the travails of ordinary French citizens (Paugam 2019).

During the first eighteen months of his presidency, Macron made a series of remarks (cited in *Politico*, October 9, 2018) suggesting that he cared only about the most economically successful people and had little regard for those who were struggling. He celebrated entrepreneurs as the "*premiers de cordée*," a mountaineering term denoting the person at the top of the rope who pulls up the others. Another time, Macron contrasted "people who are succeeding" economically to "people who are nothing." He also took jabs at the French for their supposed aversion to reform. On a visit to Denmark, Macron praised "the Lutheran people" who had embraced the transformations of recent years in contrast to "the Gaul refractory to change."

Macron's remarks toward those who were struggling were especially insensitive. When an unemployed gardener asked Macron for advice on how to find a job as a gardener, Macron's response was that if the person was "ready and motivated," he could "cross the street" and find a job waiting tables in a café. Macron also lamented that France is spending "crazy dough" on antipoverty measures that he claimed give the unemployed no incentive to take jobs. Remarks such as these, when combined with mammoth tax cuts for corporations and the affluent, fueled an image of Macron as a "president of the rich" or worse, a kind of Marie Antoinette, telling the poor to eat cake. Many yellow vests responded with a Jacobin enthusiasm for beheading the king, and observers noted that the yellow vest movement, like the French Revolution, had begun as a tax revolt (Vandepitte 2019: 42–44).

It is difficult to overstate the antipathy that the yellow vests harbored toward Macron. When the president visited a prefecture that had been set on fire by protestors, he was greeted with cries of "rotten" and "son of a whore" (Perrineau 2019: 74). The yellow vests also relished turning Macron's dismissive phrases against him (Mercier 2018). Graffiti left behind after a December 1 protest on a posh Parisian avenue declared "Okay Manu, cross the street," meaning get another job, perhaps working in a café, as the president had suggested to the unemployed gardener. A tweet the following day, reflecting the fact that the president had not met with the protestors, suggested that Macron "does not want to stoop to talking with the *derniers de cordée*," the last on the climbing rope or dregs of society.

The yellow vests also embraced a Jacobin, insurrectionary discourse. A banner at a yellow vest protest quoted Article 35 of the 1793 Declaration of the Rights of Man and of Citizen: "When the government violates the rights of the people, insurrection is the most sacred and indispensable duties of the people" (Perrineau 2019: 79). Other slogans went straight to the point: "Macron resign," "Macron get out," and more ominously, "Get out the guillotines" and "We've cut off heads for less" (Perrineau 2019: 106). Along with Macron's insensitive comments, two factors emphasized in this book fueled the yellow vest protests: the social anesthesia state and skinny politics.

5.4   The Social Anesthesia State and the "President of the Rich"

The social anesthesia state played a central role in triggering the yellow vest protests. As noted in previous chapters, the strategy of deploying a massive social anesthesia state meant that France's path toward a more liberal economic order proceeded in two steps: a first step to dismantle the *dirigiste* state and a second to overhaul the social anesthesia state that had made the first step politically possible. Complicating the challenge, the ramping up of the social anesthesia state had reduced the economic payoff from the rollback of *dirigiste* industrial policy, thereby fueling the sentiment that liberal economic reforms did not work.

From the perspective of many yellow vest protestors, economic liberalization had brought lots of pain, but little economic gain (Farbiaz 2019: 33–35). Their taxes had increased, while all manner of public services – from post offices, to schools, to courthouses, to rural bus and train lines – had been reduced or withdrawn entirely. As the social anesthesia state had grown, public investment had been scaled back. Working-class and lower-middle-class protestors, who swelled the ranks of the yellow vests, had also been on the receiving end of measures to make labor markets more "flexible," such as reduced job protections, the decentralization of bargaining, and the expansion of part-time and fixed-term contracts (Noiriel 2019). They were, therefore, extremely skeptical of Emmanuel Macron's upwardly redistributive tax policies and liberalizing labor market reforms (Farbiaz 2019; Noiriel 2019; Plenel 2019). In their view, such measures had been tried and failed, bringing only lower earnings and greater precarity to those at the bottom of the climbing rope. While Macron believed that France's social anesthesia state was too generous and needed to be overhauled, France's long, liberalizing road meant that the experience of many yellow vest protestors had been that such reform yielded mostly pain without gain.

The social anesthesia state fueled the yellow vest protests in a second way, by sharpening Macron's fiscal and distributional choices. Macron's top priority was to shore up the balance sheets of French companies, while reducing the government's budget deficit. As a result, he had little money for anything else. Indeed, the government sought to trim social spending in several areas, fueling the image of "Macron, president of the rich." One of the most ill-fated initiatives at the beginning of his presidency was a €5 reduction in the means-tested monthly housing allowance. The gesture inflicted hardship on a vulnerable population, all to save less than €400 million per year. Yet seeking to reduce budget deficits, while simultaneously cutting taxes, the government swept every corner for savings. Nor were housing allowances the only hard-hearted spending cut. In August 2018, the government deindexed pensions from inflation. Parliament then voted to increase pensions by only 0.3 percent annually, at a time when inflation was running at 1.8 percent (*Le Parisien*, January 17, 2019).

The social anesthesia state also compromised the government's efforts to boost the purchasing power of middle- and low-income groups. As described, the government shifted payroll taxes for unemployment (2.4 percent) and health insurance (0.75 percent) to the CSG, which is levied on all manner of earnings, not just wages. This revenue-neutral measure increased purchasing power for wage earners by 1.45 percent (*Les Echos*, October 1, 2018). Retirees fared less well, however. They do not pay Social Security charges, since they are no longer employed, but they do pay the CSG. The 40 percent of retirees with pensions below €1,400 per month were unaffected by the reform because they continued to pay a reduced CSG of 3.8 percent for those receiving modest pensions. Retirees receiving more than €1,400 per month, however, saw their CSG rise by 1.7 points from 7.5 percent to 9.2 percent (*Les Echos*, July 18, 2018). Macron might have spared senior citizens this cost by keeping their CSG at the same rate (given that they did not benefit from reduced payroll taxes), but then the government would have had to find money elsewhere. Thus, the cash-strapped social anesthesia state led to a double blow for a number of retirees: pensions that increased far less than the rate of inflation and an increase in the taxes on those pensions. The contrast between massive tax cuts for business and the affluent on the one hand, and tax increases along with a reduction in living standards for pensioners on the other hand, was grist for the mill of those claiming that Macron cared only about the rich (Noiriel 2019: 75–76).

Along with redistribution, the social anesthesia state took a toll on the government's public investment program. The GPI announced in 2017 promised €57 billion over a five-year period for training (€15 billion), ecological transformation (€20 billion), innovation (€13 billion), and the digitization of state and hospital services (€9 billion). Even as announced, the GPI included only €24 billion in additional state outlays, not €57 billion (French Government 2017a). The other €33 billion would come from three sources. The first was a redeployment of existing spending (€12 billion). The second was a loan from the state's allied financial institution, the Deposits and Consignments Fund (Caisse des Dépôts et Consignations, CDC) (€11 billion) – the same institution that Sarkozy had tapped to help finance his industrial policy initiatives during the 2008 financial crisis. The third source of money was the multi-year Investments in the Future Program (Programme d'Investissements d'Avenir, PIA) (€10 billion). As described in Chapter 3, the PIA was created by Sarkozy during the Great Recession to boost investment in strategic areas and new technologies. In its original incarnation, the program spent just under €10 billion per year from 2010 to 2013. Thus, not only was Macron repackaging Sarkozy's PIA as part of his GPI, but *Macron's spending on all the GPI programs combined (€11.4 billion per year) barely exceeded Sarkozy's spending on the PIA alone (€10 billion per year).*

As unambitious as the GPI was in its original formulation, it was even less so in its execution. The government was slow to disburse the promised funds, budgeting €3.4 billion in 2018, €6.3 billion in 2019, and €7.2 billion in 2020, for a total of only €16.9 billion over the first three years of what was supposed to be a five-year €57 billion program (*Le Figaro*, October 10, 2019). This low rate of spending raised the question if the government even intended to spend the full €57 billion. In addition, whereas the PIA kept funds in a separate account, so it was possible to trace their usage and impact, the moneys for the GPI were integrated into the regular budgets of the spending ministries (French Government 2017a; French Ministry of the Economy and Finance 2017). As a result, the GPI program was completely opaque, making it impossible to know which measures it was actually financing. Indeed, some of the GPI moneys were almost certainly used to offset cuts to normal operating budgets made under the pressure of the social anesthesia state.

The social anesthesia state also compromised the government's environmental strategy, swallowing up resources for green policies. Prior to the yellow vest conflict, France's energy tax, the Domestic Tax on the Consumption of Energy Products (Taxe Intérieure de Consommation sur les Produits Energétiques, TICPE) was expected to raise €37.7 billion in 2019. Yet less than 25 percent of the €37.7 billion was slated for the development of alternative energy sources (€7.2 billion) or transportation infrastructure (€1.2 billion) (*Le Monde*, November 6, 2018). Of the remainder, €12 billion was destined for local government authorities to cover the cost of apprenticeship programs and the Active Solidarity Income (Revenu de Solidarité Active, RSA), while €17 billion would go into state coffers. Yellow vest protestors were infuriated that they were being forced to pay more for energy and the government was not even using the money for environmental purposes. Instead, energy tax revenues were helping backfill the hole in the state budget created by massive tax cuts for corporations and the rich. As sociologist Alexis Spire put it, the yellow vests had "the feeling that under the pretext of ecology, [the government] is picking their pockets" (Spire 2019: 18). Thus, instead of shared sacrifice to restore France's public finances, the "president of the rich" was cutting taxes for corporations and the well-heeled, while cutting benefits and services for the rest of the French and raising their taxes to boot.

This critical view of Macron's economic policies was widely shared by the French public. According to a poll in late October 2018, 72 percent of respondents believed that their purchasing power had decreased under Macron (*Le Monde*, October 30, 2018). The yellow vests called for a reversal of the policies that had squeezed ordinary citizens: a repeal of all planned energy tax increases, an increase in the minimum wage, a reindexation of pensions, and a repeal of the 1.7 percent increase in the CSG on pensions (*Le Monde*, November 12, 2018).

The combination of the president's belief that he needed to prioritize the well-being of business and the affluent for economic reasons and the fiscal constraints imposed by the social anesthesia state fueled the image of Macron as "president of the rich." On the one hand, the government tendered massive tax cuts to the rich and the affluent. On the other hand, it chased budgetary savings with sometimes ruthless determination, raised taxes on ordinary citizens, and emptied public investment and ecological promises of much of their substance. These sharp distributional choices, which were made necessary by the social anesthesia state, contributed centrally to Macron's unpopularity.

5.5   Skinny Politics and the Backlash against Jupiter

Along with the social anesthesia state, the second factor emphasized in this book that contributed to the yellow vest protests was Macron's extreme skinny-politics approach to reform. Of course, presidents under the Fifth Republic have generally operated in a top-down manner, but Macron, embracing a Jupiterian governing style, took this approach to a whole new level. Part of the reason is the insular, technocratic structure of his government. The president, both of his prime ministers during his first term (Edouard Philippe from May 2017 to July 2020 and Jean Castex from July 2020 to May 2022), and his minister of the economy and finance, Bruno Le Maire, all graduated from the ultra-elite National School of Administration (Ecole Nationale d'Administration, ENA). All of their respective cabinet directors graduated from ENA as well. Macron is known for relying on a very narrow circle of technocrats, who think like he does, without seeking wider input from either members of parliament, local elected officials, or leaders of interest groups.

Macron held little regard for established political elites and interest groups. In his mind, they were the losers of the 2017 elections, the people he had defeated. They were also losers in the sense of having failed to reform and modernize France when they had been in power. Given Macron's dim view of the political establishment, it is perhaps no surprise that he titled the book that he published on the eve of his presidential run, *Révolution* (Macron 2016). In the spirit of revolution, Macron created an entirely new political party and recruited as candidates for the legislative elections people from civil society, most of whom had never run for office. Also in the spirit of revolution, Macron had little regard for the members of the *ancien régime*. Political economist Elie Cohen, who helped advise Macron in 2017, notes that Macron showed no interest in working with political elites, even those who offered their support prior to the elections: "He didn't negotiate with the existing political forces. Instead, he dynamited the system. He got rid of everyone and refused to negotiate with politicians on the left and the right who supported him" (interview by author with Elie Cohen, Research Director,

National Center for Scientific Research (CNRS) at the Institute of Political Studies of Paris and member of the Prime Minister's Council of Economic Analysis, Paris, March 19, 2019).

Macron wanted a free hand in governing, and working with existing elites might limit his room to maneuver. What is more, he did not really respect traditional political elites. The PS, in his view, was a conservative party of ideological apparatchiks who were out of touch with the real world, and the Republicans were scarcely any better. Elie Cohen voiced frustration at Macron's unwillingness to work with deputies in the National Assembly, who were prepared to support him and would have provided valuable governing experience:

During the run-up to the presidential election, fifty or so Socialist deputies as well as some Republicans wanted to forge an alliance with Macron. They would keep their party affiliations but endorse Macron for president. I encouraged him to go this route. I called is the "Catamaran strategy" because in a Catamaran, the center steers, but the boat is kept balanced by the left and right wings. The Catamaran strategy would have expanded Macron's electoral base. He could have won over other deputies. He could have benefited from the political experience of elected officials. He could have incorporated a block of local elected officials into LREM party structures. Macron refused. He just didn't want to share power. (Interview by author with Elie Cohen, Research Director, National Center for Scientific Research (CNRS) at the Institute of Political Studies of Paris and member of the Prime Minister's Council of Economic Analysis, Paris, March 19, 2019)

Macron was equally disdainful of the trade unions and employers. Indeed, one of his main reproaches of previous presidents, especially François Hollande, was that they had been too solicitous of the social partners. Instead of identifying a clear line of action and working with the unions and employers to implement it, Hollande and other leaders had sought to forge compromises, often at the expense of their agenda. Macron and his team felt that the government needed to be more assertive, imposing its will even in the face of opposition from the social partners. Otherwise, as a high-level political adviser related, Macron would fail just like his predecessors: "We aren't going to negotiate for the sake of negotiating or agree to a compromise for the sake of compromise. That's what our predecessor did. That's what all the people who lost in 2017 did" (interview by author with high-level political adviser to Macron, March 2019).

Macron's approach to concertation reduced the role of the social partners dramatically. The government was not looking for compromises. It was also not looking for input from the unions and employers. Rather, the presumption was that the government knew what had to be done, and the social partners were welcome to participate, but only if they followed the government's agenda:

When we give an orientation letter to the social partners, we state our goals and tell the social partners that if they find a solution, we will translate it into law. Previous governments would accept a solution that was very far from their objectives. We insist on our objectives. A compromise has no intrinsic value. (Interview by author with high-level political adviser to Macron, March 2019)

The government had no intention of diluting its agenda for the sake of an agreement: "We won't sacrifice reforms to French totems and taboos like the need to work with the social partners" (interview by author with high-level political adviser to Macron, March 2019). Rather, if the social partners declined to go along, the government would implement its agenda anyway:

The difference between us and previous governments is that we don't consider an agreement, a compromise, as the objective. It is a means. If it works, fine, but if not, we'll go a different way. (Interview by author with high-level political adviser to Macron, March 2019)

The government's relationship with the CFDT was especially revealing of Macron's disdain for the social partners. Not only is the CFDT the largest trade union in France, but it also shares much of the government's economic and social agenda. Like Macron, the CFDT sees social investment as the key to fighting poverty and creating equality of opportunity. The CFDT also supports labor market activation measures combining greater job search requirements with more secure benefits and training opportunities. In addition, it favors increased reliance on collective bargaining, as opposed to legislation, and expanded company-level bargaining, provided that such agreements require the approval of a majority of employees. Finally, the CFDT has long championed the creation of a Swedish-style pension system that treats all contributors equally – exactly the kind of system that Macron was advancing as the signature social justice initiative of his presidential term. Yet for all these convergences between the positions of the government and the CFDT, Macron showed little inclination to work with the union, as Laurent Berger, the General Secretary of the CFDT, lamented:

The CFDT supported pension reforms in 1995, 2003, and 2013. We also supported the more flexible layoff system established in 2008. Fifty percent of CFDT members voted for Macron on the first round [of the 2017 presidential election]. Yet with this government, we are limited to a role of commentator, not negotiator or decision maker. My beef with the government is that it won't work with those who know how and want to reform. This makes no sense. The country is traumatized. The government needs buy-in for its reforms. (Interview by author with Laurent Berger, General Secretary, CFDT, March 21, 2019)

Macron was not looking for a partner, however. He believed that the role of unions was to negotiate in the factories, not to shape policy. He also felt that Berger was overstepping his authority. As the economist Jean Pisani-Ferry noted, "Macron doesn't want to let the CFDT decide what is acceptable and what is not. He wants to affirm his freedom vis-à-vis the CFDT" (interview by author with Jean Pisani-Ferry, March 14, 2019).

Macron and his circle of advisers did not see any real benefit to working with the CFDT. The government already knew what it wanted to do, and there was no sense that the CFDT or other actors had anything to add to the government's reforms. Consultation would just slow things down, and the government wanted to move fast. In addition, Macron was very concerned about appearing weak like his predecessors. If the government started making concessions to the CFDT, his opponents would smell blood and mobilize to block his every move. As Bernard Cazeneuve, the Socialist prime minister from 2016 to 2017, observed, this outlook had the unfortunate effect of equating negotiation with weakness: "The current government believes that if it negotiates, it becomes weaker. And that holding the line in an authoritarian manner is the way to triumph over the resistance to change" (*Le Monde*, December 4, 2018).

Along with technocratic arrogance and disdain for established political and social leaders, Macron's ultra-skinny approach was driven by an overestimation of his democratic mandate. Macron and his defenders point out that he has been more faithful to his campaign platform than any French president in memory. Just about all of the government's reforms, popular and controversial alike, were in his program, including the hated tax on gasoline. As a top Macron economic adviser remarked, Macron made his intentions very clear when he was running for president: "It is better to say what you are going to do before doing it. Macron made clear declarations during the [presidential] campaign. Already in 2016, all of the major reforms were articulated by Macron" (interview by author with high-level economic adviser to Macron, March 2019).

Given that Macron was faithfully implementing the platform on which he had run successfully for president, he and his advisers felt that he had a democratic mandate for these reforms and that there was no reason to compromise or delay. This reading reinforced the government's disdain for dissenting voices and refusal to back down when challenged. The problem is that it did not represent an entirely accurate reading of the motivations of those who had voted for Macron in 2017. Macron received less than 25 percent of the vote on the first ballot, and many of those votes stemmed from strategic calculations by voters, as opposed to an endorsement of Macron's agenda. According to an Ipsos poll, only 43 percent of Macron voters said that they voted "to support a candidate who suits you," far less than the 61 percent of Mélenchon voters, 67 percent of Le Pen voters, and 66 percent of Fillon voters (Mercier 2018). Conversely, 26 percent of Macron voters said that they gave him their vote "to prevent another candidate from reaching the second round," versus just 14 percent of Mélenchon voters, 9 percent of Le Pen voters, and 14 percent of Fillon voters.

Another sign that Macron's voters did not endorse his liberalizing economic agenda is that 46 percent of his votes on the first round came from people who had cast ballots for the Socialist Hollande in 2012 (Perrineau 2019: 47). In the absence of a credible Socialist candidate and with the expectation that the far right's Marine Le Pen would qualify for the runoff, many leftist supporters voted for Macron in order to prevent what they deemed an even worse candidate from facing off against Le Pen – the hard-right, scandal-plagued François Fillon. Macron won the runoff easily by a two-to-one margin against Marine Le Pen. Again, though, most voters were expressing their opposition to having a far-right xenophobe as president, rather than supporting Macron's agenda.

The institutions of the Fifth Republic more or less automatically converted Macron's election as president into a majority in the legislature. Legislative elections are held one or two months after the presidential election. Consequently, French voters know who the president will be for the next five years when they cast their votes for the National Assembly and have almost given the newly elected president a legislative majority.[4] In 2017, Macron's LREM won an absolute majority in the National Assembly, even though the party had existed for barely one year. Thanks to the institutional logic of the Fifth Republic, a presidential candidate who received less than 25 percent of the vote, much of it for strategic reasons, found himself with more than 50 percent of the seats in the National Assembly. This overrepresentation gave Macron tremendous power to legislate his agenda, but that power far exceeded popular support for this agenda. Indeed, in the 2022 legislative elections, disgruntled voters, tired of top-down policymaking and distrustful of Macron, took the unprecedented step of depriving the newly reelected president of a majority in the National Assembly for the first time since the 2000 constitutional reform aligned the presidential and legislative terms.

Another limit to Macron's democratic mandate is that his campaign platform was not as probusiness and neoliberal as he and his supporters claimed subsequently. As noted, slogans like "liberate, protect" and "on the other hand" suggested a careful balancing of economic and social objectives. There were also important public investment and social investment planks in Macron's platform. Consequently, even those voters who supported Macron for programmatic rather than strategic reasons may have expected a more social agenda than the government delivered.

The government's ultra-skinny-politics approach led to the yellow vest protests in several ways. For starters, secure in its supposed democratic mandate, the government aggressively pursued policies that lacked popular support (Noiriel 2019: 118). Even before the yellow vest protests, the president's approval rate had fallen from 62 percent in May 2017 to 29 percent in September 2018, a loss of 33 points. According to Pascal Perrineau, the two main reasons for this slide were the sense that Macron cared only about people who succeed and dissatisfaction among the elderly, who had been hurt by his policies (Perrineau 2019: 60–61). An Ipsos poll showed that 65 percent of respondents disapproved of the replacement of the ISF with a narrower real estate tax, while just 19 percent approved it (*Le Monde*, November 22, 2018). In addition, 67 percent of those surveyed believed that the government's fiscal policy was increasing inequality, as against only 4 percent who thought it was reducing inequality. Finally, on the issue that triggered the yellow vest protests, 63 percent of respondents to the Ipsos poll disapproved of "the increase in the price of diesel gasoline to fight global warming," more than double the 27 percent who approved of it.

Skinny politics also contributed to the government's failure to heed concerns voiced by its own supporters in the National Assembly. A group of LREM deputies had been calling for more social measures for over a year. They complained that "We are a majority of the center left that has been taken hostage by a minority of the center right" (*Le Monde*, December 14, 2018). In addition, they denounced the stranglehold of technocrats over government decisions and the marginalization of those seeking a more social approach.

Even as the yellow vests began to mobilize, Macron was slow to apprehend the danger, no doubt thinking that he could ride out this protest just like he had the earlier movements against the labor market and SNCF reforms. Three days before the first protest, the government tried to nip the movement in the bud by offering several small concessions worth a total of €500 million. The main measures included a doubling of the subsidy for the purchase of fuel-efficient cars from €2,000 to €4,000, an increase in the subsidy from €2,500 to €4,000 for low-income households purchasing new, less polluting home heating systems, and the expansion of eligibility for home heating and electricity subsidies to 2 million new households (for a total of 5.6 million households) (*Libération*, November 16, 2019). The yellow vests were not impressed, and critics noted that even with the subsidies, few average- or low-income households could afford to purchase expensive new electric cars or home heating systems

(Combes 2019). In addition, the €500 million in subsidies paled in comparison to the energy tax increases, which totaled €3.7 billion in 2018 and a planned €2.8 billion in 2019 (*Le Monde*, November 6, 2018).

Following the first yellow vest protest on November 17, Macron and his prime minister, Edouard Philippe, dug in their heels, refusing to entertain any modification of the gasoline tax hike. Philippe declared, "It's not when the wind blows that you should change direction. We will stay the course" (*Le Monde*, November 18, 2018). Other members of the government were openly dismissive. Benjamin Griveaux, the spokesperson for the government, described the protestors as "guys who smoke cigarettes and drive diesel cars," before adding, "This is not the France of the twenty-first century that we want" (Perrineau 2019: 95).

Even when seeking to strike a conciliatory tone, Macron remained intransigent. On November 27, the president allowed that he needed to change his methods, but not the substance of his policy: "I take away from the last few days that we should not abandon the course, which is right, but that we must change the method, since citizens have felt that we are imposing this course from above" (*Le Monde*, November 27, 2018). Driving home the stay-the-course message the next day, Prime Minister Philippe rejected one of the central demands of the yellow vests, an increase in the minimum wage to help those struggling to get by. The following day, Macron declared that he heard "the legitimate anger, the impatience, the suffering of part of the population," but that nonetheless, future decisions "would never involve a retreat" (*Le Monde*, November 30, 2018). Macron added that his refusal to backtrack set him apart and above previous governments that had abandoned needed reforms for reasons of political expediency: "I know that those accustomed to politics are expecting me to renounce or side-step ... but it is because we have always acted that way that we find ourselves in such a predicament" (*Le Monde*, November 30, 2018).

The government's inflexible and disdainful stance only egged on the protestors. What is more, while talking a tough line, the government lost control of the streets. The December 1 protests were especially shocking. That day, yellow vests and *casseurs* or "wreckers," who inserted themselves into the protests to wreak havoc, set cars on fire and vandalized buildings and monuments. A prefecture was torched, and the fabled Arc de Triomphe was damaged and covered in graffiti. The yellow vests now had the government's attention.

As the government began to reconsider its refusal to compromise, it ran up against another problem stemming from its top-down, skinny-politics approach: it had no interlocutors with whom to negotiate an end to the crisis. The yellow vests were an amorphous movement, lacking any clear structure or leadership. They were also a radical movement, fueled by an accumulation of material grievances and slights by Macron and those around him, with many members opposed to any kind of negotiation with the government.

Efforts to set up negotiations with the yellow vests floundered. A group of yellow vest leaders were supposed to meet with Prime Minister Philippe on November 30, but only two showed up, and one left almost immediately when the government would not agree to have the meeting filmed and broadcast live (*Le Monde*, November 30, 2018). Three days later, a delegation of ten yellow vests, who had issued a public manifesto calling for negotiations and for giving the government a way out of the crisis, was supposed to meet with Philippe. The delegation cancelled, however, because the government rejected its demand to withdraw the energy tax hikes and tougher auto inspection rules as a precondition for meeting. In addition, the delegates feared that they would be used as a public relations prop by government leaders, who wanted to look good without negotiating in earnest. Finally, the delegates had received death threats from other yellow vests if they participated (*Le Monde*, December 4, 2018). CFDT General Secretary Berger noted that the government was paying the price for its disdain of intermediary associations:

Macron denies the existence of social democracy, of intermediary associations. When things go well, it's not a problem. When things go badly or when people make contradictory demands (for more services and lower taxes), you need intermediaries, organizations that represent various groups, to sell reforms to members, to allow reforms to be implemented. (Interview by author with Laurent Berger, General Secretary, CFDT, March 21, 2019)

The government added to its difficulties by refusing an olive branch extended by the CFDT. When Berger issued a communiqué calling for negotiations to define a more inclusive and socially just ecological transition, Prime Minister Philippe bluntly rejected the proposal, noting that the unions did not represent the people who were protesting. Although there was certainly some truth to Philippe's observation, the government missed an opportunity to reduce its isolation. In return for some concessions, the unions could have countered the image of Macron as caring only about the rich and successful. An agreement with the unions might also have lowered the social thermostat and begun winding down the crisis. Instead, the government continued its skinny-politics approach, refusing to enlarge the circle of participants to include the social partners.

The final way in which the government's skinny-politics approach contributed to the yellow vest crisis was in focusing the anger and hostility of the protestors on Macron himself. Macron's Jupiterian governing style, marked by an extreme concentration of power in the presidency and a micromanaging of seemingly every detail of government policy, made the president the focal point for popular dissatisfaction. There could be no blame-sharing when there had been no power-sharing. Instead, all of the hatred and rage that the yellow vests felt about the tone and direction of government policy was directed at Macron. When French prefects were consulted by the government in early December, they reported that the most common theme among the yellow vests was "hatred for Macron" (*Le Monde*, December 3, 2018). François Ruffin, a member of parliament for the far-left France Unbowed (La France Insoumise, LFI), captured the tenor of yellow vest feelings toward the president: "From anger, we have moved on to rage. The pride of the President of the Republic – his tone deafness, his obstinacy, his absence of concessions – is a machine for [generating] hatred" (*Le Monde*, December 3, 2018).

5.6   The Retreat from Reform

Following the destructive December 1 protests, Macron deployed both the carrot and the stick to try to regain control of events. Once again, the government tendered concessions in the hope of appeasing the yellow vests. On December 4, Prime Minister Philippe announced a series of measures worth some €4 billion. Declaring that "no tax is worth endangering the unity of the nation," Philippe postponed the gasoline and home heating fuel taxes that were scheduled to go into effect on January 1, 2019 for six months (*Libération*, December 4, 2018). He also froze electricity and gas rates for six months and did the same for the new automobile inspection regime. In addition, Philippe promised a "broad debate" on taxes and public spending. Philippe's concessions failed to calm the yellow vest movement, which was demanding the cancellation of the energy tax increases, not just a postponement for six months.

Along with carrots, the government wielded powerful sticks. In the run-up to the December 8 protests, the government locked down Paris. Museums, along with theaters and libraries, were closed. France's celebrated department stores, the *grands magasins*, also shut their doors. To prevent the yellow vests from reaching the protest areas, the government closed thirty-six subway (*métro*) and suburban Regional Express Network (Réseau Express Régional, RER) train stations. Most striking, the government deployed 8,000 heavily armed police in Paris and 89,000 officers throughout the country (Vandepitte 2019: 98–99). Twelve tanks capable of destroying barricades were also deployed in Paris. That day, the police made some 1,500 arrests.

December 8 would be far from the last conflict. Over the next two months, between mid-December 2018 and mid-February 2019, yellow vests and police forces engaged in a series of battles in the streets, and the police made over 8,000 arrests (*Le Monde*, February 14, 2019). Moreover, the indiscriminate use of supposedly "nonlethal" police weapons, such as Flash-Ball riot guns (*lanceurs de balles de défense*, LBD), produced a stream of horrific injuries. More than 3,000 protestors were injured, a significant number of them seriously (Vandepitte 2019: 94). There were over 300 serious head injuries, 24 people lost an eye to police projectiles, and 5 people lost hands. In addition, two people died, including one 81-year-old woman, who was killed when a police grenade landed in her apartment. The government was widely criticized for its excessive use of force, including by the United Nations (*Le Monde*, March 6, 2019).

Despite the physical damage caused by the protests, the yellow vests garnered considerable public support (Perrineau 2019: 110). Surveys in November and December showed that 66 to 72 percent of respondents held a favorable opinion of the movement. By contrast, in December 2018, Macron's approval rating was only 23 percent (*Le Monde*, December 17, 2018). To put that figure in perspective, Nicolas Sarkozy, a highly divisive figure, who was defeated in his reelection bid, had a 45 percent approval rating at the same point in his term. Macron barely edged out François Hollande, who had a 22 percent approval rating at the time and would prove so unpopular that he would not even run for reelection (*Le Monde*, December 17, 2018).

On December 10, with the protests showing no sign of abating and public opinion running strongly in favor of the yellow vests, Macron threw in the towel. In a TV speech that was watched by 23 million people, the largest audience for a political speech in French history, the president cancelled all of the planned increases in energy taxes (Vandepitte 2019: 15). In addition, he announced a series of measures to boost the earnings of workers and pensioners: a repeal of the planned increase of the CSG on pensions between €1,200 and €2,000 per month; an increase of €100 per month in the minimum pension beginning January 1, 2019 (a measure that the government had intended to phase in gradually by 2022); an exemption of 2018 year-end bonuses from taxes and Social Security charges; and an exemption of overtime pay throughout 2019 from taxes and Social Security charges (Macron 2018). Finally, Macron promised to conduct a broad consultation with ordinary French citizens that would come to be known as the Grand National Debate (Grand Débat National, GDN). Macron's announcement brought the total cost of concessions to the yellow vests to €10 billion: €3 billion for the canceled eco-taxes and €7 billion for the other measures (*Libération*, November 16, 2019).

Although the yellow vest protests continued after Macron's December 10 speech, his concessions reduced the protests to a manageable level. Macron still faced the challenge of showing that he had learned from the protests and rebuilding his Hollandesque approval ratings, but the insurrectionary threat to his presidency was over.

5.7   Conclusion

During his initial eighteen months as president, Macron went from victory to victory. Confident of his democratic mandate, Macron stared down opposition from the unions and leftist critics to enact a series of liberalizing reforms: tax cuts for business and the affluent, an expansion of labor market flexibility, an overhaul of the SNCF, and a reduction in public services. Strikes, protests, and other forms of contestation seemed to be no match for the determined new president.

Until they were. The yellow vest movement took the government completely by surprise. What is more, the usual tactic of standing firm and dismissing the demands of the protestors failed to defuse the crisis. This time it would be Macron who backed down, as contestation in the streets derailed his liberalizing agenda and threw his government into turmoil.

Macron's defeat at the hands of the yellow vests stemmed from personal arrogance, to be sure, but also from the legacies of France's postwar *dirigiste* model and its transformation. The long winding road away from the *dirigiste* model made Macron's agenda doubly unpopular. For one thing, it subjected a skeptical French population to yet another round of liberalizing reforms. For another, it deprived the government of the fiscal means to offer compensation or side-payments, making Macron vulnerable to the charge of being the president of the rich.

Macron's top-down, Jupiterian mode of governance made matters worse. The government imposed unpopular reforms from above, ignoring the social partners and steamrolling strikers and protestors. This skinny-politics approach worked for a while, but eventually ran up against the accumulated grievances of ordinary French citizens that fueled the yellow vest movement (Noiriel 2019: 118). Having dismissed established elites and the social partners, Macron found himself very much alone in confronting the yellow vests. He also lacked an interlocutor with whom to negotiate an exit from the crisis. In some respects, as Chapters 6 and 7 relate, Macron has never really resolved the central challenge posed by the yellow vests – that of defining a path of economic liberalization that the French population accepts as both necessary and fair.

6 Rinse and Repeat
A Mitigated *Mea Culpa* and Continued Contestation

This chapter analyzes Macron's efforts to rebound from the yellow vest crisis. His response can be described as something of a mitigated *mea culpa*. On the one hand, Macron apologized publicly and repeatedly for his top-down impositional style. He also launched two initiatives, a Grand National Debate (Grand Débat National, GDN) and Citizens' Climate Convention (Convention Citoyenne pour le Climat, CCC), that placed ordinary citizens front and center in helping define the road ahead for the government. On the other hand, the *mea culpa* was mitigated in the sense that citizen participation did not extend beyond these two extraordinary initiatives. On all other matters, it was business as usual, with Macron advancing unpopular liberalizing reforms in a top-down, skinny-politics manner that sparked significant popular contestation. This business-as-usual approach characterized the two most ambitious reforms during the fifteen months between the yellow vest crisis and COVID-19 crisis: a reform of the unemployment system and an overhaul of the pension regime.

This chapter discusses the achievements and limitations of Macron's mitigated *mea culpa*. Sections 6.1 and 6.2 describe Macron's two participatory initiatives, the GDN and the CCC respectively. Despite some criticisms, these initiatives proved quite popular. However, as Sections 6.3 and 6.4 relate, they did not define a new template for governing. Rather, Macron continued to pursue unpopular reforms, in this case, of the unemployment and pension systems, in a top-down, skinny-politics manner. As a result, these reforms generated considerable contestation, particularly in the case of the pension reform, which Macron ultimately abandoned.

6.1 The Grand National Debate

As a kind of *mea culpa* for the Jupiterian hubris of his first months in office, Macron launched two novel initiatives: the GDN and the CCC. Both initiatives were intended to respond to the criticism that Macron did not listen to the French people. The GDN and CCC also acceded to a central demand of the yellow vest movement for more participatory democracy.

The GDN was conducted over a two-month period from January 15 to March 15, 2019 (*Le Monde*, January 9, 2019). In a "letter to the French," Macron identified four broad themes for consideration: (1) taxes and public spending; (2) the organization of the state and public services; (3) ecological transformation; (4) democracy and citizenship (Macron 2019; *Le Monde*, January 14, 2019). Macron initially included immigration as a fifth topic but reversed course under criticism that he was inflaming xenophobic passions and that the yellow vests had not called for reforming immigration policy.

Macron was criticized for what he excluded as well as included. In his letter to the French, he refused a central demand of the yellow vests – to revisit the government's fiscal policy, in particular the narrowing of the Solidarity Tax on Wealth (Impôt de Solidarité sur la Fortune, ISF) and the creation of a Single Flat-Rate Levy (Prélèvement Forfaitaire Unique, PFU), at a rate of 30 percent, on income from interest, dividends, and capital gains (Plenel 2019: 70). Macron justified his position by asserting that tax increases would only hurt investment and job creation (*Le Monde*, January 14, 2019). Still, Raymond Soubie, who had been Sarkozy's social adviser, remarked that, "launching a national debate, all the while saying that you won't change your position, is a difficult position to defend" (*Le Monde*, January 10, 2019).

Macron also continued to marginalize the social partners. As noted in Chapter 5, during the yellow vest crisis, the government rejected an offer by the French Democratic Confederation of Labor (Confédération Française Démocratique du Travail, CFDT) to convene the social partners to help defuse the tension. Macron met with the social partners just once, the day that he cancelled the planned increase of energy taxes, and he made no mention of the social partners when speaking to the nation that night (Karel 2019). What is more, Macron held no subsequent meetings with the social partners prior to the GDN (*Le Monde*, January 10, 2019), and the GDN itself continued in this exclusionary spirit. While Macron acknowledged the need to listen to the French people, he felt little need to listen to the social partners, who were essentially relegated to the sidelines.

Despite these limitations, the GDN sparked considerable popular interest. Some 2 million French citizens took part in one way or another (Perrineau 2019). The government offered a variety of means to get involved, from submitting questions via an online platform to attending in-person meetings. One of the most consequential forms of participation were the so-called citizens' books (*cahiers citoyens*), evoking the "books of grievances" (*cahiers de doléances*) that French peasants had presented to King Louis XVI prior to the French Revolution. Roughly 720,000 citizens contributed to 18,000 citizens' books located in town halls throughout the country. Locally initiated meetings (réunions d'initiative locale, RIL), organized by voluntary associations and elected officials, were another important vehicle for popular engagement. Although attendance averaged only 70 people, some 700,000 citizens altogether participated in the RIL, exchanging ideas and views with their fellow citizens.

The GDN culminated in national conferences on the four main themes laid out in Macron's letter to the French. The 1,400 citizens who participated in these conferences were chosen by lots. They debated their respective themes for fourteen days and issued some policy recommendations to the government.

Macron was a frequent participant, attending sixteen meetings with mayors and citizens, totaling ninety-two hours. At these meetings, Macron faced citizens critical of his positions or approach to governing. However, the dominant sentiment was that Macron put on a brilliant performance, engaging with his critics and demonstrating a mastery of all issues, big and small (*Le Monde*, January 19 and 21, 2019). Macron also displayed tremendous stamina, fielding questions for up to seven hours at a time (*Le Monde*, January 25, 2019).

The focus on Macron points to a limitation of the GDN, though: for all the talk of bottom-up participation, there was a high degree of top-down control (Plenel 2019: 70). Macron set the agenda, which was not necessarily that of ordinary French citizens. Participants often raised themes that were of concern to much of the French population but that the government excluded from the discussion, such as unemployment, purchasing power, and tax cuts for business and the affluent (Perrineau 2019: 141). Perhaps for this reason, at the end of the GDN, only 32 percent of those polled thought that Macron would take into account the views and ideas expressed in the meetings (Perrineau 2019: 151).

Another limitation of the GDN was a lack of any sense of what this process was supposed to achieve. Citizens voiced their questions, concerns, and opinions, but it was left to Macron to decide what to do with this popular input. There was no process for translating citizen input into policy. Macron was free to do more or less as he pleased.

Finally, the GDN was, by definition, ephemeral. Citizens expressed their opinions, a number of meetings were held, then the GDN ended. The consultative process was not institutionalized; it did not become a normal part of governing. The intention was primarily to defuse the yellow vest protests and revive Macron's popularity, as opposed to forging a new mode of governance. As Pascal Perrineau, who served as one of the five official guarantors of the integrity of the GDN, observed, the process may have been pitched as a bottom-up affair, but Macron maintained tight control from start to finish:

All through the process, the president of the Republic sought to keep control over the grand national debate, setting its pace and also using it to reconstruct a personal and political image that had deteriorated. It was indeed an operation of consultative democracy, but within the framework of the institutional system of the Fifth Republic, which remained very vertical. The president originated the process, accompanied it personally, and is expected to conclude it. (Perrineau 2019: 131)

At the conclusion of the GDN, Macron again loosened the government's purse strings. In a press conference on April 25, he announced €5 billion in income tax cuts as well as the reindexation of pensions below €2,000 per month to inflation, at a cost of €2 billion (*Libération*, November 19, 2019). When added to the concessions made in November and December 2018, the tab for the yellow vest movement rose to some €17 billion (*Libération*, November 19, 2019). That figure does not include the policing expenses and the damage to the economy, notably losses suffered by the tourist industry and shopping districts, which brought the total cost of the yellow vest movement to more than €20 billion (*Le Figaro*, July 17, 2019).

6.2   The Citizens' Climate Convention

At the April 25 press conference, Macron announced the convening of a Citizens' Climate Convention (Convention Citoyenne pour le Climat, CCC). Like the GDN, the CCC was a response to the yellow vest protests. It too allowed citizens to voice their opinions, but went a step further by establishing a direct connection between these opinions and government policy. The 150 citizens selected for the CCC (a representative sample of the population chosen by lots) were each allowed to present one bill, regulation, or constitutional reform designed to improve the environment. President Macron pledged to implement the measures as quickly as possible.

Beyond giving a voice to ordinary citizens, the CCC was also a way to revive environmental policy. The yellow vest movement had been triggered by one of Macron's signature environmental initiatives, the increase in energy taxes designed to reduce CO_2 emissions. The yellow vests successfully framed the initiative as choosing the environment over the ability of struggling French citizens to meet their basic needs. In addition, many criticized the government for pursuing a largely punitive approach to ecology, taxing undesirable behaviors while doing little else to reduce France's carbon footprint. The CCC was seen as a way of relegitimizing environmental policy and providing the government with a number of concrete proposals.

Finally, as with the GDN, the CCC initiative sought to rehabilitate Macron's political image. When US President Trump quit the Paris Climate Accord in 2017, Macron mocked him by declaring a commitment to "make our planet great again," but there was a lot of skepticism about Macron's environmental commitment. In 2017, Macron had scored a coup when Nicolas Hulot, a well-known environmentalist and TV personality, agreed to join the cabinet as minister of ecological transition. However, in August 2018, Hulot resigned abruptly, complaining that he did not have the backing of the president and that the government lacked a comprehensive vision for environmental transformation (*Le Monde*, August 28, 2018). Members of Macron's own party were also increasingly dissatisfied. Indeed, one year later, sixteen Republic on the Move (La République en Marche, LREM) members of parliament would leave the party to help found Ecology, Democracy, and Solidarity (Ecologie, Démocratie, et Solidarité, EDS), a parliamentary group committed to a comprehensive ecological transformation (*Le Parisien*, May 18, 2020).[1]

As with the GDN, Macron set the parameters for the CCC. The president tasked the CCC with defining "the structural measures to achieve, in a spirit of social justice, at least a 40 percent reduction in greenhouse gas emissions by 2030 as compared to 1990" (Vie Publique Editorial Board 2021c). The 40 percent figure represents France's obligation under the 2015 Paris Accord. Macron identified five themes for the CCC: (1) food and agriculture; (2) housing; (3) employment and industry; (4) territorial planning and transportation; (5) consumption and lifestyles.

Once again, Macron was criticized for what he left out – in this case, the production of energy. Critics argued that members of the CCC should be free to craft measures promoting alternative energy sources. They also contended that rolling back France's controversial nuclear power industry should be on the table (*La Croix*, June 30, 2020). French leaders have defended nuclear power as a carbon-free alternative to fossil fuels. However, the attempt to portray nuclear power as a kind of green energy neglects the risk of a nuclear accident like Chernobyl or Fukushima. In addition, it ignores the technical challenges and cost of finding a way to safely decommission nuclear plants at the end of their life cycles as well as store waste and contaminated materials that will remain dangerous for hundreds or even thousands of years.

The work of the CCC began in October 2019. Each of the 150 members was responsible for preparing one concrete proposal, be it a regulatory reform, a bill, or a referendum. CCC members were assisted by specialists in environmental science, legislative politics, economics, and legal affairs. They also heard from 140 experts in a variety of areas. Macron cheered on the work of the CCC, promising at a meeting in January 2020 that he would implement proposals "without a filter," meaning without any modification (Vie Publique Editorial Board 2021c).

The CCC proposals ran the gamut from the sweeping to the particular (*Les Echos*, June 18, 2020). For example, one initiative proposed mandating the renovation of all buildings by 2040 to make them more energy-efficient, while another called for banning the use of outdoor heating lamps by cafés and restaurants. Some of the most significant recommendations included increasing the tax advantages for low-polluting vehicles and boosting the penalties for high-polluting vehicles (a so-called bonus–malus system); barring advertising for gas-guzzling and polluting vehicles (those consuming more than 4 liters per 100 kilometers traveled or emitting more than 95 grams of CO_2 per kilometer traveled); cutting pesticide use in half by 2025; restricting the construction of new shopping malls; imposing a sin tax on foods that are heavily processed, require a lot of energy to produce, and/or have low nutritional value; and incorporating the precautionary principle into all trade agreements.

The CCC process was supposed to take place over a six-month period, with seven (nonconsecutive) three-day meetings. However, because of protests over pension reform in winter 2019–2020 and the COVID-19 quarantine in spring 2020, the CCC did not make a formal presentation of its recommendations to President Macron until June 29, 2020. As luck would have it, the day before, a French environmental party, Europe Ecology – The Greens (Europe Ecologie – Les Verts, EELV) had been the big winner of France's municipal elections, capturing the city halls of Bordeaux, Strasbourg, Lyon, and Marseilles among others. Macron's LREM, by contrast, had fared extremely badly, winning no major cities. Moreover, in the runoff elections, LREM had mostly supported candidates of the right against EELV candidates (seventy-six alliances with the right versus only thirty-three with EELV and the left), especially in the largest municipalities (*Le Monde*, June 8, 2020). This preference for alliances with the right had not only proved to be a losing electoral strategy, but also reinforced the impression that Macron did not care about the environment (*Le Monde*, June 18, 2020). Consequently, when President Macron received the CCC proposals, he was freshly wounded politically. In addition, whereas the left had long been regarded as hopelessly weak and divided, the sweeping success of the alliance between EELV and parties of the left raised the prospect that an environmentalist candidate backed by the left might be able to mount a serious challenge to Macron in the 2022 presidential election.

In this context, Macron proved receptive to the CCC's recommendations. At the June 29 reception, he endorsed 146 out of 149 CCC proposals (*Les Echos*, June 29, 2020). Macron promised to transmit those proposals to either the cabinet (for regulations) or the parliament (for legislation). He also pledged to move on these initiatives quickly and provide his full support to make sure that they were enacted. Finally, Macron pledged an extra €15 billion over two years to support ecological initiatives (*Libération*, June 29, 2020).

Of course, there were some important omissions from the 146 proposals. Even before the CCC met for the first time, Macron took the production of energy, notably nuclear power, off the table. The CCC members themselves, who voted on all of the proposals before sending them to Macron, rejected the establishment of a carbon tax, due to concerns about the burden of the tax on ordinary citizens along with the fear of reviving the yellow vest movement. Fear of the yellow vests also prompted Macron to reject a CCC proposal to reduce the speed limit on highways from 130 kilometers to 110 kilometers per hour, since a reduction of the speed limit on rural highways had been one of the actions that had sparked the yellow vest movement (*Les Echos*, June 29, 2020). Macron rejected a second proposal, to insert the protection of the environment into the preamble of the constitution, arguing that such a move would place nature above human rights. Finally, he refused to take up a proposed increase in the tax on corporate dividends on the grounds that the French already pay a lot of taxes and that he did not wish to reduce the country's ability to attract investments. This refusal to tax the rich or companies was not only unpopular, but also left it unclear how the government would finance the promised €15 billion in additional environmental measures. Still, the CCC, like the GDN, was viewed favorably by the French citizenry, who appreciated the chance to be heard by the government and, in this instance, to design policy.

Over time, though, another concern arose – that Macron would not keep his promise to implement the 146 reforms "without a filter." The government rejected or delayed several of the most important measures, including an additional €3.6 billion per year in taxes on air travel and a revenue-neutral bonus–malus tax that would have added to the cost of vehicles that are high in CO_2 emissions, while reducing the cost of vehicles that are low in CO_2 emissions (*Les Echos*, September 25, 2020). The minister of the economy and finance argued that with Air France, Airbus, and Renault fighting for their lives due to the COVID-19 crisis, it was not the time to burden them with additional taxes. However, the bonus–malus tax was revenue-neutral, so it would not have imposed an additional burden. The government pledged that it would eventually implement the fiscal proposals once the fortunes of the French airline, aeronautics, and automobile industries recovered, but this pledge was viewed with skepticism by many CCC members. Further fueling suspicion of Macron's intentions, the president rejected a CCC proposal for a moratorium on the rollout of 5G networks pending studies of the impact on health and the environment. To add insult to injury, Macron mocked backers of the proposal as advocates of "the Amish model" and a "return to oil lamps" (*Les Echos*, September 17, 2020).

To be fair to Macron, he was hardly inactive on the environmental front. In July 2021, the government passed a far-ranging bill to fight climate change (Loi Portant Lutte Contre le Dérèglement Climatique et Renforcement de la Résilience Face à Ses Effets, commonly known as the Loi Climat et Résilience). The Climate and Resilience Law acted on many of the CCC proposals (French Ministry of Environmental Transition 2021b). It introduced a number of important changes, including banning fossil fuel advertisements beginning in 2022; prohibiting advertisements for cars that emit more than 123 grams of CO_2 per kilometer beginning in 2028; banning the sale of cars that emit more than 95 grams of CO_2 per kilometer beginning in 2030; criminalizing polluting activities, with penalties of up to ten years in jail; requiring supermarkets to reserve 20 percent of their shelf space for unpackaged bulk items by 2030; mandating the establishment of low-emission zones that limit the presence of heavily polluting vehicles in all municipalities with more than 150,000 inhabitants by 2024; providing weekly vegetarian options in all public schools and university dining services; restricting the construction of giant shopping malls in rural areas; and achieving a 50 percent reduction in the rate of conversion of farmland and forests into construction areas by 2030.

The government claims that with the passage of the Climate and Resilience Law, along with other laws and regulations, more than 100 CCC proposals have "been implemented or are in the process of [being implemented] partially or totally" (French National Assembly 2021). The problem, though, is that many of the most impactful CCC proposals were watered down significantly. Instead of requiring all residences with poor insulation, so-called thermic sieves, to be upgraded by 2028, as the CCC recommended, the Climate and Resilience Law only prohibits the renting of such residences, which means that 93 percent of all thermic sieves are unaffected (*Le Monde*, February 10, 2021). Instead of banning all domestic flights where there is an alternative train option taking less than four hours, the government made the cut-off two and

a half hours, with the effect that only three of the fifteen most polluting domestic flight routes will be decommissioned and only five routes
overall (*Le Monde*, January 21, 2021). Instead of banning advertising on
all heavily polluting products, a measure aimed at SUVs, the government narrowed the ban to ads for fossil fuels initially, with the ban on
advertisements for heavily polluting vehicles not kicking in until 2028
(*Le Monde*, February 10, 2021). Finally, instead of prohibiting the construction of shopping centers that eliminate green spaces, the law applies
only to projects of 10,000 square meters or more, exempting roughly 90
percent of new shopping center projects (*Le Monde*, January 8, 2021).
The multiplication of such retreats from the CCC agenda led critics to
jibe that when Macron said that he would implement the CCC recommendations "without a filter" (*sans filtre*), what he really meant was with
"100 filters" (*cent filtres*), the two phrases being homonyms in French (*Le
Monde*, February 28, 2021).

It was clearly a mistake for Macron to have made the "no filter" promise. The realities of politics meant that he could never implement 146
proposals without any changes. By overpromising, Macron set himself
up to disappoint CCC members, no matter how much he achieved.
Sure enough, when the CCC met February 26–28, 2021 to go over
the government's bill, there was a widespread sense of disappointment.
Members of the CCC criticized the government for not being ambitious
enough, for having no clear strategy to enable France to meet its target
of a 40 percent reduction of CO_2 emissions by 2030, for not providing
an assessment of the impact of the proposed legislation, and for ignoring or weakening the 146 CCC measures that Macron had promised to
implement without a filter (French Citizens' Convention for Climate
2021: 171–173). CCC members graded the government on a scale of 1
to 10 on a number of criteria. At the most general level, members gave
the government a grade of 3.3/10 on the question of how much it honored the pledge to implement CCC recommendations (French Citizens'
Convention for Climate 2021: 161). They gave the government a grade
of 2.5/10 on the question of the effectiveness of its bill in fighting greenhouse gases (French Citizens' Convention for Climate 2021: 163).

In its defense, the government maintained that the Climate and Resilience Bill was a major initiative, despite the need to temper some of the
reforms in order to avoid imposing significant costs on struggling French
businesses during an economic crisis. Minister of the Ecological Transition Barbara Pompili added that the government should be judged on
the entirety of its environmental action, including earlier transportation
and energy laws and the green provisions of a new public investment
program, Relaunch France (*Le Monde*, February 19, 2021). Taken in

their entirety, however, the government's actions have been judged inadequate, not only by CCC members and environmental groups like Greenpeace, which describes the Climate and Resilience Bill as "greenwashing," but also by official state bodies (*Le Monde*, February 19, 2021).

The National Environmental Transition Council (Conseil National de la Transition Ecologique) described the law as insufficient to meet France's international environmental commitments. The Economic, Social, and Environmental Council (Conseil Economique, Social, et Environnemental) decried the limitations and postponements of key environmental measures. Finally, the State Council (Conseil d'Etat) pointed to "notable insufficiencies" in the law. According to the State Council, the law will generate only 10 percent of the reductions in emissions of greenhouse gases that France has pledged to make by 2030. In response to these criticisms, the government commissioned the Boston Consulting Group (BCG) to assess all of its environmental actions, not just the Climate and Resilience Bill, yet even BCG's tally put the government on pace to achieve only 20 percent of the needed reductions by 2030 (*Le Monde*, February 19, 2021).

The GDN and CCC were designed to show that Macron had learned from the yellow vest protests, that he would listen to stakeholders, rather than imposing reforms from above, and that he would pursue a more socially inclusive economic and environmental agenda. The CCC has moved the needle on environmental policy, and the government promised to advance environmental regulations further once the economy recovered. Although the reforms did not go nearly as far as Macron led CCC members to expect, the CCC did spawn some important changes.

If the GDN and CCC marked a break from the tenor and actions of the first eighteen months of the Macron presidency, Macron's *mea culpa* remained limited. The new Macron who listened and respected his interlocutors did not extend beyond the GDN and CCC. In other areas, he continued with his skinny-politics approach to reform, dismissing the social partners and refusing to back down when challenged.

Macron's *mea culpa* was mitigated in a substantive sense as well. Macron had always made it clear that he had no intention of changing his agenda, just the way in which he pursued it. He apologized on several occasions for his high-handed manner and promised to be a better listener, but insisted that his agenda was just, that he had been elected on a pledge to implement it, and that he had no intention of reversing course (*Le Monde*, November 27, 2018). Macron had made a number of declarations along these lines during the yellow vest conflict, acknowledging that he had erred in his tone and approach to reform, while insisting that his agenda was both necessary and what the French had voted for in 2017.

In his New Year's Eve wishes to the French at the end of 2018, Macron announced his intention to pursue several highly controversial and unpopular measures, "to profoundly change the rules of unemployment indemnification to further encourage the return to employment, the organization of public service to make it more efficient, and our pension system to make it more just" (*Le Monde*, December 31, 2018). Four months later, in his April 25 press conference at the end of the GDN, Macron even made a virtue of his willingness to pursue reforms that the French public did not want: "I prefer to be responsible, to keep my promises and be unpopular, than to try to please in a way that would be purely ephemeral" (Perrineau 2019: 115).

Rather than turning over a new leaf, Macron doubled down on his original agenda. In addition, outside the GDN and CCC, he remained committed to the same top-down, skinny-politics style of policymaking. The combination of disdain for stakeholders and an unpopular agenda characterized the two most important initiatives of the period leading up to the COVID-19 crisis: a reform of the unemployment insurance system and an attempted overhaul of the pension system.

6.3   The Unemployment Insurance Reform

The unemployment insurance reform was controversial in both its process and substance. Traditionally, the social partners managed the unemployment system, the National Interprofessional Union for Employment in Industry and Commerce (Union Nationale Interprofessionnelle pour l'Emploi dans l'Industrie et le Commerce, UNEDIC), although the state also played an important role. Macron was plainly unhappy with this mode of governance, however.

In *Révolution*, Macron presented several reasons why the state should evict the social partners and assume complete control of the unemployment insurance system (Macron 2016: 150–151). For starters, the state is financially responsible for the debt of the unemployment insurance system, meaning that it bears the costs of a failure by the social partners to balance UNEDIC's budget. By 2017, UNEDIC had racked up over €33 billion in debt (UNEDIC 2022), and Macron believed that the social partners were doing a poor job managing the system: "I think that state authorities should take responsibility for decisions relating to unemployment insurance. They cannot continue to be the silent guarantors of a system that is going off the rails" (Macron 2016: 151).

There were other problems beyond the state of UNEDIC's finances. The government was especially concerned that by providing generous benefits to so-called intermittent workers, who alternated between short periods of employment and unemployment, UNEDIC made it easy for employers to offer very short-term contracts instead of recruiting workers long term. According to the government, 70 percent of fixed-term contracts were for less than one month. The system also made it more financially attractive for some intermittent workers to alternate short periods of employment with unemployment benefits than to work without interruption. A final concern was that generous benefits for highly compensated executives, generally without parallel in other European countries, were leading these employees to remain on unemployment longer than lower-paid workers, despite robust demand for their services.

Not surprisingly given his outlook on the way in which the social partners were managing the system, Macron took a skinny-politics approach to the unemployment insurance reform. As part of a reform of the worker training system in 2018, the government had gained the power to issue "framework letters" to the social partners detailing parameters for reforms of the unemployment system (Coquet 2022). In particular, the government was authorized to set out both reform objectives and financial savings, and if the social partners failed to meet these objectives, the government could take over the reform and enact changes via decree.

The framework letter issued by the government in September 2018 called for improving incentives for employers to provide stable, long-term jobs and for the unemployed to seek work (*Les Echos*, September 23, 2018). Several of the provisions came as an unwelcome surprise to the social partners, notably the requirement that they reduce UNEDIC spending by €1 to €1.3 billion annually. UNEDIC finances were trending toward a surplus, but the government argued that additional savings needed to be found in order to begin paying down UNEDIC's debt. Other controversial government objectives included the creation of a bonus–malus system that would charge higher insurance rates to employers who relied on short-term hires and made many layoffs and the reduction of benefits for the unemployed, especially higher earners and those cycling between short-term jobs and unemployment insurance. Adding to the challenge of the framework letter, the social partners were given just four months to negotiate all of these changes.

CFDT leader, Laurent Berger, described the framework letter as "a form of cynicism on the part of those who govern us" (interview by author with Laurent Berger, General Secretary of the CFDT, March 21, 2019). Berger publicly criticized the government for dictating an

outcome to the social partners while pretending to allow them to negotiate their own solutions: "The government says that it does not want to
challenge governance by the social partners, but ... if we are just pretending to manage something that is imposed, in fact, by the State, it
[governance by the social partners] holds no interest" (*Les Echos*, March
4, 2019). Berger felt that the government was putting the social partners
in the position of having to choose between implementing a painful and
unpopular government agenda and giving the government a pretext to
take over the reform.

Negotiations between the employers and the unions were unable to
meet the government's demands. Employers balked at the bonus–malus
system that would penalize companies for making layoffs, while the
unions resisted cuts in benefits. In February 2020, judging the negotiations to have failed, the government assumed control of the reform.
Macron could not resist the taking a parting shot at the social partners:
"Every day in our country, they say, 'intermediary associations, social
democracy, let us handle it.' And when we pass the baton, they say, 'but
sir, it is hard, take it back'" (*Les Echos*, October 23, 2019).

Berger countered that the negotiations were doomed from the start
because of the terms of the framework letter: "The government blames
us for the failure of the negotiations, but the government set us up to fail.
The government gave us no room to maneuver. In addition, the financial
goals of the framework law were overly ambitious" (interview by author
with Laurent Berger, General Secretary of the CFDT, March 21, 2019).
The employers were also angry. President of the Movement of French
Enterprises (Mouvement des Entreprises de France, MEDEF), Geoffroy Roux de Bézieux, declared that the employers did not want to vouch
for a system over which they had no control and were seriously considering withdrawing from UNEDIC (*Les Echos*, March 4, 2019).

If skinny politics shaped the process of the unemployment insurance
reform, the social anesthesia state shaped the substance. Macron was
determined to prune the social anesthesia state by reducing UNEDIC
spending. He was no less determined to combat the labor market effects
of the social anesthesia state by tightening eligibility rules and reducing
benefit generosity.

In June 2019, the government released its UNEDIC reform bill
(French Government 2019). From a union standpoint, the bill was
even worse than expected. The bonus–malus system, which had been
expected to impose some costs on French employers, was instead made
revenue-neutral. Consequently, all of the proposed €3.4 billion in savings over the three-year period from 2019 to 2021 would come from
employees (*Les Echos*, June 18, 2019). The bill contained one arguably

progressive measure – the reduction of reimbursements for managers and executives earning more than €4,500 per month. Henceforth, after six months, the benefits of high earners would decrease by 30 percent, with a floor of €2,261 per month. Some 80,000 executives would be affected by this degressive measure. The government argued that generous rates of compensation were incentivizing highly paid employees to remain on unemployment, pointing to the fact that the average highly compensated beneficiary stayed unemployed longer than those receiving lower payments: 575 days for recipients of benefits of more than €5,000 per month versus 475 days for recipients of benefits between €3,000 and €4,000 per month. Given that French unemployment was falling and that the unemployment rate for executives was a very low 3.8 percent, the government felt that there was no reason that highly paid workers should remain on unemployment so long.

Introducing degressive benefits for executives served a political purpose as well, demonstrating that Macron was imposing pain on higher-income groups, not just the disadvantaged. That said, the change generated only €210 million in savings out of €3.4 billion, while the rest of the government's reform did, in fact, impose losses on vulnerable citizens (*Les Echos*, June 18, 2019). The bill made it harder to qualify for unemployment benefits, requiring employees to have worked six out of the previous twenty-four months, as opposed to four out of the previous twenty-eight months under the old system. The reform also made it more difficult to requalify for benefits. Under the old rules, employees who worked for one month before the expiration of their unemployment benefits were eligible for an additional one month of benefits. Following the reform, they would need to work for a minimum of six months to qualify for additional benefits. Finally, the bill significantly reduced the benefit level for intermittent workers who cycle between short-term employment and unemployment. Under the old system, the reference wage for unemployment benefits was based on the income earned during the previous year divided by the number of days worked. The new formula divided income by the number of possible workdays in the year, regardless of how many of those days claimants actually worked, resulting in a much lower reference wage for intermittent workers.

The unemployment insurance reform struck critics, especially among the trade unions, as harsh and unnecessary (*Libération*, December 1, 2021). Unemployment was falling, and the finances of UNEDIC were approaching a surplus, so the system appeared to be working. Adding to the unpopularity of the reform, it seemed to be yet another instance of the government's picking on the little guy. It is true that highly compensated executives would see their unemployment benefits reduced after six months, but the French system was very generous to high earners by European standards. More important, the big losers of the UNEDIC reform would be people unable to secure stable jobs and forced to alternate between short periods of employment and unemployment. It also bears mentioning that the unemployment reform was one of the rare cases in which Macron unambiguously violated a campaign promise. In *Révolution*, he had ruled out precisely the kinds of measures that he was now enacting:

I do not believe at all in the debate launched by a number of political leaders on degressive unemployment insurance benefits: take away so many euro or so many months from existing rights. In that way, they suggest that transitions [between jobs] are not an issue, that professional mobility will happen all by itself, and that the unemployed are unemployed more or less due to their own failings. (Macron 2016: 131–132)

The various provisions of the unemployment reform were scheduled to go into effect on different dates (*Le Monde*, December 1, 2021). The first set of changes, degressive benefits for high earners and more restrictive rules on both qualifying and requalifying for benefits, was implemented beginning November 1, 2019. Other changes, notably the less generous benefits for intermittent workers, were slated to become operational April 1, 2020. However, in March 2020, as the COVID-19 epidemic forced France to shut down, Macron suspended the implementation of the unemployment insurance reform. Minister of Labor Muriel Pénicaud justified the reversal by noting that, "The reform was conceived on in a context that has nothing to do with that which we are experiencing now" (*Le Figaro*, March 16, 2020). In July, the government went a step further, not only suspending the implementation of provisions that had yet to go into effect, but also reversing or attenuating those changes that had already been implemented.

At first, the government expected that the postponements would be for only a few months, but as new rounds of the COVID-19 epidemic disrupted the economy, the government postponed the changes repeatedly (Vie Publique Editorial Board 2021a). Decisions by the State Council also forced the government to modify its plans. In November 2020, the State Council ruled that the new mode of calculation of the daily reference salary discriminated against intermittent workers (French State Council 2021). To meet the State Council's concerns, the government enacted a provision limiting the maximum reduction in the reference wage to 43 percent of the previous reference salary, which benefited 365,000 of the 1.15 million employees affected by the new mode of calculation (*Le Monde*, June 30, 2021). In June 2021, the State Council suspended the application of the new mode of calculation of benefits for intermittent workers, arguing that because of the difficult labor market at the time, workers were not choosing to work intermittently, but rather being forced to do so and that they, therefore, should not be punished.

The French economy recovered strongly in 2021, growing by 6.8 percent, and unemployment fell sharply. As a result, beginning in July 2021, the first provisions of the unemployment insurance reform were implemented (degressive benefits for high earners and more restrictive rules on qualifying and requalifying for benefits). On December 1, the less favorable calculation of benefits for intermittent workers went into effect after the State Council ruled that the labor market had improved to the point that workers could chose not to be employed intermittently. UNEDIC estimated that the reform would save €2.3 billion per year, with €1 billion coming from the reduced daily reference wage (UNEDIC 2020a). In addition, 1.15 million of the 2.8 million people on unemployment between July 2021 and June 2022 (41 percent) would receive lower benefits, with an average loss of 17 percent. Finally, because of tighter qualifying conditions, 475,000 people would need to work longer in order to become eligible for unemployment insurance.

The bonus–malus provision for employers, which supposedly made the reform more equitable, proved to be essentially window dressing (Vie Publique Editorial Board 2021a). Employer unemployment insurance contributions were allowed to vary only slightly, from 3 percent to 4.05 percent, providing little financial incentive for companies to change their layoff practices. What is more, the reform did not apply to small businesses with fewer than eleven employees. In addition, only seven sectors, representing 10 percent of employees in firms with more than eleven employees, were affected. Finally, the reform was implemented gradually, with a first year, beginning July 1, 2021, devoted to observing the hiring and firing behavior of companies, and the new unemployment contribution rates not going into effect until September 2022. By contrast, the more restrictive rules for employees and reductions in unemployment benefits went into effect immediately in 2021.

The unemployment insurance reform was shaped by both the fallout from the social anesthesia state and skinny politics. Concerns about high levels of social anesthesia spending led the government to try to reduce unemployment benefits. Concerns about the labor market effects of the social anesthesia state led the government to try to increase pressure on the unemployed to take jobs. Skinny politics also shaped the UNEDIC reform. The government first tried to impose detailed marching orders on the social partners, who ostensibly manage UNEDIC, then snatched responsibility from the social partners when they failed to do the government's bidding, imposing a reform opposed by both MEDEF and the unions.

6.4   The Overhaul of the Pension System

The other major reform launched during this period, the proposed overhaul of France's pension system, had the potential to be more progressive. Indeed, Macron had always pitched this reform as his signature social initiative. Under Macron's plan, France's forty-two different pension systems would be merged into a single points-based regime, with the same rules for all (French Government 2020b). By applying the same rules to all pensioners, the reform would eliminate special privileges, and ordinary workers, who rarely benefited from such privileges, would come out ahead. The reform also had an impressive progressive pedigree. It was based on Sweden's points system adopted in 1998 and was first outlined in a 2008 book coauthored by the paragon of progressive thinking, Thomas Piketty (Bozio and Piketty 2008).

In the run-up to the 2017 elections, Piketty's coauthor, Antoine Bozio, shopped the pension reform to most of the major candidates without success, before landing on Macron (*Les Echos*, December 6, 2019).[2] The shift to a points-based pension regime was just the kind of big, progressive idea that a candidate whose campaign theme was "Revolution" needed. The reform was also easy to grasp, with the slogan that 1 euro contributed would yield the same euro of pension credits for everyone. From an electoral perspective, pension reform would help shore up Macron's support with left-leaning voters by demonstrating that he cared about social justice. Finally, Macron could expect smooth sailing with the unions, since the CFDT had long been calling for precisely this kind of pension system, and the French Confederation of Christian Workers (Confédération Française des Travailleurs Chrétiens, CFTC) likewise supported the idea.

Macron wanted to move quickly and adopt a framework law by the end of 2017 (*Les Echos*, December 20, 2019). Any pension reform is a delicate matter in France, however, and Macron's advisers persuaded him to proceed more gradually. In September 2017, Macron appointed a technocrat, Jean-Paul Delevoye, as high commissioner for the reform of pensions, while still hoping that the reform could be enacted in 2018. In the end, Delevoye did not present his pension reform plan until July 2019, with the government's bill following in December 2019 (French Government 2020b).

Macron's pension reform contained a number of progressive features beyond the equal treatment of all contributors. It proposed to boost the minimum pension for a full career of contributions to €1,000 per month, and the minimum pension would continue rising until it reached 85 percent of the minimum wage. In addition, between 2022 and 2045, the regime would shift gradually from indexing pensions to prices to indexing them to wages, a more generous mode of calculation. The pension reform also offered more favorable treatment of families, who would receive pension credits beginning with the first child, as opposed to the third child under the existing system. Finally, compared with the Delevoye Report, the government's bill grandfathered significantly more people under the old rules, reassuring those who wanted to stay in the existing regime. In particular, the new pension system would apply only to employees born since 1975, as opposed to 1963 under Delevoye's proposal.

For all the progressive features of the pension reform, the government's handling of the reform provoked mass resistance. Once again, the reason can be attributed to a combination of the fiscal pressures of the social anesthesia state and the effects of skinny politics. The social anesthesia state shaped the finances of the reform. In its original formulation, the pension reform was to be revenue-neutral. In the language of pension politics, it would be a purely "systemic reform," changing the fundamental rules of the pension system, but not a "parametric reform," seeking to bolster the finances of the existing system by reducing spending or increasing revenues. The pension system was running a deficit, however, which was projected to total €12 billion through 2025, before the system's finances would return to equilibrium.

Prime Minister Edouard Philippe was the leading voice in favor of parametric reform (*Les Echos*, December 20, 2019). A former member of the conservative Republicans (Les Républicains, LR), who had left the party in 2017 but not joined Macron's more centrist LREM, Philippe was committed to curbing state spending and balancing the budget. Philippe viewed such measures as essential to retaining the support of conservative voters, declaring that "a certain part of the electorate is expecting us to deliver on budgetary equilibrium" (*Les Echos*, December 20, 2019). Philippe was supported by the budget and finance ministers, who were also former Republicans.

The introduction of parametric measures stemmed from more than the lobbying of Philippe and other Republicans. Macron and his advisers felt that if they did not act on deficits right away, they would be forced to do so during the run-up to the 2022 elections. Macron had already been bloodied politically for having cut pensions at the beginning of his tenure. The last thing that he wanted to do was cut pensions again on the eve of the next presidential election.

The pension reform presented by the government on December 12, 2019 included a very unpopular parametric measure. To eliminate the projected deficit, the government proposed to make people work longer in order to qualify for a full pension. Under the government's so-called equilibrium age or pivot age, it would still be possible to retire at age 62, but to receive a full pension a worker would need to remain on the job until age 64. The provision was a way for the government to pressure employees to work until age 64, while claiming to retain the existing retirement age of 62. The language of a "pivot age" fooled no one, however. Moreover, Macron was violating his campaign promise, having pledged that, "We will not touch the retirement age or the amount of pensions" (Macron 2017). The pivot age fueled a series of large-scale demonstrations, strikes, and transportation shutdowns in December 2019 to January 2020. No less important, it prompted the CFDT, long a major supporter of the systemic pension reform, to join the protestors.

The shift of the CFDT into the camp of opponents of the reform also stemmed from the government's skinny-politics approach to reform. On the face of things, the reform process seemed very inclusive. Delevoye's team met regularly with the unions to listen to their demands, as did government representatives. However, as CFTC representative Eric Courpotin relates, no negotiations occurred. Government representatives listened to the unions but did not bargain over the provisions of the pension reform: "We are not engaged in negotiation, but rather concertation. Instead of discussing, in contradictory fashion, all of the elements [of the pension reform], we are received, we are listened to, and we leave without knowing what will become of our proposals" (*La Croix*, December 9, 2019).

The opacity of the reform process ratcheted up popular anxiety. As part of its listening without negotiating approach, the government refused to provide any hard numbers on the reform or run simulations. As a result, future retirees had no idea how the reform would affect them. Whether a pension reform is beneficial or harmful depends on variety of complex parameters: the value of a point, the length of the phase-in period for the new system, the contribution rate, the effective retirement age, the terms of conversion of benefits from the old system into points in the new system, and so on. No one could possibly make all of these calculations. In a system of genuine negotiations, the unions might have vouched for the pension reform, but since they were kept in the dark by the government they were in no position to dampen popular concerns. On the contrary, given the lack of genuine negotiations, the unions had every incentive to bring people into the streets in order to pressure the government. Indeed, the national strike movement began one week before the government actually presented its reform.

Still, it was the addition of the pivot age of 64 that triggered mass protests. The pivot age drove the CFDT and CFTC unions, which had long supported the reform, into the camp of the protestors. The government could scarcely claim that it had received no warning. As early as 2018, CFDT General Secretary Berger stated publicly that he would oppose any pension reform that included parametric measures, which he described as "a red line" (*Les Echos*, May 31, 2020). Yet once again, the government, in its skinny-politics approach, seemed to almost go out of its way to provoke a union that should have logically been one of its closest allies. When Prime Minister Philippe presented the government's pension reform on December 12, he took a direct shot at Berger, declaring, "Red lines, at a certain point, it's too bad. We have to govern" (*Les Echos*, December 12, 2019).

Philippe's remarks attested to the government's frustration with the CFDT (*Les Echos*, December 20, 2019). Macron and Philippe bristled at receiving public ultimatums from Berger. They also felt that they had done a lot for the CFDT, proposing a reform that the union had long advocated and introducing important progressive measures like the minimum pension and the reindexation of pensions to wages. Moreover, Philippe had announced his intention to include a pivot age months before the December protests, so he was scarcely taking the CFDT by surprise. CFDT leaders had grievances of their own, though. They had stood up for the government's pension reform, the only major trade union to do so, in the face of criticisms by the General Confederation of Labor (Confédération Générale du Travail, CGT) and Workers' Power (Force Ouvrière, FO), only to have the government make them look like fools by introducing the pivot age.

Regardless of who was right and who was wrong, from a tactical perspective the government's dismissal of the CFDT's concerns would prove costly. The 2017 labor market reform had shown that without CFDT support, a CGT-led movement lacked clout and staying power. This time, however, the CGT would not be alone. Beginning December 5, 2019, all of the unions organized ten so-called national days of protests and strikes over a seven-week period (*Les Echos*, March 3, 2020). The biggest protect occurred December 17, 2019, with 1.8 million demonstrators taking to the streets, according to the unions, and 806,000, according to the police. The protests were accompanied by widely observed strikes in public transportation and, to a lesser degree, public education. Despite the disruptions, French public opinion revealed 60 to 70 percent support for the strikers. In a January Elabe–BFM poll, 61 percent of those surveyed thought that the government should "take the protests into account and withdraw the reform" (*Les Echos*, January 24, 2020). Only 9 percent of blue-collar workers, the presumed beneficiaries of the pension reform, supported it. Macron's popularity was also being hurt by the protests, with 72 percent of respondents describing him as "authoritarian" and only 19 percent believing that he possessed "a capacity to unite."

In the end, the CFDT got its way. On January 11, 2020, Prime Minister Philippe announced the abandonment of the pivot age (*Les Echos*, January 13, 2020). At the same time, he made the social partners responsible for finding the necessary €12 billion in savings. A "financing conference" would be tasked with balancing the pension system budget, and Philippe reserved the right to impose the pivot age if the social partners failed. Nonetheless, with the government's retreat, the CFDT and CFTC ceased to oppose the reform, and the protests flagged.

The government was not out of the woods yet, however. Having refused to negotiate the terms of the reform with the unions, it now found itself besieged by groups who would be made worse off by the new pension regime, particularly public-sector employees and workers covered by the "special regimes" (*Les Echos*, December 5, 2019). All the negotiations that the government had refused to undertake with the social partners during the preparation of the pension reform now occurred with categorical interests under the pressure of the streets. In response, a politically weakened government made a series of concessions.

Within the "special regimes," police officers, firefighters, prison guards, and military personnel were allowed to retain their existing pension system and continue retiring in their fifties (*Le Point*, December 20, 2019). Other categories of special regime workers, such as employees in the transportation, gas, and electric industries, were protected by generous grandfather clauses. Whereas the new pension system was supposed to apply to those born since 1975, for the special regimes the new system would apply only to those born since 1980 (for office employees) or 1985 (for those working in the field). Given the older age profile of these workers, somewhere between 60 and 70 percent of them would have their pensions determined entirely by the rules of the old system. What is more, those special regime employees who were moved into the new pension regime would benefit from a generous calculation of the value of their accrued pension rights.

Civil servants were also concerned about losing benefits under the new regime (*Les Echos*, December 5, 2019). Under the existing pension system, workers in the public sector receive better pensions than workers in the private sector (*Le Monde*, December 12, 2019). The reference wage for their pensions is calculated on the basis of their last six months of earnings, as opposed to a twenty-five-year average for workers in the private sector. In addition, civil servants receive 75 percent of the reference wage for their pension, versus just 50 percent in the private sector. Consequently, civil servants had a lot to lose from a move to an egalitarian pension regime. To limit their losses, the government agreed to include the bonuses of civil servants, averaging 22.5 percent of annual wages, in the calculation of the reference wage.

The government's concessions to categorical interests encouraged every group to protest in the hope of securing more favorable terms. What is more, no matter how many concessions the government made, some groups would still be disadvantaged by the reform. For example, the inclusion of bonuses into the reference wage for civil servants worked well for most employees, but teachers do not generally receive significant bonuses. Prime Minister Philippe's reassurance that teachers would not lose "a single euro in pensions from the reform" failed to dissuade skeptical teachers from taking to the streets (*Les Echos*, December 5, 2019). The multiplication of backdoor arrangements also sparked a feeling that others were getting a better deal, as one journalist noted with a touch of humor: "The office worker discretely rages against the benefits of his neighbor, a professor, who feels that he is getting a raw deal compared to the bonuses of the secretary working for the prefecture, who herself feels that the railroad workers have it really good ..." (*La Croix*, May 9, 2019). A supposedly uniform and egalitarian regime was incorporating many of the inequalities and privileges of the old system, thereby making the emerging system more opaque, unequal, and unpopular.

Even after the protests died down, the government still needed to get its law approved by the legislature. Here, too, there was considerable resistance (*Le Monde*, December 12, 2019). The parties of the left opposed the general orientation of the pension reform, which they regarded as a rollback of social rights. On the other side of the political spectrum, LR wanted to keep the existing system, while raising the retirement age from 62 to 65 to balance the pension regime's finances.

When the National Assembly began examining the pension bill on February 17, 2020, the government confronted more than 40,000 amendments, most proposed by parties of the left. Twelve days later, Prime Minister Philippe announced that he was using the Article 49.3 to cut off the debate (*Les Echos*, March 1, 2020). Only 11,000 amendments had been examined to that point, but the government argued that opponents were simply stalling for time. Moreover, the government had made a number of concessions during the parliamentary debates to win support: to the Communists by allowing sewer workers employed before 2022 to retire at age 52; to the Socialists by adding measures to boost teacher pensions; to centrists by making partners in civil unions eligible for spousal survival pensions; and to the Republicans by increasing the transition period for independent workers from fifteen to twenty years. Prime Minister Philippe also insisted that "the text remains open," that is, that the government was still willing to negotiate on critical issues like early retirement for workers in physically taxing or dangerous occupations and unemployed older workers who, because of the reluctance of employers to hire seniors, might be unable to find a new job to carry them until retirement.

The deployment of Article 49.3 was the ultimate skinny-politics maneuver. Moreover, it was the first time in Macron's presidency that the government had used the procedure. Once again, the CFDT felt victimized by the government (*Les Echos*, March 1, 2020). The CFDT had been able to extract concessions from the National Assembly and was counting on continuing to improve the bill in this way. Many CFDT concerns had yet to be addressed, notably the problem of civil servants with small bonuses and early retirement opportunities for workers in taxing or dangerous occupations. The CFDT was skeptical of Philippe's promise to make further changes in the future to deal with these issues. The employer association was also critical of the recourse to Article 49.3, with MEDEF president, Geoffroy Roux de Bézieux, voicing his disappointment that there had not been "a real debate" in parliament. Roux de Bézieux also noted that "Too many questions remain without answers, notably concerning the financing [of the pension system]" (*Les Echos*, March 1, 2020). Validating MEDEF's concern, two of the unions, FO and the CGT, withdrew from the financing conference in protest over the use of Article 49.3.

Both the left and the right put forward motions of no confidence against the government. Early in the morning of March 4, the two motions were rejected, which was no surprise, given LREM's majority in the National Assembly (*Le Monde*, March 4, 2020). The failure of the no confidence motions meant that the pension reform was considered to have been adopted by the National Assembly. To become law, though, the bill had to be approved by the Senate. In case of differences, negotiations between the two chambers of parliament would be needed to harmonize the text. Depending on the stance of the Senate, the National Assembly could be required to adopt the bill as many as three times.[3] Still, following the deployment of Article 49.3, the ultimate adoption of the pension reform seemed like a foregone conclusion.

The COVID-19 crisis interrupted the process, however. Despite the considerable political capital that Macron had invested in what was supposed to be his signature social reform, he put the reform on hold for several reasons. For one thing, he needed to focus the nation's energies on the health crisis. Appearing on television on March 16, 2020, Macron announced that France was "at war" with the coronavirus and that "all of the action of the government and parliament must henceforth be turned, day and night, toward the fight against the epidemic" (*Le Monde*, March 17, 2020). In other words, Macron had time for one priority only, fighting the epidemic, and everything else would have to wait: "I decided that all reforms currently underway will be suspended, starting with the pension reform" (*Le Monde*, March 17, 2020).

Fiscal considerations also militated against the pension reform, not to mention the unemployment reform, which Macron paused as well. The economic crisis plunged both UNEDIC and the pension system deep into the red. UNEDIC's deficit was €1.9 billion in 2019, and the initial forecast for 2020 was for a deficit of just €0.9 billion, before the system returned to surplus in 2021 (UNEDIC 2020a). Instead, the economic collapse provoked by the national quarantine sent the deficit for 2020 skyrocketing to more than €17.4 billion (UNEDIC 2022). The figures for the pension system were nearly as bleak, with the deficit jumping from €1.9 billion in 2019 to €13.0 billion in 2020 (Vie Publique Editorial Board 2021b).

Pursuing pension or unemployment insurance reform in this fiscal environment would have been politically fraught. On the one hand, having made a big issue of deficits in the unemployment and pension systems, going so far as to seize control of UNEDIC reform in order to squeeze out €1 billion to €1.3 billion in annual savings, the government could not well look askance at the vastly larger deficits exceeding €30 billion for the two programs. On the other hand, to restore financial equilibrium, the government would have to enact deep and painful cuts that would undoubtedly damage Macron's popularity and could easily spark mass protests. Moreover, the government did not want to weaken aggregate demand at a time when the economy was ailing. Consequently, Macron decided that discretion was the better part of budget-cutting valor and put both reforms on hold.

Macron did not give up on either, however. As discussed, the unemployment reform was eventually implemented in the second half of 2021. Macron also remained committed to pension reform. In a speech on June 24, 2020, he declared that the French needed to work more, adding that France would not be able to rebuild its economy after the COVID-19 pandemic if it remained "one of the countries in Europe in which people work the least during their lifetimes" (*Libération*, July 3, 2020). As the reference to the amount of work during "their lifetimes" suggested, pension reform was definitely on the table. Indeed, so, too, was parametric pension reform: "the question of the number of years during which we pay [into the pension system] is posed" (*Le Monde*, July 2, 2020).

Macron voiced such sentiments on a regular basis. On July 6, 2020, he declared, "I think that the direction to which I committed myself in 2017 remains true" and again called for pension reform (*Le Monde*, July 6, 2020). In an interview on July 14, Macron stated that he would not abandon the pension reform, although he remained open to negotiating changes (*Le Figaro*, July 14, 2020).

Macron's appointment of Jean Castex as prime minister in July 2020 was made, in part, with an eye toward pension reform. Castex, a self-described "social Gaullist," has a warm demeanor and reputation as a fair and open negotiator. He seemed like just the person to work with the social partners and legislature to bring the pension reform to a successful conclusion. Macron wanted to go to the voters in 2022 having enacted the main reforms, notably the pension reform, that had been part of his 2017 campaign. At best, the French electorate would reward him for modernizing the French economy and social relations. At worst, he would lose the election, but on his own terms, leaving behind an important legacy of reform.

The pension reform ran up against two powerful obstacles, however. The first is that the government had more pressing economic priorities. The administration was managing the economic and social fallout from a pandemic. The government's top concerns were to save companies and prevent mass layoffs. Completing the pension reform would have allowed Macron to honor a major campaign promise, one that he consistently depicted as a measure of social justice, but it would have done nothing to fix the French economy or save jobs.

The second obstacle was that the social partners, including the employers, were dead set against the pension reform, at least during the crisis, and the government wanted their support in other areas. Yves Veyrier, the General Secretary of FO, which opposed the pension reform, argued that the government's priorities were misplaced: "What is urgent is not to make people with jobs work longer; it is to ensure that everyone has a job" (*Le Monde*, July 3, 2020). Even those unions that supported the principle of the pension reform questioned the government's timing. CFDT General Secretary Berger urged the government to deal with the economy and employment first: "The CFDT does not see how, during this period when layoff plans keep coming, when the difficulties of finding a job keep piling up, that pensions should be the priority for social concertation" (*France Inter*, July 3, 2020). MEDEF President Roux de Bézieux made much the same argument, calling for the government and social partners "to put all of our energy into what matters, which is the production system" (*La Croix*, July 6, 2020).

The united opposition of the social partners forced the government to choose between trying to impose an unpopular reform from above and advancing the rest of its agenda with the cooperation of the social partners. A strategy of top-down imposition was at odds with Prime Minister Castex's concertational governing style. Pushing full steam ahead also risked triggering another round of mass protests, which could easily spiral into threats to the government itself. Finally, even if the government prevailed, such an approach would alienate the social partners, whose support Castex wanted for other employment and labor market reforms. The government was planning to negotiate a number of important dossiers with the social partners, including the implementation of the CCC environmental recommendations, youth employment measures, and the creation of a new Social Security branch for the dependent elderly (*Le Monde*, July 17, 2020; *Les Echos*, July 17, 2020). Steamrolling the social partners to impose pension reform would have placed all of these negotiations in jeopardy.

In the end, Macron acceded to the social partners' wishes. On July 17, 2020, Castex convened the first so-called social summit between the government and the social partners to establish a framework for negotiations across a range of issues. At the summit, Castex announced that the government was postponing both the pension and UNEDIC reforms until at least 2021 (*Les Echos*, July 17, 2020; *Le Monde*, July 17, 2020). Macron still hoped to enact the pension reform before the 2022 elections. However, new variants of the COVID-19 crisis forced the government to focus on often-unpopular public-health measures, such as local quarantines, curfews, business shutdowns, mask mandates, and actions to pressure the population to get vaccinated. In such a context, there was simply no room for a controversial pension reform. Macron first conceded that pension reform would have to wait until after the 2022 elections, then abandoned the reform altogether.

In the run-up to the 2022 elections, Macron floated several alternative ideas for pension reform. Instead of creating a single pension regime with the same rules for all, he proposed reducing France's forty-two pension regimes to three: one for the private sector, one for the public sector (including the *régimes spéciaux*), and one for independent workers (*Les Echos*, February 8, 2022). Macron also called for raising the retirement age from 62 to 65. This proposal was very unpopular, leading him to retreat to the position of raising the retirement age to 64 by 2028, then convening key stakeholders to assess whether to continue increasing the retirement age to 65. In addition, Macron sweetened the reform by promising to set the minimum pension for a full career of contributions (forty-three years) at €1,100 per month, instead of the €1,000 in his original plan. Still, the weight of the social anesthesia state, aggravated by the COVID-19 crisis, clearly moved Macron's project away from its original social justice objectives and toward standard parametric measures to curb spending and deficits.

As of this writing, Macron's pension reform is still under construction, but the contours of his reform have taken shape (*Le Monde*, October 26, 2022). Macron remains determined to raise the retirement age, probably to 64. He has also declared his intention to put an end to the special regime pensions, albeit only for new hires. As in the case of the French National Railway Company (Société Nationale des Chemins de Fer Français, SNCF) reform discussed in Chapter 5, existing employees would be grandfathered under the current, more generous rules. The minimum pension for a complete career will be raised to €1,200 per month instead of the previously announced €1,100 per month, a gesture meant to soften the blow of the higher retirement age and to demonstrate that more years of contributions help finance better benefits. The government has also extended an olive branch to the unions, expressing a willingness to negotiate exemptions, allowing employees in physically demanding jobs or who began working in their teens and have accumulated a long record of payroll tax contributions to retire a few years earlier than the general retirement age.

Still, the unions are united in their opposition to the reform, especially the increase in the retirement age. Despite several rounds of consultations with the government, they intend to mobilize their members to oppose the pension reform via both demonstrations and strikes. Macron also faces the challenge of getting his pension reform approved by the National Assembly, where he no longer has an absolute majority. Thus, the future of Macron's pension reform remains very much up in the air. One thing appears certain, though: Macron's original pension reform, his signature progressive social initiative, is no more. In its place is a more modest and regressive set of parametric measures focused on saving money by making the French work longer.

Macron's pension overhaul was felled by the familiar combination of the fiscal pressures of the social anesthesia state and the government's skinny-politics approach to reform. Worries about the size of the social anesthesia state and the finances of the pension system prompted the government to introduce the pivot age. That move, while understandable from a fiscal perspective, displayed blatant disregard for the concerns of the CFDT, a classic instance of skinny politics. As a result, the government confronted united union opposition, which delayed the reform for over a month and increased its unpopularity. Had the government stuck to its original formulation without the pivot age, in all likelihood the reform would have been more popular, would have avoided the CFDT's opposition, and could have been sent to parliament much sooner. In this scenario, the government likely would have had enough time to enact the reform into law before the onset of the COVID-19 crisis. Instead, the pivot age will go down in history as the poison pill that killed Macron's signature social reform.

6.5   Conclusion

Macron's response to the yellow vest movement was a mitigated *mea culpa*. True, he adopted a humbler tone in the GDN, and the CCC put a number of environmental measures onto the legislative calendar. Both initiatives were well received and revealed a strong desire among the French to be listened to and participate in key decisions affecting their lives. Rather than serve as a template for a new agenda and mode of governance, however, the GDN and CCC remained isolated instances, a hint of what might have been under a more inclusive leadership.

In retrospect, the GDN and CCC appear as exceptions to the Jupiterian rule. Both the unemployment insurance reform and pension reform displayed the same features that had mobilized the yellow vests and made Macron unpopular: an arrogant, skinny-politics mode of governance on behalf of measures that seemed to impose unnecessary or excessive costs on ordinary French citizens. The snatching of control over the unemployment reform from the social partners and the recourse to Article 49.3 to pass the pension reform were especially heavy-handed. Because of both the style and substance of the reforms, the UNEDIC and pension initiatives were hotly contested. Although the UNEDIC reform eventually took effect, the pension reform was abandoned, with Macron now proposing a set of changes that are a far cry from what was supposed to be the signal social reform of his presidency.

7 "Whatever It Costs"
Macron's Statist Response to the COVID-19 Crisis

The initial phase of Macron's presidency, culminating in the yellow vest protests, was marked by top-down imposition on behalf on an unpopular liberal agenda. In the second phase of his presidency, as he sought to rebound from the yellow vest crisis, Macron offered conciliatory gestures in the form of the Grand National Debate (Grand Débat National, GDN) and Citizens' Climate Convention (Convention Citoyenne pour le Climat, CCC), but he basically continued as before on matters of importance like the unemployment insurance and pension reforms. In contrast to the second phase, the third phase of Macron's presidency saw a significant inflection, with Macron embracing statist remedies in response to the COVID-19 crisis.

France, like most of Europe, has suffered greatly from the COVID-19 virus. As of July 2022, the World Health Organization (WHO) reported that France had registered more than 30 million confirmed cases and over 146,000 confirmed deaths from the disease (WHO 2022). The COVID-19 crisis has also wreaked havoc with the French economy. In March 2020, Macron imposed a strict nationwide quarantine that lasted fifty-five days, bringing most businesses to a standstill. Although many hoped that with the end of the quarantine in May 2020 the COVID-19 crisis would be over, a second, then a third wave struck France in the fall and winter, followed by new waves when the Delta and Omicron variants arrived in 2021. Macron declined to impose another national quarantine, but he did institute more targeted public-health measures to limit the spread of the disease, including local quarantines, curfews, mask mandates, and the closing of a variety of businesses (bars, restaurants, museums, discotheques, movie theaters, health clubs, etc.). The COVID-19 crisis and accompanying public-health measures caused considerable damage to the French economy. Indeed, France experienced its worst economic crisis since the Great Depression, with the economy shrinking by 7.8 percent in 2020 (INSEE 2022c).

Just as there are no atheists in a foxhole, there are no neoliberals in an economic catastrophe. The COVID-19 crisis pushed governments everywhere to stimulate demand, provide benefits to those who could not work, and succor strategic industries. Still, Macron made this turn with exceptional alacrity. In his first major response to the crisis, March 12, 2020, Macron declared that "Everything will be done to protect our employees and our companies, whatever it costs" (*La Croix*, March 15, 2020). "Whatever it costs" became Macron's mantra, which he repeated so often that French media and the government began using it as a noun ("the whatever it costs" or "Macron's whatever it costs"). Such unbridled faith in public spending, the belief that the solution to any social or economic problem during the COVID-19 crisis was to just spend more, could not be further from liberal economic principles. Like Nicolas Sarkozy in 2008, Macron turned away from economic liberalism in a crisis.

Whereas Chapters 5 and 6 emphasized the impact of the social anesthesia state and skinny politics in fueling the contestation of Macron's liberal economic reforms, in this chapter the main source of resistance has come from Macron himself. Not only have the political voices for economic liberalization generally been weak in France, but even when those voices have seemed to be in the ascendency, leaders inclined toward liberal economic reform have displayed a striking willingness to embrace statist policies in times of crisis. Macron's response to the COVID-19 crisis is emblematic of this fair-weather liberalism, with the president adopting a statist, interventionist stance across a range of areas and, in some cases, launching statist initiatives that had little to do with the crisis at hand.

This chapter analyzes Macron's statist response to the COVID-19 crisis. Section 7.1 describes Macron's aggressive deployment of state powers and spending in the area of public health. Section 7.2 reviews a number of expensive new programs designed to keep businesses afloat during the COVID-19 crisis and to protect and steer French industry over the longer term. Section 7.3 presents several major social anesthesia programs that Macron launched to limit unemployment, in many cases reversing his prior stance against such programs. Section 7.4 discusses the impact of Macron's statist turn on French public finances. Section 7.5 details a more recent set of statist initiatives, beginning in late 2021, to protect French households against surging inflation, notably in energy prices. Section 7.6 analyzes how Macron's statist turn and the continued contestation of economic liberalization in France impacted the 2022 presidential and legislative elections.

7.1   Statist Public-Health Policy

The COVID-19 crisis prompted Macron to pivot away from his liberal agenda and take up the mantle of statist protector. In the area of public health, he deployed the full powers of the French state to both combat COVID-19 and address vulnerabilities in the public-health system revealed by the COVID-19 crisis. Macron imposed a lengthy quarantine at the beginning of the COVID-19 outbreak, lasting nearly two months, but he did not stop there. He continued to take aggressive public-health measures in response to subsequent waves of the disease, ordering curfews, business shutdowns, mask mandates, and local quarantines in COVID-19 hot spots. These restrictions imposed significant hardship on French businesses and citizens alike, but despite considerable criticism, Macron persisted.

Macron's boldest statist move occurred with the arrival of vaccines in 2021. Initially, he thought that persuasion would suffice to ensure widespread vaccination. The French population displayed a high degree of vaccine hesitancy however, dampening vaccination rates (Cracknell 2021). After several months of disappointing results, Macron ramped up the pressure on French citizens to get vaccinated (Finnegan 2021).

In a television appearance July 12, 2021, Macron announced a vaccination requirement for all staff (health-care and otherwise) working in hospitals, retirement homes, establishments for persons with disabilities, or any other jobs that brought them into contact with elderly or vulnerable people (Macron 2021). Staff who failed to get vaccinated by mid-September would be suspended without pay. In addition, the government made proof of vaccination or a negative COVID-19 test, the so-called health pass, a precondition for an increasingly lengthy list of everyday activities, including eating in restaurants, exercising at gyms, accessing shopping malls, and taking long-distance public transportation. To encourage people to opt for vaccination over repeated COVID-19 tests, Macron put an end to free COVID-19 tests except upon presentation of a doctor's prescription. Six months later, in January 2022, Macron tightened the screws further by transforming the "health pass" into a "vaccine pass," that is, requiring proof of vaccination (a "vaccine pass"), as opposed to just a negative COVID-19 test (a "health pass").

Faced with such restrictions, most French citizens fell into line, albeit not always happily. Over 1 million people made vaccine appointments within twenty-four hours of Macron's July 12 announcement (*Le Figaro*, July 13, 2021; *Libération*, July 13, 2021). One year later, in July 2022, France boasted one of the highest vaccination rates in Europe, with 81.0 percent of the population fully vaccinated, a higher percentage than Germany, Italy, the Netherlands, Sweden, Switzerland, and the UK among others (Johns Hopkins University of Medicine 2022). Macron has deployed the same tactics to induce older French citizens to get booster vaccines.

Macron's shift to a statist protective stance in public health was financial as well as regulatory. In particular, he has spent heavily to try to remedy critical weaknesses revealed by the COVID-19 crisis. Early in the crisis, on March 12, 2020, Macron issued a whatever-it-costs promise for health-care spending: "Health has no price. The government will mobilize all the financial means necessary to provide aid, take care of the sick, and save lives, whatever it costs" (Macron 2020). Health care does have a price, however, and for years, governments of the left and right alike had sought to reduce that price (Tumasjan 2020). Cost-containment efforts had proven more successful in public hospitals, which are directly controlled by the government, than in the private sector. The problem is that austerity left public hospitals, the main providers in the country, ill-prepared for the COVID-19 crisis. As the number of patients skyrocketed, French hospitals ran out of beds, leading the government to use high-speed trains (Trains à Grande Vitesse, TGV) and military aircraft to transfer patients to less affected parts of France or even neighboring countries. In addition, many hospitals were short-staffed and lacked personal protective equipment (PPE), especially masks (*Libération*, April 27, 2020 and June 18, 2020).

As France exited the first COVID-19 lockdown, Macron came under pressure to reward the heroic efforts of health-care workers, who had labored tirelessly under difficult and even dangerous circumstances, due to the initial shortage of PPE. The president also acknowledged the need to reinvest in the health-care sector, particularly public hospitals. Following a series of negotiations with health-care stakeholders, the government announced some €30 billion in additional spending (French Ministry of Health and Solidarity 2020; *Le Monde*, July 3, 2020; *Les Echos*, July 15, 2020). The administration committed €8.2 billion to raising the wages of health-care workers in hospitals and retirement homes, €13 billion to reducing the debt of public hospitals, and €6 billion to modernizing hospitals. The government also pledged to hire 15,000 new health-care workers. The French Court of Auditors, the national administrative court responsible for conducting financial and legislative audits of the government and other public institutions, notes that France spent an additional €29.9 billion on health care in 2020 and 2021 (French Court of Auditors 2022b: 36).

Macron's commitment of significant resources to the French health-care system was necessary for both political and public-health reasons. It also attests to the long-term crowding-out effects of the social anesthesia state. Even as France became the biggest social spender in the Organisation for Economic Co-operation and Development (OECD), French public hospitals and health-care workers suffered from underfunding. Indeed, the €34.9 billion in extra spending is widely regarded as insufficient (*Le Monde*, July 14, 2020). Driving home the point, in summer 2022 French public hospitals experienced an extraordinary staffing crisis, with many forced to reduce the hours of operation of their emergency rooms or even close them altogether due to a shortage of personnel. The combination of stress, overwork, and low pay has made it increasingly difficult for public hospitals to recruit and retain the staff they need. Thus, the case of health care shows that the social anesthesia state is not just expanding French public spending overall, but also, within that public spending, crowding out critical investment priorities like public hospitals.

Another vulnerability revealed by the COVID-19 crisis concerns the situation of the dependent elderly. Many French senior citizens live in retirement homes, where COVID-19 took a devastating toll, and there is a more general sentiment that the quality of life and care of the most fragile elderly is inadequate. During his 2017 presidential campaign, Macron had pledged to create a set of programs to help the dependent elderly, declaring, "It is not enough to add years to life; we must above all add life to one's years" (Macron 2016: 152). The COVID-19 crisis added urgency to this pledge, and in August 2020 Macron honored his promise. To address the social risk of "a loss of autonomy," the government established a fifth branch of the Social Security system alongside the health, workplace accident, family, and retirement branches (French Ministry of Solidarity and Health 2021; Vie Publique Editorial Board 2020; *Les Echos*, September 30, 2020). The inaugural 2021 budget for this "Autonomy Branch" of Social Security was €31.6 billion, most of it redeployed from existing programs. The main expenditures were for retirement homes and assistance to the handicapped. In 2022, the Autonomy Branch budget rose by 8.8 percent, to €34.4 billion (CNSA 2022). The Autonomy Branch is expected to continue growing rapidly in the years ahead, as the elderly population increases and the branch takes on more missions.

Across the affluent democracies, governments face the challenge of providing a safe and fulfilling life to a growing cohort of dependent elderly citizens. Still, Macron was the only leader to establish a sweeping new program for the dependent elderly during the COVID-19 crisis. Launching an entirely new branch of Social Security amidst the worst fiscal crisis of the postwar period is not exactly the work of a liberal economic reformer. Yet it made perfect sense for a leader seeking to reassure and protect an elderly population traumatized and frightened by the ravages of the coronavirus.

7.2   Supporting Business in the Short Term, Steering Business in the Long Term

Macron's protective statism has extended beyond public-health measures. Support for French business has also figured prominently. Of course, in all countries, governments moved to protect sectors and enterprises made vulnerable by the COVID-19 crisis. Macron did much the same, but he also went a step further. Like President Sarkozy in 2008, Macron launched new industrial policies that had little to do with short-term crisis management.

The most pressing economic challenge facing Macron at the beginning of the pandemic was to prevent French companies from going bankrupt as a result of the economic disruption caused by the COVID-19 crisis and accompanying public-health measures. In response, the government quickly established a €300 billion loan guarantee program for French firms. Thanks to state guarantees, companies were able to access credit at low interest rates at a time when most banks balked at lending to businesses laid low by the crisis.

On the face of it, governments in other countries created larger loan guarantee programs than France: €756 billion in Germany and €360 billion in the UK. These headline numbers are misleading, however, because the French program had a higher take-up rate, especially initially (Anderson et al. 2020). As of September 2021, the French government had guaranteed €140.3 billion in loans to business, nearly 6 percent of GDP, as compared with €119.4 billion in the UK and €59.1 billion in Germany (Bruegel 2022).[1] Minister of the Economy and Finance Bruno Le Maire captured the spirit of the government's effort to get money quickly to struggling businesses: "Before, to get approval for a credit of over 1 million euro, you had to go through an inter-ministerial meeting. During the crisis, we are releasing 1 billion [euro] in 24 hours" (*Le Monde*, December 12, 2020). The loan guarantee program was slated to run until the end of 2020 initially, but it was extended through 2021, then to July 2022. In the end, some 700,000 French businesses received a total of €143 billion in loan guarantees through the program (French Ministry of the Economy and Finance 2022).

The state loan guarantee program is not without risks. As guarantor, the state is responsible for 70 to 90 percent of the value of the loans should French businesses default. When the program was launched, French banks anticipated a default rate of 5 to 10 percent (*Capital*, January 15, 2021). Of course, most of the loans are to otherwise-viable companies that are suffering from the economic fallout from the COVID-19 crisis. Thanks to state support, well-managed enterprises have a chance to survive the crisis. That said, some businesses are in deep trouble, and French authorities are well aware that the loans to so-called zombie companies may never be repaid (French Senate Finance Commission 2021; *Le Monde*, October 13, 2020). For example, a large number of the loans have gone to small shops, hotels, bars, cafés, and restaurants that are reeling from multiple rounds of closures in response to surging COVID-19 cases. There is widespread concern that these businesses will be unable to repay their state-guaranteed loans or even continue operating once exceptional support measures are withdrawn.

The state has provided not just loans to French companies, but also direct aid. The biggest initiative has been the Solidarity Fund (Fonds de Solidarité) aimed at small businesses, such as restaurants, bars, cafés, hotels, clubs, shops, and auto repair facilities, that have been forced to limit their activities or close temporarily due to COVID-19 public-health restrictions (French Government 2022d). The program generally covers 100 percent of the lost revenues up to €10,000 per month, then 20 percent up to €200,000 per month. The French government reports that as of July 1, 2022, the Solidarity Fund had provided €41.5 billion in direct aid to over 2 million French businesses (French Government 2022d). Roughly one-half of the aid has gone to companies in the hotel, restaurant, and commerce sectors.

In September 2021, with the French economy seemingly on the mend, the government established a €3 billion Transition Fund (Fonds de Transition) for companies that still needed help (French Ministry of the Economy and Finance 2021b). The mission of the Transition Fund is to provide loans and capital injections to medium and large firms that continue to experience significant difficulties as a result of the COVID-19 crisis. The Transition Fund is meant to substitute temporarily for other programs that are being wound down with the (apparent) end of the economic crisis. Given that Transition Fund is targeting companies that demonstrate continued vulnerability despite a strong economic recovery in 2021, the state has assumed a nonnegligible risk in lending to or investing in these companies.

Macron has not stopped at helping French business weather an extraordinary crisis. Much like Sarkozy in 2008, he has also taken advantage of the crisis to launch a series of policies designed to protect and promote French industry over the long term. One of Macron's first economic initiatives in response to the COVID-19 crisis was to reinforce protections against foreign takeovers of strategic French companies. As described in Chapter 3, notwithstanding Macron's promarket reputation, he had already moved in this direction in 2019. Key changes at the time included adding new sectors to the list of protected strategic sectors, extending the restrictions on takeovers to European Union (EU) companies, lowering the threshold for government review from 33 percent to 25 percent foreign ownership, making links with foreign governments a basis for denying acquisitions, and establishing strict penalties for foreign companies that do not follow procedures laid out by French law or violate promises made as a condition for acquiring a French company.

With the COVID-19 outbreak, Macron added biotechnology to the list of strategic sectors, a reflection of its importance in the fight against COVID-19. He also gave the ministry of the economy and finance the means to intervene earlier to forestall foreign takeovers of French companies. Concerned that foreign investors would take advantage of falling stock prices to scoop up French firms on the cheap, Macron "temporarily" reduced the threshold for triggering a government review of foreign holdings from 25 percent to 10 percent of a listed French company's shares, a measure that has been renewed several times, most recently through 2023 (French Treasury 2021; *Les Echos*, December 23, 2022).

For the most part, Macron has intervened to protect French firms involved in national defense or possessing valuable technologies. However, in January 2021, the government shocked the business community in France and abroad when, invoking "food sovereignty," it blocked a €16.2 billion friendly takeover of France's largest supermarket chain, Carrefour, by a Canadian company, Couche-Tard (*Financial Times*, January 18, 2021; *Les Echos*, January 22, 2021). The move was surprising for a number of reasons: the acquisition was friendly, Couche-Tard had pledged to invest €3 billion in Carrefour, and Macron had signed a free-trade treaty with Canada in 2018. What is more, the veto came just as France's Alstom was completing an acquisition of the Canadian Bombardier's railroad business, a seemingly more strategic sector than supermarkets (*Les Echos*, January 14, 2021). In addition, although Carrefour is the biggest supermarket chain and employer in France, the country has no shortage of large supermarket chains (Casino, Intermarché, Auchan, Leclerc, Super U, etc.). Finally, the notion that the domestic ownership of a supermarket chain, however large, is essential to "food sovereignty" strains credulity. Foreign supermarket chains like Aldi and Lidl have continued to sell groceries in France during the COVID-19 crisis, and French supermarket chains are notorious for squeezing domestic farmers and food suppliers, presumably eroding France's capacity to produce food at home. In the end, the government's veto was motivated more by the symbolism of preserving French ownership of a household name than any national security or economic logic. The action was also completely at odds with liberal economic principles.

The same can be said of Macron's embrace of industrial policy. The government has provided considerable aid to ailing national champions through sectoral industrial policies. The automobile and aeronautics industries are the most prominent examples, but the government has developed sectoral policies for a number of ailing activities, from books to tourism (French Government 2022b; French Ministry of Culture 2021). The automobile and aeronautic policies aim not just to stabilize national champions in a crisis, but also to steer their business strategies over the long term.

Announced in May 2020, the "Automobile Plan" pledged €8 billion to the industry, with most of the money going to Renault and Peugeot Group (Peugeot Société Anonyme, PSA) (French Government 2020e). The plan has three main "axes": (1) to revive demand for automobiles; (2) to relocalize production in France; (3) to improve competitiveness via investment, particularly in electric vehicles. Only the first of those three axes can be considered a response to the economic crisis, seeking to boost demand for cars and soak up excess production. The second and third axes represent more traditional industrial policy initiatives, pushing Renault and PSA to accelerate the transition to electric cars and to site production in France. Even the first axis is not altogether independent of industrial policy considerations. The incentives of the €1.0 to €1.3 billion program are most generous for the purchase of the kinds of fuel-efficient hybrid and especially electric cars that the government is trying to get PSA and Renault to manufacture.

The government's Automobile Plan seeks to reverse a longstanding delocalization of auto production to other countries, notably in Eastern Europe. Between 2000 and 2012, PSA and Renault closed twelve automobile plants in Western Europe, while opening eleven automobile plants in Eastern Europe (*Le Monde*, June 3, 2020). Today, no small cars are produced in France. Relatedly, whereas the French auto industry ran a trade surplus of €12 billion in 2004, by 2018 the situation had reversed completely, with the auto industry running a trade deficit of €12 billion (*Le Monde*, June 3, 2020). Minister of the Economy and Finance Bruno Le Maire declared that delocalizations by Renault and PSA have been harmful for France and must be halted: "We are going to break with 30 years of massive delocalization by the automobile industry. It may have been good for the companies, but the cost to the nation has been prohibitive and, collectively, we all lost out" (*Le Monde*, May 27, 2020). Le Maire, who hailed from the conservative Republicans (Les Républicains, LR), has long been regarded as dedicated to balanced budgets and free markets. Like many French conservatives, however, Le Maire has proven to be something of a fair-weather liberal, declaring that "We will privilege support for our employees and companies over the balancing of public finances" and insisting that the auto industry bring production back to France in return for government aid (*Libération*, June 10, 2020).

The Automobile Plan imposed a number of obligations on Renault and PSA (*Le Monde*, May 26, 2020; *Les Echos*, May 26, 2020). Renault was required to produce a future electric engine at a factory in Normandy instead of China, as the company had originally intended. Renault was also required to quadruple the number of electric vehicles assembled in France by the year 2024. Finally, the government pushed Renault to enter the capital of the Automotive Cell Company, often described as the "Airbus of Batteries" because it involves French and German producers. Launched in January 2020, the Automotive Cell Company started as a joint venture between Total, a French energy company, with its wholly owned Saft battery manufacturer, on the one hand, and PSA, with its German Opel subsidiary, on the other hand. Renault had not wanted to partner with its domestic rival, PSA, but agreed to join the consortium at the government's insistence.[2]

PSA likewise incurred a number of obligations under the Automobile Plan (*Le Monde*, May 26, 2020; *Les Echos*, May 26, 2020). The company was required to source all of the key components for its electric engines in France, quintuple the production of rechargeable vehicles, manufacture its future electric 308 model automobile in France, and go from zero electric vehicles produced in 2019 to 130,000 in 2021, at an estimated cost to the firm of €360 million. In addition, the government made both PSA and Renault sign a "good conduct charter" pledging to integrate social and environmental costs, as opposed to just financial costs, in all sourcing decisions.

Macron's €15 billion "Aeronautics Plan" displays more than a passing resemblance to the Automobile Plan (French Government 2020d). The government provided €7 billion in direct loans and loan guarantees to the ailing Air France-KLM airline. In addition, some 80 percent of Air France employees were put into a government program (discussed later in this chapter) that temporarily paid their wages (*Le Monde*, March 17, 2020). In return, Air France was required to reduce CO_2 emissions from its domestic flights by 50 percent by the year 2024. The simplest way to hit this target, and one that the government strongly encouraged, was for Air France to eliminate all domestic flights shorter than 2.5 hours for which a high-speed rail alternative existed (*Les Echos*, April 29, 2020). To make sure that low-cost airlines did not take advantage of Air France's withdrawal from short domestic flights, the government promised to prevent other airlines from using Air France's vacated airport slots for flights within France (*Les Echos*, June 19, 2020).

The Aeronautics Plan offered support to the ailing Airbus aircraft manufacturer as well as Air France. The government committed €3.8

billion to boost airplane sales, €3 billion in export guarantees, and €800 million in direct purchases. It also kicked in €1.5 billion for research and €1.3 billion to bolster small aeronautics suppliers. In return, Airbus pledged to produce a carbon-neutral airplane by 2035 (*Les Echos*, June 17, 2020).

In addition to explicit industrial policies, the government packaged long-term support for industry in what it presented as a short-term stimulus measure. In September 2020, the government announced a fiscal package called France Relance (Relaunch France), which it later supplemented with a smaller initiative, France 2030, in October 2021. Despite its name (*relance* is the French word for demand stimulus), Relaunch France is more of a long-term industrial policy than a short-term, Keynesian support for demand, as Macron himself related (French Government 2020c). Almost all of the money is being channeled to business, rather than consumers, and mostly over the long term. Key measures include support for investments in environmental industries (€30 billion) and new technologies (€11 billion), business tax cuts (€20 billion), government payment of wages in the place of employers (€7.6 billion), subsidies for youth hires (€6.7 billion), and direct injections of capital into small enterprises (€3 billion). The business business tax cuts, totaling €10 billion per year, are the only permanent measure. Even the ostensibly social measures, such as support for employment, operate through subsidies to business. By contrast, just €800 million, less than 1 percent of the money, is dedicated to poverty relief, although some measures, such as the government's payment of wages and provision of subsidies for youth hires, help ordinary workers and prop up demand in a Keynesian fashion (*Libération*, September 3, 2020; *Les Echos*, September 6, 2020). Still, over 80 percent of the spending in Relaunch France is dedicated to long-term industrial policy, aiming to build a world-class French industry by the year 2030 (French Government 2020; *Libération*, September 2, 2020).

Voluntarist institutions have also made a comeback under Relaunch France. As part of the initiative, Macron reestablished the symbol of postwar *dirigiste* industrial policy, the planning commissariat, now known as the High Commission for Planning (Haut-Commissariat au Plan). The planning commissariat had fallen into disuse decades ago, before being abolished in 2006. Macron's selection of François Bayrou, a key center-right ally, to head the High Commission for Planning attests to the importance of the institution in the president's mind. Macron charged Bayrou with helping plan the French economy of 2030. In addition, Macron hopes that the High Commission for Planning will inject long-term, strategic thinking into government decision-making, which he believes is driven too often by short-term pressures and constraints. Macron has given Bayrou a wide-ranging mandate "to animate and coordinate the work of planning and prospective reflection conducted on behalf of the State and to illuminate the choices of public authorities regarding demographic, economic, social, environmental, health, technological and cultural challenges" (French Government 2022c). Thus, Macron has revived not only *dirigiste* practices, but also an institutional thinking capacity for developing new *dirigiste* initiatives across a wide range of areas.

In October 2021, Macron launched another industrial policy initiative, France 2030. As its name indicates, France 2030 seeks to promote French industry over the course of the 2020s, just like Relaunch France. The program pledges €34 billion to, in the words of Macron, "help the future technological champions of tomorrow emerge and accompany the transitions of our sectors of excellence in automobiles, aeronautics, or even space" (French Presidency 2021). France 2030 lists ten very ambitious objectives, including developing small nuclear reactors, making France a world leader in green hydrogen, manufacturing the world's first low-carbon airplanes, reducing greenhouse gases by 35 percent over 2015, and placing France in a leadership position in the production of cultural and creative content.

The Automobile Plan, Aeronautics Plan, Relaunch France, and France 2030 seek to accelerate the greening of French industry, whether through new cars, new engines, new aircraft, or new sources of energy, and to revive manufacturing on French soil. The green development strategy appeals to Macron for several reasons. Green technologies are a growing, high-value-added segment that could buoy French industry. In addition, as part of his strategy for rebounding from the yellow vest protests, Macron wanted to cast environmental policy as a source of new businesses and jobs, not just higher taxes. What is more, promoting green industries was in line with the recommendations of the CCC. Finally, this tack offered a way to steal some of the thunder from the environmental party, Europe Ecology – The Greens (Europe Ecologie – Les Verts, EELV), that triumphed in the 2020 municipal elections. Macron has portrayed his approach to ecology, with its emphasis on the development of new technologies and industries, as an alternative to the supposedly punitive and anti-growth approach of Green parties like the EELV. Significant investments in green technologies allow Macron to argue that he is reducing France's carbon footprint, but in ways that promote economic growth.

Macron is betting on France's capacity to become a leader in green technologies like electric cars and zero-emission aircraft. As industrial policies go, the government's approach has a lot to recommend it. In particular, it focuses on high-cost, high-value-added products that take advantage of Europe's excellent research and advanced manufacturing capacities. For example, an electric car battery is worth on the order of one-third of the price of the vehicle. As one auto industry consultant noted, "It is a lot smarter to fight to produce batteries in France, which represent 35 percent of the value of a vehicle, than to bring back the production of lightweight plastic parts made in China and easily transported" (*Le Monde*, June 3, 2020).

Still, Macron's strategy is not without concerns and risks. One is the familiar question, in the age of the social anesthesia state, of how much additional money the government is actually committing. As usual, the government is not just providing new financial resources, but also redeploying existing resources. In particular, the Investments in the Future Program (Programme d'Investissements d'Avenir, PIA) created by Nicolas Sarkozy in 2010 and renewed three times since seems to be serving as a piggy bank for several of Macron's industrial policies (Bellaiche 2022). The third iteration of the PIA ran from 2017 to 2020, and its entire €10 billion allotment went to Macron's €57 billion Grand Investment Plan (Grand Plan d'Investissement, GPI). The fourth iteration of the PIA is running from 2021 to 2025 and providing €11 billion of its €20 billion to Relaunch France along with an unspecified amount to France 2030. Relaunch France is also covering part of the cost of France 2030. Such Rube Goldberg systems of financing make it impossible to assess the total financial outlay of Macron's industrial policy measures, but there is clearly less fresh money than the government suggests.

The challenges to Macron's green industrial strategy are not just financial. China has a substantial lead in batteries for electric cars and is investing far more than the Europeans in building and supporting an electric car industry. As for zero-emissions aircraft, while there are some promising engine technologies, the prospects for such an airplane are far off in the future. Adding to the risk of these green initiatives, Macron wants new products like electric cars to be built in France, yet France is not a technological leader; nor does France have the kind of strong manufacturing base found in Germany. Macron's strategy is, therefore, very much a gamble.

It is also very much at odds with liberal economic principles. Macron is picking winners, conditioning economic aid on support for his green industrial policy objectives. Moreover, he is pressing companies to produce in France, even when they believe that foreign sourcing offers a better option. These initiatives may be smart, or they may be foolish, but the one thing that they are not is liberal. The same can be said of Macron's restrictions on foreign acquisitions of French companies and his decision to establish the High Commission of Planning, reviving a symbol of postwar French voluntarism.

7.3   The Revival of Social Anesthesia

Macron has revived social anesthesia policies as well as industrial policies. In March 2020, with the economy collapsing and many businesses unable to pay their workers, the administration stepped in to limit the social fallout. Such actions may have been understandable, but they have been very expensive and passively oriented, with the government committing vast amounts of money to programs that mitigate or mask unemployment.

Some of the new measures are directly at odds with the government's previous emphasis on moving away from social anesthesia policies that do little more than disguise unemployment. When Macron came to power, one of his first initiatives was to shut down subsidized employment programs that provided payments and exemptions from taxes to companies hiring unskilled, young, and/or low-wage workers (*Les Echos*, November 14, 2019). Minister of Labor Muriel Pénicaud repeatedly denounced subsidized employment as wasteful and ineffective, and analyses of these programs backed her up (French Court of Auditors 2011). French employers were being paid for hires that they mostly would have made anyway, or else they were simply replacing nonsubsidized hires with subsidized hires. What is more, the subsidized hires rarely received training and were often let go once the subsidies expired. To add insult to injury, the very same employers who dismissed these subsidized workers could then hire new subsidized workers under the same or other public programs.

Macron's government moved quickly to wind down subsidized employment. The number of subsidized hires plummeted from 458,000 in 2016 to 293,000 in 2017 and 134,000 in 2018 (Lamar 2020). The COVID-19 crisis interrupted the process of phasing out subsidized hires, however. Macron was especially concerned that the estimated 750,000 young people entering the labor market in 2020 would be unable to find any kind of employment (French Government 2020a: 5). A delayed entry into the labor market would be not only painful to youths in the short term, but also potentially harmful to their lifetime employment trajectories and earnings. To try to limit such labor scarring, Macron revved up precisely the kinds of subsidized employment programs that he had previously sought to eliminate.

Relaunch France budgeted €6.5 billion for a panoply of measures to occupy youths entering the labor market (French Ministry of Labor 2020). Dubbed "One Youth, One Solution" (Un Jeune, Une Solution), Macron's plan has relied heavily on employment subsidies, offering up to €4,000 for the hire of low-wage youths under the age of 25. Eligible jobs can be temporary, although only €1,000 is paid every quarter, so the job must last at least one year for employers to receive the full subsidy. According to the government, during the final six months of 2020, 1 million youths were hired under the One Youth, One Solution program, receiving job contracts of at least three months (French Ministry of the Economy and Finance 2021a).

One Youth, One Solution has also spent heavily on apprenticeships. Beginning July 2020, the government offered employers subsidies of €5,000 for apprentices under the age of 18 and €8,000 for those aged 18 to 29. In most cases, the subsidies essentially cover the cost of the apprentice for the first year. Not surprisingly, employers have taken on apprentices with alacrity. Even though the program only began halfway through 2020, the number of apprentices increased that year by nearly 50 percent, from 354,000 to 510,000 (French Ministry of Labor 2022). In 2021, the number of apprentices surged by an additional 200,000, to an all-time high of 718,000, more than double the pre-COVID-19 figure.

One Youth, One Solution included other initiatives that ramped up in 2021 (*Le Parisien*, July 23, 2020; *Les Echos*, September 3, 2020). To stem the flow of youths into the labor market, the government allowed 200,000 students to pursue an extra year of education, focusing on training for "the occupations of the future," such as green industries, health care, and digital technologies. In addition, some 300,000 young people who were "the most distant from employment," generally high school dropouts, received training and subsidies to help place them in jobs. According to Elisabeth Borne, the minister of employment at the time (and future prime minister), some 3 million youths have participated in One Youth, One Solution (*Le Figaro Etudiant*, September 10, 2021). Meanwhile, the Court of Auditors pointed out that the cost of the program rose from €6.5 billion to €10 billion (French Court of Auditors 2022b: 19).

The Court of Auditors has voiced skepticism about the long-term impact of One Youth, One Solution and criticized the government for not conducting any evaluations to assess the effectiveness of the initiative (French Court of Auditors 2022b: 135–155). Although some of the programs involve continuing education or training, others are little more than subsidized employment of a kind that Macron previously combatted. The Court of Auditors is especially critical of the apprentice-ship program (French Court of Auditors 2022a). The court points out that in doubling the number of apprentices, the government has mostly enrolled students in higher education above the Bac+2 level, who do not need an apprenticeship to land a job.[3] Students above the Bac+2 level now make up roughly 60 percent of the apprentices, while the proportion of unskilled youths, whose employment and career prospects *do* benefit from participation in an apprenticeship, has declined significantly. Consequently, the apprenticeship program has become not only more expensive, but also less centered on the population of unskilled youths, who have the most to gain from participation in the program.

In addition to subsidized employment, a second social anesthesia initiative has sought to keep companies afloat at government expense in order to preserve jobs. Many state-guaranteed loans discussed in Section 7.2 fall into this category, supporting businesses for reasons of employment maintenance, rather than economic potential. As noted, France has guaranteed more business borrowing than either the UK or Germany. The subsidies provided by the Solidarity Fund and Transition Fund likewise aim to sustain ailing enterprises.

A third important social anesthesia initiative has been so-called partial unemployment (*chômage partiel*), which covers the wages of employees, while allowing them to remain formally attached to their companies (Masson 2020; UNEDIC 2020b). According to the Court of Auditors, France spent €35.8 billion on partial employment measures in 2020 and 2021 (French Court of Auditors 2022b: 16). Partial employment was pioneered in Germany, where it is known as *kurzarbeitergeld*, or short-time work allowance. During the 2008 economic crisis, Germany deployed *kurzarbeitergeld* on a wide scale. By keeping employees attached to their companies, rather than laying them off, as France did, *kurzarbeitergeld* prevented German businesses from losing workers with valuable skills and know-how. When the macroeconomic context improved in Europe, German companies were able to respond quickly to increased demand, whereas French firms often had to rehire and retrain workers, adding to their costs and slowing their response.

French authorities were determined not to let the same thing happen this time around. Beyond economic arguments, *kurzarbeitergeld* or *chômage partiel* offered a handy way of disguising unemployment, even as there is little difference between employees who are being paid not to work and employees who have been laid off and are receiving unemployment benefits. Indeed, given the generally lower skill levels of French workers compared with German workers, the economic rationale for keeping them attached to their company, that is, the difficulty of finding replacements quickly, is probably less compelling. In the French case, *chômage partiel* seems like yet another social anesthesia measure, with the state substituting for employers by paying the wages of workers without work. It is also important to note that despite the label of "partial unemployment," in most cases *chômage partiel* recipients are not working part-time; they are simply not working at all.

A number of countries adopted the German *kurzarbeitergeld* approach, but France took it the furthest, offering the most generous terms in Europe (Masson 2020; UNEDIC 2020b). Compared with Germany, for example, French *chômage partiel* pays at least the minimum wage, whereas there is no legal floor for German *kurzarbeitergeld*. At the other end of the wage spectrum, France pays benefits of up to €4,848 per month, compared with a ceiling of €2,892 in Germany. The mode of calculation of the benefit is also more generous in France: 84 percent of the net wage, as opposed to 60 percent in Germany (although the German benefit is 67 percent for households with children and rises to 70 percent after three months and 80 percent after six months). In addition, the French benefit covered more employees: 11.3 million recipients in 2020, versus 10.1 million in Germany, even though the German workforce is roughly 40 percent larger than the French workforce. Thus, if Germany invented a system for paying workers not to work while remaining attached to their companies, the French student has surpassed (or, at least, outspent) the master.

As the French economy began to reopen in May 2020, with the end of the fifty-five-day national quarantine, the Macron administration sought to scale back *chômage partiel* (Journal du Net Editorial Board 2022; Lachaise 2022). The government reduced its financial contribution, effective June 1, 2020, from 100 to 85 percent of the cost of partial unemployment, with employers required to pay the remaining 15 percent. Beginning October 1, 2020, the employer share was supposed to increase from 15 percent to 40 percent and employees to receive only 72 percent of their net wage instead of 84 percent. These changes were postponed, however, as the French economy remained weak, and the government feared rising unemployment rates. Renewed waves of COVID-19 also interrupted the scaling back of *chômage partiel*. Still, the government eventually reduced its reimbursement of employer costs to 74 percent beginning June 1, 2021 and 60 percent one month later. The government also reduced the amount paid to employees from 84 to 72 percent of the net wage, effective July 1, 2021.

While seeking to scale back *chômage partiel*, the government created a new program, Long-Term Partial Employment (Activité Partielle de Longue Durée, APLD), designed to continue such provisions in hard-hit sectors like automobiles, aeronautics, and tourism (French Government 2020c: 167–168). Modeled on an agreement signed in the metalworking and mining sector, APLD allows companies to reduce employee hours and wages up to 40 percent for any twenty-four months during a thirty-six-month period (Journal du Net Editorial Board 2022). Like the initial *chômage partiel*, employees receive 84 percent of their net wage, with the state paying 85 percent of the cost of hours not worked and the employer paying 15 percent, but in contrast to the *chômage partiel*, these rates will remain in place through June 2025 (Fédération Nationale des Travaux Publics 2021). In order to be eligible, companies must either sign an agreement with workforce representatives or be covered by a sectoral collective bargaining agreement.[4] In theory, APLD is available to companies "confronted with a long-term reduction in their activity that is not of a nature to compromise their survival" (French Ministry of Labor, Full Employment, and Integration 2021). Such a determination is extremely difficult to make, however, creating a risk that under pressure to limit job losses the government will permit APLD to be deployed by companies whose prospects for survival are, in fact, quite compromised.

The COVID-19 crisis prompted Macron to relaunch social anesthesia measures on a grand scale. Where the government once sought to eliminate subsidized employment, it is now shunting hundreds of thousands of French youths into such positions – when it is not parking young people in education and training programs to keep them out of the labor force entirely. The government has also engaged in employment maintenance by helping struggling companies remain in business. Finally, France has become a world "leader" in substituting for employers by paying the wages of workers who are not, in fact, working. Macron has made no secret of his determination to protect wages from the effects of the COVID-19 crisis. Indeed, in an interview with a news magazine, Macron declared proudly that his government had "nationalized the payment of salaries," adding that it was something that "has never existed in contemporary economic history" (*Le Point*, April 15, 2020). Macron's extraordinary effort to ensure the continuing flow of wages in the absence of actual jobs is another instance in which the statist protector has supplanted the liberal reformer.

7.4   The High Cost of Statist Revival

Macron's statist, activist turn has ramped up public spending. The shift is especially jarring given that, during the initial years of his presidency, Macron focused on curbing the social anesthesia state and bringing down the budget deficit. On behalf of these objectives, the government swept every corner for budgetary savings, sometimes – as in the case of the €5 reduction in the monthly housing allowance – with shocking inattention to popular opinion and the hardships of the disadvantaged. In 2019, the budget deficit stood at 3.1 percent of GDP (INSEE 2021b), and Macron still hoped to eliminate the deficit altogether by the end of his term. Under the banner of "whatever it costs," however, Macron has presided over a massive increase in public spending, deficits, and debt.

Although Macron's statist turn echoed that of Sarkozy, he has been deliberately more ambitious when it comes to deficit spending. Specifically, with Relaunch France, the government sought to avoid what it regarded as two macroeconomic errors made by the Sarkozy administration in its response to the 2008 financial crisis (*Le Figaro*, September 3, 2020). The first was to not make the stimulus package big enough. Whereas the Sarkozy stimulus plan totaled €34 billion or 1.5 percent of GDP, Relaunch France is nearly three times the size, at €100 billion, or close to 4.0 percent of GDP (*La Croix*, September 3, 2020). Relaunch France is also slightly bigger than the German plan of 3.7 percent of GDP (*Libération*, September 2, 2020; *La Croix*, September 3, 2020). With the addition of France 2030, costing €34 billion, France's fiscal stimulus is almost 5 percent of GDP.

Sarkozy's other error, in the view of the administration, was to reverse fiscal stimulus and seek to reduce the budget deficit too quickly (*Le Figaro*, September 3, 2020). Fearing a Greek-style sovereign debt crisis, Sarkozy cut spending and increased taxes to bring down the deficit, but at the cost of weakening France's recovery. This time, Macron promised not to raise taxes, and Prime Minister Philippe, evoking Sarkozy's ill-fated U-turn, reaffirmed the pledge: "I will say it again and I want all the French to be convinced; there will not be an increase in taxes. That was the mistake that was made during the last crisis and we will not repeat it" (*Le Figaro*, September 2, 2020). Public spending has likewise continued to grow apace. Thus, Macron's whatever-it-costs fiscal policy is designed to protect the French economy against a prolonged recession like the nearly decade-long slump that followed the 2008 financial crisis.

The combination of falling revenues as a result of the crisis and increased government spending on public-health measures, support for business, social anesthesia, and stimulus programs has had a dramatic impact on French public finances. In 2020, the budget deficit nearly tripled from 3.1 percent to 8.9 percent of GDP, while public expenditures, which had edged down from 56.5 percent of GDP in 2017 to 55.4 percent in 2019, shot up to a postwar high of 61.4 percent of GDP (INSEE 2022a, 2022c). Part of the erosion in French public finances occurred because the economy shrank by 7.8 percent of GDP in 2020, meaning that public spending, deficits, and debt measured as a share of GDP grew as a result of not only an increase in the numerator, but also a sharp decrease in the denominator (size of GDP). The French economy bounced back in 2021, however, growing by 6.8 percent of GDP, and by early 2022, it had recovered to its pre-COVID-19 level, yet France's public finances did not recover to the same extent. Despite rapid growth in 2021, France still ran a budget deficit of 6.4 percent of GDP (INSEE 2022b).

A February 2022 report by the French Court of Auditors observed that public spending in 2021 was 2 percent of GDP higher than in 2019 (French Court of Auditors 2022b). The 2022 deficit is projected to be 5 percent of GDP, compared with 3.1 percent of GDP in 2019. What is more, the Court of Auditors points out that the structural deficit has doubled from 2.5 percent of GDP to 5 percent of GDP as a result of tax cuts and higher social spending.

Macron shows little interest in bringing down France's budget deficit. According to the government's five-year projection, the deficit will not return to its pre-pandemic level of 3 percent of GDP until 2027. What is more, the Court of Auditors contends that for France to reach even this modest deficit target, the government would need to both refrain from additional tax cuts (whereas Macron plans some €15 billion in tax cuts) and find an extra €9 billion in spending reductions every year compared with the pace of expenditure growth from 2010 to 2019 (French Court of Auditors 2022b: 51).

The same limited ambitions characterize Macron's approach to the structural budget deficit. The Court of Auditors observes that Germany and Italy, like France, have presented fiscal plans beyond 2022 (to 2025 for Germany and 2024 for Italy). From 2021 to 2024, Germany intends to reduce its structural deficit by 5.75 points, Italy by 3.8 points, and France by just 2.3 percentage points (French Court of Auditors 2022b: 47–48). If all goes as planned, Germany will have eliminated its structural deficit, while France and Italy will still have structural deficits of around 4 percent of GDP.[5]

Not surprisingly, France's public debt has grown substantially during the COVID-19 crisis. OECD data show that French debt surged by 15.3 percent of GDP in two years, from 97.3 percent of GDP in 2019 to 112.6 percent in 2021 (OECD 2021c). Figure 7.1 compares the increase in debt in France with that of the leading European economies referenced in Chapter 1 (Denmark, Germany, the Netherlands, and Sweden), on the one hand, and a heavily indebted group composed of Belgium and the Southern European countries (Greece, Italy, Portugal, and Spain), on the other hand. France's performance clearly aligns with

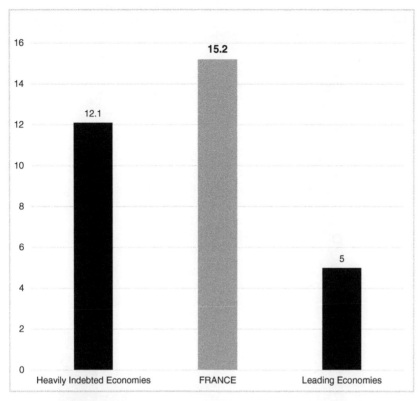

Figure 7.1 Increase in public debt as a percentage of GDP in 2020 and 2021 combined
Note: Heavily indebted economies = Greece, Italy, Portugal, Spain, and Belgium; leading economies = Denmark, Germany, Netherlands, and Sweden.
Source: OECD (2021c)

that of the heavily indebted countries. Indeed, France's debt increased by more than the debt of Belgium and the Southern European countries (15.2 percent versus 12.1 percent of GDP).

As Figure 7.2 reveals, France's public debt is approaching Belgian and Southern European levels. The French Court of Auditors warns that the eurozone is splitting into two groups (French Court of Auditors 2022b: 45). A first group, which includes France, Belgium, Spain, and Italy, has a structural deficit of more than 5 percent of GDP and public debt of more than 110 percent of GDP. A second group, which includes Germany, the Netherlands, and Austria (Denmark and Sweden are not members of the eurozone, but their public finances are comparable)

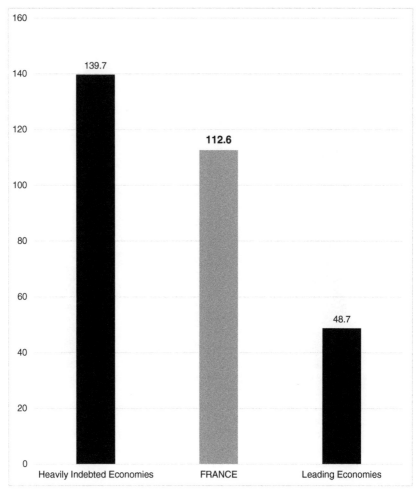

Figure 7.2 Gross public debt as a percentage of GDP, 2021
Note: Heavily indebted economies = Greece, Italy, Portugal, Spain, and Belgium; leading economies = Denmark, Germany, Netherlands, and Sweden.
Source: OECD (2021c)

has a structural deficit of around 3 percent of GDP and debt of 60–80 percent of GDP. Germany has a relatively large structural deficit and public debt compared with the other countries in the second group, but as discussed, it is undertaking an ambitious fiscal adjustment program to reduce those levels significantly and, by 2025, its public debt is projected to be some 50 percent of GDP lower than that of France.

The coronavirus crisis was the primary cause of the deterioration in French public finances, pushing emergency spending up, while pushing economic growth down. Still, other European countries suffered the same shock without as steep an erosion of their public finances. Clearly, Macron's policy choices also contributed to the increase in French debt and deficits. Macron shifted fiscal gears, from championing deficit reduction to spending "whatever it costs" to repair the health-care system, protect the dependent elderly, save jobs and businesses, launch new industrial policies, and deploy social anesthesia programs to sustain incomes. What is more, as Section 7.5 details, Macron has recently found new reasons unrelated to the COVID-19 crisis to ramp up state spending and launch additional industrial policy measures.

7.5   The Statist Response to Inflation and Surging Energy Prices

The surge of vaccinations in France in the second half of 2021 and beginning of 2022 seems to have brought the acute phase of the COVID-19 crisis to an end. While cases have still spiked at times with new variants of the coronavirus, hospitalization and fatality rates have declined significantly. In response, Macron has lifted all mask mandates and public-health measures. Of course, the possibility of a future more lethal variant of the coronavirus cannot be ruled out, but for now at least, life in France has largely returned to normal.

The reasons for protective statism have not disappeared with the waning of COVID-19, however. The approach of the 2022 presidential election, coupled with rising inflation and a dramatic spike in energy prices, prompted Macron to spring back into action. Macron has deployed expensive and market-distorting measures to protect the French from the effects of inflation in general, but especially rising energy prices. Thus, if Macron's pivot from liberal reformism to statist protection during the COVID-19 crisis was a response to a world-historical pandemic, he has also displayed a willingness to take up the role of statist protector in response to less extreme circumstances.

Part of the reason for Macron's anti-inflationary activism has been electoral. In the run-up to the 2022 presidential election, French voters consistently indicated that their number one priority was purchasing power (OpinionWay-Kéa Partners 2022). Moreover, Marine Le Pen, Macron's opponent in the second round of the presidential election, made purchasing power central to her campaign (*Le Monde*, March 19, 2022). Le Pen railed against Macron for spending billions of euro helping businesses during the COVID-19 crisis, while leaving ordinary citizens to fend for themselves in the face of unprecedented inflation. To combat rising energy prices, Le Pen promised to slash the value-added tax (VAT) on natural gas, electricity, and gasoline from 20 percent to 5.5 percent, along with other measures.

Marine Le Pen was not Macron's only concern. The 2018 yellow vest movement had been touched off by sharp increases in energy taxes against a backdrop of rising global prices. These taxes had been slated to nearly double between 2018 and 2022 as part of the government's strategy for reducing energy consumption and curbing CO_2 emissions (Dusanter 2022). However, in response to the yellow vest protests, Macron froze energy taxes at their 2018 level. The prospect of renewed protests touched off by rising energy prices spurred Macron to further action.

Whether to protect vulnerable households, preempt protests, or safeguard his electoral standing, Macron launched a number of initiatives to shelter consumers from the effects of rising inflation, especially for energy. In November 2021, the government added €100 to the "energy check" paid to low-income households, which typically ranges from €48 to €277 per year, at a cost of €580 million (French Ministry of Environmental Transition 2021a). The government followed up, during the winter months, by providing so-called inflation compensation in the amount of €100 to 38 million citizens, at a cost of €3.8 billion (French Government 2021). These measures provided a modicum of relief to the needy, while allowing energy prices to continue incentivizing the French to reduce consumption and migrate to more fuel-efficient home heating systems and automobiles.

The same cannot be said of Macron's most significant protective initiative, the establishment of the so-called rate shield (*bouclier tarifaire*) on natural gas and electricity rates. Announced in September 2021, the rate shield – a protective image if ever there were one – froze natural gas rates and capped electricity rate hikes at 4 percent from October 1, 2021 to July 1, 2022 (*Le Monde*, February 16, 2022). With the presidential election scheduled for April 2022 and the legislative elections for June, the timing of the rate shield raised more than a few eyebrows. In addition, unlike direct payments, the rate shield prevents price signals from incentivizing French consumers to reduce their energy consumption.

In March 2022, shortly after launching his presidential campaign, Macron announced a further measure to protect French consumers. With the price of gasoline climbing above the politically sensitive mark of €2 per liter (around $10 per gallon), the government established a "gasoline rebate" (*remise carburant*) of €0.18 per liter (around $0.90 per gallon) (French Prime Minister's Office 2022). As with the rate shield, the timing of the gasoline rebate, which was scheduled to run for four months, from April 1 to August 1, 2022, prompted accusations of vote buying (*Les Echos*, March 12, 2022). Also like the rate shield, the gasoline rebate interferes with price signals, blunting incentives for the French to drive less, take public transportation, and purchase more fuel-efficient cars.

The rate shield and gasoline rebate are very expensive. The gasoline rebate of €0.18 per liter costs €750 million per month, but at least that cost is independent of global energy prices, much like the inflation compensation and energy checks (*Libération*, June 28, 2022). By contrast, the cost of the gas and electricity rate shields is tied directly to global energy prices and has skyrocketed. When the rate shield for natural gas was first announced in September 2021, the government estimated that it would cost €1.2 billion, but as natural gas prices shot up, so too did the cost of the rate shield. According to the government, absent the rate shields, natural gas rates would have been 39.2 percent higher as of March 1, 2022 and electricity prices 35 percent higher as of February 1, 2002 (French Government 2022a: 9). In an interview in March 2022, Minister of the Economy and Finance Bruno Le Maire indicated that the rate shield for natural gas would probably be extended by six months, to the end of 2022, and estimated that the cost through 2022 would be €10 billion instead of €1.2 billion (BFM Business, March 7, 2022). The estimated cost of the rate shield for electricity is €8 billion, bringing the total price of the government's energy initiatives – including the gasoline rebate, inflation compensation, and energy check – to €24 billion (*Les Echos*, March 12, 2022). What is more, the cost of the rate shields on natural gas and electricity could increase further if global energy prices continue to rise in the wake of the Russian invasion of Ukraine.

The future of the rate shields remains uncertain. Macron authorized a 15 percent increase in natural gas and electricity rates for 2023, but rates remain far below market levels (*Le Figaro*, January 2, 2023). The latest estimate is that the rate shields will cost the government €21 billion in 2023 (*Le Figaro*, December 12, 2023). In addition, to protect those least able to afford the 2023 rate hikes, the government is sending some 12 million households a check in the amount of €100 or €200, depending on their incomes.

While the future of the rate shields remains uncertain, Macron did put an end to the gasoline subsidy as of January 1, 2023. At the same time, to ease the pain for low-income households, the government provided a "gasoline check" in the amount of €100 per adult driver to up to 10 million citizens (*Le Figaro*, December 28, 2023). This amount is roughly equal to the savings provided by a rate shield of €0.18 per liter for the purchase of 550 liters of gasoline, enough for the average French automobile to drive around 10,000 kilometers.

A government true to liberal principles could have provided relief from surging inflation to the French population without distorting price signals. For example, Macron could have increased the energy check or inflation compensation to offset some or all of the higher cost of natural gas, electricity, and gasoline. A direct payment, as opposed to the rate shield and the gasoline rebate, would have preserved market incentives to reduce energy consumption. It would also have helped with Macron's stated objective of lowering France's CO_2 emissions. Instead, Macron leaned on protective measures that blunt price signals, an expensive and decidedly illiberal approach.

While limiting energy price increases in the short term, Macron embraced voluntarist industrial policy to expand zero-carbon French electricity production in the long term. At his first campaign rally in February 2022, Macron pledged to multiply solar energy tenfold, build fifty offshore windmill farms, and launch the construction of a minimum of six (and as many as fourteen) of the latest generation of nuclear reactors by the year 2050 (*Les Echos*, February 10, 2022). All three projects are exceptionally ambitious, to put it mildly. France has next to no experience building offshore windmill farms, for example. Moreover, in addition to constructing six or more nuclear plants, Macron mandated that existing reactors be kept operating beyond their normal life span of fifty years.

The commitment to nuclear power dovetails with Macron's productivist approach to environmentalism. As against the supposedly zero-growth approach of France's environmental movement, Macron sees the challenge of reducing greenhouse gas emissions as an opportunity to develop new advanced industries that generate high-paying jobs and exports the world over. Because nuclear power is carbon-free, it occupies a central place in Macron's strategy for reducing France's CO_2 emissions. Indeed, it was the first measure listed (followed by the solar energy and offshore windfarm proposals) under the heading, "Planning the ecological transition" in Macron's 2022 presidential campaign platform (Macron 2022: 15). The implication is that France will industrialize itself into a zero-carbon future. In short, the commitment to a new generation of nuclear reactors allows Macron to have his productivist cake and eat his greenhouse gas reductions too.

Strategic considerations have also boosted the appeal of nuclear power. Macron views nuclear power as critical for achieving energy independence. Such independence is especially important given the authoritarian regimes of many oil-producing countries, most notably Russia. The invasion of Ukraine has heightened the urgency of weaning France and Europe from dependence on Russian oil and natural gas.

Macron's strategy is risky, however. His intention to continue operating nuclear plants beyond their fifty-year life expectancy is running up against the fact that France's nuclear plants are already showing their age. At the end of 2021, cracks in pipes caused by corrosion threatened the ability of the plants' operators to cool reactor cores in an emergency, necessitating lengthy shutdowns for inspections and repairs. During 2022, roughly half the reactors were out of commission at any given time. As a result, French nuclear electricity production fell to its lowest level since the early 1990s, where it is expected to remain at least through 2023 (*Les Echos*, February 8, 2022).

The challenges to the construction of six to fourteen new-generation European Pressurized Reactors (EPR2) are no less daunting. The nuclear industry has not built a reactor in France since 1999, and the first domestic EPR2, the Flamanville project in northern France, is running years behind schedule and billions of euro over budget (*Les Echos*, February 11, 2022). According to a report by the French Court of Auditors, the Flamanville reactor was supposed to be built in 54 months, at a cost of €3.3 billion, but will instead take 187 months to construct and cost €19.1 billion (French Court of Auditors 2020).

Finally, there are questions about whether the France's electricity operator, Electricité de France (EDF) is up to the task of building the next generation of nuclear reactors. Technical glitches and cost overruns are part of the problem. No less important, EDF lacks the financial capacity for Macron's ambitions. Electricity rates, even before the rate shield, barely covered operating costs, and the electricity shield is adding to EDF's financial difficulties. In addition, EDF's massive debt, totaling €44 billion at the end of 2021, makes it difficult for the company to continue borrowing (*Les Echos*, July 8, 2022). Given that the first new reactor is not expected to see the light of day (and generate revenues) before 2037 at the earliest, EDF will need considerable financial support to weather the intervening years (*Le Monde*, March 18, 2022).

EDF's financial weakness has led Macron to embrace an extraordinarily illiberal solution – the renationalization of the company. EDF was partially privatized in 2005, with private investors holding around 15 percent of EDF's shares and EDF employees another 1 percent. During his 2022 presidential campaign, Macron indicated that a repurchase of the outstanding 16 percent of EDF shares was under consideration. On July 6, 2022, Macron's newly appointed prime minister, Elisabeth Borne, confirmed in her general policy declaration to the French parliament that the government would indeed take full ownership of EDF (*Le Monde*, July 6, 2022). The government has offered €9.7 billion for the outstanding EDF shares but may have to up its bid (*Le Monde*, July 19, 2022).

Nationalizing EDF will give the government a freer hand to reorganize the company. Macron has considered doing so previously as part of a plan to separate the nuclear power generation business from the operation of the electricity transmission network and the production of hydroelectric power (the so-called Hercules Plan). In addition, the government could borrow much more easily and at a lower rate than EDF to finance the next generation of nuclear reactors. The government also intends to transform EDF's nuclear business into a so-called Service of General Economic Interest, which would be eligible for state aid under EU law, since governments are allowed to provide subsidies to such companies in line with the cost of the public services that they provide (European Commission 2022).

Macron's commitment to nuclear power deviates in important ways from liberal principles. He is clearly picking winners, despite significant grounds for caution. EDF has experienced a variety of technical problems, delays, and cost overruns on the new generation of EPR2 reactors. Moreover, the company lacks the financial wherewithal to cover the costs of the nuclear project. Macron's solution is not to give EDF the means to finance the project by letting it raise prices, as a liberal approach would entail, but rather to renationalize EDF in order to increase government control, facilitate borrowing, and get around EU restrictions on state subsidies. Once again, it would be difficult to imagine a less liberal approach.

During his presidential campaign, Macron promised additional measures to protect purchasing power (*Les Echos*, March 7, 2022). These measures included the elimination of the €138 annual audiovisual license fee, which supports public television and radio; a "food check," in the amount of €150 per household plus €50 for each dependent child, paid to 9 million low-income households; and a tripling of the so-called Macron bonus, which allows employers to pay bonuses free of taxes and Social Security charges (from a maximum of €1,000 per year to a maximum of €3,000 per year, or even €6,000 per year if the company has a profit-sharing plan in place). Macron also indicated that the government was preparing actions to attenuate the impact of rising gasoline prices for drivers, which eventually became the gasoline rebate described earlier in this section.

Following the 2022 presidential and legislative elections, all of these measures were bundled into a law on purchasing power (*Le Monde*, July 14, 2022). The purchasing power law also boosted pensions, family allowances, and various social assistance payments by 4 percent and the public-sector pay scale by 3.5 percent. It capped rent hikes at 3.5 percent for one year and increased the housing subsidy by 3.5 percent. In addition, the purchasing power law committed the government to maintaining the electricity and natural gas rate shields until the end of 2022. Under the initial draft of the purchasing power legislation, the gasoline subsidy of €0.18 per liter was slated to be phased out between October and December, then replaced with a program targeted at low-income households and people who drive long distances to get to work or as part of their work. This provision was modified in the National Assembly, however.

During consideration of the bill by the National Assembly, the government made two concessions to secure the support of LR. The first was to increase the ceiling for the exemption of overtime hours from taxes and Social Security charges from €5,000 to €7,500 annually (*Le Figaro*, July 14, 2022). The second was to prolong the gasoline subsidy to the end of 2022, increasing it to €0.30 per liter (around $1.50 per gallon) in September and October, then reducing it to €0.10 per liter ($0.50 per gallon) in November and December, before replacing it with a more targeted measure in 2023 (*Les Echos*, July 22, 2022). The LR delegation voted for the purchasing power bill in its first reading by the National Assembly, ensuring that the bill would pass.

Altogether, the purchasing power law is expected to add another €25 billion to the cost of the government's anti-inflationary measures for a total of around €50 billion from fall 2021 to the end of 2022 (*Le Figaro*, June 28, 2022). Again, the figure could go higher if energy prices continue to rise. The government claims that its measures have reduced inflation by 1.5 percent in 2022 and that they are one of the reasons why France has the lowest inflation rate in the eurozone, albeit a historically high 5.8 percent for the year ending June 2022 (*Libération*, June 28, 2022).

7.6   Contested Liberalization and the 2022 Elections

Macron's presidency was marked by the recurring contestation of economic liberalization, whether by protestors or the president himself. Not surprisingly, the contestation of economic liberalization also played an important role in the 2022 French presidential election, held April 10 and 24, and especially the ensuing legislative elections, June 12 and 19. On the one hand, Macron's statist response to the COVID-19 crisis helped revive his popular support and secure his reelection as president. On the other hand, Macron floated several controversial liberal economic ideas toward the end of the campaign, most notably a proposal to increase the retirement age from 62 to 65, which antagonized many voters, particularly on the left and the far right. Although their dissatisfaction was not enough to prevent Macron from winning the presidency, it was a major reason for Macron's surprising setback in the ensuing legislative elections.

Macron's shift from liberal reformer to statist protector in response to the COVID-19 crisis worked to his political advantage. Public opinion polls indicate that Macron's greatest electoral assets were his handling of the COVID-19 health crisis and his whatever-it-costs policy (*Le Monde*, February 15, 2022). His vaccine pass, for example, was approved of by 62 percent of French voters (*Le Monde*, February 22, 2022), while his whatever-it-costs policy garnered 71 percent approval (Elabe 2021). These policies also elicited a (grudging) respect for Macron's competence as a leader, which proved to be especially important in the run-off against Marine Le Pen. For example, 62 percent of respondents viewed Macron as "better [than Le Pen] in a crisis," as against only 34 percent who thought that Le Pen was better in a crisis (*Le Monde*, April 20, 2022).

Despite the general public approval of his statist turn, Macron adopted several high-profile liberal economic positions during his presidential campaign. He pledged to cut taxes by €15 billion, with a €7 billion reduction in corporate VAT (on top of the €10 billion reduction in Relaunch France), and a 50 percent increase in the amount of wealth exempt from inheritance taxes. In addition, Macron promised to deepen the 2017 labor market reform, further reform the unemployment system, and make the receipt of the guaranteed minimum income, the Active Solidarity Income (Revenu de Solidarité Active, RSA), conditional on engaging in some kind of activity designed to move the recipient toward employment for fifteen to twenty hours per week.

Macron's most controversial proposal was to increase the retirement age from 62 to 65. Although Macron insists that the French have no choice but to work longer, his proposal triggered a strong political backlash, with all of the unions and most of the presidential candidates denouncing the idea. Opinion polls indicate that more than three-quarters of the French also oppose raising the retirement age to 65 (IFOP 2022). Such opposition should come as no surprise, given that it was the proposed "pivot age" of 64 that spawned giant protests against Macron's original 2019 pension reform.

Macron advanced these liberal economic promises for two main reasons. The first was to siphon away voters from the Republican candidate, Valérie Pécresse. With the Socialist Party (Parti Socialiste, PS) still in disarray and the left unable to unite around a single candidate, Macron did not fear a challenger on his left. The right was another story, though. In 2017, the LR candidate, François Fillon, had managed to score more than 20 percent on the first ballot of the presidential election, despite being engulfed in a scandal over the payment of some €1 million to his wife for fictitious parliamentary jobs. Many believed that had the scandal not erupted Fillon would have won the presidency and that, in any case, LR could regain its traditional vote share in 2022. During his presidency, Macron had sought to appeal to LR voters by adopting conservative positions on policing, antiterrorism, immigration and assimilation, and racial inequality. Macron's move to the right on economic policy reflected a similar strategy, narrowing the distance between himself and the LR presidential candidate. Indeed, Pécresse and her supporters complained that Macron's liberal economic promises on the retirement age and RSA conditionality had been cut and pasted from her platform (*Le Monde*, March 18, 2022).

The other reason why Macron put forward liberal economic proposals was to claim a democratic mandate for such reforms. Of course, voters have many reasons for supporting presidential candidates, and much of Macron's liberal economic platform was unpopular. However, by making pension reform, lower inheritance taxes, and RSA conditionality part of his program, Macron hoped to put himself in a position to contend that the voters, in electing him president, had given him a mandate to implement his liberal agenda – just as he had maintained following the 2017 elections.

Macron's strategy largely succeeded as planned in the presidential election. On the first round of balloting, Macron placed first, while Pécresse, hemorrhaging electors to Macron on her left and Marine Le Pen and the xenophobic, far-right pundit Eric Zemmour on her right, received a dismal 4.8 percent of the vote (French Ministry of the Interior 2022b). The left failed to place a candidate in the run-off, with the leader of France Unbowed (La France Insoumise, LFI), Jean-Luc Mélenchon, falling just short, despite increasing his score from 19.6 percent to 22.0 percent. As in 2017, Macron came in first, with 27.9 percent, and got his preferred adversary, Marine Le Pen, who received 23.2 percent of the vote. Faced once again with the choice between Macron and a candidate viewed by many as unfit and a threat to democracy, mainstream conservative and leftist voters largely fell into line. Although Le Pen raised her score from 33.1 percent in the 2017 run-off to 41.5 percent in 2022, Macron still won reelection handily, with 58.5 percent of the vote (French Ministry of the Interior 2022b).

The strategy of tacking to the right that served Macron so well in the presidential election hurt him in the ensuing legislative elections, however. Many electors, particularly on the left, were angry at having to give their votes to Macron again. Left-leaning voters felt that Macron had misled them in 2017, suggesting that he was a centrist, who would choose the best ideas from the left and the right, only to govern as a conservative, not just economically, but also on societal issues like law and order, immigration, race, and civil liberties. In the presidential election, left voters held their noses and did their republican duty by barring the door to Le Pen, but in the legislative elections they would have other options.

Ever since the 2000 constitutional reform aligning the presidential and legislative terms, voters had always given the newly elected president a majority in the National Assembly. The presidency was the key prize, with a legislative majority flowing automatically to the victor. Macron's team, along with most observers of French politics, fully expected the same thing to happen in 2022. There was no obligation for voters to throw their support to the party of the newly elected president, however. Indeed, signs of trouble for Macron were visible almost immediately after his reelection.

At the beginning of May, Macron's approval rate was a mere 34 percent, as compared with 45 percent at the same point in 2017 (*Les Echos*, May 5, 2022). Former Prime Minister Edouard Philippe was more popular than Macron not just in general, but also among The Republic on the Move (La République en Marche, LREM) voters, despite the fact that Philippe did not even belong to LREM, having founded his own Horizons movement in October 2021. Bernard Sananès, the president of the Elabe polling agency, pointed to the "paradox between the great success [of Macron] in the voting booths and the low level of approval that the country gives him" (*Les Echos*, May 5, 2022). That paradox would resolve itself in the June legislative elections.

In the legislative elections, French voters chose to rein in their president, depriving Macron of a parliamentary majority. Macron's LREM, renamed Renaissance (meaning Rebirth or Revival in English) in May 2022 (*Le Figaro*, May 5, 2022), lost nearly one-half its representatives in the National Assembly, falling from 305 to 164 seats (French Ministry of the Interior 2017a, 2022a). Renaissance had run in a coalition called Ensemble (Together), encompassing François Bayrou's Democratic Movement (Mouvement Démocratique or MoDem) to its left and Edouard Philippe's Horizons to its right, but the three parties earned just 250 seats combined, falling 39 seats short of a majority. Part of the reason is that leaders of the left, tired of being penalized by their divisions – of having to support Macron in the presidential run-off not just once, but twice – set aside their differences and ran a single slate of candidates under the banner of the New Popular Ecological and Social Union (Nouvelle Union Populaire Ecologique et Sociale, NUPES). It was able to more than double its seats in the National Assembly from 64 to 131 (French Ministry of the Interior 2017a, 2022a).

Macron's coalition was also hurt by the unexpectedly strong performance of the far right. Marine Le Pen's National Rally (Rassemblement National, RN) was arguably the biggest winner of the legislative elections, going from eight to eighty-nine seats and becoming the largest opposition party. RN's breakthrough was made possible by the crumbling of the Republican Front, as Ensemble and NUPES candidates eliminated on the first round mostly instructed their supporters not to vote for the RN, while stopping short of telling them to vote in favor of the remaining Ensemble or NUPES candidates (*Le Figaro*, June 20, 2022). The right had always been more ambivalent than the left about the Republican Front, and this ambivalence, amplified by Macron's suggestion that Mélenchon's LFI, the main party in the NUPES coalition, was just as threatening to the republic as Le Pen's RN, helped RN candidates win thirty-four of sixty-five run-offs against NUPES candidates

(*Le Monde*, June 21, 2022). What was different this time is that the left, angered by Macron's conservative policies, promises of additional liberal economic reforms, and vilification of NUPES, likewise turned its back on the Republican Front. Whereas in 2017, LREM candidates had won 97 of 104 run-offs (93.3 percent) against candidates from Le Pen's party, in 2022, Ensemble candidates won only 54 of 107 run-offs (50.4 percent) against RN candidates (*Le Monde*, June 21, 2022).

Ironically, Macron's setback also stemmed from a major change in the French party system that he, more than anyone, had brought about. By defeating and marginalizing the mainstream Republicans and Socialists, Macron has transformed the historic bipolar division between the left and the right into a tripolar system with three main pillars: a radical left around Mélenchon's LFI, a radical right around Le Pen's RN, and Macron's center-right Ensemble coalition in the middle. While this tripolar structure served Macron perfectly in the presidential election, forcing voters of the left to support him in the run-off against Le Pen, tripartism operated against Macron in the legislative elections.

The main reason why voters had given every newly elected president since 2000 a majority in the National Assembly is that in a bipolar party system, to vote against the president's party necessarily meant to give the opposition a majority and force the newly elected president into a cohabitation. It made no sense to elect a president, only to immediately strip him of most of his powers by imposing a cohabitation. In a tripolar system, by contrast, voting against Macron's party did not necessarily mean voting in favor of a cohabitation. Because there were two main opposition movements to Macron, the two combined could earn enough seats to deprive Macron of a legislative majority without creating an alternative, anti-Macron governing majority, especially since LFI and the RNs occupy opposite ends of the political spectrum. Thus, following the legislative elections, Macron's Ensemble remained the biggest coalition and Renaissance was still the biggest party, but Ensemble lacked a majority, meaning that Macron would have to work with other parties in order to govern.

This need to reach out to other parties points to a final reason for Macron's defeat – weak popular support for both his agenda and method of governing. In a poll between the two rounds of the presidential election, respondents were given a choice of three reasons for supporting Macron. The largest group, 39 percent, chose the response "to prevent the other candidate [Le Pen] from being elected." The second most popular answer, with 36 percent, was that respondents "have confidence in him," attesting to Macron's perceived competence in managing the COVID-19 public-health and economic crisis. The third and least popular response, at 25 percent, was that Macron was "the closest to their ideas." In other words, only one Macron voter in four supported him because they agreed with his program. By way of comparison, 42 percent of Le Pen voters supported her for this reason.

Voters had also tired of Macron's Jupiterian, top-down governing style. Stunningly, in an April 2022 Ipsos–Sopra Steria poll, more respondents found Macron than Le Pen to be "too authoritarian" (55 vs. 51 percent) (*Le Monde*, April 20, 2022). Instead of making all decisions unilaterally and imposing them from above, voters wanted Macron to negotiate with other parties and stakeholders, seek consensus, and engage in genuine compromise. They had had enough of skinny politics. For this reason, in an Elabe poll just after the legislative elections, 71 percent of respondents agreed with the statement that the fact that Macron does not have a parliamentary majority is "a good thing for democracy and debate" (*Les Echos*, June 22, 2022). Similarly, in an Odoxa Backbone Consulting poll, 64 percent agreed with the statement that the outcome of the legislative elections is "rather a good thing because it gives a real role to the National Assembly [and] the government will have to convince part of the opposition to vote for its laws," while only 33 percent viewed the outcome of the elections as "rather a bad thing because it makes France ungovernable and could block France for months or even years to come" (*Le Figaro*, June 23, 2022).

It is too soon to tell how Macron's new presidency will unfold. Unable, at least initially, to forge a coalition with other parties, Macron has instructed Prime Minister Elisabeth Borne to seek majorities on a case-by-case basis for each major piece of legislation. Whether this strategy can work for five years remains to be seen. Attesting to the difficulty of the task, Prime Minister Borne deployed Article 49.3 ten times during her first eight months in office, from May through December 2022 (*Le Monde*, December 6, 2022). By contrast, Macron's government resorted to Article 49.3 only once (for the pension reform) during his entire first five-year term as president.

Of course, Macron may eventually find some way to win over another party or enough unaffiliated deputies to secure a durable majority. Alternatively, many believe that if Macron is unable to achieve his objectives with the current legislature, he will blame the opposition for making France ungovernable, dissolve the National Assembly, and call new elections in the hope of securing an absolute majority. That said, Chirac's disastrous 1997 dissolution stands as a warning that such a move is by no means assured of success.

The 2022 elections showed that an agenda of economic liberalization, particularly in the form presented by Macron, remains highly contested among French voters. Combining that agenda with a Jupiterian or skinny-politics approach to reform has only added to its unpopularity. As discussed in Chapter 8, the challenge for Macron and other French liberalizers will be to forge a more inclusive process of liberalization and a more equitable substance of liberalization than what Macron has offered during the past five years – and, to be fair, than what most French reformers have been offering for decades.

7.7   Conclusion

Economic liberalization has been contested throughout Emmanuel Macron's presidency. It has been contested in the streets, most notably by the yellow vest protestors and opponents of Macron's pension reform. It has been contested at the ballot box, with voters using the 2022 legislative elections to try to put an end to Macron's Jupiterian pursuit of liberal economic reforms. And it has been contested within the government itself, as Macron responded, first to the COVID-19 crisis, then to the recent surge in energy prices, with an array of statist initiatives.

The three legacies of the *dirigiste* state – social anesthesia, the right's ambivalence toward economic liberalization, and skinny politics – have retained all their salience in the Macron years. The combination of skinny politics and uncompensated liberal reform has been a recipe for contestation. In addition, Macron himself has followed in the footsteps of Giscard d'Estaing and Sarkozy before him, pivoting from liberal reformer to statist protector in a crisis. Only time will tell how Macron's second term as president plays out. One thing is certain, though: for now, at least, the ghosts of the postwar *dirigiste* model show no sign of going quietly into the night.

8   Beyond Contestation

In 1983, a government of the left, which had been elected on a pledge to take France's postwar *dirigiste* model to new heights, made a spectacular U-turn. Whether because of European constraints or recognition of the growing dysfunctions of statist economic policy, the left reversed course and launched a process of *dirigiste* rollback. Governments of the right and the left alike continued the process, dismantling not only specific industrial policy programs, but also the institutions and regulatory powers that abetted voluntarist policymaking. By the mid-1990s, little remained of France's postwar *dirigiste* model.

If the *dirigiste* model is no more, this book has shown that the legacies of that model continue to shape French economic and social policy decades later. Specifically, the policy, party-political, and institutional legacies of the *dirigiste* model have fueled the persistent contestation of economic liberalization. Liberalizing reforms have been contested in the streets and, in a number of cases, defeated. They have also been contested within governing circles, as leaders, including those on the right, have regularly sacrificed liberalization to higher priorities, such as national ownership or the preservation of social order. Finally, the contestation of economic liberalization has spilled over to the contestation of the leaders who have initiated such reform – Balladur, Juppé, de Villepin, and Macron – with more than one political career being ruined as a result.

Of course, not all liberalizing reforms in France have been contested. What is more, even when opponents have mobilized against reform, French governments have still been able to prevail on many occasions. That said, as Chapter 1 demonstrated, economic liberalization has made less headway in France than in the leading European political economies. France also stands out for the frequency with which liberalizing initiatives have elicited protests and derailed political careers.

This concluding chapter draws out the implications of the French experience for liberalizing reformers in France and elsewhere. Section 8.1 summarizes the evidence that the policy, party-political, and institutional legacies of the postwar *dirigiste* model have driven the contestation

of economic liberalization in France. Section 8.2 extrapolates beyond the
French case, describing the circumstances that are most likely to prompt
contestation in other countries and applying the argument to East Asia
and Latin America. Section 8.3 points to changes in the process and
substance of economic liberalization that might reduce contestation.
Finally, Section 8.4 discusses the links between France's contested liberalization and the rise of populist parties along with ways to possibly
mitigate populist gains.

8.1   Summary of the Evidence

This book presented the argument in two steps. Chapters 2 to 4 focused
on one strand of the argument each. Chapter 2 described France's movement in the 1980s from the *dirigiste* state to the social anesthesia state. It
showed how the social anesthesia state resolved the challenge of breaking with the *dirigiste* model, but then generated economic, social, and
political problems of its own. The social anesthesia state is expensive and
primarily passive in orientation, keeping the social peace by sustaining
incomes independent of activity.

Chapter 2 showed that the movement from the *dirigiste* state to social
anesthesia state bequeathed two legacies that have contributed to the
contestation of economic liberalization. The first is a two-step trajectory
of reform – a movement from the *dirigiste* state to the social anesthesia
state, then an overhaul of the social anesthesia state – that has prompted
liberalization fatigue or skepticism. Liberal reformers and the French
public often seem to be talking past each other, drawing radically different lessons from the movement from the *dirigiste* state to the social
anesthesia state in the 1980s. Liberal reformers see a bloated, passive
social anesthesia state and argue that government spending must be cur-
tailed and labor market regulations eased if the French economy is ever
to recover. Much of the French public, by contrast, having already experienced the pain of economic liberalization in the 1980s with little economic benefit to show for it, has no faith in a new liberalizing strategy.
They see reform without results. Indeed, many regard economic liberalization and globalization as the *cause* of France's economic difficulties,
rather than a potential *solution*.

The second legacy of the movement from the *dirigiste* state to the social
anesthesia state is the crowding out of state resources. Whereas the break
with the *dirigiste* model in the 1980s was accompanied by massive social
compensation in the form of the social anesthesia state, contemporary
reformers lack the fiscal resources to offer substantial side-payments to
the opponents and victims of liberalizing reform. They are reforming

without resources. Yet as the Balladur and de Villepin labor market reforms demonstrated, asking ordinary citizens to accept liberalization purely on its own terms – in this case, lower wages or reduced job security in return for the hypothetical benefits of a more flexible labor market – is a very tough sell. Indeed, liberalization without compensation is a recipe for contestation.

Chapter 3 focused on the party-political obstacles to economic liberalization. France is essentially a case of liberalization without liberals. On the left of the political spectrum, the main governing party, the Socialist Party (Parti Socialiste, PS), has long stood out for its hostility to capitalism and market forces (Spector 2017). Moreover, in order to forge a governing majority, the Socialists have needed to rally voters and establish alliances with parties representing far-left movements – historically, the Communists, but more recently, self-styled Trotskyists and Jean-Luc Mélenchon's France Unbowed (La France Insoumise, LFI). Consequently, there has been little room for the kind of accommodation to liberalism practiced by the center-left parties across Northern Europe. With LFI apparently supplanting the PS as the dominant party of the left, the prospects for left-led liberalization have become more remote than ever.

The French right has also been less committed to economic liberalization than its counterparts elsewhere in Europe. Chapter 3 focused on the actions of leaders of the right, most notably Jacques Chirac, Edouard Balladur, Dominique de Villepin, and Nicolas Sarkozy. All of these leaders sought to move France (more or less cautiously) in a liberal direction. As heirs to Gaullist and *dirigiste* traditions, however, their liberalism was tempered in important ways. Chirac and Balladur placed nationalism ahead of liberalism, notably during the privatization campaign, which they rigged to prevent France's national champions from falling under foreign control. Similarly, a decade later, under the banner of "economic patriotism," Chirac's prime minister, de Villepin, established a list of sectors requiring government permission for any foreign acquisition, a list that has grown steadily longer in the ensuing years. The liberalism of Chirac and especially Balladur was also tempered by the experience of May 1968, the lingering fear for social order, which led both leaders to retreat from liberalizing initiatives when confronted by mass protests and strikes.

The inability or unwillingness of the right to develop a legitimating discourse for economic liberalization has further fueled contestation. Instead of defending liberalization on its own terms, as good for the French economy, the right, like the left, has tended to blame external forces, notably European integration. Chirac's first term as president revealed the limitations of this strategy. In 1995, Chirac campaigned for president on an anti-liberal platform, calling for intensified state intervention to heal France's "social fracture." While this anti-liberal discourse worked as a campaign strategy, it prompted mass protests when Chirac tried to pivot back to liberal austerity with the Juppé Plan. The attempt to justify austerity with reference to the need to qualify for the European Monetary Union (EMU) was also contested, this time in the ballot box. Chirac suffered a surprising defeat at the hands of the left in the 1997 legislative elections, as many French voters refused to make further sacrifices for the sake of a European Union (EU) that was increasingly associated with unpopular liberal reforms. In short, the failure to articulate a coherent discourse of reform left liberalization without legitimation – and delegitimized European integration as well.

The experience of Chirac's successor as president, Nicolas Sarkozy, illustrated another limitation of the right's commitment to liberal economic reform – a kind of thin or fair-weather liberalism that tends to give way to statist solutions in times of crisis. Sarkozy came to power in 2007 on a clear probusiness agenda. He was openly critical of France's "social model" for generating high rates of unemployment and embraced a number of liberalizing reforms, including tax cuts, spending cuts, and expanded labor market flexibility. Yet when the 2008 financial crisis hit, Sarkozy turned against economic liberalism, denouncing the notion that "the market is always right" and calling for "a new balance between the State and the market" (Sarkozy 2008). Sarkozy also launched a variety of industrial policy initiatives, including a sovereign wealth fund and a program to invest in industries of the future, which went well beyond the economic needs of the moment. Moreover, Sarkozy accompanied these voluntarist initiatives with a kind of neo-*dirigiste* discourse not heard since the early 1980s. Sarkozy's experience illustrates the limited commitment to liberal reform of even ostensibly promarket French leaders.

Chapter 4 analyzed the institutional features driving the contestation of liberal economic reform. Cutting government social spending or labor market protections is invariably unpopular and politically treacherous (Pierson 1994, 1996). In those European countries that have achieved major changes, the government has generally negotiated the terms of reform with other actors, such as the political opposition or social partners (Hinrichs 2000, 2010; Palier 2003b; Schludi 2003, 2005). Broadening the array of actors helps insulate the government against contestation, whether in the form of protests in the streets or punishment at the polls.

France's politico-institutional landscape is ill-suited to this kind of concertational approach. Under the "bipolar" logic of the Fifth Republic, government and opposition have generally been cleaved into two warring camps due to the two-round, winner-take-all electoral law and presidential run-off system. In addition, the instruments of rationalized parliamentarism, notably the ordinance procedure (Article 38), package vote (Article 44.3), and confidence vote (Article 49.3), encourage governments to ram through controversial or unpopular reforms, instead of negotiating to build a broader basis of support. The weakness of French societal organizations, which tend to have few members, reinforces this temptation. As a result, French governments almost invariably act alone. No retrenchment initiative in France has ever been the product of an all-party alliance, and governments have mostly chosen to ignore or bypass stakeholders, imposing reforms from above.

Chapter 4 illustrated the problems of this skinny-politics, go-it-alone strategy in three ways. The first concerned the employer-initiated effort, known as the "Social Refoundation." Launched in the 1998, the Social Refoundation sought to overhaul French labor markets and the welfare state through bilateral negotiations between employers and reformist trade unions. Shifting reform out of the political arena offered an ideal method of blame avoidance, yet governments of both the left and the right resisted the Social Refoundation, which they saw as a threat to their power, and the Social Refoundation was eventually disbanded.

The second way of illustrating the effects of the skinny-politics strategy was through the case of pension reform. French governments have advanced no less than seven different pension reforms since the early 1990s. Some have gone through, while others have been checked by protesters. What is striking, though, is that for all the attention to pension reform during the past quarter-century, the French system remains beset by problems: France devotes a higher share of GDP to pensions than every European country except the notoriously corrupt Greece and Italy; French citizens spend the most years in retirement of any European country; the pension regime consistently runs a deficit; and the system remains fragmented into forty-two different schemes, with some groups favored over others in ways that are difficult to justify. Using comparisons both across different French pension reforms and between pension reform in France and Sweden, Chapter 4 showed that France's go-it-alone, skinny approach has produced modest results and continued contestation, as compared with the concertational approach embodied by Sweden.

The third way of illustrating the limitations of skinny politics was through an analysis of Chirac's reforming record following his decision, at the beginning of his second term as president, to forego the Social Refoundation. Over the next five years, from 2002 to 2007, Chirac's administration pursued liberalizing reforms in fiscal policy, labor market policy, and pension policy. However, fearful of provoking another mass movement like the one that destroyed the Juppé Plan and Chirac's first term as president, the government proposed modest changes, so as to minimize the likelihood of large-scale protests. The problem is that such reforms, even when successful, did not have a very big impact. Indeed, across the board, the reforms of Chirac's second presidency hewed to a kind of perverse Goldilocks pattern: they were painful enough to anger many ordinary citizens, but not ambitious enough to resolve the fiscal and economic problems that had motivated reform in the first place.

Chapters 5 to 7, analyzing the policies of President Emmanuel Macron, presented the second step in the argument of this book. Collectively, they demonstrated that the three legacies of *dirigisme* have not faded into irrelevance with the passage of time, but rather continue to foster the contestation of liberalization in the current era. Chapter 5 focused on the first eighteen months of Macron's presidency, culminating in the yellow vest crisis of fall 2018. It showed that the social anesthesia state and skinny politics contributed centrally to this crisis. The social anesthesia state deprived Macron of the resources to offer side-payments or compensation in return for liberal economic reform, but reforming without resources proved politically explosive. Seeking to bolster business through tax cuts, while reducing France's budget deficit, Macron had no choice but to raise taxes on ordinary citizens and reduce public services and social benefits. The combination of tax cuts for business and the affluent, on the one hand, and tax hikes and program cuts for ordinary French citizens, on the other hand, gave rise to the depiction of Macron as the "president of the rich," helping spark the yellow vest protests.

Macron's top-down "Jupiterian" approach to reform further fueled contestation. Macron interpreted the 2017 elections as having given him a mandate for liberalizing reforms, a questionable interpretation in light of the fact that fewer than one voter in four had supported him on the first ballot of the presidential election and that much of his support stemmed from opposition to Marine Le Pen, as opposed to an endorsement of his agenda. Nonetheless, Macron pursued an extreme form of skinny politics, disdaining negotiations with the social partners and imposing unpopular reforms from above. Over time, such actions earned Macron the image of an arrogant, out-of-touch Parisian technocrat, dismissive of others, and concerned only about the rich. The yellow vests tapped into the accumulated grievances of ordinary French citizens, in particular, the sentiment that their president was picking on the little guy, deploying the full powers of the state to weaken job protections and take away benefits from workers struggling to make ends meet, while showering favors on corporations and the affluent.

Chapter 6 analyzed Macron's effort to rebound from the yellow vest crisis. Macron apologized repeatedly for his arrogance and top-down impositional style. He also launched two intriguing initiatives to provide opportunities for popular input into the government's agenda. The first was a Grand National Debate (Grand Débat National, GDN) that allowed ordinary citizens to voice their opinions on a range of issues, including taxes and public spending, the organization of the state and public services, ecological transformation, and democracy and citizenship. Some 2 million citizens participated in the GDN, and Macron himself made several appearances at local meetings, facing criticism from unhappy citizens and responding to their questions for hours. The second novel vehicle for popular input was the Citizens' Climate Convention (Convention Citoyenne pour le Climat, CCC), which gave 150 citizens the chance to develop one specific reform each, with the help of a team of experts, academics, and technocrats. Macron met with the participants on several occasions and promised to implement their ideas quickly and "without a filter."

Although the GDN and CCC constituted a novel, participatory approach and were quite popular with the French, Macron used them more as a sop to public opinion than as a template for a new approach to governing. In other areas, Macron continued to operate as before, combining top-down imposition with an unpopular agenda. The two most important initiatives of this period, a tightening of eligibility and reduction of benefits in the unemployment insurance program and an overhaul of the pension system, operated in this manner. While the unemployment reform was eventually implemented after much delay, the pension reform did not survive. A proposal to increase the minimum age for receiving a complete pension triggered mass protests and strikes in December 2019–January 2020. The government eventually acceded to the demands of the protesters, but the delay proved fatal to the pension reform. Despite strong-arm tactics like the use of Article 49.3 to pass the first version of the bill in the National Assembly, Macron was unable to complete the reform by the time the COVID-19 crisis hit. In March 2020, citing the need for national unity to fight the pandemic, Macron put the reform on hold, then postponed it until after the 2022 elections, before abandoning it altogether.

Chapter 7 analyzed Macron's response to the COVID-19 crisis. It showed that much like Nicolas Sarkozy in 2008, Macron retreated from liberal principles and pivoted toward statism in a crisis. Macron deployed the full powers of the French state to both combat the disease and sustain French business and employment through the accompanying economic dislocation, as symbolized by his pledge to spend "whatever it takes" to preserve French companies and jobs. True to his words, Macron rolled out social anesthesia measures, such as subsidized jobs, youth employment programs, and government payment of wages (*chômage partiel*). He also took advantage of the crisis to launch new industrial policy initiatives to encourage French automobile and aircraft companies to invest in green technologies and domestic manufacturing. In so doing, Macron boosted French spending and indebtedness to new highs; indeed, France's deficits and debt are approaching the levels of Belgium and the Southern European countries and are far above the levels of the advanced economies of Northern Europe.

Chapter 7 also described Macron's statist response to surging inflation, in particular energy prices. The government committed €50 billion through 2022 to limit the impact of inflation on French households. What is more, it is doing so in often illiberal ways. Macron has not hesitated to interfere with price signals by capping rates for natural gas and electricity and subsidizing gasoline purchases, thereby dampening incentives for households to reduce their energy consumption. Macron also used the energy crisis as a justification for a voluntarist initiative to construct six new-generation nuclear European Pressurized Reactor (EPR2) at an estimated cost of €50 billion. Furthermore, because the nuclear power operator, Electricité de France (EDF), lacks the means to finance such a long-term investment, Macron has moved to renationalize the company, at a projected cost of nearly €10 billion. Public ownership will make it easier to the state to provide subsidies and raise capital on behalf of EDF. Needless to say, blunting price signals and nationalizing a company so that it can better do the government's industrial policy bidding are not exactly the hallmarks of economic liberalism.

Chapter 7 concluded by showing how the contestation of economic liberalization influenced the 2022 presidential and legislative elections. Macron's statist turn in response to the COVID-19 crisis – particularly his "health pass" and "vaccine pass" that essentially forced citizens to get vaccinated and his "whatever-it-costs" policy to protect businesses and workers from the economic effects of the crisis – proved popular, raising his standing and reputation for competent leadership. However, during the presidential campaign, Macron floated several liberal ideas, notably a very unpopular proposal to increase the retirement age from 62 to 65. Although Macron still managed to win the presidential election, the ensuing legislative elections produced a shocking setback. For the first time since the 2000 constitutional reform aligning the presidential and legislative terms, French voters declined to give the newly elected president a legislative majority. Wary of Macron's liberal economic agenda and tired of his top-down governance, the voters sought to rein him in and force him to work with other parties.

France has yet to emerge from the shadow of its *dirigiste* past. In a first step of this book's argument, Chapters 2 through 4 showed that the policy, party-political, and institutional legacies of *dirigisme* – reform without results or resources (Chapter 2), liberalization without liberals (Chapter 3), and politics without partners (Chapter 4) – played a central role in fomenting the contestation of economic liberalization during the 1990s and 2000s. In a second step, Chapters 5 through 7 demonstrated that these legacies have continued to fuel contestation under President Macron. Emmanuel Macron may have been elected in 2017 on a campaign slogan of "Revolution," but he has repeatedly found himself on the wrong side of the barricades. Macron, like his predecessors, has been able to enact some liberalizing reforms; France has not stood still. That said, Macron has confronted more than his share of protests and strikes, been forced to retreat on several occasions, and even seen his legitimacy and capacity to rule eroded, as in the yellow vest protests and the June 2022 legislative elections. If the future of Macron's liberalizing agenda remains uncertain, there can be no doubt about the continued salience of France's *dirigiste* past.

8.2   Extending the Argument to East Asia and Latin America

The French case points to a number of hypotheses about the conditions that may contribute to the contestation of economic liberalization. At least some of these conditions are present in just about every country, but the greatest overlap would appear to be with nations in East Asia and Latin America. The following discussion translates the French experience into more general hypotheses about the economic, institutional, and political sources of contestation of economic liberalization. It also discusses, in an admittedly cursory and broad-brush manner, how these hypotheses might apply to East Asia and Latin America.

From an *economic* standpoint, France's postwar boom period coincided with the heyday of the *dirigiste* model. While covariation is not causation, in the eyes of many French citizens the *dirigiste* state delivered full employment and steadily rising living standards, so an embrace of economic liberalization, which could not be further from *dirigiste* principles, makes little sense. *The more generalizable hypothesis is that in countries that experienced rapid economic growth and rising living standards at a time of interventionist policy, the population is likely to display considerable attachment to interventionist models and a corresponding distrust of economic liberalization.* The statist political economies of Japan and East Asia clearly fall into this category. The same could be said of many Latin American countries, where the era of import-substitution industrialization (ISI) likewise coincided with a period of economic growth and prosperity.

Just as France's postwar boom coincided with the *dirigiste* heyday, the country has struggled with slow growth and persistent mass unemployment since the break with *dirigisme*. Again, covariation may not be causation, but it is easy to see why many French citizens may be skeptical of economic liberalization. The fact that liberalizing reforms have not revived growth and employment has fueled liberalization fatigue, an unwillingness to accept immediate hardship in exchange for liberalization's promise of a brighter tomorrow. *A second economic hypothesis is that in countries in which the break with an interventionist model was followed by poor economic performance, proposed additional rounds of liberalization risk contestation by a skeptical population.*

The East Asian countries have not broken as sharply with the statist model as France. Liberalizing reforms have been more gradual and incremental (Pempel 1998; Vogel 2006). Yet, as in France, these reforms have brought mostly disappointing results. Japan's movement toward liberalization coincided with a "lost decade" of very slow growth, while the liberalization of capital flows in East Asia set the stage for the 1997 financial crisis. Similarly, Latin American countries that abandoned ISI and adopted the "Washington consensus" generally experienced slow economic growth and a surge in poverty and inequality. Although neoliberal pundits might blame disappointing results on other factors – such as the overhang of past dysfunctional policies, the debt burden, the failure to fully implement a liberalizing agenda, or corrupt "crony capitalism" – many ordinary citizens regard neoliberal reforms as the culprit.

From an *institutional* standpoint, both the political and social institutions of France have encouraged governments to act alone and ram through reforms from above. The institutions and electoral laws of the Fifth Republic have fostered a sharp divide between government and opposition, limiting the incentives for cooperation. With governments almost invariably enjoying an absolute majority in the legislature and having the instruments of rationalized parliamentarism at their disposal, they have felt little need to temper their initiatives in order to win support from the opposition. While the go-it-alone approach is well suited for launching popular new programs, it offers little shelter for governments seeking to avoid blame for painful or controversial liberalization measures. *The third more generalizable hypothesis, this one institutional in nature, is that in those countries with institutions that generate a sharp division between government and opposition, such as majoritarian electoral laws and powerful presidents, governments are more likely to act in a unilateral manner and a marginalized political opposition to respond by contesting liberalizing reforms in the streets.*

Many Latin American and East Asian countries have strong presidents enjoying quasi-legislative powers. These presidents can be tempted to act unilaterally, with the risk of prompting protests against controversial or poorly prepared initiatives. What is more, presidential elections tend to sharpen the divide between government and opposition, and in a number of Latin American countries that divide is reinforced by a pronounced left–right cleavage, expanding the ideological and policy distance between the government and the opposition. In East Asia, left parties have found it more difficult to compete for power, and much of the struggle for power takes place within or among conservative parties, as opposed to between the left and the right. The sharper ideological divide between government and opposition in Latin America could be expected to lead to greater popular contestation than in East Asia.

Another institutional variable, state–society relations, operates along similar lines. In this instance, it is a sharp division between the government and societal organizations that contributes to contestation. The weakness and divisions of French societal organizations have increased the temptation for policymakers to bypass these organizations, rather than engaging in protracted and potentially fruitless negotiations. The resulting politics without partners concentrates blame, however, and also encourages marginalized groups to take to the streets to make their voices heard. *The fourth hypothesis is that in countries where societal interests are weak and divided, governments are more likely to ignore these interests, often leading opponents of liberalizing reforms to take to the streets to force the government to modify or retract its proposals.* East Asian and Latin American countries have low rates of unionization, and the unions are often ignored by liberal reformers. Transitions to democracy opened the door to a variety of new associations, but they too have struggled to gain the ear of policymakers. Like the unions, they have often sought to influence the government through protests.

Finally, from a *party-political* standpoint, the ideology and governing approach of French conservative parties have fueled the contestation of economic liberalization in several ways. Parties of the left can be expected to be ambivalent, at best, toward economic liberalization, making parties of the right the seeming natural voice for liberalization and, therefore, the pivotal actor. In France, that actor has diverged from parties of the right in other European countries. Whereas most European conservative parties, notably Christian Democrats, have supported a market-centered, ordoliberal political economy accompanied by a large welfare state, the French right was forged in the Gaullist template and ran the *dirigiste* model for decades. The nationalist and statist orientation of French conservatives has often put them at cross-purposes with liberalization. *The fifth more general hypothesis, this one party-political in nature, is that where governing parties of the right have been forged in nationalist ideals and administered statist economic models, these experiences and ideals are likely to temper their commitment to liberalizing reform.* The most obvious parallel is with the conservative movements that presided over the statist models of Japan and East Asia. These movements have approached liberalizing reform cautiously and incrementally, seeking to preserve their capacity to steer economic development and prevent foreign takeovers of cherished domestic champions. In Latin America, by contrast, where the ISI system was run by populist parties displaying features of both left and right, parties of the right have hewed to a more conventional liberal economic ideology. Consequently, the expectation is that the contestation of economic liberalization by conservative parties would be more prevalent in Japan and East Asia than Latin America.

Another party-political variable concerns the public case made for economic liberalization. French conservatives joined the left in blaming unpopular liberalizing reforms on external factors, notably European integration. This recurring blame-shifting worked for a while, but, over time, it chipped away at the legitimacy of liberalization, not to mention European integration. *The sixth general hypothesis is that in countries in which liberalization is blamed on external forces, especially unpopular external forces, the lack of a legitimating discourse is likely to weaken popular support for liberalization.* Both East Asia and Latin America display such dynamics. In the Japanese case, US trade negotiators have long pressed for greater trade openness, opportunities for foreign direct investment (FDI), financial deregulation, and expanded domestic competition. Whatever the economic arguments for such changes, the politics of reform in Japan has been complicated by the fact that undertaking these changes is associated in the minds of many with capitulating to US demands. The same is true in East Asia, with the International Monetary Fund (IMF) joining the USA in the role of external bogey, especially following the 1997 financial crisis. Whereas French authorities could justify liberalizing reform, at least initially, as a way of supporting the then-popular cause of European integration, in Japan and East Asia liberalizing reform has never had such a positive external valence and has been associated instead with subservience to the USA and IMF. In Latin America, too, liberalization has often been driven by US and IMF demands, especially during the debt crisis of the 1980s and subsequent moments of economic difficulty. As in France, perhaps even more so, economic liberalization in Japan, East Asia, and Latin America has been regarded as an unwelcome foreign imposition, adding a nationalist motive to the economic motive for contesting liberalization.

A final party-political variable concerns protest dynamics. The May 1968 upheaval, which nearly toppled the Fifth Republic, scarred a generation of French leaders. As a result, conservatives have often retracted liberalizing reforms in response to disruptive strikes and protests. Prominent examples include two youth labor reforms, the Professional Integration Contract (Contrat d'Insertion Professionnelle, CIP) and First Employment Contract (Contrat Première Embauche, CPE), as well as the Juppé Social Security Plan. Protests have also prompted conservatives to accept substantial modifications of their initiatives, as Macron did with his proposed pension overhaul in 2020, abandoning the pivot age and negotiating a series of concessions to groups that stood to lose from the reform. For conservative leaders, sacrificing liberalizing reforms was a small price to pay for the preservation of social order. *The seventh and final hypothesis is that in countries that have experienced regime change or political instability as a result of popular protests, conservatives will be less willing to stare down strikes and demonstrations against liberalizing reforms.* Many countries in East Asia and Latin America transitioned to democracy on the heels of popular protest movements, and, in these countries, regime collapse is a living memory for conservatives, elevating the importance of political and social stability relative to liberal economic reform. As a result, protests and strikes remain important vehicles for bringing governments to the bargaining table or inducing them to abandon liberalizing initiatives altogether.

The French experience with economic liberalization offers an array of hypotheses concerning the economic, institutional, and party-political conditions that may foster the contestation of economic liberalization. Obviously, it is beyond the scope of this book to test these hypotheses in a rigorous manner. Yet, even a cursory examination of the East Asian and Latin American cases suggests that many of the forces that have fueled the contestation of economic liberalization in France may operate in other national contexts.

Beyond identifying factors that fuel contestation, the comparison of France, East Asia, and Latin America speaks to contemporary debates about the relationship between conservative parties and economic liberalization. Scholars have noted that parties of the right do not always gravitate toward aggressive, across-the-board liberalization in the manner of Thatcherite neoliberalism or the "Washington consensus" (Gamble 1994; Moran 2007; Williamson 1990). Many Christian Democratic parties in Europe, most notably the German Christian Democratic Union (Christlich-Demokratische Union), have long combined an "ordoliberal" economic order with generous social policies to integrate the working class and protect those dislocated by competition (Esping-Andersen 1990; Katzenstein 1984, 1985).

A more recent, critical perspective on conservative parties like the US Republican Party and the British Conservatives accuses the right of defending the interests of corporations and the rich, as opposed to neoliberal ideals. Such parties are claimed to be hypocritically imposing liberalization on ordinary citizens and the disadvantaged, who are subjected to reduced public services, weakened job protections, and lower benefits, while handing out tax cuts to business and the rich and limiting competition that threatens corporate allies (Crouch 2017; Hacker and Pierson 2020). Thus, the relationship between parties of the right and economic liberalization ranges from across-the-board support (Thatcherism), to a balancing of ordoliberalism with extensive social protection (German Christian Democracy), to a combination of liberalism for the poor and state favors for corporations and the rich (recent US and UK conservatism).

The French case points to a fourth kind of relationship between parties of the right and economic liberalization – an ambivalent, halfhearted, easily revocable liberalization. It is a liberalization by parties and leaders who harbor deep qualms and shallow commitments to economic liberalism, whether of the broad economic order or social protection. France is not the only such case, however. Some of the historical legacies that have contributed to the French right's ambivalence are present in East Asia and Latin America as well.

In Japan and the East Asian "tigers," conservative ambivalence stems primarily from previous stewardship of statist models that were associated with tremendous economic success and rapidly rising living standards. In Latin America, conservative ambivalence is more rooted in fear of popular protests that could potentially unseat the government or even the regime. Given that both channels operate in France, it is not surprising that economic liberalization is so subject to contestation. Yet, extending the analysis to other countries makes it clear that the French right's ambivalence toward economic liberalization is not a subset of one, but rather a particularly striking example of a fourth conservative party stance on economic liberalization – a deep ambivalence and trepidation toward liberal economic reform, whether of the broad economic order or the welfare state.

Again, the claims in this section are meant to be suggestive, not conclusive. A task for future research would be to assess the extent to which the factors highlighted in the French case apply to specific countries in East Asia and Latin America. It would likewise be interesting to probe the variation both within and across the two regions. Finally, while this discussion has centered on the East Asian and Latin American regions, scholars of economic liberalization in other parts of the world might also find elements of the French experience to be relevant to the countries that they research.

8.3   A More Inclusive and Just Economic Liberalization

This book has emphasized the weight of policy, party-political, and institutional legacies in fueling contestation and limiting French liberalization, but governments are not just prisoners of history. The experiences of French governments, both successful and unsuccessful, point to strategies that can enhance the prospects for liberal economic reform. For presentational purposes, this section divides the strategies into those relating to the *process* of liberalization and those relating to the *substance* of economic liberalization, but the two are often intertwined. The broader point is that French authorities can reduce contestation by making the process of economic liberalization more inclusive and the substance more equitable.

8.3.1   The Process of Liberalization: "Thickening" the Politics of Reform

At first glance, the French skinny-politics approach to economic liberalization might seem like an effective way of enacting far-reaching change. Negotiations with stakeholders take time, slowing the process. They also require the government to make concessions. The skinny approach avoids such delays and concessions and is generally effective when governments are establishing popular new programs. The problem is that economic liberalization is not very popular, especially in France.

Scholars have shown that sharing responsibility and blame for controversial or unpopular liberalizing reforms with other actors improves the chances of success (Hinrichs 2000, 2010; Palier 2003b; Schludi 2003, 2005). In particular, expanding the circle of participants narrows the circle of potential opponents and backers of popular resistance. Although the institutions of the Fifth Republic and French political traditions are geared toward top-down imposition, there are a number of ways that leaders might cultivate a "thicker," more inclusive mode of policymaking.

One change that has been promised again and again by French presidential candidates, including Macron, would be to allocate some or all of the seats in the National Assembly on the basis of proportional representation (PR). PR would likely increase the number of parties in the French legislature. In addition, it would decrease the bonus currently enjoyed by the party of the president, a system in which 25 percent of the vote on the first round of the presidential election generally translates to more than 50 percent of the seats in the National Assembly. PR would thus generate a party structure that more faithfully reflects the will of the voters.

Beyond considerations of democratic representation, PR would reduce the possibilities for skinny-political rule, as a single party would be less likely to hold an absolute majority in the National Assembly. PR would "thicken" French governments by forcing the first-place party to forge alliances with other parties in order to obtain a majority. The first-place party would also have to make concessions to those allies when devising policy. A "thicker" mode of governance might help French authorities build support for and diminish protest against liberalizing measures. It is probably no coincidence that most of the countries in Europe that have successfully overhauled their economies in a reasonably consensual manner, while preserving robust social protection – including Germany, the Netherlands, and the Nordic countries – operate under PR electoral laws.

PR is no panacea, of course. Even when French governments have included more than one party, leaders have still acted in a top-down manner. If a single party holds nearly enough seats in the legislature to rule on its own and can choose from a number of possible coalition partners, then those partners will have limited influence over government policy. The plight of green parties under Socialist-led governments offers a clear illustration, as they have often been compelled to swallow their objections to pronuclear, productivist policies preferred by the PS, while obtaining only minor concessions in return.

PR also presents potential dangers. The current two-round, majoritarian system was chosen in no small part as a backlash against the pure PR of the Fourth Republic, which produced a multitude of small parties and revolving-door governments. Those governments lacked the capacity to undertake bold or decisive action, since the defection of even one of the several parties in the ruling coalition would cause the government to fall.

Another concern is that PR would give greater representation to extremist parties, such as the National Rally (Rassemblement National, RN) of Marine Le Pen, that are unable to forge the kinds of alliances necessary to contest run-offs successfully under the current system. At this point, though, the RN horse has already left the barn. In the 2022 legislative elections, the collapse of the "Republican Front" against the RN allowed Marine Le Pen's movement to become the largest opposition party in the National Assembly. Consequently, the argument that PR should be avoided in order to prevent the RN from gaining representation has become significantly less compelling.

In any case, French reformers have generally proposed a limited dose of PR. Macron, for example, has spoken of allocating 15 percent of

National Assembly seats via PR.[1] A high minimum threshold for receiving seats, on the order of 5 percent or even 10 percent of votes, could provide a further safeguard by preventing the emergence of small, single-issue parties. Although no reform is ever risk-free, attenuating the incentives for skinny politics through a modicum of PR poses a relatively small risk. On the plus side, it could potentially "thicken" French politics, making French governments more inclusive, broadening their support base, and incorporating a wider range of views and interests into liberalizing reforms.

The next five years, from 2022 to 2027, may offer a kind of limited test run, as Macron lacks a legislative majority and will have to work with at least one other party. If the current situation leads to inertia and gridlock or an early dissolution, it could dampen support for a PR reform that would make it more difficult for future presidents to achieve a legislative majority. Conversely, if Macron "thickens" his governance, moving away from the Jupiterian ways of his first term and consulting and compromising with other parties, it could boost support for institutionalizing a PR electoral rule that increases the role of bargaining and coalitions.

Another way to reduce the incentives for skinny politics would be to curtail the instruments of "rationalized parliamentarism" like the confidence vote (Article 49.3), package vote (Article 44.3), and ordinance procedure (Article 38). All three mechanisms have been used regularly to ram through controversial liberalizing measures with little or no debate and, in the case of Article 49.3, no vote by the legislature. Such procedures violate democratic norms of accountability and trample legislative prerogatives. They also limit the opportunities to fix problematic liberalizing initiatives through negotiation and adjustment during the legislative process. What is more, by closing off participation in the formulation of liberalizing reforms, rationalized parliamentarism provides strong incentives for opponents or critics of liberalization to engage in popular contestation in order to secure changes or beat back liberalizing reforms altogether.

As with electoral laws, the politicians campaigning for president often promise to reform the system of rationalized parliamentarism or, at least, to refrain from using controversial techniques, particularly Article 49.3. To his credit, Nicolas Sarkozy did, in fact, enact a constitutional amendment in 2008 restricting the use of Article 49.3 and never once resorted to Article 49.3 during his presidency. In the wake of Sarkozy's constitutional reform, governments may use Article 49.3 to pass the general budget and the Social Security budget as needed, but are otherwise allowed to deploy Article 49.3 only once per parliamentary session. Given that there are typically two parliamentary sessions per year, governments still have plenty of chances to use Article 49.3.[2] Several of the most important social and labor market reforms have been enacted via Article 49.3, including the first reading of Macron's pension reform in February 2020. In almost all other cases of major reform, the government has relied on the ordinance procedure.

Narrowing the scope for rationalized parliamentarism could help move French governments away from skinny politics. Once again, an incremental approach could be deployed. For example, the use of Article 49.3 outside the budget and Social Security funding bill could be limited to once per year or even once per five-year legislative term. The modalities of Article 49.3 could also be made less favorable to the government. For instance, the government's deployment of Article 49.3 could automatically trigger a confidence vote, which is the general practice in parliamentary democracies, as opposed to the French rule requiring 10 percent of the members of the National Assembly to sign up for a no confidence vote (which they are only allowed to do a limited number of times) in order for a vote to even be held. In a similar vein, the use of the ordinance procedure could be capped at one time per year or per legislative term. By narrowing the opportunities for skinny, top-down imposition, such changes would compel the government to vet its proposals more carefully and pay greater heed to the opinions of the legislators. Thick governance would make controversial legislation more difficult to enact, but the resulting legislation would be more responsive to the concerns of critics and opponents of reform and, therefore, more likely to be actually implemented, as opposed to derailed by protests and strikes.

Constitutional changes are not the only way to thicken the politics of economic liberalization. In some instances, simple shifts in norms or outlooks are all that is required. In 2002, President Chirac missed a golden opportunity to empower the Social Refoundation, a forum for negotiations between the unions and the employer associations, to tackle controversial welfare state and labor market reforms. Instead of supporting the Social Refoundation, while perhaps establishing some parameters to safeguard the government's priorities and prerogatives, Chirac refused to share power. His decision to pursue reform via the conventional legislative process instead yielded limited results.

Similarly, Macron has repeatedly chosen to marginalize and steamroll the social partners, even though the largest French union, the French Democratic Confederation of Labor (Confédération Française Démocratique du Travail, CFDT), shares much of Macron's agenda. Had Macron opted to work more closely with the CFDT, he would have had to make some concessions, to be sure, but those concessions would have probably made his liberalizing reforms fairer. They also might have spared Macron from being tarred with the sobriquet "president of the rich," a key driver of the yellow vest protests. In addition, while a unified front of the unions has often forced governments to back down, when the CFDT has supported reforms it has generally been much easier for governments to stand their ground and prevail. The concessions extracted by the CFDT would have thus reduced contestation and perhaps saved Macron from some of his worst setbacks.

One of Macron's arguments against working with the unions is that they do not necessarily represent the groups who are protesting. When the leader of the CFDT offered to meet with the government to try to defuse the yellow vest protests, Prime Minister Edouard Philippe noted that there were few union members among the yellow vests. That said, concertational policymaking does not always have to be with the unions. Indeed, Macron's participatory innovations in the wake of the yellow vest protests point to another way of thickening the reform process.

Both the GDN and CCC gave ordinary citizens a way of expressing their concerns and ideas to the government and were very popular. The CCC went a step further than the GDN by allowing 150 citizens to each formulate a specific edict, legislative bill, or constitutional amendment to reduce France's carbon footprint, with Macron promising to enact 146 of the 150 proposals "without a filter." This approach was a source of not only ideas, but also legitimacy. In the wake of the yellow vest protests against central elements of Macron's environmental agenda, notably an increase in gasoline taxes and other measures to dissuade driving, the president needed both new proposals and a way of making them politically acceptable. The CCC filled this need by giving concrete form and a kind of popular legitimacy to a host of environmental measures. Indeed, Macron himself has felt pressure to honor his promise to enact the CCC proposals, as CCC members have continued to monitor the government's actions and criticize Macron whenever he has postponed or watered down their recommendations. Macron probably regrets his promise to implement the CCC proposals "without a filter." Yet, by enlarging the circle of participants on environmental policy, he created political momentum for reform, an approach that could potentially be replicated in other areas.

One option would be to create the equivalent of the CCC for different kinds of liberalizing reforms. Instead of devising a pension reform on its own, the government could establish a "Citizens' Pension Convention," composed of ordinary citizens, to formulate proposals with the help of experts. Likewise, a "Citizens' Transportation Convention" could develop proposals for reducing vehicle emissions and expanding public transportation, or a "Citizens' Health Convention" could suggest ways of reforming the health-care system. Macron's initial liberalizing reforms would have looked very different and probably been better received had they been negotiated with such citizens' conventions. Many French legislators object to citizens' conventions on the grounds that they bypass and reduce the role of parliament in fashioning legislation. That said, whatever the proposals from citizens' conventions (or any other advisory body), the legislature would still retain the ultimate authority to determine which measures, if any, were enacted into law.

Citizens' conventions need not be temporary organizations that sunset once they have issued their recommendations. As the case of the CCC indicates, citizens' conventions could continue to play a role in monitoring the government's implementation of their proposals and perhaps negotiating adjustments as needed. The government might even consider making such organizations permanent by paying members, providing staff and offices, privileging citizens' conventions as the preferred government partner for developing reform proposals, and/or giving the conventions a central role in the administration of policy. Such techniques have long been used to bolster producer associations in corporatist countries (Schmitter 1979; Streeck and Schmitter 1985).

Another option would be for the government to make greater use of existing organizations. A variant of the Social Refoundation that incorporated a greater role for the government might well be able to tackle some of the thornier reform issues like pensions, especially if the government were to provide resources to grease the wheels of corporatist bargaining. Beyond the social partners, the government could work with organizations representing narrower interests, such as physicians, teachers, and the elderly. It could also partner with religious and/or charitable associations that work on specific challenges, such as poverty, homelessness, and food insecurity.

The more general point is that when it comes to controversial liberalizing reforms, French governments would be better served by refraining from formulating policies in a technocratic bubble and instead negotiating and compromising with the political opposition, the legislature, the social partners, citizens' conventions, voluntary associations, and other stakeholders. Majoritarian electoral laws, presidentialism, rationalized parliamentarism, and the weakness of societal interest groups incline French leaders toward a divisive, skinny-politics approach to reform. This insular, top-down approach has demonstrated its limits, spurring contestation that has not only blocked many reforms, but also compromised the capacity of French leaders to govern. Weakening the incentives to engage in skinny politics, while building channels for thick, concertational politics, could improve democratic deliberation and the quality of policymaking. It could also reduce the frequency and intensity of contestation by marginalized and excluded groups.

8.3.2   The Substance of Liberalization: A More Equitable Distribution of Costs and Benefits

France's social anesthesia state has weighed heavily on the politics of economic liberalization. The expansion of the social anesthesia state that accompanied the movement away from the *dirigiste* model has limited the fiscal resources available to reformers, making it difficult to offer side-payments or compensation to the opponents of new rounds of liberalization. Yet liberalization without compensation is a very hard sell politically and leaves the government open to charges of favoring the rich.

To limit contestation, French governments need to do more than portray distributionally skewed reforms, *pace* Thatcher, as the only alternative for turning around the economy. Perceptions of fairness matter greatly. It is much easier to rally support for painful reforms if there is a sense of shared sacrifice, a collective understanding that everyone is pitching in to restore public finances and revive the economy. Conversely, as the yellow vest and other French protest movements have demonstrated, an agenda of tax cuts for corporations and the affluent along with spending cuts and tax increases for ordinary citizens invites contestation. Although the social anesthesia state places fiscal constraints on the government, there are still opportunities for addressing perceptions of fairness and equality of sacrifice.

One strategy would be to structure proposals in a way that builds room for walking back some of the most painful or controversial provisions. At a minimum, if a government seeks to reduce spending by €10 billion, it could propose €11 billion in spending cuts, so that it could then scale the cuts back by €1 billion in the course of negotiations. Such a minimalist approach would, at least, give the government's negotiating partners a chance to push the government away from its initial proposal and remove the cuts that they find most objectionable.

A more ambitious version of this strategy would be to structure proposals to also allow for spending on compensation or side-payments. To continue with the previous example, instead of proposing €10 billion in cuts, the government could propose €14 billion in cuts, then make two concessions in the course of negotiations: one reducing the cuts from €14 billion to €12 billion and the other providing €2 billion in new spending on measures of compensation and/or social justice favored by the stakeholders. Politically, the more ambitious approach would allow the government's bargaining partners to tell their constituents that they were able to both force the administration to cancel €2 billion in spending cuts and extract €2 billion in new spending for progressive priorities. It would also allow the government's partners to participate in defining the €2 billion in concessions. Distributionally, some €2 billion could be dedicated to important compensatory or social justice measures. A reform that allows for give and take between the government and its interlocutors would likely be easier to conclude, more equitable, and less susceptible to contestation.

Silja Häusermann suggests that many contemporary reforms offer possibilities for compensation even without additional government spending (Häusermann 2010). The growing complexity of pension, health-care, and labor market systems means that just about any attempt to control spending involves changes to a host of parameters. Some of these parameters could be adjusted to offer concessions to key groups. Even if the overall outcome were still a reduction in public spending, the multiple parameters in flux would allow for progressive tweaks and side-payments. The 1993 Balladur pension reform, described in Chapter 4, offers an example. The reform was an undeniable austerity measure, reducing the generosity of pensions and increasing the number of years required to qualify for a full pension. However, through a series of technical adjustments that shifted the financing of noncontributory pensions from payroll taxes, which are levied only on wages, to the General Social Contribution (Contribution Sociale Généralisée, CSG), which is imposed on all earnings, Balladur acceded to a longstanding union demand to "separate Bismarck from Beveridge" and boosted worker take-home pay. Having secured an important gain, moderate unions were then able to end their protests against the pension reform without losing face.

The heightened complexity of liberalizing reform is a source of risks as well as potential benefits. Precisely because the calculations are so complex, trust between the government and the relevant stakeholders is essential for dampening contestation. The failed Macron pension reform, analyzed in Chapter 6, offers a telling illustration. Whereas the Balladur pension reform was an indisputable austerity measure, the Macron reform was primarily an effort to make the pension system more equitable. Indeed, Macron championed the reform as the most important social justice measure of his presidency because it would end special privileges and instead treat all pensioners equally. It also included a generous minimum pension. Presumably, then, it should have faced less opposition than the Balladur reform.

With so many parameters being modified simultaneously under the Macron reform, however, it was almost impossible to determine who would win and who would lose. Low-trust relations added to popular wariness. Because the unions were at loggerheads with the government and had been excluded from the drafting of the pension bill, they felt no obligation to vouch for it. Unable to calculate the impact of Macron's reform themselves, many employees assumed the worst and mobilized against it – even though the reform was considerably more progressive than that of Balladur. Thus, complex multidimensional reform may create opportunities to offer compensation to key stakeholders and defuse contestation, but only if the representatives of those stakeholders are given a place in forging the reform and an incentive to vouch for it to the rank and file. In other words, concessions without genuine negotiation and concertation may not suffice to demobilize anxious citizens.

The literatures on varieties of liberalization, welfare state recalibration, and social/public investment described in Chapter 1 of this book point to other possibilities for a more progressive approach to liberalization. In several European countries, the expansion of labor market flexibility has been conducted on the basis of negotiations between the government, employer associations, and trade unions, and has provided important concessions to employees. The Danish so-called flexicurity model, a merging of "flexibility" and "security," gives employers considerable flexibility in laying off excess workers, while providing security to employees in the form of generous unemployment benefits and retraining opportunities (Madsen 2004; Schulze-Cleven 2014). The liberalization of work time in the Netherlands was the product of a similar give-and-take process (Visser 2002). On the one hand, restrictions on part-time employment were essentially eliminated, with the result that more than one-third of Dutch employees work part-time, the highest percentage in the Organisation for Economic Co-operation and Development (OECD 2019g). On the other hand, employers were required to pay the same pro rata wages and benefits to part-time workers as full-time workers, so part-time employment could not be used as a way of circumventing and undercutting the wages and benefits of full-time workers. In both the Danish and Dutch cases, labor market liberalization was carefully negotiated, resulting in win-win games that accommodated both employers seeking flexibility and employees seeking security and protection.

Not all measures of economic liberalization revolve around painful measures like fiscal austerity or the weakening of worker protections. Tax cuts, for example, distribute *benefits* to the affected groups. Here again, there is room for liberal reformers to do more than shower favors on corporations and the affluent. Ordinary and low-income citizens pay taxes too, notably value-added taxes (VAT) and Social Security charges.

Reducing the fiscal burden on low-income or disadvantaged segments of society holds far greater political appeal than Macron's narrowing of France's wealth tax and slashing of the capital gains rate. It can also have a huge impact on poverty and inequality. For example, as part of an effort to encourage work and reduce child poverty, Britain's New Labour government in the late 1990s and early 2000s targeted tax cuts and tax credits at working families. In combination with a rising minimum wage, this policy produced a nearly 25 percent reduction in child poverty in just five years (Brewer et al. 2004).

Of course, tax cuts are generally justified on economic more than social grounds. Corporate tax cuts increase the capacity of companies to provide goods that society values, like investment and employment. The economic argument is less clear with respect to tax cuts for high earners or reductions in inheritance taxes, however. Moreover, there are significant efficiency arguments to be made on behalf of cutting the income taxes and especially payroll taxes of the lowest earners. During hard economic times, such as the 2008 financial crisis, the most effective vehicle for Keynesian demand stimulus is to give money to the poor, who will spend it, rather than corporations and the affluent, who will mostly save it.

Even in prosperous times, it often makes good economic sense to cut the taxes of low-income groups, notably to reduce so-called poverty traps or inactivity traps. Many of the disadvantaged in France, such as single parents and recipients of the minimum income benefit, the Active Solidarity Income (Revenu de Solidarité Active, RSA), confront high effective marginal tax rates in moving from benefits to work or from part-time jobs to full-time jobs. As they enter the workforce or increase their working hours, their means-tested benefits are reduced, they confront new costs for childcare and transportation, and they have to pay Social Security charges. One way of limiting work disincentives is to lower these Social Security charges. By increasing the returns to paid employment, the government could help expand the labor supply, boosting the economy.

Income and payroll tax cuts targeted at low earners could also bolster the economy in other ways. In the early 1980s, Dutch unions accepted wage restraint in order to revive anemic employer profits (Visser and Hemerijck 1997). Even after corporate profits revived, the unions agreed to continue restraining wages in return for reductions in employee payroll taxes. Dutch businesses flourished, thanks to stable wages, and made new investments and hires, bringing down unemployment. At the same time, despite largely unchanged pretax wages, employee take-home pay increased significantly, due to much lower Social Security charges (Bakker and Halikas 1999). In a logic that should appeal to French liberal reformers, liberalization in one area (a reduction in employee payroll taxes) supported liberalization in another area (wage restraint to boost employer profits). In a logic that should appeal to French unions, employee take-home pay still enjoyed steady growth, and the Netherlands returned to full employment.

As related in Chapter 1, *dirigiste* legacies have tended to steer French reformers away from these kinds of inclusive, distributionally equitable liberalizing packages. The fiscal demands of the social anesthesia state have not left much money for measures of compensation. In any case, French reformers deploying a top-down, skinny-politics approach to reform have seen little need for trying to accommodate the demands of stakeholders or subordinate groups.

Despite these obstacles, there are still possibilities for a more inclusive and equitable form of liberalization in France. The process reforms discussed would compel would-be liberalizers to deal with the demands of stakeholders and those potentially harmed by proposed changes. In other words, a more inclusive *process* of reform could yield a more progressive *substance* of reform. Moreover, for all the fiscal constraints of the social anesthesia state, many reforms, notably of labor markets, involve regulatory changes, and writing slightly different rules does not require increased state outlays. Likewise, to the extent that tax relief is part of the liberal agenda, channeling such relief to average and low-income groups is not only plausible, but also socially impactful, as in the British case. What is more, it can provide important economic benefits in the form of wage restraint (as in the Netherlands) or increased labor market participation as a result of reduced poverty traps. Finally, even in the case of painful austerity measures, some of the savings can be used to provide either compensation or, as exemplified by the Nordic countries, social investment in childcare, education, and technology that increases opportunities for less advantaged workers and their children.

Economic liberalization in France has repeatedly triggered contestation over the substance and process of reform. Yet there are ways to attenuate both problems. Despite the skinny logic of the Fifth Republic, liberalizing reforms need not be prepared in secrecy and imposed from above. Thicker, more inclusive policymaking is often more effective than the kind of high-handed, skinny policymaking that destroyed the Juppé Plan and led the yellow vests to confront Macron. In a similar vein, despite the fiscal constraints of the social anesthesia state, economic liberalization need not mean austerity for the poor and tax cuts for business and the affluent. Liberalizing reforms can attenuate inequities instead of increasing them, depending on how the costs and benefits of liberalization are distributed. Taken together, a thicker, more concertational, and distributionally equitable approach to economic liberalization could go a long way toward dampening the contestation that has repeatedly beset liberalizing reformers in France.

8.4 Paring Populism

Changing the direction of economic liberalization could provide political as well as economic and social benefits. A number of studies have attributed the rise of populist parties, both on the left and the right, to resentment among working-class and less-educated citizens against globalization and neoliberalism (Cayla 2021; Crouch 2019). Populist parties have tapped into the sentiment that cosmopolitan elites have sold out the interests of ordinary citizens by enacting free-trade policies that benefit multinational corporations and international investors, while hollowing out manufacturing and devastating once-thriving industrial communities. The 2008 financial crisis and the apparent impunity of the bankers who caused it added to popular outrage (Kriesi and Pappas 2015). In addition, populists blast the mainstream governing parties for allegedly allowing waves of often undocumented immigrants to enter the country, drive down wages, take opportunities away from ordinary workers, live off government benefits, and commit crimes or even acts of terrorism.

Blue-collar and unemployed workers in rustbelt communities have been very receptive to the populist message, flocking to populist parties that promise to defend national economic interests, secure the border, and restore a bygone era of economic prominence. In many cases, the agenda of restoration extends beyond the economy, with a promised return to "traditional values" and – sometimes implicitly, sometimes explicitly – a racial and gendered hierarchy (Inglehart and Norris 2019; Kaufmann 2019). Of course, once in power, many populists like Donald Trump have been no better for ordinary workers, to put it mildly, than the mainstream parties they denounced. Yet, they have retained mass support due to widespread popular resentment of the globalizing and liberalizing policies of the mainstream parties. To a considerable extent, then, the rise of populist parties has been the political price for untrammeled neoliberal reform and the abandonment of subordinate groups.

If an excessive embrace of neoliberal globalization has exposed mainstream parties to a populist backlash, the French experience points to another risk. France is a case of contestation and considerable resistance to neoliberal globalization. As Chapter 1 demonstrated, to an extent unparalleled in other leading European political economies, liberal reformers in France have confronted popular opposition and frequent setbacks. Yet resisting neoliberal globalization has failed to keep populism in check, as populist parties have made deep inroads in France.

The far-right National Front (Front National, FN), renamed the National Rally (RN) in 2018, has been a fixture of French politics since the mid-1980s. The FN placed a candidate in the run-off for the presidency three times – Jean-Marie Le Pen in 2002 and his daughter, Marine Le Pen, in 2017 and 2022. The FN/RN was the leading vote-getter in both the 2014 and 2109 elections to the European parliament. In the 2022 legislative elections, the RN became the biggest opposition party in the National Assembly. The RN is also the leading party of the working class and the unemployed. What is more, the FN/RN's ceiling has risen dramatically, as Marine Le Pen has "de-demonized" the party by clearing away some of the most inflammatory themes, such as the defense of the Vichy regime and the minimization of Nazi crimes. If contesting liberalization were the key to paring populism, then the RN should have secured fewer votes in France than radical-right, xenophobic parties in other leading European countries. While electoral scores do not always mean the same thing from one country to the next, due to different electoral rules and offices at stake, the least that can be said is that France does not stand out for its ability to limit the electoral appeal of radical-right populism. Indeed, in the second round of the 2022 presidential election, Marine Le Pen hit a new high for a far-right candidate, with 41.5 percent of the vote, and in the legislative elections, the RN became France's largest opposition party.

Nor is populism in France confined to the right of the political spectrum. On the left side, Jean-Luc Mélenchon, a far-left populist firebrand, who has sung the praises of repressive leftist regimes in Cuba and Venezuela, federated a number of "Left of the Left" or "anti-liberal left" groups into a single movement, LFI. LFI then supplanted the PS as the dominant party of the left, with Mélenchon trouncing the Socialist candidates in the 2017 and 2022 presidential elections, and LFI earning more seats in the legislature in 2022 than all the other parties of the left combined (Communists, Socialists, Greens, and smaller movements).

The French case suggests that neglectful neoliberalism is not the only pathway to populism. Contested liberalization also presents risks. Repeated liberalizing initiatives threaten the interests of many groups, feeding the sentiment that the government cares more about global markets than the well-being of its own citizens. At the same time, the repeated failure of such initiatives conveys the sense that the government is unable to govern, tempting conservative voters to support a "stronger" regime that will regain control of the streets. With mainstream parties having continued to disappoint, frustrated and desperate French voters have grown increasingly receptive to the siren songs of populist leaders on both ends of the political spectrum.

There is another possible pathway, however. The approach to economic liberalization of the Scandinavian countries, Germany, and the Netherlands differs from both the Thatcherite and the French approaches in two important ways. First, it is more concertational. Liberalizing reforms have generally been negotiated with the opposition parties, social partners, and other critical stakeholders, rather than imposed from above. Second and related, the costs and benefits of economic liberalization have been distributed more equitably, with special attention to compensating the losers of liberalization.

Scholars have observed that where robust welfare states protect and compensate workers for the dislocation produced by globalization, populists have made less headway than in liberal countries like the USA and UK that have left unemployed rustbelt workers to their own devices (Eichengreen 2018; Rodrik 2018). Yet this domestic compensation argument does not go far enough. Other kinds of liberalization, such as tax reduction and efforts to make labor markets more flexible and employment-friendly, also potentially threaten worker interests. Thus, the need for compensation to accompany liberalization extends well beyond free trade.

The Northern European countries have mostly pursued liberalization in tandem with compensation. This compensation has been the direct result of concertation. Precisely because governments have sought to preserve social consensus by reforming through agreements with key stakeholders, they have been compelled to make concessions in order to secure such deals. These concessions, in turn, have taken some of the harsh edges off liberalizing reforms, for example by offering workers longer and more generous unemployment benefits or expanded opportunities for retraining as compensation for greater trade openness or the relaxation of restrictions on layoffs. In other words, concertational reform politics may play an important role in generating the kind of compensation that is central to keeping populists at bay.

Although poverty and inequality have increased across the OECD, the phenomenon has been much less pronounced among Northern European countries than in the USA and UK (OECD 2008). In addition, Northern European countries have preserved generous systems of social protection. In a sense, they have threaded the needle between neoliberalism and no liberalism. As against France's contested liberalization, they have reformed their welfare states and labor markets; as against Anglo-American neoliberalism, they have done so in an inclusive manner that sustains and, in some cases, enhances social protection.

Of course, populist parties are fueled by factors beyond the economy, including a general distrust of elites, racism, and fears about immigration, terrorism, and national identity (Eatwell and Goodwin 2018; Inglehart and

Norris 2019). What is more, even if liberalizing reforms are carefully calibrated, they can still make some people worse off. Economic liberalization also triggers concerns among ordinary citizens that they are being abandoned by the state. Perhaps for these reasons, populist parties have registered breakthroughs in almost all the affluent democracies, whatever their economic performance. That said, populist scores have mostly ranged from 10 to 15 percent in Germany, the Netherlands, and the Nordic countries, which is significantly lower than in France. Moreover, Northern European populists have never won a national election outright in the manner of Donald Trump in the USA or pro-Brexit forces in the UK.

It goes without saying that limiting radical-right populist parties to "only" 10 to 15 percent of the vote is no grounds for rejoicing. Moreover, populist parties in Northern Europe have sometimes scored higher. In addition, the combination of fragmented party systems and opportunistic conservative leaders has led to the inclusion of populist parties in governing coalitions in several Northern European countries, including the Netherlands, Denmark, Norway, and Sweden. Finally, even when populist parties have not entered governing coalitions, many of their ideas, particularly on immigration and law and order, have been picked up by mainstream parties. Thus, if populism has been contained somewhat more effectively in Northern Europe than elsewhere (for now, at least), it has certainly not been defeated. Yet, with all these caveats, it is clear that the Northern European countries have outperformed France in limiting the growth of populist parties.

France's contested liberalization is a political problem as much as an economic problem. It has fueled a multidimensional loss of faith in French government, elites, and the state. For those who believe that France needs a shot in the arm of market forces, the limits and failures of liberalizing reformers indicate that French elites are incompetent and cowardly in the face of protests. For those fearful of globalization and market forces, the continuous efforts to impose unpopular liberalizing reforms from above indicate that French governments are not listening, but instead sacrificing ordinary citizens on the altar of neoliberal globalization and *la pensée unique*. Such an environment of disappointment, frustration, and anxiety, reinforced by poor economic performance, provides fertile ground for demagogic leaders and populist parties. For this reason, finding a pathway for a version of economic liberalization that is fair, inclusive, and widely accepted is critical, not only for the French economy, but also for French democracy.

Notes

1   Three Legacies of *Dirigisme*

1 The Bolkestein Directive proposed to extend the "country-of-origin principle" to services, meaning that a company deploying a worker from a low-income country to provide a service in a high-income country could theoretically employ that worker under the less generous prevailing wages and benefits of the low-income country. That said, the company would still be required to abide by the statutory rules of the country where the work is performed, notably minimum-wage laws. It is no coincidence that one of the first cases to trigger concern about the Bolkestein Directive involved the use of low-paid Eastern European workers to build schools in Sweden. Because Sweden relies on collective bargaining to set wages and does not have a statutory minimum wage, the company was free to pay whatever the (East European labor) market would bear. The Bolkestein Directive triggered a firestorm of criticism and denunciations of "social dumping." It was ultimately adopted in 2006, but not before it had been emptied of much of its substance, including the country-of-origin principle.

2 This book uses the word "liberalization" or "liberalism" in the European sense, meaning a commitment to limited government spending and intervention in the market along with maximum individual choice and autonomy. The closest US equivalents would be "neoliberalism," "libertarianism," or the traditional free-market, small-government orientation of the Republican Party (pre-Trump). It goes without saying that the concept of liberalism in this book has nothing to do with the common US usage designating the tax-and-spend, interventionist wing of the Democratic Party that is historically associated with progressive leaders like the late Edward Kennedy.

3 Neither Balladur nor de Villepin was ever appointed to a cabinet position again, let alone as prime minister. Juppé was similarly damaged after 1997, although he did manage to eventually resurrect his political career, becoming the mayor of Bordeaux and holding several major ministerial portfolios from 2010 to 2012. Juppé attempted to run for president in 2017, but he was defeated in the party primary and has since retired from politics.

4 The Southern European countries do not score consistently lower than France on indices of economic liberalization. The sovereign debt crisis moved the Southern European countries in a sharply liberal direction, as the "Troika" (composed of the European Commission, European Central

Bank, and IMF), urged on by Germany, conditioned bailouts on severe austerity programs and far-reaching labor market reforms. As a result, the gap between France and Southern Europe on indicators of fiscal liberalization has narrowed considerably, while the Southern European countries often score higher than France on indices of labor market liberalization. The fact that France's indices of economic liberalization are similar or even lower than those of the Southern European countries, countries that are plagued by patronage politics and state capture, reinforces the notion that France's low indices of economic liberalization are a real puzzle in need of explanation.

5 In 2020, the French budget deficit nearly tripled from 3.1 to 9.1 percent of GDP, public spending increased by over 6 percent of GDP to 62.1 percent of GDP, and public debt jumped from 97.6 to 115.7 percent of GDP (INSEE 2021b). France's fiscal response to the COVID-19 crisis is discussed in Chapter 7.

6 In January 2021, PSA merged with Fiat Chrysler Automobile to create a new company called Stellantis. PSA CEO Carlos Tavares became the CEO of Stellantis. For purposes of familiarity and because the period covered in this book largely predates the merger, I continue to use "PSA" to designate what is now a part of a larger automotive enterprise.

7 Indeed, as pointed out in note 4, on most of the measures of economic liberalization reviewed in this chapter, France scores closer to interventionist Southern European countries like Italy, marked by corruption and state capture, than to the advanced political economies of Continental and Northern Europe.

8 Under the rules of the Fifth Republic, if no presidential candidate wins an absolute majority on the first round of voting, the two highest scorers face off in a second round of voting two weeks later.

9 In May 2022, Macron changed the name of his party from LREM to Renaissance (meaning Rebirth or Revival in English).

10 Jean-Baptiste Colbert was the finance minister to King Louis XIV from 1661 to 1683. Colbert deployed a combination of tariffs, public works projects, imperialist conquests, and aid to domestic industries to support the development of the French economy. For this reason, he is often regarded as the founder of mercantilism, and the term "Colbertism" is used by the French as a synonym for economic "statism" or "*dirigisme.*"

11 In this book, all translations from the French are by the author.

12 In a similar vein, Bruno Amable shows that when presented with a proposal to replace the French system of open-ended and fixed-term labor contracts with a single contract providing little job security but unemployment insurance benefits for all job seekers, most fixed-term workers opposed the single contract, even though it would have improved their unemployment benefits (Amable 2014). The reason is that these fixed-term workers expected to eventually obtain an open-ended contract and, with it, the job security enjoyed by the stably employed. Support for the proposed single contract was actually higher among the more wealthy, experienced, and educated employees on open-ended contracts, even though the reform would have eliminated their job protections, presumably because these employees felt that they were unlikely to be laid off and that, in the event that they were, they would have no trouble finding another attractive job. Amable also identifies a strong partisan effect, with voters on the right supporting the Single

Labor Contract (Contrat de Travail Unique, CTU) reform, which had been advanced by parties of the right, and voters on the left opposing the CTU reform, which had been criticized by parties of the left. In other words, not only do insiders and outsiders hold different preferences from those ascribed by the insider–outsider literature, but these preferences are a function of partisanship as much as position in the labor market.

13 Bruno Palier writes, for example: "The French, Austrian, or Belgian welfare systems are … certainly not identical to the German one, but they *are* considerably closer to it than to the Swedish system, and thus reflect both similar principles of welfare and comparable 'ways of doing' welfare. A central hypothesis of this research project is that these Continental European systems should therefore experience some shared difficulties and show similar reform dynamics" (Palier 2010a: 25, emphasis in the original).

14 Emmanuel Macron probably comes closest among French leaders to a consistent advocate of liberal reforms. Still, as related in Chapter 5, Macron's platform when he ran for president in 2017 carefully balanced promises of liberalization with new measures of social protection and public investment. In addition, as described in Chapter 7, in response to the COVID-19 crisis, Macron pivoted away from liberal reform, embracing a statist protector role, as exemplified by his promise to spend "whatever it takes" to protect French companies and workers from the economic consequences of the pandemic.

2   From the *Dirigiste* State to the Social Anesthesia State

1 In April 2019, in response to the yellow vest protestors and their denunciations of out-of-touch elites, President Macron announced that he was closing ENA. Two years later, after much debate, Macron opted to reform rather than abolish ENA (*Le Monde*, April 9, 2021). The school's name has been changed to the National Institute of Public Service (Institut National du Service Public, INSP), and Macron promises that the INSP will recruit much more widely than the notoriously narrow, elitist ENA. In addition, graduates will have to work in local administration in the provinces for several years, as opposed to the ENA tradition of installing them immediately in the upper reaches of the state administration in Paris.

2 In this book, the terms "Social Security charges" and "payroll taxes" are used interchangeably.

3 All figures prior to the introduction of the euro in 1999 have been converted from French francs to euro at the rate of €1 = 6.56 French francs.

4 In 2010, the RSA was made available to young adults, aged 18 to 25 (French National Council of Policies to Fight Poverty and Exclusion 2010). However, in contrast to claimants over the age of 25, young adults do not qualify solely on the basis of being poor and out of work. In addition, they must have been employed for two or more of the previous three years. As a result, most disadvantaged young adults remain ineligible for the RSA.

5 In the late 1990s, Japanese leadership finally began shifting from buying time to introducing elements of structural reform (Vogel 2006, 2013).

3   Liberalization without Liberals

1 Of course, the rise of Trumpism in the USA has called into question many of the fundamental principles, including economic, of the US Republican Party.
2 Names for the Gaullist movement include Union for the New Republic (Union pour la Nouvelle République, UNR), 1958–1967; Democratic Union for the Fifth Republic (Union des Démocrates pour la Cinquième République, UD-Ve), 1967–1968; Union for the Defense of the Republic (Union pour la Défense de la République, UDR), 1968; Union of Democrats for the Republic (Union des Démocrates pour la République, UDR), 1968–1976; and Rally for the Republic (RPR), 1976–2002. In 2002, most of the UDF joined the RPR in a new Union for the Presidential Majority (Union pour la Majorité Présidentielle, UMP), which changed its name a few months later to Union for a Popular Movement (UMP). Most recently, in 2015, the UMP became the Republicans (Les Républicains, LR). Gaullists have always avoided the label "party," since Charles de Gaulle disliked political parties, viewing them as selfish, corrupt, and shortsighted.
3 There was one puzzling sector on the list: for whatever reason, the government deemed "gambling outside casinos" to be a strategic sector, necessitating state protection.
4 Critics of Juppé's claim that Thomson Multimédia was worthless appear to have been right. In 2000, the Jospin government received €1.7 billion from the sale of a 16 percent share in Thomson Multimédia (*Le Parisien*, September 19, 2000).

4   Skinny Politics

1 For example, under a system with a retirement age of 62 and a requirement that a worker have forty-two years of contributions to qualify for a full pension, the unions argue that a manual laborer who started working at age 18 and remained employed continuously should be allowed to retire with a full pension at age 60.
2 What is more, in the event that a confidence vote is held, several rules favor the government. For the government to lose, the confidence vote must receive a majority of votes, including deputies who are not present or abstain. In addition, the government wins any tie vote.

5   Jupiter's Limits

1 Le Maire and Darmanin left LR and joined Macron's LREM when they entered the government in 2017, while Philippe left LR without becoming a member of LREM. In October 2021, Philippe launched his own center-right party, Horizons, which has worked closely with LREM/Renaissance.
2 A ruling by the French Constitutional Council required the government to extend the exemption from the housing tax to all citizens. Extending the reform to the wealthiest 20 percent was expensive, costing an additional €7 billion per year, as compared with €10 billion per year to end the tax for the

bottom 80 percent of the population (*Le Monde*, January 8, 2019; *Les Echos*, September 28, 2020). Not only was the court-ordered change expensive, but, politically, it transformed one of the government's most high-profile initiatives on behalf of ordinary and low-income citizens into a tax cut that provides a disproportionate share of its benefits (41 percent) to the wealthiest 20 percent of the population. While the housing tax was completely eliminated for 80 percent of earners in 2020, the government put off the first reduction in the tax for the top 20 percent of earners until 2021. The tax for high earners is being phased out over a three-year period, with a total reduction of 30 percent in 2021, 65 percent in 2022, and 100 percent in 2023, at which point the housing tax will have been abolished for rich and poor alike (French Ministry of the Economy and Finance 2020).

3 Dollar figures are calculated at the rate of $1.20 per euro.

4 Only twice in the history of the Fifth Republic has a newly elected president failed to secure an absolute majority in the ensuing legislative elections. In 1988, François Mitterrand's PS won 275 seats, leaving it 14 seats short of a majority, but it should be noted that during the legislative campaign, Mitterrand himself suggested that it might not be good for the PS to have all the power. The other newly elected president who failed to secure a legislative majority was, of course, Macron in 2022. His three-party coalition performed significantly worse than the PS in 1988, winning only 250 seats and falling 39 seats short of a majority. The 2022 elections are discussed in Chapter 7.

6   Rinse and Repeat

1 In October 2020, defections to other parties left EDS below the minimum of fifteen National Assembly members required for a parliamentary group. EDS was dissolved, and its members became independents.

2 Piketty has been very critical of Macron for increasing inequalities in France, even comparing Macron's economic agenda to that of Donald Trump (*Le Monde*, December 12, 2017). Piketty opposed Macron's pension reform primarily because of the light taxation of high earners (*Le Monde*, December 10, 2020; *Libération*, January 22, 2020). Under the government's plan, for incomes up to €10,000 per month, everyone would pay a flat rate of 28 percent, with the contributions conferring corresponding pension benefits. Above that figure, contributions would confer no pension benefits, but the contribution rate would drop to only 2.8 percent (one-tenth of the rate applied to earnings below €10,000 per month). Piketty wanted a much higher contribution rate for earnings of more than €10,000 per month, so that the revenues from high earners would help cover expenses elsewhere in the pension system and avoid the need for painful measures, such as pension cuts or a higher retirement age, to reduce future deficits in the pension regime. Piketty also favored more redistribution toward low-income pensioners who, because of shorter life expectancies, tend to receive pensions for significantly fewer years than high-income pensioners.

3 Under the Fifth Republic, bills are considered by the Senate as well as the National Assembly. In case of disagreement, a "shuttle" between the two

legislative bodies attempts to reconcile the different versions. If an agreement cannot be reached after two readings of the bill in both chambers, the prime minister can call a meeting of the Joint Mediation Committee, composed of seven representatives from each chamber. If the Joint Mediation Committee is unable to reach an agreement, the prime minister can ask the National Assembly to vote for a third time and enact this version into law. Around 10 percent of French laws are enacted in this manner (French Senate 2021). A reform as complex and controversial as Macron's pension overhaul would, therefore, have probably needed to be approved three times by the National Assembly.

7   "Whatever It Costs"

1 Although France provided the largest amount of state loan guarantees during the first wave of the COVID-19 epidemic, from March to June 2020, Italy surged past France with €245.8 billion in loan guarantees at the end of 2021, and Spain nearly caught up, with €135.3 billion in loan guarantees (Bruegel 2022).

2 Almost immediately, Renault began seeking to wiggle out of its agreement to join the Automotive Cell Company (*Usine Nouvelle*, January 21, 2021). In January 2021, it announced that it was preparing to create its own battery factory on French soil in partnership with another company. Renault justified the move by arguing that it had agreed to participate in the Automotive Cell Company only if it was treated as an equal partner, suggesting that it had somehow been mistreated. In addition, Renault contended that the Automotive Cell Company was focused on developing the battery of the future, whereas Renault's site would produce batteries for the here and now. In June 2021, Renault signed a partnership agreement with the Chinese battery maker, Envision AESC, and a French startup, Verkor, to supply electric batteries for Renault's electric vehicle hub in northern France. The deal seemingly eliminated any reason for Renault to work with the Automotive Cell Company (*Automotive News Europe*, June 28, 2021). Three months later, the Automotive Cell Company fired back, announcing that Mercedes Benz had agreed to take a one-third stake in the venture (*Elective.com*, September 24, 2021). In the wake of these moves, Renault does not appear poised to join the "Airbus of Batteries" anytime soon.

3 The main reason why young people enrolled in higher education sign up for apprenticeships is to top up meager, government-provided student stipends. In other words, apprenticeships function as an alternative to dead-end, part-time jobs (or more generous student stipends) as a way to make ends meet.

4 Responding to criticism that the *chômage partiel* program was paying employees to do nothing, the government is requiring companies enrolled in APLD to conduct worker training. Employees are allowed to work no more than 60 percent of the time, with the remaining 40 percent reserved for training to enhance worker skills and facilitate the securing of a new job, if necessary. The state pays 80 percent of the cost of the training.

5 Of course, deficit projections are shrouded in uncertainty. On the plus side, France's economy grew faster than expected in 2021, and a continued robust performance could accelerate deficit reduction. On the minus side, as of December 2022, France's economic prospects are looking anything but robust. Several developments in 2022 are threatening to push France and its trading partners into a recession, including surprisingly high rates of inflation, spiraling energy prices, the fallout from the Russian invasion of Ukraine, and the move by central bankers to raise interest rates in order to reduce inflation. Higher interest rates not only slow growth, but also increase the cost of financing France's sizable public debt. Should these various headwinds continue, it would be extremely difficult for Macron to reduce France's budget deficits, absent a commitment to a painful austerity program. It goes without saying that the emergence of a new more virulent strain of COVID-19 or the extension of the Ukraine war to other European countries would also disrupt France's economy and public finances.

8   Beyond Contestation

1 Even a 15 percent "dose of proportional" appears to be too much for Macron, at least for the time being. Like Sarkozy and Hollande before him, Macron abandoned a campaign promise to allow for the election of some deputies in the National Assembly via PR. In early 2021, Macron announced that the 2022 legislative elections would be held under the existing two-round, majoritarian system, while holding out the possibility of introducing a degree of PR during an eventual second term as president (*Libération*, February 22, 2021).
2 As noted in Chapter 7, lacking an absolute majority in the National Assembly, Macron deployed Article 49.3 ten times during the first eight months of his second presidency, compared with just once (on pension reform) during the entire five years of his first presidency.

Bibliography

Adam, G. (2000), "La refondation sociale," *La Croix*, October 26, 2000.

Adam, G. (2002), *La refondation sociale à réinventer*, Paris: Editions Liaisons.

Adam, G., J.-D. Reynaud, et al. (1972), *La négociation collective en France*, Paris: Editions Ouvrières.

Aghion, P., G. Cette, et al. (2014), *Changer de modèle*, Paris: Odile Jacob.

Aleksynska, M. and S. Cazes (2014), *Comparing Indicators of Labour Market Regulations across Databases: A Post Scriptum to the Employing Workers Debate*, Conditions of Work and Employment Series, No. 50, Geneva: ILO. Available at: www.ilo.org/wcmsp5/groups/public/---ed_protect/---protrav/---travail/documents/publication/wcms_245349.pdf. Consulted: December 10, 2022.

Allaire, M.-B. and P. Goulliaud (2002), *L'incroyable septennat: Jacques Chirac à l'Elysée, 1995–2002*, Paris: Fayard.

Allègre, C. and D. Montalvon (2012), *Sarkozy ou le complexe de Zoro*, Paris: Plon.

Amable, B. (2014), "Who Wants the *Contrat de Travail Unique*? Social Support for Labor Market Flexibilization in France," *Industrial Relations*, 53(4): 636–662.

Amable, B. and S. Palombarini (2017), *L'illusion du bloc bourgeois: Alliances sociales et avenir du modèle français*, Paris: Raisons d'Agir Editions.

Amable, B. and S. Palombarini (2021), *The Last Neoliberal: Macron and the Origins of France's Political Crisis*, London: Verso.

Amsden, A. (1989), *Asia's Next Giant: South Korea and Late Industrialization*, Oxford: Oxford University Press.

Anderson, J., F. Papadia, et al. (2020), *Government-Guaranteed Bank Lending in Europe: Beyond the Headline Numbers*, Peterson Institute for International Economics, July 21, 2020.

Anderson, K. (2001), "The Politics of Retrenchment in a Social Democratic Welfare State: Reform of Swedish Pensions and Unemployment Insurance," *Comparative Political Studies*, 34(9): 1063–1091.

Anderson, K. and E. Immergut (2006), "Sweden: After Social Democratic Hegemony," in Ellen Immergut and Karen Anderson, Eds., *West European Pension Politics*, Oxford: Oxford University Press: 349–395.

Anderson, K. and T. Meyer (2003), "Social Democracy, Unions, and Pension Politics in Germany and Sweden," *Journal of European Public Policy*, 23(1): 23–54.

Armingeon, K. and G. Bonoli, Eds. (2006), *The Politics of Post-Industrial Welfare States: Adapting Post-War Social Policies to New Social Risks*, London: Routledge.

Attali, J. (2008), *Rapport de la Commission pour la Libération de la Croissance Française*, Paris: La Documentation Française.

Baccaro, L. and R. Locke (1996), "Public Sector Reform and Union Participation: The Case of the Italian Pension Reform," Paper presented to the 1996 annual meeting of the American Political Science Association, San Francisco, CA, August 29–September 1, 1996.

Bakker, B. B. and I. Halikas (1999), "Policy Reforms and Employment Creation," in C. Maxwell Watson, Bas B. Bakker, et al., Eds., *The Netherlands: Transforming a Market Economy*, Washington, DC: IMF: 16–41.

Balladur, E. (1979), *L'arbre de mai: Chronique alternée*, Paris: Plon.

Balladur, E. (1995), *Deux ans à Matignon*, Paris: Plon.

Barbier, C. (2017), *Deux présidents pour rien, 2007–2017: Chronique d'une décennie*, Paris: Presses de la Cité.

Barnier, M., J. Barrot, et al. (2001), *Notre contrat pour l'alternance*, Paris: Plon.

Bauchet, P. (1986), *Le plan dans l'économie française*, Paris: Fondation Nationale des Sciences Politiques.

Baudoin, J. (1990), "Le 'moment néo-libérale' du RPR: Essai d'interprétation," *Revue française de science politique*, 40(6): 830–844.

Bauer, M. (1988), "The Politics of State-Directed Privatisation: The Case of France, 1986–1988," *West European Politics*, 11(4): 49–60.

Baverez, N. (2012), *Réveillez-vous!* Paris: Fayard.

Baverez, N. (2017), *Chroniques du déni français*, Paris: Albin Michel.

Bellaiche, A. S. (2022), "Vous ne comprenez plus rien aux plans d'investissements français? C'est normal!" *Usine nouvelle*, January 14, 2022.

Berger, S. (1981), "Lame Ducks and National Champions: Industrial Policy in the Fifth Republic," in William Andrews and Stanley Hoffmann, Eds., *The Fifth Republic at Twenty*, Albany, NY: SUNY Press: 160–178.

Berger, S. (1985), "The Socialists and the *Patronat*: The Dilemmas of Coexistence in a Mixed Economy," in Howard Machin and Vincent Wright, Eds., *Economic Policy and Policy-Making Under the Mitterrand Presidency, 1981–1984*, New York: Saint Martin's: 225–244.

Berger, S. (1986), "Liberalism Reborn: The New Liberal Synthesis in France," in Jolyon Howorth and George Ross, Eds., *Contemporary France: A Review of Interdisciplinary Studies*, London: Frances Pinter: 86–108.

Berstein, S. (2002), *Histoire du gaullisme*, Paris: Perrin.

Berstein, S. (2006), *The Republic of de Gaulle, 1958–1969*, Cambridge: Cambridge University Press.

Bigorgne, L., A. Baudry, et al. (2017), *Macron, et en même temps*, Paris: Plon.

Birnbaum, P. (1977), *Les sommets de l'Etat: Essai sur l'élite du pouvoir en France*, Paris: Seuil.

Birnbaum, P. (1978), *La classe dirigeante française: Dissociation, interpénétration, intégration*, Paris: PUF.

Bloch-Lainé, F. (1982), *Profession: Fonctionnaire*, Paris: Seuil.

Bloch-Lainé, F. and J. Bouvier (1986), *La France restaurée, 1944–1954: Dialogue sur les choix d'une modernisation*, Paris: Fayard.

Boisguérin, B. (2001), "Les bénéficiaires de la couverture maladie universelle au 30 juin 2001," *Etudes et résultats*, No. 141.

Bonoli, G. (1997), "Pension Politics in France: Patterns of Cooperation and Conflict in Two Recent Reforms," *West European Politics*, 20(4): 160–181.

Bonoli, G. and B. Palier (1997), "Reclaiming Welfare: The Politics of French Social Protection Reform," in Martin Rhodes, Ed., *Southern European Welfare States: Between Crisis and Reform*, Portland, OR: Frank Cass: 240–259.

Boublil, A. (1977), *Le socialisme industriel*, Paris: PUF.

Boublil, A. (1990), *Le soulèvement du sérail*, Paris: Albin Michel.

Bozio, A. and T. Piketty (2008), *Pour un nouveau système de retraites: Des comptes individuels de cotisations financés par répartition*, Paris: Editions Rue d'Ulm.

Brewer, M., A. Goodman, et al. (2004), *Poverty and Inequality in Britain: 2004*, London: Institute for Fiscal Studies.

Brigouleix, B. (1995), *Histoire indiscrète des années Balladur: Matignon durant la seconde cohabitation*, Paris: Albin Michel.

Brizay, B. (1975), *Le Patronat: Histoire, structure, stratégie du CNPF*, Paris: Seuil.

Bruegel (2022), Loan Guarantees and other National Credit-Support Programmes in the Wake of COVID-19, June 10, 2022.

Bruneau, I., J. Mischi, et al. (2019), "Les 'gilets jaunes' en campagne: une ruralité politique," in Sylvain Bourneau, Ed., *'Gilets jaunes': Hypothèses sur un mouvement*, Paris: La Découverte, Analyse Opinion Critique (AOC) Cahier #1: 89–94.

Buch-Hansen, H. and A. Wigger (2010), "Revisiting 50 Years of Market-Making: The Neoliberal Transformation of European Competition Policy," *Review of International Political Economy*, 17(1): 20–44.

Buchanan, J., R. Tollison, et al., Eds. (1980), *Toward a Theory of the Rent-Seeking Society*, College Station, TX: Texas A&M University Press.

Buffotot, P. and D. Hanley (1996), "Chronique d'une victoire annoncée: Les élections présidentielles de 1995," *Modern and Contemporary France*, 4(1): 15–29.

Buigues, P.-A. and E. Cohen (2020), "The Failure of French Industrial Policy," *Journal of Industry, Competition, and Trade*, 20(2): 249–277.

Bunel, J. and J. Saglio (1979), *L'action patronale du CNPF au petit patron*, Paris: PUF.

Burgin, A. (2012), *The Great Persuasion: Reinventing Free Markets since the Depression*, Cambridge, MA: Harvard University Press.

Business France (2020), *Annual Report 2019: Foreign Investment in France*.

Cable, V. (1995), "The Diminished Nation-State: A Study in the Loss of Economic Power," *Daedalus*, 124(2): 23–53.

Cahiers, Français (1983), *La politique industrielle*, Paris: La Documentation Française, No. 212.

Cahuc, P. and A. Zylberberg (2009), *Les réformes ratées du Président Sarkozy*, Paris: Flammarion.

CNSA (Caisse Nationale de Solidarité pour l'Autonomie) (2022), *Le Conseil de la CNSA adopte un budget provisoire dans l'attente de la convention d'objectifs et de gestion*, December 21, 2021. Available at: www.cnsa.fr/actualites-agenda/ actualites-du-conseil/le-conseil-de-la-cnsa-adopte-un-budget-provisoire-dans-lattente-de-la-convention-dobjectifs-et-de-gestion. Consulted: July 29, 2022.

Caldwell, B. (2011), "Hayek, the Chicago School, and Neoliberalism," in Robert Van Horn, Philip Mirowski et al., Eds., *Building Chicago Economics*, Cambridge: Cambridge University Press: 301–334.

Camdessus, M. (2004), *Le sursaut: Vers une nouvelle croissance pour la France*, Paris: La Documentation Française.

Cameron, D. (1991), "Continuity and Change in French Social Policy: The Welfare State under Gaullism, Liberalism, and Socialism," in John Ambler, Ed., *The French Welfare State: Surviving Social and Ideological Change*, New York: New York University Press: 58–93.

Campbell, A. (2012), "Policy Makes Mass Politics," *Annual Review of Political Science*, 15: 333–351.

Campbell, J. and O. Pedersen, Eds. (2001), *The Rise of Neoliberalism and Institutional Analysis*, Princeton, NJ: Princeton University Press.

Cayla, D. (2021), *Populism and Neoliberalism*, Milton Park, UK: Routledge.

Charpin, J.-M. (1999), *L'avenir de nos retraites*, Paris: La Documentation Française.

Chauvel, L. (2006), *Les classes moyennes à la dérive*, Paris: Seuil.

Chauvel, L. (2010), "The Long-Term Destabilization of Youth, Scarring Effects, and the Future of the Welfare Regime in Post-*Trente Glorieuses* France," *French Politics, Culture, and Society*, 28(3): 74–96.

Chauvel, L. (2013), "Welfare Regimes, Cohorts, and the Middle Class," in Janet Gornick and Markus Jänti, Eds., *Income Inequality: Economic Disparities and the Middle Class in Affluent Countries*, Stanford, CA: Stanford University Press: 115–141.

Chevènement, J.-P. (2011), *La France est-elle finie?* Paris: Fayard.

Chiroux, R. (1994), "Edouard Balladur et l'inévitable échéance présidentielle," *Revue administrative*, 47(277): 98–107.

Chiroux, R. (2006), "Dominique de Villepin face à l'adversité," *La revue administrative*, 59(352): 438–445.

Claeys, A., J.-P. Gores, et al. (2011), Rapport d'information sur les financements extrabudgétaires de la recherche et de l'enseignement supérieur, Paris: Finance, Economy, and Budgetary Commission, French National Assembly, Report, No. 4031.

Clifford Chance (2020), *France Amends Its Foreign Investment Regime*, July 29, 2020. Available at: www.cliffordchance.com/briefings/2020/02/france-amends-its-foreign-investment-regime.html. Consulted: November 27, 2020.

Clift, B. (2006), "The New Political Economy of *Dirigisme*: French Macroeconomic Policy, Unrepentant Sinning, and the Stability and Growth Pact," *British Journal of Politics and International Relations*, 8(3): 388–409.

Clift, B. (2009a), *French Economic Patriotism: Legislative, Regulatory, and Discursive Dimensions*, Paper prepared for the PSA Annual Conference, Manchester, UK, April 7–9, 2009.

Clift, B. (2009b), "The Second Time as Farce? The EU Takeover Directive, the Clash of Capitalisms, and the Hamstrung Harmonization of European (and French) Corporate Governance," *Journal of Common Market Studies*, 47(1): 55–79.

Clift, B. (2013), "Economic Patriotism, the Clash of Capitalisms, and State Aid in the European Union," *Journal of Industry, Competition, and Trade*, 13(1): 101–117.

Clift, B. and C. Woll (2012), "Economic Patriotism: Reinventing Control Over Open Markets," *Journal of European Public Policy*, 19(3): 307–323.

Clift, B. and C. Woll, Eds. (2013), *Economic Patriotism in Open Economies*, London: Routledge.

Cohen, E. (1989), *L'Etat brancardier: Politiques du déclin industriel (1974–1984)*, Paris: Calmann-Lévy.

Cohen, E. (1992), *Le Colbertisme "high tech": Economie des télécom et du grand projet*, Paris: Hachette.

Cohen, E. (2004), "De la CGE à Alstom: Une histoire bien française," *Sociétal*, No. 43.

Cohen, E. (2007), "Industrial Policies in France: The Old and the New," *Journal of Industry Competition and Trade*, 7(3–4): 213–227.

Cohen, E. (2008), "Les trois erreurs de Nicolas Sarkozy," *Telos*, May 9, 2008.

Cohen, E. (2017), "Elie Cohen: 'C'est le capital qui a le dernier mot'," *La Croix*, September 27, 2017.

Cohen, E. (2018), *Testimony to French National Assembly*, Commission d'enquête chargée d'examiner les décisions de l'État en matière de politique industrielle, au regard des fusions d'entreprises d'Alstom, d'Alcatel, et de STX, ainsi que les moyens susceptibles de protéger nos fleurons industriels. French National Assembly, January 18, 2018. Available at: www.assemblee-nationale .fr/dyn/15/comptes-rendus/cepolind/l15cepolind1718013_compte-rendu. Consulted: January 12, 2021.

Cohen, E. and M. Bauer (1985), *Les grandes manoeuvres industrielles*, Paris: Belfond.

Cohen, E. and P.-A. Buigues (2014), *Le décrochage industriel*, Paris: Fayard.

Cohen, S. (1977), *Modern Capitalist Planning: The French Model*, Berkeley, CA: University of California Press.

Cole, A. (1999), "The *Service Public* under Stress," *West European Politics*, 22(4): 166–184.

Cole, A. and H. Drake (2000), "The Europeanization of the French Polity: Continuity, Change, and Adaptation," *Journal of European Public Policy*, 7(1): 26–43.

Cole, A., P. Le Galès, et al. (2003), "Introduction: The Republican Model in Transition," in Alistair Cole, Patrick Le Galès et al., Eds., *Developments in French Politics 3*, London: Palgrave: 1–17.

Combes, M. (2019), "'Gilets jaunes' vs. Macron: La transition écologique dans l'impasse," in Sylvain Bourneau, Ed., *'Gilets jaunes': Hypothèses sur un mouvement*, Paris: La Découverte, Analyse Opinion Critique (AOC) Cahier #1: 21–29.

Complémentaire Solidaire Santé (2021), *Rapport annuel de la Complémentaire Solidaire Santé*, 2021 edition. Available at: https://solidarites-sante.gouv .fr/IMG/pdf/rapport_dc_la_complementaire_sante_solidaire_-_2021.pdf. Consulted: February 13, 2021.

Coquet, B. (2022), *Les deux réformes de l'assurance chômage*, Etude OFCE N° 03/2022, March 2022.

Cracknell, E. (2021), *Why Are the French the Most Skeptical about COVID-19 Vaccines in the EU?* FleishmanHillard, April 7, 2021. Available at: https:// fleishmanhillard.eu/2021/04/why-are-the-french-the-most-skeptical-about-covid-19-vaccines-in-the-eu/. Consulted: March 2, 2022.

Crespy, A. (2015), "The Vanishing Promise of a More 'Social' Europe: Public Services Before and After the Debt Crisis," in Amandine Crespy, Ed., *Social Policy and the Euro Crisis*, London: Palgrave Macmillan: 114–139.

Crouch, C. (2011), *The Strange Non-Death of Neo-Liberalism*, Cambridge: Polity.

Crouch, C. (2017), *Can Neoliberalism Be Saved from Itself?* London: Social Europe Edition.

Crouch, C. (2019), *The Globalization Backlash*, Cambridge: Polity.

Crozier, M. (1964), *Le phénomène bureaucratique*, Paris: Seuil.

Crozier, M. (1970), *La société bloquée*, Paris: Seuil.

Crozier, M. (1979), *On ne change pas la société par décret*, Paris: Grasset.

Daley, A. (1996), *Steel, State, and Labor: Mobilization and Adjustment in France*, Pittsburgh, PA: University of Pittsburgh Press.

Daniel, J.-M. (2015), *Le gâchis français: 40 ans de mensonges économiques*, Paris: Tallandier.

DARES (1996), *40 ans de politique de l'emploi*, Paris: Direction de l'Animation de la Recherche, des Etudes, et des Statistiques.

DARES (2000), *La politique de l'emploi en 1999*, Paris: Direction de l'Animation, de la Recherche, des Etudes, et des Statistiques.

De Gaulle, C. (2007), *Mémoires*, Paris: Bibliothèque de la Pléiade, No. 465.

De la Porte, C. and E. Heins, Eds. (2016), *The Sovereign Debt Crisis, the EU, and Welfare Reform*, London: Palgrave Macmillan.

Deeg, R. (1999), *Finance Capitalism Unveiled: Banks and the German Political Economy*, Ann Arbor, MI: University of Michigan Press.

Depraz, S. (2019), "La France contrainte des 'gilets jaunes'," in Sylvain Bourneau, Ed., *'Gilets jaunes': Hypothèses sur un mouvement*, Paris: La Découverte, Analyse Opinion Critique (AOC) Cahier #1: 75–80.

Domenach, N. and M. Szafran (1997), *Le roman d'un président*, Paris: Plon.

DREES (2021), "Le Revenu de Solidarité Active (RSA)," *Minima sociaux et prestations sociales*, Direction de la Recherche, des Etudes, de l'Evaluation, et des Statistiques: 184–191.

Dusanter, C. (2022), *TICGN: Fonctionnement, montant, et exonération en 2022*, Opéra Energie, January 4, 2022. Available at: https://opera-energie.com/ticgn/. Consulted: March 25, 2022.

Duval, G. (2009), "Le grand emprunt en questions," *Alternatives économiques*, November 1, 2009, No. 285.

Eatwell, R. and M. Goodwin (2018), *National Populism: The Revolt against Liberal Democracy*, London: Pelican.

Eichengreen, B. (2018), *The Populist Temptation: Economic Grievance and Political Reaction in the Modern Era*, Oxford: Oxford University Press.

Elabe (2021), "Les Français et le 'quoi qu'il en coûte'," *Etudes et sondages*, February 4, 2021. Available at: https://elabe.fr/le-quoi-quil-en-coute. Consulted: July 12, 2022.

Ehrmann, H. (1957), *Organized Business in France*, Princeton, NJ: Princeton University Press.

Esping-Andersen, G. (1990), *The Three Worlds of Welfare Capitalism*, Princeton, NJ: Princeton University Press.

Esping-Andersen, G. (1996a), "Welfare States without Work: The Impasse of Labor Shedding and Familialism in Continental European Social Policy," in

Gøsta Esping-Andersen, Ed., *Welfare States in Transition: National Adaptations in a Global Economy*, Thousand Oaks, CA: Sage: 66–87.

Esping-Andersen, G. (1996b), "After the Golden Age? Welfare State Dilemmas in a Global Economy," in Gøsta Esping-Andersen, Ed., *Welfare States in Transition: National Adaptations in a Global Economy*, Thousand Oaks, CA: Sage: 1–31.

Esping-Andersen, G., Ed. (2002), *Why We Need a New Welfare State*, Oxford: Oxford University Press.

Etchemendy, S. (2011), *Models of Economic Liberalization: Business, Workers, and Compensation in Latin America, Spain, and Portugal*, Cambridge: Cambridge University Press.

European Commission (2010), *Europe 2020: A European Strategy for Smart, Sustainable, and Inclusive Growth*, Com (2010) 2020, March 3, 2010. Available at: https://ec.europa.eu/eu2020/pdf/COMPLET%20EN%20BARROSO%20%20%20007%20-%20Europe%202020%20-%20EN%20version.pdf. Consulted: July 22, 2022.

European Commission (2020), *France: Report Prepared in Accordance with Article 126(3) of the Treaty on the Functioning of the European Union*, COM (2020) 538 Final, May 20, 2020. Available at: https://ec.europa.eu/economy_finance/economic_governance/sgp/pdf/30_edps/126-03_commission/com-2020-538-fr_en.pdf. Consulted: July 22, 2022.

European Commission (2022), *Services of General Interest*. Available at: https://ec.europa.eu/info/topics/single-market/services-general-interest_en. Consulted: July 29, 2022.

Farbiaz, P. (2019), *Les gilets jaunes: Documents et textes*, Vulaines-sur-Seine: Editions du Croquant.

Faugère, J.-P. and C. Voisin (1994), *Le système financier français: Crises et mutations*, Paris: Nathan.

Fédération Nationale des Travaux Publics (2021), *Tableau récapitulatif des différences entre l'activité partielle de droit commun et l'APLD*. Available at: www.fntp.fr/sites/default/files/content/fntp_tableau_recap_activite_partielle_112020.pdf. Consulted: February 25, 2022.

Fenby, J. (2010), *The General: Charles de Gaulle and the France He Saved*, London: Simon and Schuster.

Ferrera, M., A. Hemerijck, et al. (2000), "Recasting European Welfare States for the 21st Century," *European Review*, 8(3): 427–446.

Ferrera, M. and M. Rhodes, Eds. (2000), *Recasting European Welfare States*, London: Frank Cass.

Finnegan, G. (2021), "How France Overcame COVID-19 Vaccine Hesitancy," *Vaccines Today*, September 8, 2021.

Forrester, V. (1996), *L'horreur économique*, Paris: Fayard.

Foucault, M. (2007), "Nicolas Sarkozy: 100 jours plus tard …" *Policy Options*, November 1, 2007: 75–79.

Fourastié, J. (1979), *Les trente glorieuses ou la révolution invisible de 1946 à 1975*, Paris: Fayard.

France, A. (2018), *Capital Gains Tax on Property, Shares, and Goods*. Available at: www.angloinfo.com/how-to/france/money/general-taxes/capital-gains-tax. Consulted: September 12, 2020.

Frazier, M. (1986), "The French Revolution of 1986," *Reason: Free Minds and Free Markets*, November 1986.

French Citizens' Convention for Climate (2021), *Avis de la Convention Citoyenne pour le Climat sur les réponses apportées par le gouvernement à ses propositions*, March 2, 2021. Available at: https://propositions.conventioncitoyennepourleclimat.fr/. Consulted: February 20, 2022.

French Court of Auditors (2011), *Communication à la commission des finances, de l'économie générale, et du contrôle budgétaire de l'Assemblée nationale: Les contrats aidés dans la politique de l'emploi*. Available at: www.ccomptes.fr/sites/default/files/2018-01/05-mise-en-oeuvre-contrats-aides-Tome-2.pdf. Consulted: October 20, 2020.

French Court of Auditors (2020), *La filière EPR*. Available at: www.ccomptes.fr/fr/publications/la-filiere-epr. Consulted: February 21, 2022.

French Court of Auditors (2022a), *La formation en alternance*. June 23, 2022. Available at: www.ccomptes.fr/fr/publications/la-formation-en-alternance. Consulted: July 8, 2022.

French Court of Auditors (2022b), *Les acteurs public face à la crise: Une réactivité certaine, des fragilités strcturelles accentuées*, 2022 Annual Report, February 2022. Available at: www.ccomptes.fr/fr/publications/le-rapport-public-annuel-2022. Consulted: February 17, 2022.

French Government (2017a), *Annexe au projet de loi de finances pour 2018, Grand plan d'investissement*. Available at: www.budget.gouv.fr/sites/performance_publique/files/farandole/ressources/2018/pap/pdf/jaunes/Jaune2018_grand_plan_investissement.pdf. Consulted: July 18, 2022.

French Government (2017b), *Le grand plan d'investissement, 2018–2022*. Available at: www.gouvernement.fr/action/le-grand-plan-d-investissement-2018-2022. Consulted: October 2, 2020.

French Government (2018), *Un an d'action pour libérer, protéger, et unir les Français*. Available at: www.gouvernement.fr/un-an-d-action-pour-liberer-proteger-et-unir-les-francais. Consulted: September 12, 2020.

French Government (2019), *Document de cadrage en vue de la négociation de la convention d'assurance chômage*. Available at: www.actuel-rh.fr/sites/default/files/article-files/document_de_cadrage.pdf. Consulted: February 22, 2022.

French Government (2020a), *#1jeune1solution: Au sortir de la crise de la Covid-19, accompagner les 16–25 ans pour construire leur avenir*, July 23, 2020. Available at: https://solidarites-sante.gouv.fr/IMG/pdf/plan_jeunes_dossier_de_presse.pdf. Consulted: February 27, 2022.

French Government (2020b), *Projet de loi n° 2623 instituant un système universel de retraite*, January 24, 2020. Available at: www.assemblee-nationale.fr/dyn/15/textes/l15b2623_projet-loi. Consulted: February 22, 2022.

French Government (2020c), *France Relance*, September 3, 2020. Available at: www.economie.gouv.fr/files/files/directions_services/plan-de-relance/annexe-fiche-mesures.pdf. Consulted: September 9, 2020.

French Government (2020d), *Le plan de soutien à l'aéronautique: Pour une industrie verte et compétitive*, Dossier de presse, June 9, 2020. Available at: https://minefi.hosting.augure.com/Augure_Minefi/r/ContenuEnLigne/Download?id=94C9F4D9-0CB4-4D85-9026-7801E5E7F1E7&filename=2196%20

DP%20-%20Plan%20de%20soutien%20à%20l%27aéronautique.pdf. Consulted: July 22, 2022.

French Government (2020e), *Le plan de soutien à l'automobile: Pour une industrie verte et compétitive*, Dossier de Presse, May 26, 2020. Available at: www.economie.gouv.fr/plan-soutien-filiere-automobile. Consulted: February 26, 2022.

French Government (2021), *Une indemnité inflation pour protéger le pouvoir d'achat des Français face à la hausse des prix*, November 3, 2021. Available at: www.gouvernement.fr/actualite/une-indemnite-inflation-pour-proteger-le-pouvoir-d-achat-des-francais-face-a-la-hausse-des-prix. Consulted: February 28, 2022.

French Government (2022a), *Plan de résilience économique et sociale: Face à l'urgence, l'Etat se mobilise*, Dossier de presse, March 16, 2022. Available at: www.gouvernement.fr/upload/media/default/0001/01/2022_03_dossier_de_presse_-_plan_de_resilience_economique_et_sociale_-_16.03.2022.pdf. Consulted: July 22, 2022.

French Government (2022b), *Plan relance tourisme*. Available at: www.plan-tourisme.fr/. Consulted: February 28, 2022.

French Government (2022c), *Présentation du Haut-Commissariat au Plan*. Available at: www.gouvernement.fr/haut-commissariat-au-plan/presentation. Consulted: February 28, 2022.

French Government (2022d), *Fonds de solidarité: Echelle Nationale*. Available at: https://aides-entreprises.data.gouv.fr/fds/. Consulted: July 7, 2022.

French Ministry of Culture (2021), *Plan de relance livre: Aide à la modernisation des librairies 2021*. Available at: www.culture.gouv.fr/Aides-demarches/Appels-a-projets/Tous-les-appels-a-projets-France-Relance/Plan-de-relance-livre-aide-a-la-modernisation-des-librairies-20212. Consulted: February 28, 2022.

French Ministry of Environmental Transition (2020), *Fiscalité des énergies*, January 28, 2020. Available at: www.ecologie.gouv.fr/fiscalite-des-energies. Consulted: October 2, 2020.

French Ministry of Environmental Transition (2021a), *Le chèque énergie: L'Etat accompagne les ménages à revenus modestes pour payer leurs factures d'énergie*. Available at: https://chequeenergie.gouv.fr/. Consulted: February 28, 2022.

French Ministry of Environmental Transition (2021b), *Dossier de presse - Loi Climat et Résilience: Décryptage de la loi promulguée et publiée au journal officiel le 24 août 2021*. Available at: www.ecologie.gouv.fr/dossier-presse-loi-climat-et-resilience. Consulted: July 22, 2022.

French Ministry of Health and Solidarity (2020), *Ségur de la santé: Les conclusions*. Available at: https://solidarites-sante.gouv.fr/systeme-de-sante-et-medico-social/segur-de-la-sante-les-conclusions/. Consulted: October 31, 2020.

French Ministry of Industry (2004), L'effort français de recherche et développement (R&D).

French Ministry of Labor, Employment, and Integration (2022), *Les chiffres de l'apprentissage en 2021: Des emplois pour les jeunes, des compétences pour les entreprises*, February 2022. Available at: https://travail-emploi.gouv.fr/IMG/pdf/chiffres-apprentissage-2021.pdf?TSPD_101_R0=087dc22938ab200041f54271b2027c2550471bbbf1e138fc73b09c5e3e32e6cc91b0c034e621c28c0

89d31a2c514300065f5dc5c94bb5e392bc3d44b74d9303c293cc4c89db552 9e383afcd9344cbd682a48ef9827c6428cef9ac110e90eaa66. Consulted: July 22, 2022.

French Ministry of Labor, Employment, and Social Integration (2020), *Dossier de presse - Plan #1JEUNE1SOLUTION*, July 23, 2020. Available at: https://travail-emploi.gouv.fr/actualites/presse/dossiers-de-presse/dp-1jeune1solution? TSPD_101_R0=087dc22938ab200087fb15f206d431994821ef537bc81c4 2df1d6aa3439e6fbeef516f254ff9d8f708bf098d151430003ba68eb31b7360 5c3d892406894db982f961b03671c6e9c465a26d321eb3101f0807b6d82f 6c7f7f2e76fbf758ca537d. Consulted: July 22, 2022.

French Ministry of Labor, Full Employment, and Integration (2021), "Quel est l'objectif du dispositif d'activité partielle de longue durée?" *Questions – réponses "Activité partielle de longue durée (APLD),"* November 10, 2022. Available at: https://travail-emploi.gouv.fr/emploi-et-insertion/accompagne ment-des-mutations-economiques/activite-partielle-chomage-partiel/faq-apld#objectif. Consulted: December 10, 2022.

French Ministry of Solidarity and Health (2021), *Adoption en Conseil des ministres d'un projet d'ordonnance relatif à la mise en œuvre de la nouvelle 5ème branche autonomie*, December 1, 2021. Available at: https://solidarites-sante.gouv .fr/actualites/presse/communiques-de-presse/article/adoption-en-conseil-des-ministres-d-un-projet-d-ordonnance-relatif-a-la-mise-en. Consulted: February 27, 2022.

French Ministry of the Economy and Finance (2012), R*apport relatif à la mise en oeuvre et au suivi des investissements d'avenir.* Annexe au projet de loi de finances pour 2012, Paris: French Government. Available at: www.budget .gouv.fr/sites/performance_publique/files/farandole/ressources/2013/pap/pdf/ Jaune2013_investissements_avenir.pdf. Consulted: February 26, 2022.

French Ministry of the Economy and Finance (2017), *Projet de loi de finances: Les moyens de l'action 2018*, September 27, 2017. Available at: www.economie .gouv.fr/files/files/PLF2018/DP_PLF_2018.pdf. Consulted: October 2, 2020.

French Ministry of the Economy and Finance (2020), *La taxe d'habitation: Comment ça marche?* November 30, 2020. Available at: www.economie .gouv.fr/particuliers/taxe-habitation#:~:text=Pour%2080%20%25%20 des%20foyers%20fiscaux,puis%20de%2065%20%25%20en%202022. Consulted: January 19, 2021.

French Ministry of the Economy and Finance (2021a), *Bilan de l'exécution du plan de relance à la fin 2020*, January 21, 2021. Available at: www.economie .gouv.fr/plan-de-relance/bilan-execution-plan-relance-fin-2020. Consulted: February 8, 2021.

French Ministry of the Economy and Finance (2021b), *Entreprises en difficultés: Lancement du fonds de transition de 3 milliards d'euros*, September 27, 2021. Available at: www.economie.gouv.fr/covid19-soutien-entreprises/entreprises-difficultes-lancement-fonds-transition. Consulted: February 28, 2022.

French Ministry of the Economy and Finance (2022), *Prêt Garanti par l'Etat: Situation au 31 août 2022.* Available at: www.economie.gouv.fr/files/files/ directions_services/covid19-soutien-entreprises/PGE_20220831.pdf?v= 1669368415. Consulted: December 6, 2022.

French Ministry of the Interior (2017a), *Résultats des élections législatives 2017*. Available at: www.interieur.gouv.fr/Elections/Les-resultats/Legislatives/ elecresult__legislatives-2017/(path)/legislatives-2017//FE.html. Consulted: July 2, 2022.

French Ministry of the Interior (2017b), *Résultats de l'élection présidentielle 2017*. Available at: www.interieur.gouv.fr/Elections/Les-resultats/Presidentielles/ elecresult__presidentielle-2017/(path)/presidentielle-2017/FE.html. Consulted: July 2, 2022.

French Ministry of the Interior (2022a), *Elections législatives 2022*. Available at: www.resultats-elections.interieur.gouv.fr/legislatives-2022/FE.html. Consulted: July 2, 2022.

French Ministry of the Interior (2022b), *Résultats de l'élection présidentielle 2022*. Available at: https://mobile.interieur.gouv.fr/Elections/Les-resultats/ Presidentielles/elecresult__presidentielle-2022/(path)/presidentielle-2022/ FE.html. Consulted: July 2, 2022.

French National Assembly (2021), *Projet de loi n° 3875 portant lutte contre le dérèglement climatique et renforcement de la résilience face à ses effets*. Available at: www.assemblee-nationale.fr/dyn/15/textes/l15b3875_projet-loi. Consulted: February 20, 2022.

French National Council of Policies to Fight Poverty and Exclusion (2010), *L'ouverture du RSA aux jeunes de moins de 25 ans: Une mesure d'équité, un soutien aux jeunes actifs*, August 27, 2010. Available at: www.cnle.gouv.fr/l-ouverture-du-rsa-aux-jeunes-de.html. Consulted: February 9, 2021.

French Presidency (2009), *Pacte automobile: Dossier de presse*, February 9, 2009. Available at: www.pfa-auto.fr/wp-content/uploads/2016/02/Pacte-Automobile-2009.pdf. Consulted: January 7, 2021.

French Presidency (2010), *Conclusion des Etats Généraux de l'Industrie*, Dossier de Presse, Marignane, France, March 4, 2010. Available at: www.yumpu.com/ fr/document/read/30925341/conclusion-des-etats-generaux-de-lindustrie. Consulted: January 19, 2021.

French Presidency (2021), *France 2030: La France de 2030 se prépare aujourd'hui!* Available at: www.elysee.fr/emmanuel-macron/france2030. Consulted: July 18, 2022.

French Prime Minister's Office (2022), "Prix des carburants: Remise de 15 à 18 centimes par litre à partir du 1er avril," *Service-publique.fr*, March 29, 2022.

French Senate (2006), *Recherche et innovation en France: Surmonter nos handicaps au service de la croissance*. Available at: www.senat.fr/rap/r07-392/r07-3924 .html. Consulted: January 19, 2021.

French Senate (2021), *The Legislative Process*. Available at: www.senat.fr/lng/en/ the_senates_role/the_legislative_process.html. Consulted: March 15, 2021.

French Senate Commission on Social Regimes and Retirement (2010), *Projet de loi de finances pour 2020: Régimes sociaux et retraites*. Available at: www.senat .fr/rap/a09-103-3/a09-103-39.html. Consulted: January 7, 2021.

French Senate Finance Commission (2021), *Comment réussir la sortie des prêts garantis par l'État (PGE)?* Rapport d'information n° 583 (2020–2021), May 12, 2021. Available at: www.senat.fr/rap/r20-583/r20-583_mono.html#toc50. Consulted: February 26, 2022.

French State Council (2021), *Assurance-chômage: Les nouvelles règles de calcul de l'allocation sont suspendues*, June 22, 2021. Available at: www.conseil-etat.fr/actualites/assurance-chomage-les-nouvelles-regles-de-calcul-de-l-allocation-sont-suspendues. Consulted: February 19, 2022.

French Treasury (2021), "Bruno Le Maire et Franck Riester annoncent la prolongation d'un an de l'abaissement exceptionnel du seuil de contrôle des investissements étrangers en France de 25 à 10%," November 30, 2021. Available at: www.tresor.economie.gouv.fr/Articles/2021/11/30/bruno-le-maire-et-franck-riester-annoncent-la-prolongation-d-un-an-de-l-abaissement-exceptionnel-du-seuil-de-controle-des-investissements-etrangers-en-france-de-25-a-10. Consulted: February 23, 2022.

Friedberg, E. (2006), "Le CPE est mort: et maintenant?" *French Politics, Culture, and Society*, 24(3): 89–95.

Friedman, T. (1999), *The Lexus and the Olive Tree*, New York: Farrar, Straus and Giroux.

Fukuyama, F. (1992), *The End of History and the Last Man*, New York: Free Press.

Fulmer, R. (2010), "The Paradox of the Welfare State," Foundation for Economic Education, Wednesday 22. Available at: https://fee.org/articles/the-paradox-of-the-welfare-state/. Consulted: January 31, 2022.

Gamble, A. (1994), *The Free Economy and the Strong State: The Politics of Thatcherism*, Houndmills, UK: Macmillan.

Gao, B. (2001), *Japan's Economic Dilemma: The Institutional Origins of Prosperity and Stagnation*, Cambridge: Cambridge University Press.

Garritzmann, J., S. Hausermann, et al., Eds. (2022), *The World Politics of Social Investment*, two volumes. Oxford: Oxford University Press.

Geay, B. (2009), *La protestation étudiante: Le mouvement du printemps 2006*, Paris: Broché.

Germain, J.-M. (2015), *Tout avait si bien commencé: Journal d'un 'frondeur'*, Paris: Les Editions Ouvrières.

Gerschenkron, A. (1962), *Economic Backwardness in Historical Perspective*, Cambridge, MA: Harvard University Press.

Giesbert, F.-O. (2014), *Jacques Chirac, une vie*, Paris: Flammarion.

Giroux, B. (2013), *Du CNPF au MEDEF: Confidences d'un apparatchik*, Paris: l'Archipel.

Giscard d'Estaing, V. (1976), *Démocratie française*, Paris: Fayard.

Glennerster, H. (2010), "The Sustainability of Western Welfare States," in Francis Castles, Stephan Leibfried et al., Eds., *The Oxford Handbook of the Welfare State*, Oxford: 689–702.

Gordon, P. and S. Meunier (2001), *The French Challenge: Adapting to Globalization*, Washington, DC: Brookings Institution.

Greciano, P.-A. (2008), "Economie: Une année mitigée," in Frédéric Charillon, Pierre-Alain Greciano et al., Eds., *La France en 2007: Chronique politique, économique, et sociale*, Paris: La Documentation Française: 67–88.

Greciano, P.-A. (2010), "Economie: Vers l'éclaircie?" in Frédéric Charillon, Pierre-Alain Greciano et al., Eds., *La France en 2009: Chronique politique, économique, et sociale*, Paris: La Documentation Française: 67–92.

Griotteray, A. (1994), *Mieux privatiser: Evolution du secteur public en France et en Europe–Bilan et perspectives*, Paris: La Documentation Française.

Griotteray, A. (1997), *La droite molle: Chronique d'une déroute méritée*, Paris: Plon.

Groux, G. and R. Mouriaux (1990), "Le cas français," in Geneviève Bibes and René Mouriaux, Eds., *Les syndicats européens à l'épreuve*, Paris: Fondation Nationale des Sciences Politiques: 49–68.

Guené, C. (2012), *Rapport d'information sur les conséquences pour les collectivités territoriales, l'État, et les entreprises de la suppression de la taxe professionnelle et de son remplacement par la contribution économique territoriale*, French Senate Report, No. 611, June 26, 2012. Available at: www.senat.fr/rap/r11-611/r11-6111.pdf. Consulted: January 14, 2021.

Guette-Khiter, C. (2020), "La détention par les non-résidents des actions des sociétés françaises du CAC 40 à fin 2019 et début 2020," *Le Bulletin de la Banque de France*, 231(4): 1–9.

Guyon, Y., Ed. (1995), *Les privatisations en France, en Allemagne, en Grande-Bretagne, et en Italie*, Paris: La Documentation Française.

Hacker, J. (2011), "The Institutional Foundations of Middle-Class Democracy," *Policy Network*, May 6, 2011.

Hacker, J. and P. Pierson (2020), *Let Them Eat Tweets: How the Right Rules in an Age of Extreme Inequality*, New York: W. W. Norton & Company.

Hainsworth, P. (1998), "The Return of the Left: The 1997 French Parliamentary Election," *Parliamentary Affairs*, 51(1): 71–83.

Hall, P. (1986), *Governing the Economy: The Politics of State Intervention in Britain and France*, Oxford: Oxford University Press.

Hall, P. (1990), "The State and the Market," in Peter Hall, Jack Hayward et al., Eds., *Developments in French Politics 2*, London: Macmillan: 172–188.

Hall, P. (1992), "The Movement from Keynesianism to Monetarism: Institutional Analysis and British Economic Policy in the 1970s," in Sven Steinmo, Kathleen Thelen et al., Eds., *Structuring Politics: Historical Institutionalism in Comparative Analysis*, Cambridge: Cambridge University Press: 90–113.

Hall, P. and D. Soskice, Eds. (2001), *Varieties of Capitalism: The Institutional Foundations of Comparative Advantage*, Oxford: Oxford University Press.

Hamon, H. and P. Rotman (1982), *La deuxième gauche: Histoire intellectuelle et politique de la CFDT*, Paris: Ramsay.

Hassenteufel, P. (1997), *Les médecins face à l'Etat: Une comparaison internationale*, Paris: Presses de la Fondation Nationale des Sciences Politiques.

Häusermann, S. (2010), *The Politics of Welfare State Reform in Continental Europe: Modernization in Hard Times*, Cambridge: Cambridge University Press.

Hay, C. (2001), "The 'Crisis' of Keynesianism and the Rise of Neoliberalism in Britain: An Institutionalist Approach," in John Campbell and Ove Pedersen, Eds., *The Rise of Neoliberalism and Institutional Analysis*, Princeton, NJ: Princeton University Press: 193–218.

Hemerijck, A. (2013), *Changing Welfare States*, Oxford: Oxford University Press.

Hemerijck, A., Ed. (2017), *The Uses of Social Investment*, Oxford: Oxford University Press.

Hemerijck, A. and M. Vail (2006), "The Forgotten Center: State Activism and Corporatist Adjustment in Holland and Germany," in Jonah Levy, Ed., *The*

State after Statism: New State Activities in the Age of Liberalization, Cambridge, MA: Harvard University Press: 57–92.

Hinrichs, K. (2000), "Elephants on the Move: Patterns of Public Pension Reform in OECD Countries," *European Review*, 8(3): 353–378.

Hinrichs, K. (2010), "A Social Insurance State Whithers Away: Welfare State Reforms in Germany – Or: Attempts to Turn Around in a Cul-de-Sac," in Bruno Palier, Ed., *A Long Goodbye to Bismarck? The Politics of Welfare Reform in Continental Europe*, Oxford: Oxford University Press: 45–72.

Hoffmann, S., Ed. (1963), *In Search of France: The Economy, Society, and Political System in the Twentieth Century*, Cambridge, MA: Harvard University Press.

Hoffmann, S. (1978), *France: Decline or Renewal?* New York: Harper and Row.

Horn, R. V. and P. Mirowski (2009), "The Rise of the Chicago School of Economics and the Birth of Neoliberalism," in Philip Mirowski and Dieter Plehwe, Eds., *The Road from Mont Pèlerin*, Cambridge, MA: Harvard University Press: 139–178.

Horsman, M. and A. Marshall (1994), *After the Nation-State: Citizens, Tribalism, and the New World Disorder*, London: HarperCollins.

Howell, C. (1992a), *Regulating Labor: The State and Industrial Relations Reform in Postwar France*, Princeton, NJ: Princeton University Press.

Howell, C. (1992b), "The Dilemmas of Post-Fordism: Socialists, Flexibility, and Labor Market Deregulation in France," *Politics and Society*, 20(1): 71–99.

Howell, C. (1996), "French Socialism and the Transformation of Industrial Relations since 1981," in Anthony Daley, Ed., *The Mitterrand Era: Policy Alternatives and Political Mobilization in France*, New York: New York University Press: 141–169.

Howell, C. (2006), "The State and the Reconstruction of Industrial Relations after Fordism: Britain and France Compared," in Jonah Levy, Ed., *The State after Statism: New State Activities in the Age of Liberalization*, Cambridge, MA: Harvard University Press: 139–184.

Howell, C. (2008), "Between State and Market: Crisis and Transformation in French Industrial Relations," in Alistair Cole, Patrick Le Galès et al., Eds., *Developments in French Politics 4*, London: Palgrave: 209–226.

Howell, C. (2009), "The Transformation of French Industrial Relations: Labor Representation and the State in a Post-*Dirigiste* Era," *Politics and Society*, 37(2): 229–256.

Howell, C. (2018), "The French Road to Neoliberalism," *Catalyst*, 2(3), Fall 2018.

Huber, E. and J. Stephens (1998), "Internationalization and the Social Democratic Model: Crisis and Future Prospects," *Comparative Political Studies*, 31(3): 353–398.

Huber, E. and J. Stephens (2001), *Development and Crisis of the Welfare State: Parties and Policies in Global Markets*, Chicago: University of Chicago Press.

Huber, J. (1992), "Restrictive Legislative Procedures in France and the United States," *American Political Science Review*, 86(3): 675–687.

Huber, J. (1996), *Rationalizing Parliament: Legislative Institutions and Party Politics in France*, Cambridge: Cambridge University Press.

Huo, J. and J. Stephens (2015), "From Industrial Corporatism to the Social Investment State," in Stephan Leibfried, Evelyne Huber et al., Eds., *Oxford*

Handbook of Transformations of the State, Oxford: Oxford University Press: 410–425.

Huo, J., M. Nelson, et al. (2008), "Decommodification and Activation in Social Democratic Policy: Resolving the Paradox," *Journal of European Social Policy*, 18(1): 5–10.

IFOP (2010), *Regards croisés sur la mondialisation dans dix pays*, Institut Français d'Opinion Publique poll for *La Croix*. Available at: www.ifop.com/publication/regards-croises-sur-la-mondialisation-dans-dix-pays/. Consulted: March 12, 2019.

IFOP (2011), *Les valeurs des Français à 6 mois de l'élection présidentielle*, Institut Français d'Opinion Publique poll for *Europe 1/Paris Match*. Available at: www.ifop.com/publication/les-valeurs-des-francais-a-6-mois-de-lelection-presidentielle/. Consulted: March 12, 2019.

IFOP (2014), *1994–2006: Les Français et les propositions de 'smic jeunes'*, Institut Français d'Opinion Publique Collectors, No. 30. Available at: www.ifop.com/publication/ifop-collectors-n30-1994-2006-les-francais-et-les-propositions-de-smic-jeunes/. Consulted: June 2, 2019.

IFOP (2022), *Les Français et la suppression de la retraite à 65 du programme d'Emmanuel Macron*, IFOP Poll for the *Journal du Dimanche*, April 2022. Available at: www.ifop.com/publication/les-francais-et-la-suppression-de-la-retraite-a-65-ans-du-programme-demmanuel-macron/. Consulted: July 8, 2022.

ILO (2016), *Collective Bargaining Coverage Rate: Share of Employees Covered by One or More Collective Agreements (in Percent)*, Latest Year. Available at: https://ilostat.ilo.org/topics/collective-bargaining/. Data extracted: January 25, 2021.

ILO (2017), *Statistics on Union Membership*. Available at: https://ilostat.ilo.org/topics/union-membership/. Consulted: January 28, 2021.

ILO (2021), *Labour Income Distribution - ILO Modelled Estimates, November 2021 (%)*. Available at: www.ilo.org/shinyapps/bulkexplorer27/?lang=en&segment=indicator&id=LAP_2LID_QTL_RT_A. Data extracted: July 18, 2022.

IMF (2019), *General Government Gross Debt (Percent of GDP)*. Available at: www.imf.org/external/datamapper/GGXWDG_NGDP@WEO/FRA/DNK/DEU/NLD/SWE. Data extracted: February 6, 2019.

Immergut, E. (1992a), *Health Politics: Interests and Institutions in Western Europe*, Cambridge: Cambridge University Press.

Immergut, E. (1992b), "The Rules of the Game: The Logic of Health Policy-Making in France, Switzerland, and Sweden," in Sven Steinmo, Kathleen Thelen et al., Eds., *Structuring Politics: Historical Institutionalism in Comparative Analysis*, Cambridge: Cambridge University Press: 57–89.

Inglehart, R. and P. Norris (2019), *Cultural Backlash: Trump, Brexit, and Authoritarian Populism*, Cambridge: Cambridge University Press.

INSEE (1998), *L'économie française, Edition 1998–1999*, Paris: Institut National de la Statistique et des Etudes Economiques.

INSEE (2018), *Tableaux de l'économie française*, Institut National de la Statistique et des Etudes Economiques. Available at: www.insee.fr/fr/information/3361360. Consulted: February 8, 2021.

INSEE (2021a), *Flux d'investissements directs entre la France et l'étranger: Données annuelles de 2000 à 2020*, September 3, 2021. Available at: www.insee.fr/fr/statistiques/2381422. Consulted: March 17, 2022.

INSEE (2021b), En 2020, le déficit public s'élève à 9,2 % du PIB, la dette notifiée à 115,7 % du PIB, Institut National de la Statistique et des Etudes Economiques. Available at: www.insee.fr/fr/statistiques/5347882. Consulted: February 2, 2022.

INSEE (2021c), Dépenses et recettes publiques en % du PIB, données annuelles, Institut National de la Statistique et des Etudes Economiques. Available at: www.insee.fr/fr/statistiques/2381414#graphique-Donnes. Data extracted: April 20, 2021.

INSEE (2022a), *En 2021, le déficit public s'élève à 6,5 % du PIB, la dette notifiée à 112,9 % du PIB*, Institut National de la Statistique et des Etudes Economiques (INSEE), March 29, 2022. Available at: www.insee.fr/fr/statistiques/6324844. Consulted: March 30, 2022.

INSEE (2022b), "Le compte des administrations publiques en 2021," *INSEE Première*, No. 1903, May 31, 2022.

INSEE (2022c), "Les comptes de la nation en 2021," *INSEE Première*, No. 1904, May 31, 2022.

Istria, R. (2010), *L'Etat: Le grand naufrage*, Paris: Editions du Rocher.

Jabko, N. (2005), *Playing the Market: A Political Strategy for Uniting Europe*, Ithaca, NY: Cornell University Press.

Jacot, H. (2001/2), "La 'refondation sociale' n'est pas un long fleuve tranquille," *Mouvements*: 8–14.

Jarreau, P. (1997), *Chirac, la malédiction*, Paris: Stock.

Johanet, G. (1999), *Le plan d'action stratégique*, Paris: CNAM.

Johns Hopkins University of Medicine (2022), *The Race to Vaccinate the World*, Coronavirus Resource Center, July 2022. Available at: https://coronavirus.jhu.edu/vaccines/international#race-to-vaccine-world. Consulted: July 6, 2022.

Johnson, C. (1982), *MITI and the Japanese Miracle: The Growth of Industrial Policy*, Stanford, CA: Stanford University Press.

Jones Day (2020), *French Foreign Direct Investment Rules Set for Overhaul*, January 2020. Available at: www.jonesday.com/en/insights/2020/01/french-fdi-rules-set-for-overhaul. Consulted: November 27, 2020.

Journal du Net Editorial Board (2022), "APLD: Tout sur le chômage partiel de longue durée," *Journal du net*, January 25, 2022.

Julliard, J. and J.-C. Michéa (2014), *La gauche et le peuple*, Paris: Flammarion.

Karel, Y. (2019), "Les syndicats dans la roue des 'gilets jaunes'?" in Sylvain Bourneau, Ed., *'Gilets jaunes': Hypothèses sur un mouvement*, Paris: La Découverte, Analyse Opinion Critique (AOC) Cahier # 1: 101–106.

Katzenstein, P., Ed. (1978), *Between Power and Plenty: Foreign Economic Policies of Advanced Industrial States*, Madison, WI: University of Wisconsin Press.

Katzenstein, P. (1984), *Corporatism and Change: Austria, Switzerland, and the Politics of Industry*, Ithaca, NY: Cornell University Press.

Katzenstein, P. (1985), *Small States in World Markets: Industrial Policy in Europe*, Ithaca, NY: Cornell University Press.

Katzenstein, P. (1989), *Industry and Politics in West Germany: Toward the Third Republic*, Ithaca, NY: Cornell University Press.

Kaufmann, E. (2019), *White Shift: Populism, Immigration, and the Future of White Majorities*, New York, NY: Abrams Press.

Keating, M. and D. McCrone, Eds. (2015), *The Crisis of Social Democracy in Europe*, Edinburgh: Edinburgh University Press.

King, D. and S. Wood (1999), "The Political Economy of Neoliberalism: Britain and the United States in the 1980s," in Herbert Kitschelt, Peter Lange et al., Eds., *Continuity and Change in Contemporary Capitalism*, Cambridge: Cambridge University Press: 371–397.

Knapp, A. (1994), *Gaullism since de Gaulle*, Abingdon, UK: Routledge.

Kocka, J. (1981), "Class Formation, Interest Articulation, and Public Policy: The Origins of the German White-Collar Class in the Late Nineteenth and Early Twentieth Centuries," in Suzanne Berger, Ed., *Organizing Interests in Western Europe: Pluralism, Corporatism, and the Transformation of Politics*, Cambridge: Cambridge University Press: 63–82.

Kriesi, H. and T. Pappas, Eds. (2015), *European Populism in the Shadow of the Great Recession*, Colchester, UK: ECPR Studies Press.

Kuisel, R. (1981), *Capitalism and the State in Modern France: Renovation and Economic Management in the Twentieth Century*, Cambridge: Cambridge University Press.

Labbé, D. and M. Croisat (1992), *La fin des syndicats?* Paris: L'Harmattan.

Lachaise, A. (2022), "Chômage partiel: Evolutions de l'activité partielle 2022," *Juritravail*, February 28, 2022.

Lagneau-Ymonet, P. (2002), "Quand le patronat français impose sa refondation sociale," *Le Monde Diplomatique*, 583 (October): 22–23.

Lallement, M. and O. Méraux (2003), "Status and Contracts in Industrial Relations: La 'Refondation Sociale,' a New Bottle for an Old (French) Wine," *German Journal of Industrial Relations*, 10(3): 418–437.

Lamar, D. (2020), "Que reste-il des contrats aidés?" *Tout pour l'emploi*.

Landes, D. (1951), "French Business and the Businessman: A Social and Cultural Analysis," in Edward Earle, Ed., *Modern France: Problems of the Third and Fourth Republics*, Princeton, NJ: Princeton University Press: 334–353.

Landes, D. (1957), "Observations on France: Economy, Society, and Polity," *World Politics*, 9(3): 329–350.

Laot, L. (1997), "La réforme Juppé-Barrot de la Sécurite Sociale," in René Mouriaux, Ed., *L'année sociale 1996*, Paris: Editions Ouvrières: 135–151.

Levy, J. (1999a), "Vice into Virtue? Progressive Politics and Welfare Reform in Continental Europe," *Politics and Society*, 27(2): 239–273.

Levy, J. (1999b), *Tocqueville's Revenge: State, Society, and Economy in Contemporary France*, Cambridge, MA: Harvard University Press.

Levy, J. (2000), "France: Directing Adjustment?" in Fritz Scharpf and Vivien Schmidt, Eds., *Welfare and Work in the Open Economy: Diverse Responses to Common Challenges, Vol. II.*, Oxford: Oxford University Press: 308–350.

Levy, J. (2005a), "Economic Policy," in Alistair Cole, Patrick Le Galès et al., Eds., *Developments in French Politics 3*, London: Palgrave: 170–194.

Levy, J. (2005b), "Redeploying the French State: Liberalization and Social Policy in France," in Kathleen Thelen and Wolfgang Streeck, Eds., *Beyond Continuity: Explorations in the Dynamics of Advanced Political Economies*, Oxford: Oxford University Press: 103–126.

Levy, J. (2008), "From the *Dirigiste* State to the Social Anesthesia State: French Economic Policy in the *Longue Durée*," *Modern and Contemporary France*, 16(4): 417–435.

Levy, J. (2010), "Welfare Retrenchment," in Francis Castles, Stephan Leibfried et al., Eds., *Oxford Handbook of the Welfare State*, Oxford: Oxford University Press: 552–565.

Levy, J. (2013), "Directionless: French Economic Policy in the 21st Century," in John Zysman and Dan Breznitz, Eds., *The Third Globalization: Can Wealthy Nations Stay Rich in the Twenty-First Century?* Oxford: Oxford University Press: 323–349.

Levy, J. (2015), "The Transformation of the Statist Model," in Stephan Leibfried, Evelyne Huber et al., Eds., *The Oxford Handbook of Transformations of the State*, Oxford: Oxford University Press: 393–409.

Levy, J. (2017), "The Return of the State? France's Response to the Financial and Economic Crisis," *Comparative European Politics*, 15(4): 604–627.

Levy, J. and C. Skach (2008), "The Return to a Strong Presidency," in Alistair Cole, Patrick Le Galès et al., Eds., *Developments in French Politics 4*, London: Palgrave-Macmillan: 111–126.

Levy, J., M. Miura, et al. (2006), "Exiting *Etatisme*? New Directions in State Policy in France and Japan," in Jonah Levy, Ed., *The State after Statism: New State Activities in the Age of Globalization and Liberalization*, Cambridge, MA: Harvard University Press: 92–146.

Lindbeck, A. and D. Snower (1988), *The Insider-Outsider Theory of Unemployment*, Cambridge, MA: MIT Press.

Lindbeck, A., P. Molander, et al. (1994), *Turning Sweden Around*, Cambridge, MA: MIT University Press.

Lipietz, A. (1984), *L'audace ou l'enlisement: Sur les politiques économiques de la gauche*, Paris: La Découverte.

Lisbon European Council (2000), *Presidency Conclusions, 23 and 24 March 2000*, Available at: http://aei.pitt.edu/43340/. Consulted: January 31, 2022.

Lithuanian Free Market Institute (2018), *Employment Flexibility Index, 2018: EU and OECD Countries*. Available at: https://en.llri.lt/wp-content/uploads/2017/12/Employment-Flexibility-Index-2018_-LFMI.pdf. Data extracted: March 4, 2019.

Lorriaux, A. (2018), "Ce que révèlent les sondages sur l'identité des 'gilets jaunes'," *Slate.fr*, December 4, 2018.

Lundberg, E. (1986), "The Rise and Fall of the Swedish Model," *Journal of Economic Literature*, 23(1): 1–36.

Lussault, M. (2019), "La condition périurbaine," in Sylvain Bourneau, Ed., *'Gilets jaunes': Hypothèses sur un mouvement*, Paris: La Découverte, Analyse Opinion Critique (AOC) Cahier #1: 171–179.

Macron, E. (2016), *Révolution*, Paris: XO Editions.

Macron, E. (2017), *Programme En Marche! Election présidentielle - 23 avril et 7 mai 2017*. Available at: https://en-marche.fr/emmanuel-macron/le-programme. Consulted: September 12, 2020.

Macron, E. (2018), *Faire de cette colère une chance*, Speech delivered December 10, 2018. Available at: www.elysee.fr/emmanuel-macron/2018/12/10/adresse-du-president-de-la-republique-du-lundi-10-decembre-2018. Consulted: September 20, 2020.

Macron, E. (2019), *Lettre aux Français,* January 13, 2019. Available at: www .elysee.fr/emmanuel-macron/2019/01/13/lettre-aux-francais.   Consulted: October 28, 2020.

Macron, E. (2020), *Adresse aux Français - 12 mars 2020.* Available at: www .elysee.fr/emmanuel-macron/2020/03/12/adresse-aux-francais.   Consulted: April 6, 2022.

Macron, E. (2021), *Adresse aux Français - 12 juillet 2021.* Available at: www .elysee.fr/emmanuel-macron/2021/07/12/adresse-aux-francais-12-juillet-2021. Consulted: March 3, 2022.

Macron, E. (2022), *Emmanuel Macron avec vous: Election présidentielle - 10 et 24 avril 2022.* Available at: https://avecvous.fr/wp-content/uploads/2022/03/ Emmanuel-Macron-Avec-Vous-24-pages.pdf. Consulted: July 18, 2022.

Madsen, P. K. (2004), "The Danish Model of 'Flexicurity': Experiences and Lessons," *European Review of Labour and Research,* 10(2): 187–207.

Marian, M. (1993), "Balladur: Un homme de bonne volonté," *Esprit,* 195: 163–165.

Marthaler, S. (2005), "The French Referendum on Ratification of the EU Constitutional Treaty, 29 May 2005," *Representation,* 41(3): 228–236.

Massé, P. (1965), *Le plan ou l'anti-hasard,* Paris: Gallimard.

Massoc, E. and N. Jabko (2012), "French Capitalism under Stress: How Nicolas Sarkozy Rescued the Banks," *Review of International Political Economy,* 19(4): 562–585.

Masson, J.-R. (2020), "Le soutien au chômage partiel de crise en France et en Europe," *Metis,* June 8, 2020.

Mathieu, F. (1994), "Les bénéficiaires du RMI au 31 décembre 1993," *Recherches et prévisions,* No. 38: 101–106.

Maus, D., Ed. (1995), "Election présidentielle des 23 avril et 7 mai 1995," *Notes et études documentaires,* No. 5025, Paris: La Documentation Française.

McLauchlin, A. (2005), "Will the 'Bolkestein Directive' Really Kill Europe's Social Model?" *Politico,* February 16, 2005.

Mercier, A. (2018), "'Gilets jaunes' contre Emmanuel Macron, aux racines de l'incommunication," *The Conversation,* December 3, 2018.

Michon, S. (2008), *Les étudiants et le contrat première embauche,* Paris: L'Harmattan.

Miura, M. (2002), "Playing without a Net: Employment Maintenance Policy and the Underdevelopment of the Social Safety Net," Paper presented to the Annual Meeting of the American Political Science Association, Boston, MA, August 29–September 1, 2002.

Miura, M. (2012), *Welfare through Work: Conservative Ideas, Partisan Dynamics, and Social Protection in Japan,* Ithaca, NY: Cornell University Press.

Monnier, J.-M. (2009), "Politique fiscale: Une mise en perspective," in Elisabeth Lau, Ed., *L'Etat de la France, Edition 2009–2010,* Paris: La Découverte: 182–192.

Montbrial, T. (2000), *Pour combattre les pensées uniques,* Paris: Flammarion.

Moran, M. (2007), *The British Regulatory State: High Modernism and Hyper-Innovation,* Oxford: Oxford University Press.

Morel, N., B. Palier, et al., Eds. (2012), *Towards a Social Investment Welfare State? Ideas, Policies, and Challenges,* Bristol, UK: Policy Press.

Mouriaux, R., Ed. (1997), *L'année sociale 1996*, Paris: Editions Ouvrières.

Murillo, M. V. (2009), *Political Competition, Partisanship, and Policy Making in Latin American Public Utilities*, Cambridge: Cambridge University Press.

Murray, C. (1984), *Losing Ground: American Social Policy, 1950–1980*, New York: Basic Books.

Nay, C. (1994), *Le dauphin et le régent*, Paris: Editions Grasset et Fasquelle.

Nay, C. (2012), *L'impétueux: Tourments, tourmentes, crises, et tempêtes*, Paris: Bernard Grasset.

Noiriel, G. (2019), *Les gilets jaunes à la lumière de l'histoire*, Paris: Le Monde.

Northcutt, G. (1998), "Juppé's Two-Year Descent into Hell: The Re-emergence of the Left in France in the 1997 Legislative Elections," *Contemporary French Civilization*, 22(1): 89–105.

OECD (1998), *Economic Survey: Netherlands, 1997–1998*, Paris: OECD.

OECD (2008), *Growing Unequal? Income Distribution and Poverty in OECD Countries*, Paris: OECD.

OECD (2009), *Economic Survey of France, 2009*, Paris: OECD.

OECD (2017a), *Expected Number of Years in Retirement by Sex*. Available at: https://stats.oecd.org/index.aspx?queryid=54758. Data extracted: January 24, 2019.

OECD (2017b), *General Government Debt as Percentage of GDP, 1995–2015*. Available at: https://data.oecd.org/gga/general-government-debt.htm. Data extracted: June 13, 2019.

OECD (2017c), *Regulation in Network Sectors (Energy, Transport, and Communications)*. Available at: www.oecd.org/economy/reform/indicators-of-product-market-regulation/. Data extracted: January 25, 2021.

OECD (2018a), *Indicators of Product Market Regulation (PMR): Country Fiches*. Available at: www.oecd.org/economy/reform/indicators-of-product-market-regulation/. Data extracted: January 25, 2021.

OECD (2018b), *OECD Data: Harmonized Unemployment Rate, Total % of Labour Force, 1985–2017*. Available at: https://data.oecd.org/unemp/harmonised-unemployment-rate-hur.htm. Data extracted: January 21, 2021.

OECD (2018c), *OECD Data: Employment Rate, Total % of Working Age Population, 2003–2017*. Available at: https://data.oecd.org/emp/employment-rate.htm. Data extracted: January 21, 2019.

OECD (2019a), *OECD Data, Pension Spending*. Available at: https://data.oecd.org/socialexp/pension-spending.htm. Consulted: January 3, 2021.

OECD (2019b), *Public Spending on Labour Markets*. Available at: https://data.oecd.org/socialexp/public-spending-on-labour-markets.htm. Consulted: January 18, 2019.

OECD (2019c), *Social Expenditure*. Available at: https://stats.oecd.org/Index.aspx?DataSetCode=SOCX_AGG#. Data extracted: January 24, 2019.

OECD (2019d), *Tax Revenue*. Available at: https://data.oecd.org/tax/tax-revenue.htm. Data extracted: January 20, 2019.

OECD (2019e), *Strictness of Employment Protection: Temporary Contracts*. Available at: https://stats.oecd.org/Index.aspx?DataSetCode=EPL_T. Data extracted: July 18, 2022.

OECD (2019f), *General Government Deficit*. Available at: https://data.oecd.org/gga/general-government-deficit.htm. Data extracted: January 20, 2019.

OECD (2019g), *OECD Data: Part-Time Employment Rate.* Available at: https://data
.oecd.org/emp/part-time-employment-rate.htm. Data extracted: March 15, 2021.

OECD (2019h), *Strictness of Employment Protection: Individual and Collective
Dismissals (Regular Contracts).* Available at: https://stats.oecd.org/Index
.aspx?DataSetCode=EPL_OV#. Data extracted: February 8, 2022.

OECD (2020a), *Gross Domestic Spending on R&D, Total % of GDP, 1990–2020.*
Available at: https://data.oecd.org/rd/gross-domestic-spending-on-r-d.htm.
Data extracted: February 8, 2022.

OECD (2020b), *Poverty Rate Total / 0-17 year-olds / 66 year-olds or more, Ratio,
2020 or latest available.* Available at: https://data.oecd.org/inequality/poverty-
rate.htm. Data extracted: January 27, 2022.

OECD (2021a), *Poverty Rate.* Available at: https://data.oecd.org/inequality/
poverty-rate.htm. Data extracted: January 27, 2022.

OECD (2021b), *Strictness of Activation Requirements, 2020.* Available at: https://stats
.oecd.org/Index.aspx?DataSetCode=SBE. Data extracted: January 24, 2021.

OECD (2021c), *Economic Outlook, No. 111 - June 2022.* Available at: https://stats
.oecd.org/index.aspx?DataSetCode=EO#. Consulted: July 7, 2022.

OECD (2021d), *General Government Spending, Total, % of GDP, 1995–2017.*
Available at: https://data.oecd.org/gga/general-government-spending.htm.
Data extracted: January 22, 2021.

OECD (2021e), *Tax Revenue: Total, % of GDP, 2007–2012.* Available at: https://
data.oecd.org/tax/tax-revenue.htm. Data extracted: January 7, 2021.

OECD (2021f), *Minimum Relative to Average Wages of Full-Time Workers.* Available
at: https://stats.oecd.org/Index.aspx?DataSetCode=MIN2AVE. Data extracted:
September 3, 2021.

OECD (2021g), *GDP Per Hour Worked, 1970–2020.* Available at: https://data
.oecd.org/lprdty/gdp-per-hour-worked.htm. Consulted: February 14, 2022.

OECD (2022), *Income Inequality.* Available at: https://data.oecd.org/inequality/
income-inequality.htm. Data extracted: January 27, 2022.

Offe, C. (1981), "The Attribution of Public Status to Interest Groups:
Observations on the West German Case," in Suzanne Berger, Ed., *Organizing
Interests in Western Europe: Pluralism, Corporatism, and the Transformation of
Politics*, Cambridge: Cambridge University Press: 123–158.

Offe, C. (1985), *Disorganized Capitalism: Contemporary Transformations of Work
and Politics*, Cambridge, MA: MIT Press.

OpinionWay-Kéa Partners (2022), *Baromètre quotidien pour "Les Echos" et
Radio classique.* Available at: www.lesechos.fr/elections/sondages/sondage-
presidentielle-2022-les-resultats-de-presitrack-1357211. Consulted: March
25, 2022.

Ornston, D. (2012), *When Small States Make Big Leaps: Institutional Innovation
and High-Tech Competition in Western Europe*, Ithaca, NY: Cornell University
Press.

Ottenheimer, G. (1996), *Le fiasco*, Paris: Albin Michel.

Overtveldt, J. V. (2009), *The Chicago School: How the University of Chicago
Assembled the Thinkers Who Revolutionized Economics and Business*, Evanston,
IL: Agate.

Palier, B. (2000), "Defrosting the French Welfare State," *West European Politics*,
23(2): 113–136.

Palier, B. (2002), *Gouverner la Sécurité Sociale*, Paris: Fondation Nationale des Sciences Politiques.

Palier, B. (2003a), *La réforme des retraites*, Paris: Presses Universitaires de France (PUF). Collection "Que sais-je?" No. 3667.

Palier, B. (2003b), "La réforme des retraites," in Sarah Netter and Serge Cordellier, Eds., *L'Etat de la France*, Paris: La Découverte: 316–319.

Palier, B., Ed. (2010a), *A Long Goodbye to Bismarck? The Politics of Welfare Reform in Continental Europe*, Amsterdam: Amsterdam University Press.

Palier, B. (2010b), "The Dualizations of the French Welfare System," in Bruno Palier, Ed., *A Long Goodbye to Bismarck? The Politics of Welfare Reform in Continental Europe*, Amsterdam: Amsterdam University Press: 73–99.

Palier, B. and G. Bonoli (2007), "When Past Reforms Open New Opportunities: Comparing Old-Age Insurance Reforms in Bismarckian Welfare Systems," *Social Policy and Administration*, 41(6): 555–473.

Palier, B. and K. Thelen (2010), "Institutionalizing Dualism: Complementarities and Change in France and Germany," *Politics and Society*, 38(1): 119–148.

Palme, B. (2014), *100 ans d'erreurs de la gauche française: Va-t-elle recommencer?* Paris: La Boîte à Pandore.

Palme, J. and I. Wennemo (1998), *Swedish Social Security in the 1990s: Reform and Retrenchment*, Stockholm: Print Works of the Cabinet Office and Ministries.

Paradis, E. and J.-M. Salmon (1994), "Du CIP à la marche des chômeurs," *Esprit*, 204(8/9): 181–187.

Paugam, S. (2019), "Face au mépris social, la revanche des invisibles," in Sylvain Bourneau, Ed., *'Gilets jaunes': Hypothèses sur un mouvement*, Paris: La Découverte, Analyse Opinion Critique (AOC) Cahier #1: 37–42.

Pedder, S. (2012), *Le dénis français: Les derniers enfants gâtés de l'Europe*, Paris: Jean-Claude Lattès.

Pempel, T. J. (1998), *Regime Shift: Comparative Dynamics of the Japanese Political Economy*, Ithaca, NY: Cornell University Press.

Pempel, T. J. (2010), "Between Pork and Productivity: The Collapse of the Liberal Democratic Party," *Journal of Japanese Studies*, 36(2): 227–254.

Perrier, J. (2015), "La parenthèse libérale de la droite française des années 1980," *Histoire@politique*, 1(25): 176–196.

Perrineau, P. (2019), *Le grand écart: Chronique d'une démocratie fragmentée*, Paris: Plon.

Pew Research Center (2018), *A Decade after the Financial Crisis, Economic Confidence Rebounds in Many Countries*. Available at: www.pewresearch.org/global/2018/09/18/a-decade-after-the-financial-crisis-economic-confidence-rebounds-in-many-countries/. Data extracted: January 21, 2021.

Pew Research Center (2019a), *Pew Global Indicators Database: Percent Responding that the Economic Situation Is Bad*, March 2019. Available at: www.pewresearch.org/global/database/indicator/5. Data extracted: January 26, 2021.

Pew Research Center (2019b), *Pew Global Indicators Database: Percent Who Say Their Country's Overall Economy Has Been* Strengthened *by the Economic Integration of Europe*. Available at: www.pewresearch.org/global/2019/10/14/the-european-union/. Consulted: July 18, 2022.

Peyrelevade, J. (2014), *Histoire d'une névrose: La France et son économie*, Paris: Albin Michel.

Pierson, P. (1993), "When Effect Becomes Cause: Policy Feedback and Political Change," *World Politics*, 45(4): 595–628.

Pierson, P. (1994), *Dismantling the Welfare State? Reagan, Thatcher, and the Politics of Retrenchment*, Cambridge: Cambridge University Press.

Pierson, P. (1996), "The New Politics of the Welfare State," *World Politics*, 48(2): 143–179.

Pierson, P., Ed. (2001a), *The New Politics of the Welfare State*, Oxford: Oxford University Press.

Pierson, P. (2001b), "Coping with Permanent Austerity: Welfare State Restructuring in Affluent Democracies," in Paul Pierson, Ed., *The New Politics of the Welfare State*, Oxford: Oxford University Press: 410–456.

Piore, M. and C. Sabel (1984), *The Second Industrial Divide: Possibilities for Prosperity*, New York: Basic Books.

Pisani-Ferry, J. (2017), *Le grand plan d'investissement, 2018–2022: Rapport au premier ministre*, September 25, 2017. Available at: www.gouvernement.fr/partage/9535-rapport-de-m-jean-pisani-ferry. Consulted: February 21, 2022.

Plenel, E. (2019), *La victoire des vaincus: A propos des gilets jaunes*, Paris: La Découverte.

Plenel, E. and S. Dufau (2015), *Qu'ont-ils fait de nos espoirs? Faits et gestes de la présidence Hollande*, Paris: Don Quichotte.

Polanyi, K. (1944), *The Great Transformation*, Boston, MA: Beacon.

Poncins, M. (2009), "Un conte fantastique: Le grand emprunt," *Tocqueville Magazine*, April 30, 2009.

Pontusson, J. (2010), "Once again a Model: Nordic Social Democracy in a Globalized World," in James Cronin, George Ross et al., Eds., *What's Left of the Left? Democrats and Social Democrats in Challenging Times*, Durham, NC: Duke University Press: 89–115.

Quénel, G. (2016), *Denis Kessler, de la recherche au CNRS à la direction du Medef (1976–1998)*, Paris: Edilivre.

Reisenbichler, A. and K. Morgan (2012), "From 'Sick Man' to 'Miracle': Explaining the Robustness of the German Labor Market During and After the Financial Crisis, 2008–09," *Politics and Society*, 40(4): 549–579.

Renard, T. and V. Cleyre (2001), *Medef: Un projet de société*, Paris: Editions Syllepse.

Rey, H. (2004), *La gauche et les classes populaires: Histoire et actualité d'une mésentente*, Paris: La Découverte.

Rhodes, M. (1997), "Southern European Welfare States: Identity, Problems, and Prospects for Reform," in Martin Rhodes, Ed., *Southern European Welfare States: Between Crisis and Reform*, Portland, OR: Frank Cass: 1–22.

Rhodes, M. (2001), "The Political Economy of Social Pacts: 'Competitive Corporatism' and European Welfare Reform," in Paul Pierson, Ed., *The New Politics of the Welfare State*, Oxford: Oxford University Press: 165–194.

Riboud, A. (1987), *Modernisation, mode d'emploi*, Paris: Union Générale d'Editions.

Rodrik, D. (2018), "Populism and the Economics of Globalization," *Journal of International Business Policy*, 1(1–2): 12–33.

Roger, P. (2001), "Refondation sociale, année zéro," in René Mouriaux, Ed., *L'année sociale 2001*, Paris: Editions Syllepse: 77–93.

Romanet, A. (2012), *Non aux trente douloureuses*, Paris: Plon.

Ross, G. (1997), "Europe and the Misfortunes of Mr. Chirac," *French Politics and Society*, 15(2): 3–8.

Ross, G. (2006), "Myths and Realities in the 2006 'Events'," *French Politics, Culture, and Society*, 24(3): 81–88.

Rothé, B. (2013), *De l'abandon au mépris: Comment le PS a tourné le dos à la classe ouvrière*, Paris: Editions du Seuil.

Rousso, H., Ed. (1986), *De Monnet à Massé: Enjeux politiques et objectifs économiques dans le cadre des quatre premiers plans (1945–1965)*, Paris: Centre National de la Recherche Scientifique (CNRS).

Rueda, D. (2007), *Social Democracy Inside Out: Partisanship and Labor Market Policy in Industrialized Democracies*, Oxford: Oxford University Press.

Saint-Etienne, C. (2014), "Alstom à vendre: 'La France est un pays capitaliste … sans capital'," *L'Obs Economie*, April 28, 2014.

Sarkozy, N. (2007), *Ensemble, tout devient possible*. Available at: https://archive .org/details/EL235_P_2007_008/page/n1/mode/2up. Consulted: July 18, 2022.

Sarkozy, N. (2008), "Le discours de Nicolas Sarkozy à Toulon en 2008," *Le Figaro*, March 27, 2014.

Sawyer, M. (1976), "Income Distribution in OECD Countries," *OECD Economic Outlook*, July 1976: 3–36.

Scharpf, F. (2013), "Monetary Union, Fiscal Crisis, and the Disabling of Democratic Accountability," in Fritz Scharpf and Armin Schäfer, Eds., *Politics in the Age of Austerity*, Cambridge: Polity: 108–142.

Scharpf, F. and V. Schmidt, Eds. (2000), *Welfare and Work in the Open Economy: From Vulnerability to Competitiveness*, Oxford: Oxford University Press.

Scherman, K. G. (1999), *The Swedish Pension Reform*, Geneva: International Labour Organization (ILO).

Schludi, M. (2003), "Politics of Pension Reform: The French Case in a Comparative Perspective," *French Politics*, 1(2): 199–224.

Schludi, M. (2005), *The Reform of Bismarckian Pension Systems: A Comparison of Pension Politics in Austria, France, Germany, Italy, and Sweden*, Amsterdam: Amsterdam University Press.

Schmidt, V. (1996), *From State to Market? The Transformation of French Business and Government*, Cambridge: Cambridge University Press.

Schmidt, V. (2002a), "Does Discourse Matter in the Politics of Welfare Adjustment?" *Comparative Political Studies*, 35(2): 168–193.

Schmidt, V. (2002b), *The Futures of European Capitalism*, Oxford: Oxford University Press.

Schmidt, V. (2003), "French Capitalism: Transformed, Yet Still a Third Variety of Capitalism," *Economy and Society*, 32(4): 526–554.

Schmidt, V. (2007), "Trapped by Their Ideas: French Elites' Discourses of European Integration and Globalization," *Journal of European Public Policy*, 14(7): 992–1009.

Schmidt, V. (2008), "European Political Economy: Labour Out, State Back In, Firm to the Fore," *European Political Economy*, 31(1–2): 302–320.

Schmidt, V. (2009), "Putting the Political Back into Political Economy by Bringing the State Back in Yet Again," *World Politics*, 61(3): 516–546.

Schmidt, V. (2012), "What Happened to the State-Influenced Market Economies (SMEs)? France, Italy, and Spain Confront the Crisis as the Good, the Bad, and the Ugly," in Wyn Grant and Graham Wilson, Eds., *The Consequences of the Global Financial Crisis: The Rhetoric of Reform and Regulation*, Oxford: Oxford University Press: 156–186.

Schmidt, V. and M. Thatcher, Eds. (2013), *Resilient Liberalism in Europe's Political Economy*, Cambridge: Cambridge University Press.

Schmitter, P. (1979), "Still the Century of Corporatism?" in Philippe Schmitter and Gerhard Lehmbruch, Eds., *Trends Toward Corporatist Intermediation*, Beverly Hills, CA: Sage: 7–52.

Schulze-Cleven, T. (2014), "Labor Market Policy: Toward A 'Flexicurity' Model in the US?" in R. Daniel Kelemen, Ed., *Lessons from Europe? What Americans Can Learn from European Public Policies*, Washington, DC: Congressional Quarterly Press: 77–96.

Seillière, E.-A. (2005), *Qu'est-ce que le MEDEF?* Paris: L'Information citoyenne.

Shonfield, A. (1965), *Modern Capitalism: The Changing Balance of Public and Private Power*, Oxford: Oxford University Press.

Skocpol, T. (1992), *Protecting Soldiers and Mothers: The Politics of Social Provision in the United States, 1870s to 1920s*, Cambridge, MA: Harvard University Press.

Smith, T. (2004), *France in Crisis: Welfare, Inequality, and Globalization since 1980*, Cambridge: Cambridge University Press.

Soskice, D. (1999), "Divergent Production Regimes: Coordinated and Uncoordinated Market Economies in the 1980s and 1990s," in Herbert Kitschelt, Peter Lange et al., Eds., *Continuity and Change in Contemporary Capitalism*, Cambridge: Cambridge University Press: 101–134.

Spector, D. (2017), *La gauche, la droite, et le marché: Histoire d'unee idée controversée (XIXe-XXIe siècle)*, Paris: Odile Jacob.

Spire, A. (2019), "Voir les 'gilets jaunes' comme des citoyens mobilisés contre l'écologie serait une erreur," in Sylvain Bourneau, Ed., *'Gilets jaunes': Hypothèses sur un mouvement*, Paris: La Découverte, Analyse Opinion Critique (AOC) Cahier #1: 11–20.

Statista (2022), *Taux de chômage des jeunes de 15 à 24 ans en France de 2006 à 2020, selon le sexe*. Available at: https://fr.statista.com/statistiques/474246/chomage-des-jeunes-en-france/. Consulted: March 7, 2022.

Steinmo, S. (1993), *Taxation and Democracy: Swedish, British, and American Approaches to Financing the Modern State*, New Haven, CT: Yale University Press.

Steinmo, S. (2003), "Bucking the Trend? Social Democracy in a Global Economy: The Swedish Case Up Close," *New Political Economy*, 8(1): 31–48.

Stephens, J. (1996), "The Scandinavian Welfare States: Achievements, Crisis, and Prospects," in Gøsta Esping-Andersen, Ed., *Welfare States in Transition: National Adaptations in a Global Economy*, Thousand Oaks, CA: Sage Publications: 32–65.

Stephens, J., E. Huber, et al. (1999), "The Welfare State in Hard Times," in Herbert Kitschelt, Peter Lange et al., Eds., *Continuity and Change in Contemporary Capitalism*, Cambridge: Cambridge University Press: 164–193.

Stigler, G. (1971), "The Theory of Economic Regulation," *Bell Journal of Economics and Management Science*, 2(1): 3–21.

Stiglitz, J. (2007), *Globalization and Its Discontents*, New York: W. W. Norton & Company.

Stiglitz, J. (2010), *Freefall: America, Free Markets, and the Sinking of the World Economy*, New York: W. W. Norton & Company.

Stoffaës, C. (1985), "The Nationalizations: An Initial Assessment, 1981–1984," in Howard Machin and Vincent Wright, Eds., *Economic Policy and Policy-Making under the Mitterrand Presidency*, New York: Saint-Martin's: 144–169.

Strange, S. (2000), *The Retreat of the State: The Diffusion of Power in the World Economy*, Cambridge: Cambridge University Press.

Streeck, W. (1987), "The Uncertainties of Management in the Management of Uncertainty," *International Journal of Political Economy*, 17(3): 57–87.

Streeck, W. (1991), "On the Institutional Conditions of Diversified Quality Production," in Egon Matzner and Wolfgang Streeck, Eds., *Beyond Keynesianism: The Socio-Economics of Production and Full Employment*, Brookfield, VT: Edward Elgar: 21–61.

Streeck, W. (1995), "From Market Making to State Building? Reflections on the Political Economy of European Social Policy," in Stephan Leibfried and Paul Pierson, Eds., *European Social Policy: Between Fragmentation and Integration*, Washington, DC: Brookings: 389–431.

Streeck, W. and P. Schmitter, Eds. (1985), *Private Interest Government: Beyond Market and State*, Beverly Hills, CA: Sage.

Streeck, W. and K. Yamamura, Eds. (2005), *The Origins of Nonliberal Capitalism: Germany and Japan in Comparison*, Ithaca, NY: Cornell University Press.

Suleiman, E. (1974), *Politics, Power and Bureaucracy in France: The Administrative Elite*, Princeton, NJ: Princeton University Press.

Suleiman, E. (1978), *Elites in French Society: The Politics of Survival*, Princeton, NJ: Princeton University Press.

Tanner, M. (2008), "Welfare State," in Ronald Hamowy, Ed., *The Encyclopedia of Libertarianism*, Los Angeles, CA: Sage: 540–542.

Thelen, K. (2014), *Varieties of Liberalization and the New Politics of Social Solidarity*, Cambridge: Cambridge University Press.

Tilton, M. (1996), *Restrained Trade: Cartels in Japan's Basic Materials Industries*, Ithaca, NY: Cornell University Press.

Titmuss, R. (1987), "Welfare State and Welfare Society," in Brian Abel-Smith and Kay Titmuss, Eds., *The Philosophy of Welfare: Selected Writings of Richard Titmuss*, London: Allen and Unwin: 141–156.

Tocqueville, A. (1893), *Souvenirs*, Paris: Calmann-Lévy.

Tocqueville, A. (1955), *The Old Régime and the French Revolution*, Garden City, NY: Anchor Books.

Tocqueville, A. (1969), *Democracy in America*, Garden City, NY: Anchor Books.

Tompson, W. (2010), *L'Economie politique de la réforme: Retraites, emplois, et déréglementation dans dix pays de l'OCDE*, Paris: OECD.

Tumasjan, A. (2020), "Hôpitaux publics: Comment la réduction des budgets augmente à la fois les coûts et les risques," *The Conversation*, October 16, 2020. Available at: https://theconversation.com/hopitaux-publics-comment-la-reduction-des-budgets-augmente-a-la-fois-les-couts-et-les-risques-142589. Consulted: November 1, 2020.

UNEDIC (2020a), *Prévisions financières de l'Unédic - juin 2020*, Union Nationale pour l'Emploi dans l'Industrie et le Commerce, June 18, 2020. Available at: www.unedic.org/publications/previsions-financieres-de-lunedic-juin-2020. Consulted: October 17, 2020.

UNEDIC (2020b), *Tableau de données comparatives sur les dispositifs de chômage partiel dans 8 pays d'Europe*, Union Nationale pour l'Emploi dans l'Industrie et le Commerce. Available at: www.unedic.org/sites/default/files/2020-04/ comparatif_europe_chomage_partiel%20%283%29.pdf. Consulted: August 30, 2020.

UNEDIC (2022), "Prévisions financières: L'Unédic confirme un retour aux excédents et l'amorce d'une trajectoire de désendettement, toutefois le régime reste fortement endetté," UNEDIC Press Release, February 24, 2022. Available at: www.unedic.org/espace-presse/actualites/previsions-financieres-lunedic-confirme-un-retour-aux-excedents-et-lamorce. Consulted: July 17, 2022.

Vail, M. (2010), *Recasting Welfare Capitalism: Economic Adjustment in Contemporary France and Germany*, Philadelphia, PA: Temple University Press.

Vail, M. (2018), *Liberalism in Illiberal States: Ideas and Economic Adjustment in Contemporary Europe*, Oxford: Oxford University Press.

Van der Veen, R. and W. Trommel (1999), "Managed Liberalization of the Dutch Welfare State," *Governance*, 12(3): 289–310.

Vandepitte, F. (2019), *Le petit livre des gilets jaunes*, Paris: Editions First.

Verdier-Molinié, A. (2013), *60 milliards d'économies!* Paris: Albin Michel.

Verdier-Molinié, A. (2015), *On va dans le mur*, Paris: Albin Michel.

Vie Publique Editorial Board (2020), "Allocation autonomie, maintien à domicile, 5e risque: Quelle politique pour la dépendance?" *Vie publique*, June 9, 2020.

Vie Publique Editorial Board (2021a), "Six questions sur la réforme de l'assurance chômage," *Vie publique*, November 30, 2021.

Vie Publique Editorial Board (2021b), "Retraites: Un déficit moins important que prévu," *Vie publique*, June 15, 2021.

Vie Publique Editorial Board (2021c), "Loi 'Climat et Résilience': Des avancées et des limites," *Vie publique*, October 28, 2021.

Visser, J. (2002), "The First Part-Time Economy in the World: A Model to Be Followed?" *Journal of European Social Policy*, 12(1): 23–42.

Visser, J. and A. Hemerijck (1997), *'A Dutch Miracle?' Job Growth, Welfare Reform, and Corporatism in the Netherlands*, Amsterdam: Amsterdam University Press.

Vogel, S. (1996), *Freer Markets, More Rules: The Paradoxical Politics of Regulatory Reform in the Advanced Industrial Countries*, Ithaca, NY: Cornell University Press.

Vogel, S. (2006), *Japan Remodeled: How Government and Industry Are Reforming Japanese Capitalism*, Ithaca, NY: Cornell University Press.

Vogel, S. (2013), "Japan's Information Technology Challenge," in Dan Breznitz and John Zysman, Eds., *The Third Globalization: Can Wealthy Nations Stay Rich in the Twenty-First Century?* Oxford: Oxford University Press: 350–372.

Wade, R. (1990), *Governing the Market: Economic Theory and the Role of Government in East Asian Industrialization*, Princeton, NJ: Princeton University Press.

Wadensjö, E. (1999), "Sweden: Revisions of the Public Pension Programmes," *Industry and Trade*, Reprint No. 535, Swedish Institute for Social Research: 101–115.

WHO (2022), *WHO Coronavirus (COVID-19) Dashboard: France*, World Health Organization. Available at: https://covid19.who.int/region/euro/country/fr. Consulted: July 6, 2022.

Williamson, J. (1990), "What Washington Means by Policy Reform," in John Williamson, Ed., *Latin American Adjustment: How Much Has Happened?* Washington, DC: Peterson Institute for International Economies: 7–40.

Woll, C. (2006), "La réforme du Medef: Chroniques des difficultés de l'action collective patronale," *Revue française de science politique*, 56(2): 253–279.

Woll, C. (2014), *The Power of Inaction: Bank Bailouts in Comparative Perspective*, Ithaca, NY: Cornell University Press.

World Bank (1994), *Averting the Old Age Crisis: Policies to Protect the Old and Promote Growth*, Oxford: Oxford University Press.

World Bank (2018), *World Development Indicators: Manufacturing Value Added (% GDP)*. Available at: https://databank.worldbank.org/reports.aspx?source=2&series=NV.IND.MANF.ZS. Data extracted: January 26, 2021.

World Bank (2019a), *Doing Business 2019*. Available at: www.worldbank.org/content/dam/doingBusiness/media/Annual-Reports/English/DB2019-report_web-version.pdf. Consulted: February 8, 2019.

World Bank (2019b), *World Development Indicators: GDP Per Capita Growth (Annual %)*. Available at: https://databank.worldbank.org/reports.aspx?source=2&series=NY.GDP.PCAP.KD.ZG&country=. Data extracted: February 10, 2019.

World Economic Forum (2018), *The Global Competitiveness Report 2018*. Available at: www.weforum.org/reports/the-global-competitveness-report-2018. Consulted: February 12, 2019.

Young, Z. (2018), "Emmanuel Macron's 9 Greatest Gaffes," *Politico*, October 9, 2018.

Zysman, J. (1977), *Political Strategies for Industrial Order: State, Market, and Industry in France*, Berkeley, CA: University of California Press.

Zysman, J. (1978), "The French State in the International Economy," in Peter Katzenstein, Ed., *Between Power and Plenty: Foreign Economic Policies in Advanced Industrial States*, Madison, WI: University of Wisconsin Press: 255–293.

Zysman, J. (1983), *Governments, Markets, and Growth: Financial Systems and the Politics of Industrial Change*, Ithaca, NY: Cornell University Press.

Index

Ingram Content Group UK Ltd.
Milton Keynes UK
UKHW040143050523
421267UK00012B/134